To Secure These Rights

To Secure These Rights

The Declaration of Independence
and Constitutional Interpretation

Scott Douglas Gerber

New York University Press
New York and London

NEW YORK UNIVERSITY PRESS
New York and London

© 1995 by New York University
All rights reserved

Library of Congress Cataloging-in-Publication Data
Gerber, Scott Douglas, 1961–
To secure these rights : the Declaration of Independence and
constitutional interpretation / Scott Douglas Gerber.
p.   cm.
Includes bibliographical references and index.
ISBN 0-8147-3066-3 (acid-free paper)
1. United States—Constitutional law—Interpretation and
construction.   2. Natural law—Philosophy.   I. Title.
KF4550.G46   1995
342.73′02—dc20
[347.3022]   94-46414
                        CIP

New York University Press books are printed on acid-free paper,
and their binding materials are chosen for strength and durability.

Manufactured in the United States of America

10   9   8   7   6   5   4   3   2   1

This work is dedicated to the memory of Bonnie Groff.

Contents

II Natural Rights and the Role of the Court

Foreword

How to interpret the evolving Constitution contemporarily, and the Supreme Court's crucial role in the process, has been the abiding concern of its students and observers—whether they are lawyers, political scientists, historians, other social scientists, or humanists ... or the public at large. It has been a central question since the basic document was formulated on Fifth and Chestnut Streets in Philadelphia during that hot summer of 1787. The answers have been as diverse as they have been numerous, informed by wisdom as well as nebulousness, by sophistication as well as naïveté—with the Court quite naturally at the center of gravity of the controversy. For in the final analysis it is the high tribunal that decides what the Constitution means. To be sure, the Court is not the Constitution, pace Charles Evans Hughes's facile and catchy yet misleading famed political-stump-speech observation that "the Constitution is what the Justices say it is."

But the Court does inexorably draw lines and, in doing so, it interprets (or misinterprets) the document. In a very real sense these lines are born of the cardinal dual fact of politico-governmental life: the quality cum capability of the individual justices and their perception of the parameters of judicial power, to wit, their stance on the fundamental dichotomy of judicial activism and judicial restraint.

The last two decades have witnessed intriguing intellectual combat between, to employ John Hart Ely's challenging terminology, "interpretivists" and "noninterpretivists": the former presumably cautiously faithful conservative adherents to specific constitutional language, the latter devotees of an expansive ad hominem, liberal philosophy, arguably substituting a commitment to "equal justice at any cost" for "equal justice under law." Or, to categorize the cardinal difference somewhat differently, if oversimplifiedly, it represents a clash between "originalist" champions, generally personified by Chief Justice William Rehnquist and Robert Bork, and "what-do-the-words-mean-in-our-time" proponents like Justice William Brennan and Laurence Tribe.

Scott Gerber, who possesses both law (J.D.) and political science (Ph.D.) degrees, bravely and admirably tackles the complexities of the dichotomy at issue in scholarly, imaginative, commendable compass by rejecting both poles of the basic argument. In a theory he aptly calls "liberal originalism," Gerber rejects the "what-do-the-words-mean-in-our-time" constitutional jurisprudence of modern liberals because that approach, as well-meaning as it may be, is really nothing more than legislating from the bench. And he rejects the originalism of modern conservatives because that approach, as well-meaning as it also may be, misconstrues what the Constitution is ultimately about. As Gerber persuasively demonstrates through an impressive analysis of history, political philosophy, and law, the Constitution was intended, above all else, to protect the natural rights of individuals—something that is patently at odds with the conservative originalists' emphasis on majority rule. In short, Gerber advances a theory of constitutional interpretation that will likely displease both modern liberals and modern conservatives: a sure sign that he is onto something.

Gerber, whom it was my great pleasure to have as a student, has undertaken a hugely ambitious project—and in his first book, no less. His discussion ranges from a bold revision of the character of the American Revolution to a provocative reinterpretation of many of the most famous cases in Supreme Court history, with many illuminating stops along the way. (Gerber's call for a merit-based appointment process in his chapter on checks on the Court is particularly close to my heart, as he kindly notes in the text.) With clarity, intelligence, and remarkable readability, Gerber integrates a wide range of previously isolated debates in history, political philosophy, and law into an attractive and sophisticated theory of constitutional interpretation—a theory that, in his words, is "neither consistently 'liberal,' nor consistently 'conservative,' in the modern conception of those terms." In constructing his theory, Gerber shows not only that scholars from different disciplines *should* talk to each other, but that they *must*—"especially," as he puts it, "where the Constitution is concerned." There is much to be learned from this important book.

HENRY J. ABRAHAM
James Hart Professor of Government and Foreign Affairs
University of Virginia
Charlottesville, Virginia

Preface

This is a study in American constitutional theory. In essence, it is an effort to expound a systematic theory of constitutional interpretation. To that end, two questions are addressed. First, *how* should the Constitution of the United States be interpreted? Second, *who* should be ultimately responsible for making that interpretation?[1] Answers are sought by examining the two fundamental documents of the American regime: the Declaration of Independence and the Constitution of the United States.

My approach to constitutional theory is through history, political philosophy, and law. And while I am directing this work chiefly to the public-law community, I try to take history and political philosophy seriously. I am therefore often engaged in an "interdisciplinary conversation" (to borrow historian Peter Onuf's useful phrase): sometimes approaching an issue through history, at other times through political philosophy, and at still others through law. Although it is difficult to please such justifiably demanding audiences as historians, political philosophers, and lawyers, I have come to believe that it is necessary to approach constitutional interpretation from more than one discipline (something, I suggest, the Founders did). In the end, I hope my book shows it is possible for scholars from different disciplines to talk *to* each other, rather than *past* each other, as they so often do—especially where the Constitution is concerned.*

This book is broad in scope, and many of the issues I address have themselves been the subject of a vast and varied independent literature. What I endeavor to do is identify the core components of some largely isolated debates and integrate them into the specific framework of constitutional interpretation. In other words, this is *not* a book about John Locke's political philosophy or about the appointment process, to name but two of the many issues I address. Rather, this is a book that examines, for example, the roles of John Locke's political philosophy and the appointment process in constitutional interpretation.

I wrote this book because I enjoy the literature and the debate on constitutional interpretation and because I find that same literature and debate frequently troubling. To expand on the latter point, most of the previous treatments of constitutional interpretation miss a basic point: that the Constitution must be interpreted in context. And, as I explain in part 1, that context is the natural-rights political philosophy of the American Revolution. Most of the previous treatments also seem unnecessarily preoccupied with trying to reconcile judicial review and democracy. The Constitution creates a republican form of government, not a majority-rule democracy. In that republican form of government, the Court, as I describe in part 2, is to play a central role: chief guardian of the natural-rights of the American people.

In the course of writing this book I accumulated many debts. I would especially like to thank Henry J. Abraham, who was justly honored in

---

*A distinguished scholar who read my manuscript warned that I "might not have many friends." "Historians may object to your history, political philosophers to your political philosophy, and lawyers to your law," he said. Nevertheless, believing that I had something important to say—both substantively and methodologically—and that books are, at bottom, an extension of the author, he encouraged me to go forward. I will always be grateful for that encouragement.

1993 with the first Lifetime Achievement Award of the Organized Section on Law and the Courts of the American Political Science Association. Professor Abraham, whose work originally inspired me to study public law, graciously provided advice, encouragement, and support throughout this lengthy project. I would also like to single out David M. O'Brien, George Athan Billias, J. Timothy Collins, and Christopher Wolfe. Professor O'Brien, a teacher and scholar of boundless energy, enthusiasm, and dedication, was extremely generous with his time and wise counsel. Professor Billias, whom I have known and admired since I was a child, kindly read the entire manuscript and offered suggestions that only a historian of the American Founding of his enormous stature could. As for Tim, like the true friend he is, he was always willing to discuss my project and made numerous useful comments, especially concerning political philosophy, his area of expertise. With respect to Professor Wolfe, he is the epitome of a professional: he highly recommended my book for publication and offered many constructive comments, despite disagreeing with much of what I say. Many other friends also made some excellent suggestions about how to strengthen my argument. James Sterling Young, A. E. Dick Howard, William G. Weaver, Paul Robert Lucas, Charles A. Kromkowski, Mark D. Hall, and A. John Simmons were particularly helpful. Additionally, I would like to thank those who provided financial support: the Governor's Fellowship, the Scottish Rite Fellowship, the Commonwealth Fellowship, and the Bradley Fellowship. Thanks go to the editors of *Polity* as well, for their permission to use in this volume material that appears in a somewhat different form in their fine journal. Niko Pfund, Dave Updike, Despina Papazoglou Gimbel, Jennifer Hammer, and their colleagues at New York University Press made publishing this book an extremely rewarding experience. I cannot imagine a more helpful and pleasant group of editors. Thanks, too, to David Reed for his help with the index. I would also like to mention how enjoyable—and fitting—it was for me to have written so much of this exegesis on the role of the Declaration of Independence in constitutional interpretation at the University of Virginia, "Mr. Jefferson's University." Last, but certainly not least, there is my family. It is impossible for me to repay the debt I owe them. All I can say is thank you and I hope you enjoy your complimentary copy of my book!

Introduction:
Liberal Originalism

Constitutional interpretation has been a source of political debate for
most of American history. In fact, the first constitutional-law case
decided by the Supreme Court, *Chisholm v. Georgia* (1793),[1] wherein
the Court held that a citizen of one state may sue another state in
federal court, was so politically unpopular it was quickly reversed by
constitutional amendment.[2] Other examples from the early days of the
American republic are easily identified. The great debates between the
Jeffersonian Republicans and the Federalists, for instance, centered on
disagreements in constitutional interpretation, such as the power of
the national government vis-à-vis the states—disagreements that were
to continue throughout American history under different party labels.

While political debate over constitutional interpretation has a long
and rich history in the United States, it was not until the late nineteenth

century that theories of constitutional interpretation were discussed much, if at all. Indeed, in his famous *Commentaries on the Constitution of the United States* (1833), Justice Joseph Story expressly rejected the idea that he should offer a theory of constitutional interpretation in his book.[3] Story rejected the idea because during his day the declaratory theory of law, in which the law was deemed to be "declared and determined," but not "made," by judges,[4] was all but unquestioned. In the late nineteenth century, however, things began to change, as the "revolt against formalism"[5] in philosophy and the social sciences found its way into jurisprudence, largely through the efforts of Oliver Wendell Holmes. As a result, the declaratory theory of law came under increasing attack, and alternative theories of constitutional interpretation have been freely advanced ever since.

Importantly, all of the theories, whether they are the legal realism and sociological jurisprudence of Holmes's day or the economic analysis of law and critical legal studies of the present day—and whether they intend to or not[6]—appeal, at their essential level, to political philosophy. Justice Felix Frankfurter said it best: constitutional interpretation "is not at all a science, but applied politics."[7]

Surprisingly, the natural-rights political philosophy of the Declaration of Independence, the most obvious choice for interpreting the Constitution, is now all but ignored. After all, it was in the Declaration of Independence that the Founders articulated the political philosophy upon which this nation is based. In the unforgettable words of Thomas Jefferson:

We hold these Truths to be self-evident, that all Men are created equal, that they are endowed by their Creator with certain unalienable Rights; that among these are Life, Liberty and the Pursuit of Happiness—That to secure these Rights, Governments are instituted among Men, deriving their just Powers from the Consent of the Governed, that whenever any Form of Government becomes destructive of these Ends, it is the Right of the People to alter or to abolish it, and to institute new Government, laying its Foundation on such Principles and organizing its Powers in such Form, as to them shall seem most likely to effect their Safety and Happiness.[8]

A few scholars do recognize the significance of the Declaration of Independence to constitutional interpretation. The most well known of these are Walter Berns, Martin Diamond, Harry Jaffa, and Walter Murphy.[9] All but Murphy are followers of Leo Strauss. Indeed, "Straussians[,] ... more than any other single group[,] ... are attempting to set the agenda for public debate over the Constitution."[10] As will become evident, my approach differs greatly from previous efforts in several ways, most notably in its interpretation of (1) the political philosophy of the Declaration of Independence[11] and (2) the role of the Court in identifying and applying that philosophy in American life.[12] In addition, I attempt to articulate a systematic theory of the role of the Declaration of Independence in constitutional interpretation. To that end, I document historically—rather than simply assume or assert[13]—in part 1 that the Framers of the Constitution remained committed to the natural-rights principles of the Declaration, and I show in part 2 how they sought to advance those principles through political architecture, especially through a definitive power of judicial review.

Until his confirmation hearing to serve on the U.S. Supreme Court, Clarence Thomas also maintained that the political philosophy of the Declaration of Independence should have a central place in constitutional interpretation. As Thomas wrote in a 1989 law review article, "The Constitution is a logical extension of the Declaration of Independence. ... The higher-law background of the American Constitution ... provides the only firm basis for a just, wise, and *constitutional* decision."[14]

During his confirmation hearing, Thomas likely denied having ever implied in his speeches and writings that the political philosophy of the Declaration of Independence should be used as a basis for constitutional interpretation from fear of appearing out-of-date and radical.[15] Before Thomas, no member of the Supreme Court had publicly advocated interpreting the Constitution in light of the Declaration since the turn of the century. And those justices—Joseph Bradley, David Brewer, Stephen Field, and Rufus Peckham—have been widely criticized for their "simplistic" reading of that philosophy, believing as they erroneously did (see chapter 5) that the Declaration of Independence is primarily a statement of laissez-faire economics.[16]

While some consider an appeal to natural law and rights to be moving beyond an originalist methodology,[17] I endeavor to show in this volume that such is not the case for the natural-rights political philosophy of the Declaration of Independence. That is to say, the natural-rights principles embodied in the Declaration are not "above" or "beyond" the Constitution;[18] they are at the heart of the Constitution.

In essence, I advance a "jurisprudence of original intention," although one far different from that promoted by former attorney general Edwin Meese (who coined the phrase), former judge and unsuccessful Supreme Court nominee Robert Bork, Chief Justice William Rehnquist, and myriad other contemporary political and jurisprudential conservatives.[19] Briefly put, I employ a conservative methodology, but arrive at liberal results, as "liberal" is understood in the classic sense of seventeenth- and eighteenth-century political philosophy. I contend that originalism should not be viewed as simply a "jurisprudence of the right," as it so often is. I reject the notion that arguing that the Framers enacted abstract "concepts" in the Constitution requires one to conclude the Framers' intent is "trumped by evolving precedent, values, or needs."[20]

Conservative Originalism

Although a variety of theories of originalism have been advanced in a seemingly unending literature, the most well known and widely followed conservative originalist position is that the Court may legitimately recognize only those rights specifically mentioned in the Constitution, or ascertainably implicit in its structure or history. In all other cases, the conservatives argue, the majority is entitled to govern—to make moral choices—through the political process. According to Robert Bork, arguably the most articulate, and certainly the most controversial, champion of original intent, "The orthodoxy of our civil religion, which the Constitution has been aptly called, holds that we govern ourselves democratically, except on those occasions few in number though crucially important, when the Constitution places a topic beyond the reach of majorities."[21] The conservatives regard a jurisprudence of original intention as the only legitimate approach to constitutional interpretation, because only that "can give us law that is something other than, and superior to, the judge's will,"[22] and only that will eliminate the "anomaly of judicial supremacy in democratic society."[23]

Despite the methodological appeal of the conservatives' argument—a subject to be discussed at length below—their campaign for a jurisprudence of original intention should be seen for what it is: a quest for political results. Analyzing the conclusions to which the conservatives are led by originalism reveals that they are simply espousing politically conservative interpretations of the Constitution and labeling them "original intent."[24] In effect, the conservatives are substituting conservative result-oriented jurisprudence for liberal result-oriented jurisprudence. (The conservatives' call for a jurisprudence of original intention is clearly a reaction to the liberal jurisprudence of the Warren Court.) They are seeking radically to change constitutional law to make it conform to their preferred conception of it. For example, for the conservatives to argue, as (now Chief) Justice Rehnquist did in a dissenting opinion in *Wallace v. Jaffree* (1985),[25] an opinion for which he was publicly applauded by Meese,[26] that the establishment clause of the first amendment does *not* prohibit the majority, acting through the political process, from authorizing prayer in the public schools is to rewrite history and the Founders' political philosophy.[27] The history behind the passage of the first amendment indicates that the establishment clause was designed to erect, as Thomas Jefferson said, a strict "wall of separation between Church and State."[28] In fact, it is difficult to imagine a principle to which the Founders were more philosophically committed than the separation of church and state.[29]

Moreover, the conservative originalists mischaracterize the Constitution as establishing a majority-rule democracy, a mischaracterization that is also made by many contemporary constitutional theorists of so-called "moderate" and "liberal" political views.[30] This has led to an unfortunate portrayal of the Court as a "deviant institution in the American democracy,"[31] because judicial review is outside the processes of majoritarian politics. As discussed in chapters 2 and 3, the Constitution does *not* establish a majority-rule democracy. Indeed, "the framers openly and explicitly distrusted majority rule; virtually every government institution they created had strong anti-majoritarian features."[32] For example, the president is elected by the electoral college, not directly by the people, and he can veto measures passed by the popularly elected Congress; many executive officials are not electorally accountable; the Senate was originally appointed by the state legislatures, and a minority of senators can still block ratification of treaties and public officials; and the judiciary is nominated by the president, confirmed by the Senate, and given life tenure. And, of course, there is the Bill of Rights. As Justice Robert Jackson reminded the nation many years ago:

The very purpose of a Bill of Rights was to withdraw certain subjects from the vicissitudes of political controversy, to place them beyond the reach of majorities and officials and to establish them as legal principles to be applied by the courts. One's right to life, liberty, and property, to free speech, a free press, freedom of worship and assembly, and other fundamental rights may not be submitted to vote: they depend on the outcome of no elections.[33]

Because of the Framers' desire to avoid what Elbridge Gerry called the "excess of democracy,"[34] they created a "republican" form of government, not a majority-rule democracy.[35]* And in that republican form of government the Court, as part 2 explains, is to play a central role: chief guardian of the natural rights of the American people, especially of individuals and minorities. The version of a jurisprudence of original intention advanced by so many modern conservatives therefore proceeds from a faulty premise—that majority rule is the essence of the American constitutional order—and it should be rejected.

Liberal Originalism

As noted at the outset, my criticism of the conservatives' approach to constitutional interpretation is not meant to imply that there is not a jurisprudence of original intention in accordance with which the Constitution should be interpreted. As part 1 addresses in detail, the United States of America was founded to preserve the natural rights of the American people. "To secure these rights," Jefferson writes in the Declaration of Independence, is the reason "governments are instituted among men." To secure natural rights is, therefore, why the Constitution was enacted, and to secure natural rights is how the Constitution should be interpreted. That is the "original intent" of the Founders.[36]

Here, it is necessary to explain the connection between the Founders' background attitudes on the purpose of government and the interpretation of the particular provisions of the Constitution. The most important point to recognize is that, as just mentioned, the Constitution was written for a reason: to establish a form of government that would provide better security for natural rights than was provided under the Articles of Confederation. To make the point somewhat differently, the

---

*Part 1 explores why it is important to recognize the difference in the jurisprudence of the American Founding between a republican *form of government* and a republican *political philosophy.*

particular provisions of the Constitution were written with the Founders' background attitudes in mind. As chapter 2 explains, the Constitution is not an end in itself; it is a means by which the American political community's ideals—its ends—are ordered. It is therefore necessary to interpret the Constitution in light of those ideals, ideals expressed with unparalleled eloquence by Thomas Jefferson in the Declaration of Independence.

The necessity of keeping the Founders' background attitudes in mind when interpreting the particular provisions of the Constitution becomes even more apparent when one realizes that many of the most significant provisions of the Constitution are phrased in general terms, especially those concerning individual rights, the subject of this volume. For example, the first amendment's directive that Congress shall make no law "respecting an establishment of religion" is not unambiguous, nor is the eighth amendment's prohibition against "cruel and unusual punishments." Moving beyond the original ten amendments, what does it mean to say, as the fourteenth amendment does, that no state shall deny to any person "the equal protection of the laws"? Provisions as general as these—and there are many others in the Constitution—are not self-interpreting. They can be given meaning and life only when they are construed in light of the moral and political principles upon which they are based. As David O'Brien aptly observes, "Interpreting the Constitution . . . presupposes a judicial and political philosophy and poses inescapable questions of substantive value choices."[37] Although I reject the argument advanced by many proponents of the application of literary analysis to legal texts—that meaning cannot be extracted from legal texts, but can only be put into them, in other words, that the Constitution means nothing and means anything—it is difficult to deny the more modest claim that "texts can be interpreted only in some 'context.'"* And that "context," as part 1 describes, is the natural-rights philosophy of the American Revolution.

Of course, it is possible to construe the provisions of the Constitu-

---

*Levinson and Mailloux, Preface, xii. In addition to the related concerns raised by historians (discussed below), the controversy over the possibility of discerning the Framers' intent is largely a result of the efforts of legal scholars to apply the methods of literary analysis to legal texts, including the Constitution. See generally Levinson and Mailloux, *Interpreting Law and Literature* (collecting many of the leading essays on law and literature). The nuances of the highly specialized and frequently abstruse debate about the relationship between law and literature are beyond the scope of this book. In

tion in light of philosophical principles other than those embodied in the Declaration of Independence. One need only peruse the plethora of provocative theories of constitutional interpretation advanced over the years to appreciate this fact.[38] However, those advancing nonoriginalist approaches to constitutional interpretation have failed to show that the particular approach they favor is based on anything other than their own moral and political preferences. Indeed, Ronald Dworkin, a forceful critic of originalism, maintains that we should abandon the search—hopeless, in his view—for the Framers' intent in favor of the "best argument" about political morality.[39]

The problem with Dworkin's interpretive position, and a problem repeated by most lawyers attempting to articulate theories of constitutional interpretation, is that under his theory substantive values are inevitably established by those with the best argumentation skills—by clever lawyers like Dworkin himself.[40] If the rule of law means anything, it surely means that the Constitution should not be interpreted in such a subjective fashion, especially by unelected and life-tenured judges. Moreover, if the American people do wish to depart from the natural-rights principles of the Declaration of Independence and adopt, for instance, the egalitarianism of Dworkin or of retired associate justice William Brennan, or the majoritarianism of the conservative proponents of a jurisprudence of original intention, they should employ the Article 5 amendment process and so specify. To date, that has not occurred—and it is not likely to occur.

Methodological Criticisms and Responses

Because I advocate a version of originalism, it is necessary to attempt to answer here the chief criticisms leveled against that interpretive

---

my judgment, however, Richard Posner's argument that literary techniques have little relevance for interpreting constitutional and statutory texts because of the profound differences between literature and law in character, origin, and, most importantly, social function, is correct. See Posner, *Law and Literature*, 209–68. See also Kay, "Adherence to the Original Intentions in Constitutional Adjudication," 242 ("The most telling response to this objection [that discerning the Framers' intent is 'really impossible'] is simply that no one really believes it, not even the writers who make the objection. If they did, they would not use language to advance the argument"). For an illustrative opposing view, see Tushnet, *Red, White, and Blue*, 32–45.

methodology.* The most significant criticism of originalism is that the Framers could not and did not anticipate many modern needs and problems. Therefore, argue the critics, the Constitution must be a "living Constitution," one that evolves by judicial interpretation to meet modern exigencies.

The leading proponent of the notion of a living Constitution, and the leading opponent of a jurisprudence of original intention, is Justice Brennan. According to him, "the ultimate question" in constitutional interpretation "must be, what do the words of the text mean in our time? For the genius of the Constitution rests not in any static meaning it might have had in a world that is dead and gone, but in the adaptability of its great principles to cope with current problems and current needs."[41]

The "great clauses" of the Constitution were purposely phrased broadly to accomplish this goal, Justice Brennan argues. Of particular import are the Bill of Rights guarantees and the fourteenth amendment provisions requiring "due process" and "equal protection."

The notion of a living Constitution should be rejected, no matter how appealingly Justice Brennan may state the case for it.[42] The vision of the Constitution as the embodiment of "transformative overarching principles" is uncontrolled by the text of the Constitution and the political philosophy upon which the text and this nation are based. The Framers must have meant something when they *wrote* the Constitution.† Moreover, such an open-ended approach to constitutional interpretation permits judges to reject those clauses of the Constitution

---

*The debate over original intent has been dominating constitutional scholarship ever since Attorney General Meese's 1985 American Bar Association speech. See Ortiz, "The Price of Metaphysics." As anyone who has spent time reviewing the mountain of literature on originalism can attest, much has been written in the way of criticism of originalist methodology, as well as responses to that criticism. The debate over original intent has taken on such a life of its own that some now characterize Justice Brennan as an originalist! See Perry, *The Constitution in the Courts*, 213 n. 15. As much as anything else, the discussion in this Introduction attempts to bring the debate over original intent back to its moorings: to the issues of how, and whether, judges should walk the precarious line between judicial activism and judicial restraint in constitutional decision making.

† The relationship between the written words of the Constitution and the natural-rights principles underlying those written words should be made clear from the outset. That relationship is best explained by contrasting my position with Christopher Wolfe's. For Wolfe, as for most modern conservatives, the Constitution is ultimately about majority rule, with a few isolated rights, private property rights in particular, exempted from the political process. See Wolfe, *Judicial Activism*. For the Framers, as I try to show in this book, the Constitution was ultimately about securing individual rights (broadly

they do not like and to give the ones they do like whatever meaning they desire them to have. In the apt words of Harry Jaffa, "this is the negation of constitutionalism."[43] It is, in other words, nothing more than the illegitimate exercise of political power by those appointed to check political decisions.

The most conspicuous example of Justice Brennan's negation of constitutionalism is his unyielding opposition to the death penalty. Brennan's belief that the Constitution is "a sparkling vision" of the "human dignity" of every individual is at the root of his resistance to capital punishment. Brennan admits that his position is not subscribed to by a majority of the justices or a majority of Americans. However, his view of the Constitution as a transformative document embodying overarching principles required him, in his judgment, to vote as he did. For on the issue of the death penalty, Justice Brennan "hope[s] to embody a community striving for human dignity for all, although perhaps not yet arrived."[44]

As admirable as are Justice Brennan's humanitarian sentiments—sentiments with which I personally have much sympathy—a plain reading of the Constitution demonstrates how troubling is his approach to constitutional interpretation. Capital punishment is confronted in the Constitution in the eighth amendment, which forbids "cruel and unusual punishments," as applied to the states through the fourteenth amendment. Additionally, the fifth amendment speaks to capital punishment in the double jeopardy clause, and the fifth and fourteenth amendments address it in their respective due process clauses.[45] (The

---

conceived) *from* the machinations of the political process. Given his position on the essential premise of the Constitution, Wolfe is willing to let judges interpret the Constitution "in light of" natural-rights philosophy only if there is a "textual basis" for that interpretation. See Wolfe, *The Rise of Modern Judicial Review*, 108. (Unlike the vast majority of conservative originalists, Wolfe is at least willing to grant some role for natural-rights philosophy in constitutional interpretation, limited as that role may be.) Given my reading of the Framers' position on the essential premise of the Constitution, *all* of the text, especially the individual-rights provisions, is grounded in natural-rights philosophy, because the Framers enacted the Constitution to serve as the institutional framework through which the natural-rights principles of the Declaration of Independence can be advanced (the Articles of Confederation had proved a miserable failure in this regard). The Court, then, should approach the *entire* constitutional text "in light of" natural-rights philosophy, not simply the provisions dealing with private property rights, as Wolfe would have it do. Specific examples of my approach to the role of natural-rights philosophy in constitutional interpretation are found in chapter 5.

fact that the Constitution speaks to capital punishment in places other than the eighth amendment is generally overlooked by those seeking to find capital punishment unconstitutional.)[46] Moreover, the fifth amendment authorizes federal capital trials when prefaced by a "presentment or indictment of a Grand Jury," and Article 2, section 2, empowers the president "to grant Reprieves." When interpreting these provisions in light of the natural-rights principles of the Declaration of Independence it is clear that the Constitution sanctions the imposition of the death penalty on a person who intentionally takes the life of another. This is because, as is explained at length in chapters 1 and 5, such a person is violating the fundamental law of nature to preserve mankind and must be removed as a threat to the political community.[47]

Given the legitimacy of capital punishment under a natural-rights interpretation of the Constitution, the opposition to that ultimate penalty, which so typifies the notion of a living Constitution, is seen to be based on nothing other than a judge's own conception of morality. This takes the immortal words of Chief Justice Charles Evans Hughes, that "the Constitution is what the judges say it is,"[48] to an unacceptable extreme. In so doing, the role of the Court in the American constitutional order, discussed at length in part 2, is corrupted and discredited.

Those who subscribe to the notion of a living Constitution frequently appeal to *McCulloch v. Maryland* (1819) and the words of Chief Justice John Marshall: "We must never forget that it is a *constitution* we are expounding[,] ... a constitution intended to endure for ages to come, and, consequently, to be adapted to the various *crises* of human affairs."[49] Importantly, however, the passage referred to in *McCulloch* to support the notion of a living Constitution is misquoted. As Walter Berns points out, "It join[s] two sentences separated by eight pages."[50] In the first sentence Marshall is reminding his audience that the Constitution is not a detailed legal code, but is instead a "great outline" of the American form of government. In the second sentence Marshall is discussing Article 1, section 8, and the power of Congress to pass laws "necessary and proper" to the legislative function. In fact, Marshall's views on constitutional change are largely in accord with those advanced in this volume. As the chief justice stated in his most famous opinion, *Marbury v. Madison* (1803), the "principles" of the Constitution "are deemed fundamental [and] permanent" and, except by means of formal amendment, "unchangeable."[51]

To put it plainly, the Constitution provides a formal mechanism for change, and that mechanism is not judicial fiat. Instead, Article 5 is what must be invoked if the nation's views on, for example, the death penalty have "evolved."[52] The argument made by some commentators that "there is nothing inherent to the Constitution that says anything about how its meaning should evolve"[53] ignores the unequivocal language of Article 5. Similarly, those who argue that the Constitution must evolve by judicial interpretation because the Article 5 amendment process is too difficult[54] are missing a fundamental point. The Article 5 amendment process may be difficult, but that is because the Framers intended it to be. As James Madison eloquently states in *The Federalist* no. 49, the amendment process was made difficult because "frequent appeals [to the people] would, in great measure, deprive the government of that veneration which time bestows on everything, and without which perhaps the wisest and freest governments would not possess the requisite stability."[55]

In summary, the Constitution can evolve, but it should do so by the intentionally arduous Article 5 amendment process, and not by the whim of unelected and life-tenured judges. Justice Black said it best. The role of the Court is to "interpret" the Constitution, not to "rewrite" it.[56]

The next criticism that needs to be addressed is that it is impossible to determine what the Framers intended. This criticism has several levels. At its most basic level, the argument is that modern Americans cannot understand what the Framers meant because our language is different from theirs. Terrence Ball and J. G. A. Pocock state this particular criticism well:

The call for Supreme Court justices, if not for the rest of us, to return to the thoughts and intentions of the Founders would require that one recover and return to the vocabulary in which those thoughts and intentions were framed in the first place. It would mean, in short, that the law of the land would perforce be couched in a language that we no longer speak.[57]

As intellectually intriguing as this reproach may be, it is, in practical terms, unconvincing. Modern Americans can understand what the Framers meant. The language the Framers used is not irremediably different from ours[58] and, as part 1 documents, it is quite feasible to understand what they intended at the basic level of philosophical principle—that embodied in the Declaration of Independence.[59]

The next level of the criticism that modern Americans cannot determine what the Framers intended is that there is no single entity that can be called "the Framers." As Leonard Levy succinctly puts it, "The entity we call 'the Framers' did not have a collective mind, think in one groove, or possess the same convictions."[60] The problem, some argue, is exacerbated when it is realized that the true source of original intent is not the Framers who met in Philadelphia during the summer of 1787, but rather those who ratified the Constitution in the state conventions.[61] James Madison's remarks to the U.S. House of Representatives in 1796 illustrate the point:

As the instrument came from them, it was nothing more than the draft of a plan, nothing but a dead letter, until life and validity were breathed into it by the voice of the people, speaking through the several State Conventions. If we were to look, therefore, for the meaning of the instrument beyond the face of the instrument, we must look for it, not in the General Convention, which proposed, but in the State Conventions, which accepted and ratified the Constitution.[62]

The uncertainty interjected by Levy, among others, must be evaluated carefully. Indeed, the argument that the ratifiers are the true framers simply appears to be a rhetorical ploy designed to discredit the theory of original intent by multiplying the number of framers "exponentially."[63] More importantly, the general convention and the state conventions shared the same intent on the fundamental question being addressed; namely, what is the principal purpose of government in the American regime? The answer given, as part 1 explains, is that the principal purpose of government is to secure the people's natural rights. Accordingly, it seems perfectly appropriate, not merely convenient, to accept the intent of the Framers as a fair reflection of the intent of the ratifiers. (This is especially the case given the importance of intellectual leadership in the American Founding. See part 1.) Stated somewhat differently, I adopt the distinction identified by Paul Brest between "moderate originalism," or originalism at the general level of philosophical principle, and "strict originalism," or originalism at an exacting level of specificity. The methodological implications of this distinction are explained well by Brest:

Interpreters often treat the writings or statements of the framers of a provision as evidence of the adopters' intent. This is a justifiable strategy for the moderate originalist who is concerned with the framers' intent on a relatively abstract level of generality—abstract enough to permit the inference that it reflects broad social consensus rather than notions peculiar to a handful of the adopters. It is a problematic strategy for the strict originalist.[64]

The problem faced by strict originalists like Meese, Bork, and Rehnquist[65] of identifying the entity called "the Framers" is thus not shared by the interpretive approach proposed here, because I am concerned with discerning the Framers' intent at a relatively general level of social consensus, that of natural-rights philosophical principle.

The final level of the criticism that modern Americans cannot determine what the Framers intended concerns the integrity of the documentary record. This criticism has been most forcefully stated by James Hutson. After carefully examining the accuracy and reliability of the convention records—*The Journal of the Convention* (1819), Robert Yates's notes (1821), Jonathan Elliot's notes of the state convention debates (1827–30), and James Madison's notes (1840)—Hutson concludes that the records have been "comprised—perhaps fatally—by the editorial interventions of hirelings and partisans." As a consequence, Hutson argues, "to recover original intent from these records may be an impossible hermeneutic assignment."[66] Again, however, a criticism is identified that may be valid against strict originalists— those who require a judge to discern how the Framers would have applied a specific clause to a given situation, and to apply it in a like manner—but that is not damaging to the theory of constitutional interpretation advanced here, since I am interested in discovering the Framers' intent at the basic level of natural-rights principle. As part 1 shows, the documentary record is sufficiently reliable to reveal that the Framers intended the Constitution to be interpreted so as to secure the hard-won fruits of the American Revolution.

The most telling criticism against a jurisprudence of original intention is that the Framers did not intend the Constitution to be interpreted in accordance with their intent. The best accounts of this criticism are those of H. Jefferson Powell and Leonard Levy.[67] Both conclude that the Framers did not mean, want, or expect the Constitution to be construed in accordance with their intent. Levy makes the point unequivocally: "If the Framers, who met in executive sessions every day of their nearly four months of work, had wanted their country and posterity to construe the Constitution in light of their deliberations, they would have had a stenographer present to keep an official record, and they would have published it."[68] Instead, argue both Powell and Levy, the Framers expected that the Constitution would be understood through traditional common-law methods of statutory construction;

specifically, by discerning the objective meaning of the language used in the document, not the subjective intentions of the authors.

Powell and Levy correctly demonstrate that the Framers did not wish future generations of Americans to adhere to their intentions on specific issues.[69] Accordingly, strict originalism is justifiably called "a sham and an illusion,"[70] because it lacks historical foundation, and the very notion of original intent depends on history. However, Powell and Levy fail to address adequately the most essential questions, namely, what were the philosophical principles motivating the Framers, and to what obligations do those principles give rise?[71] The answers to these questions depend on remembering that the Framers wrote a *Constitution*, and it is a Constitution profoundly influenced by and committed to the philosophical ideals of the American Revolution.* English writer G. K. Chesterton made the point nicely when reflecting on his voyage across America in the early part of this century: "The American Constitution . . . is founded on a creed. America is the only nation in the world that is founded on a creed. That creed is set forth with dogmatic and even theological lucidity in the Declaration of Independence; perhaps the only piece of practical politics that is also theoretical politics and also great literature."[72]

The Constitution, in other words, is a political document in the noblest sense. It establishes a framework of government through which certain underlying philosophical principles are to be advanced. And those philosophical principles are the natural-rights principles of the Declaration of Independence. To ignore this fact is to ignore the reason we are a nation.[73] Part 1 explores the natural-rights heritage of the American regime.

* The Framers' commitment to the philosophical ideals of the American Revolution also dispels another famous concern about originalism: that *our* treasured individual rights will be lost if originalism is adopted. Senator Edward Kennedy's opening salvo against the Bork nomination is the classic statement of this concern:

Robert Bork's America is a land in which women would be forced into back-alley abortions, blacks would sit at segregated lunch counters, rogue police could break down citizens' doors in midnight raids, schoolchildren could not be taught about evolution, writers and artists would be censored at the whim or *[sic]* government, and the doors of the Federal courts would be shut on the fingers of millions of citizens for whom the judiciary is often the only protector of the individual rights that are at the heart of our democracy. (Congressional Record, 133d Cong., 1st sess., 1987, S9188–S89 [daily ed., July 1])

Chapter 5, where leading Supreme Court cases are analyzed in light of natural-rights principles, illustrates that Senator Kennedy's fears are unfounded under an originalism grounded in the political philosophy of the Declaration of Independence—though the results discerned there are not always equivalent to the senator's modern brand of liberalism.

I

The Jurisprudence of
the American Founding

The Introduction endeavored to place my project in the context of the long-standing public-law debate over constitutional interpretation. I now turn to the specific historical and philosophical support for my thesis that the Constitution should be interpreted in light of the natural-rights political philosophy of the Declaration of Independence. Here, my audience is as often historians and political philosophers as it is public-law scholars. My objective, however, remains chiefly one of public law: to discern the essential principles of the American regime in order to assess what those principles have to say about constitutional interpretation.

Chapter 1 interprets the American Revolution from the perspective of the Declaration of Independence, the founding document of the

American regime. In that chapter I explore the path-breaking scholarship of, among others, three of the most influential contemporary students of the American Founding: Bernard Bailyn, J. G. A. Pocock, and Gordon Wood. I conclude that the generally prevailing practice of minimizing the Lockean liberal basis of the American Revolution is fundamentally flawed. In essence, I show that modern students of the American Revolution have overlooked—or at least misconstrued—the significance of the Declaration of Independence for the character of that event. Importantly, however, I also explain that Lockean liberalism is not as exclusively individualistic as many modern-day political philosophers maintain.

Chapter 2 turns to the Constitution of the United States. There, I examine the leading documents of the constitutional period and conclude that the Constitution was intended by the Framers to provide the institutional framework through which the philosophical ideals of the Declaration of Independence can be advanced. I therefore identify the central role the Declaration was intended to play in constitutional interpretation.

1

The Declaration of Independence

The Founders came from England to settle America for a variety of reasons. Some sought to improve their economic condition, others were recruited by those who saw colonial development as essential to the influence and power of the mother country, and still others sought freedom from religious persecution. As the colonies grew in population and developed economically, the British government enacted more and more laws regulating them. Before 1763 that regulation was largely confined to colonial trade, and the colonists had grown accustomed to a great degree of self-government in their internal affairs. After 1763 things began to change as the British government endeavored to reform its sprawling empire and to extract revenue from the colonies to reduce the national debt resulting from the recently completed French and Indian War. As might be expected, the colonists resented the new British policies.

The road to independence was, however, cautiously taken. When, for example, in 1764 and 1765 Parliament began taxing the colonies to reduce the national debt, the colonists objected vigorously, but they also reaffirmed their allegiance to the mother country.[1] Indeed, although, as a result of increasingly determined British efforts to bring the colonies under firmer control, a series of urban riots and violence ran from the Stamp Act riots of 1765 through the Boston Massacre, the Boston Tea Party, and then the fighting at Lexington and Concord in 1775, the prevailing mood in the colonies was one of reconciliation with England. The colonists first tried to "work within the system" and based their protests on "the rights of Englishmen" and on the colonial charters. Finding their conventional appeals unsuccessful, the colonists turned increasingly to the underlying doctrine of natural rights,[2] which maintains that all persons possess certain inherent, indefeasible rights by virtue of their humanity.

Much, therefore, had transpired in what is now the United States of America before the issuance of the Declaration of Independence on July 4, 1776, and as a result many arguments were made by the colonists in opposition to the increasingly frequent British oppressions that were to lead to war. But all that had transpired culminated in the Declaration of Independence, the founding document of the American regime. It is, then, the Declaration of Independence that speaks, most fully, to who we are as a nation—our origins, purposes, and ideals. It is, in other words, the Declaration of Independence that articulates "the American philosophy of government."[3] This chapter seeks to explore that political philosophy in order to understand better what the United States of America is supposed to be about, its identity, if you will. As suggested in the Introduction, only then will we be able to discern how the Constitution should be interpreted.

"An Expression of the American Mind"

Technically, our nation's independence dates from July 2, 1776, when the Continental Congress approved a resolution of independence submitted on behalf of the Virginia delegation by Richard Henry Lee. Lee's resolution proclaimed, "These United Colonies are, and of right ought to be, free and independent States, that they are absolved from all allegiance to the British Crown, and that all political connection between them and the State of Great Britain is, and ought to be, totally dissolved."[4] The fact that the United States celebrates Independence Day on July 4 instead of July 2 is a testament to the reverence with which the Declaration of Independence is held by the American people.

The Declaration of Independence was written primarily by Thomas Jefferson. Jefferson, serving on a committee that also consisted of John Adams, Benjamin Franklin, Robert Livingston, and Roger Sherman, was chosen to draft the Declaration chiefly because of his "masterly pen."[5] According to John Adams, when Jefferson came to Congress in 1775 he "brought with him a reputation for literature, science, and a happy talent for composition. Writings of his were handed about, remarkable for the peculiar felicity of expression."[6] Indeed, the "peculiar felicity" with which the Declaration of Independence is written plays no small part in the power of its message.

The Declaration of Independence as drafted by Jefferson is largely the Declaration the American people know today.[7] Franklin and Adams did make a few changes in phraseology, as did the Continental Congress.[8] The only significant substantive change, however, was the elimination by the Congress of Jefferson's "vehement philippic against negro slavery,"[9] a charge with which Jefferson sought to conclude the list of grievances against the king. The reason for the Congress's deletion of the slavery provision is explained by Jefferson in notes he took during the deliberations:

The clause ... reprobating the enslaving the inhabitants of Africa was struck out in complaisance to South Carolina and Georgia, who had never attempted to restrain the importation of slaves, and who on the contrary still wished to continue it. Our northern brethren also I believe felt a little tender under these censures; for tho' their people have very few slaves themselves yet they had been pretty considerable carriers of them to others.[10]

Late in life Jefferson was even more critical of the deletion. "Severe strictures on the British king, in negativing our repeated repeals of the law which permitted the importation of slaves, were disapproved," Jefferson wrote, "by some Southern gentlemen whose reflections were not yet matured to the full abhorrence of that traffic."[11] Significantly, however, even those who demanded that Jefferson's "philippic" against slavery be deleted did not do so because they disagreed with the philosophical principles articulated by Jefferson in the Declaration of

Independence. They were simply self-interested and did not want their economic livelihood threatened.

The Declaration of Independence is comprised of two separate, yet interrelated, parts. The first and most important part (the first two paragraphs, principally the second) addresses issues of political philosophy. The second part (the remainder) consists of eighteen specific grievances against the king that justified, in the opinion of the Founders, the break from the crown. The part that addresses issues of political philosophy is the subject of this book.

Virtually no student of American political thought denies that the Declaration of Independence is an expression of natural-rights political philosophy.[12] The pervasiveness of that philosophy at the Founding is nicely captured by Carl Becker's remark that "where Jefferson got his ideas is hardly so much a question as where he could have got away from them."[13] In fact, John Adams, who served with Jefferson on the committee appointed to draft the Declaration of Independence, once remarked that there is "not an idea in it [the Declaration] but what had been hackneyed in Congress for two years before."[14] As might be expected, Jefferson himself most eloquently expressed the strength of the consensus:

But with respect to our rights, and the acts of the British government contravening those rights, there was but one opinion on this side of the water. All American Whigs thought alike on these subjects. When forced, therefore, to resort to arms for redress, an appeal to the tribunal of the world was deemed proper for our justification. This was the object of the Declaration of Independence. Not to find out new principles, or new arguments, never before thought of, not merely to say things which had never been said before; but to place before mankind the common sense of the subject, in terms so plain and firm as to command their assent, and to justify ourselves in the independent stand we are compelled to take. Neither aiming at originality of principle or sentiment, nor yet copied from any particular and previous writing, it was intended to be an expression of the American mind, and to give that expression the proper tone and spirit called for by the occasion. All its authority rests then on the harmonizing sentiments of the day, whether expressed in conversation, in letters, in printed essays, or in the elementary books of public right, as Aristotle, Cicero, Locke, Sidney, etc.[15]

Basic tenets of advocacy confirm Jefferson's claim to have simply penned "an expression of the American mind," to have given voice to "the harmonizing sentiments of the day." After all, it would have been less than effective to justify a revolution on principles with which his audience was unfamiliar, whether that audience be the king in Great Britain or Jefferson's fellow colonists in America. The underlying character of the American Revolution is, however, presently—as it so often has been—a subject of much debate. I now turn to that important debate.

Revising the Revisionism: Lockean Liberalism and the American Revolution

Students of the American Revolution have long been interested in the character of that event. The conclusions reached have varied dramatically. For the first generation of writers on the Revolution—those who lived through and participated in the conflict—the struggle was about fundamental principles of political philosophy. Here, the original generation of American historians maintained, the cry "no taxation without representation" was emblematic of the Founders' commitment to principle.[16]

The next generation of historians offered an interpretation of the American Revolution that bordered on the theological. The Revolution, they argued, was the decisive event in God's plan for human liberty, and the leaders of the struggle against the British were depicted as larger-than-life heroes fighting to preserve God's will.[17]

Then came "the revolt against formalism"[18] at the end of the nineteenth century and the "heroic" interpretation of the American Revolution was replaced by an account that emphasized social and economic forces. The clash of economic interests between the colonies and England and the internal social and economic divisions within the colonies themselves told the real story of the Revolution, the so-called "progressive" school contended.[19] With the rise of the progressive school we see a reading of early American history that is in stark contrast not only to the heroic interpretation just described, but to the original view of the colonists as motivated by fundamental principles of political philosophy.

The progressive school's socioeconomic interpretation of the American Revolution held sway until the 1950s,[20] when it was replaced by the "consensus" theory.[21] Proponents of the consensus theory acknowledged what the progressives had long emphasized: that conflict existed within colonial America. But, this new generation of historians insisted, the progressives had gone too far in their single-minded emphasis on socioeconomic conflict. The consensus theorists maintained that the colonists were motivated chiefly by questions of political principle. In fact, in their classic study *The Stamp Act Crisis*, Edmund and Helen Morgan show how in most cases the Stamp Act was never put into effect and that the colonists, therefore, had no opportunity to experience it as an economic hardship, something the Morgans believe called the progressives' socioeconomic thesis into doubt. With the rise of the consensus theory, historians thus came full circle back to the interpretation advanced by the first generation of students of the American Revolution.

The consensus at issue for the consensus theorists was Lockean liberalism.[22] More precisely, they argued that the founding generation was thoroughly committed to the primacy of natural rights and to government's role in protecting them. The consensus theorists did not, however, have the last word on the character of the American Revolution.

Beginning in the 1960s a republican revisionism began to take shape.[23] Led by Bernard Bailyn, J. G. A. Pocock, and Gordon Wood, the republican revisionists[24] accepted the consensus theorists' emphasis on political principle; they simply denied that the principles upon which there was a consensus were the liberal principles of Locke. Instead, the revisionists insisted, the consensus was one of "republicanism." In other words, the basis of the American Revolution was not a philosophical concern for protecting private rights; it was a widely shared commitment to sacrificing private interest for the public good.

The republican revisionism has been largely successful. One student of American political thought has gone so far as to call the fall of Lockean liberalism and the rise of classical republicanism in the historiography of the American Revolution "arguably the most stunning reversal in the history of political thought."[25] Prior to the republican revisionism, the Lockean interpretation had predominated since at least the publication of Carl Becker's *The Declaration of Independence* in 1922 and Louis Hartz's *The Liberal Tradition in America* in 1955. According to Becker, "Most Americans had absorbed Locke's work as a kind of political gospel."[26] Hartz agreed, as demonstrated by his conclusion that "Locke dominates American political thought as no thinker anywhere dominates the political thought of a nation."[27]

According to the Lockean reading of the American Revolution, "republicanism" is simply a *form* of government for securing natural rights,* not, as one commentator nicely puts it, "a dynamic ideology assuming moral dimensions and involving the very character of American society."[28] The revisionists could not disagree more with this procedural characterization of republicanism. Gordon Wood, for one, explicitly rejects it in *The Radicalism of the American Revolution*, an examination of the radical—and unexpected—social change that resulted from the War of Independence. Wood asserts: "[Republicanism] stood for something other than a set of political institutions based on popular election. In fact, republicanism was not to be reduced to a mere form of government at all; instead it was . . . 'a form of life,' ideals and values entirely compatible with monarchical institutions."[29]

Isaac Kramnick succinctly explains the implications of this substantive interpretation of republicanism—this "form of life"—in his provocative book on political ideology in late-eighteenth-century England and America:

Liberalism has been toppled in recent years and replaced by a new hegemonic ideology, republicanism. A modern self-interested, competitive, individualistic ideology emphasizing private rights has been replaced at the center of eighteenth-century political discourse by a classical-Renaissance ideology emphasizing self-less duty-based participation in the communal pursuit of the virtuous public good.[30]

In other words, the motivating force behind the American Revolution was not the protection of natural rights, but the cultivation of virtue. In Bailyn's words, "The effective, triggering convictions that lay behind the Revolution were not derived from common Lockean generalities but from the specific fears and formulations of the radical

---

* Straussians who study American political and constitutional thought argue that government protects civil, not natural, rights. See, for example, Berns, "Judicial Review and the Rights and Laws of Nature," 58–66; Nedelsky, *Private Property and the Limits of American Constitutionalism;* Storing, "The Constitution and the Bill of Rights," 44–48. The Straussians, however, are making a distinction that almost none of the Founders made (something Nedelsky seems to appreciate)—and when an occasional Founder did make a distinction among the different philosophical conceptions of rights, that Founder *explicitly rejected* the argument advanced by those who study the American Founding from a Straussian perspective. See chapter 2. Briefly put, as this book describes at length, the Founders believed the fundamental purpose of government was to protect individual rights, broadly conceived, and they believed those rights were conferred by nature, not by government.

publicists and opposition politicians of early eighteenth-century England." Those fears were of political corruption. Although the "skeleton" of the Founders' political philosophy may have been Lockean, "the flesh, the substance, the major preoccupations and the underlying motivations and mood, were quite different."[31] For the Founders, the argument goes, what made a nation great or ultimately destroyed it was the character of its people. What the Founders therefore sought to achieve with the American Revolution, Bailyn claims, was an escape from the corruption of the British Empire so that the life and integrity of the American regime could be protected.

Gordon Wood's *The Creation of the American Republic* is one of the most widely read and widely praised books ever written on the American Founding. In fact, more than twenty years after publication *The Creation of the American Republic* remains, together with Bailyn's *Ideological Origins of the American Revolution*, the benchmark on early American political thought. Continuing the work of his mentor Bailyn, Wood develops the specifics of the republican thesis in meticulous detail. Like Bailyn, Wood argues that "the sacrifice of individual interests to the greater good of the whole formed the essence of republicanism and comprehended for Americans the idealistic goal of the Revolution." And what Wood means by the greater good of the whole is plainly nonliberal—indeed, it is antiliberal. "This common interest," Wood writes, "was not, as we might today think of it, simply the sum or consensus of the particular interests that made up the community. It was rather an entity in itself, prior to and distinct from the various private interests of groups and individuals."[32] And because the various private interests of groups and individuals were frequently at odds with the common good, they sometimes had to be sacrificed. After all, Wood concludes, "the common good [was] the only objective of government" for the Founders.[33]

The most aggressive figure in the republican revisionism is J. G. A. Pocock. More than even Bailyn and Wood, Pocock seems intent on exorcising the American Founding of any traces of liberalism and "the great Mr. Locke."[34] (Even Bailyn acknowledges Locke's rhetorical influence.)[35] Pocock portrays the American Revolution "as the last great act of the Renaissance" emerging from "a line of thought which staked everything on a positive and civic concept of the individual's virtue."[36] As such, he argues, because Lockean liberalism is a rival of the classical republican tradition, Locke's influence on the Founding has been significantly overstated; in fact, it has been a "myth." Instead, the American Founding was actually, in Pocock's view, a "republican synthesis" of the political philosophy of Machiavelli and the virtuous state.[37] In effect, therefore, understanding the political philosophy of the Founding "d[oes] not necessitate reference to Locke at all."[38]

Related to the republican revisionism[39] in early American historiography is a body of work that identifies Scottish moral philosophy, not Lockean liberalism, as the motivating force behind the American Revolution. The most well-known proponent of this view is Garry Wills.[40] Wills's goal, like that of the republican revisionists, is to find and emphasize a communitarian source of the American Founding,[41] although the communitarianism of the Scots is more egalitarian than that of the republicans.[42] The focus is again on virtue, with, in the case of the Scots, man's capacity to be virtuous stemming from his disposition for sympathy and benevolence.[43] Because the Scots emphasized virtue, and Locke did not, and because the Founders followed the Scots, the Founders, the argument goes, "stood at a conscious and deliberate distance from Locke's political principles."[44]

The Conspicuous Neglect of the Declaration of Independence

To his credit, Wills recognizes the significance of the Declaration of Independence to the political philosophy of the American Revolution— he simply misreads it.* Incredibly, however, neither Wood's *The Cre-*

---

*Most scholars no longer take Wills's Scottish reading of the Declaration of Independence seriously, believing that his thesis was demolished in a superb review essay by Ronald Hamoway. See Hamoway, "Jefferson and the Scottish Enlightenment." Most notably, Hamoway shows that Francis Hutcheson, the Scottish theorist whom Wills regards as the most important influence on Jefferson, was himself a student of Locke's theory of politics, especially his doctrine of revolution. While Hamoway may be unnecessarily harsh when he calls *Inventing America* "a mass of confusions, uneducated guesses, and blatant errors of fact," it is difficult to deny that Wills has simply gone too far when he argues, "There is no indication Jefferson read [Locke's] *Second Treatise* carefully or with profit. Indeed, there is no direct proof he ever read it at all." Wills, *Inventing America*, 174. Because the republican interpretation of the American Revolution is the most widely accepted, and because Hamoway did such a definitive job of repudiating Wills's Scottish thesis, I focus most of my remaining attention in this section on the republican revisionists. For an equally devastating critique of Wills's Scottish thesis, making many of the same points made by Hamoway, see Jaffa, *American Conservatism and the American Founding*, 76–109.

ation of the American Republic nor his more recent *The Radicalism of the American Revolution* contains a discussion of the political philosophy of the Declaration. Pocock's *The Machiavellian Moment* is likewise silent, as are his other essays on the American Revolution.[45] Bailyn does address the Declaration of Independence, but his focus is on the eighteen grievances against the king—to the complete exclusion of the Declaration's preceding statement of political philosophy, an approach no doubt taken to support his corruption/conspiracy thesis.[46] As John Diggins aptly notes, "To those who interpret the Revolution as either the consummation of 'The Machiavellian Moment' or the beginnings of the Scottish movement in political thought, it must surely seem a little awkward that the idea of virtue was not even mentioned in the Declaration."[47] An examination of the phraseology and themes of the Declaration of Independence shows what most Americans have long accepted: that our founding document is an expression of Lockean natural-rights political philosophy. In fact, the similarity of phraseology and themes between the Declaration and Locke's *Second Treatise* is so obvious that "Richard Henry Lee charged [the Declaration] as copied from Locke's treatise on government."[48]

Turning first to phraseology, the Declaration of Independence's "We hold these truths to be self-evident, that all men are created equal" corresponds with the *Second Treatise*'s "Men being, as has been said, by nature, all free, equal and independent." And the Declaration's reference to every individual's natural rights to "life, liberty, and the pursuit of happiness" is traceable to Locke's "life, liberty and estate."[49]

Although many, including Wills,[50] make much of Jefferson's substitution of "the pursuit of happiness" for "property" in the enumerated trinity of natural rights, the substitution is actually not a departure from Locke. Locke uses the phrase "the pursuit of happiness" in his *Essay concerning Human Understanding.*[51] Moreover, "the pursuit of happiness" was considered by both Locke and the Founders to be synonymous with "property," when property is conceived in a broad sense, rather than simply as the ownership of material goods.[52] According to Locke, "Property ... must be understood ... to mean that property which men have in their persons as well as goods." He adds elsewhere that property involves men "united for the general preservation of their lives, liberties, and estates."[53]

The fact that Jefferson was listing only "unalienable" natural rights in the Declaration of Independence provides another explanation for the absence of the word "property" from the famous clause at issue. As Locke mentions in the *Second Treatise*, man is the creation and, hence, the property of God.[54] Every individual therefore owes a duty to his Creator to fulfill himself as an individual. To satisfy this duty, as will be explained at length below, every individual must strive to protect his life, must strive to freely control the course of his life, and must strive to achieve a good and happy life.[55] Property in the narrow sense of ownership of material goods is certainly indispensable if man is to satisfy his obligation to his Creator to preserve his life and liberty and to pursue his happiness. But as important as property is in this material sense, it is alienable. Life, liberty, and the pursuit of happiness are not, as Jefferson makes clear in the Declaration of Independence. Finally, Jefferson was a wonderful writer. "Life, liberty, and the pursuit of happiness" reads more appealingly than "life, liberty, and property."

The similarity in phraseology continues in Jefferson's expression of the social-contract theory. The Declaration's phrase "deriving their just powers from *the consent of the governed*"[56] compares favorably with Locke's account that "reason being plain on our side that men are naturally free, and the examples of history showing that the governments of the world that were begun in peace had their beginnings laid on that foundation, and were made by *the consent of the people.*"[57]

The Declaration of Independence continues by claiming that "whenever any form of government becomes destructive of these ends, it is the right of the people to alter or to abolish it, and to institute new government, laying its foundation on such principles and organizing its powers in such form, as to them shall seem most likely to effect their safety and happiness." This statement is quite similar to one written by Locke in the *Second Treatise:*

Whensoever, therefore, the Legislative shall transgress this fundamental rule of society, and either by ambition, fear, folly, or corruption, endeavor to grasp themselves, or put into the hands of any other, an absolute power over the lives, liberties, and estates of the people, by this breach of trust they forfeit the power the people had put into their hands for quite contrary ends, and it devolves to the people, who have a right to resume their original liberty and, by the establishment of a new legislative, such as they think fit, provide for their own safety and security, which is the end for which they are in society.[58]

Next, the Declaration states that "Prudence, indeed, will dictate that governments long established should not be changed for light and transient causes; and accordingly all experience hath shown, that mankind are *more disposed to suffer*, while evils are sufferable, than to right themselves by abolishing the forms to which they are accustomed." According to Locke, "till the mischief be grown general, and the ill designs of the rulers become visible, or their attempts sensible to the greater part, the people, who are *more disposed to suffer* than right themselves by resistance, are not apt to stir." [59]

The Declaration of Independence closes its exegesis on political philosophy by asserting, "But when *a long train of abuses* and usurpations, pursuing invariably the same object, evinces a design to reduce them under absolute despotism, it is their right, it is their duty, to throw off such government, and to provide new guards for their future security." This claim compares quite closely to Locke's statement:

> But if *a long train of abuses*, prevarications, and artifices, all tending the same way, make the design visible to the people, and they cannot but feel what they lie under and whither they are going, it is not to be wondered that they should then rouse themselves and endeavor to put the rule into such hands which may secure to them the ends for which government was at first erected. [60]

Although the quoted passages from the Declaration of Independence and the *Second Treatise* are not always identical, they are very similar—and sometimes even identical. Any differences can be attributed to Jefferson's immense talent as a literary stylist and to the care with which he approached his assignment to write the Declaration of Independence. Simply put, Jefferson "realized that if the colonies won their independence, this would prove to be a public document of supreme importance; and the [Declaration] ... bears ample evidence of his search for the right word, the right phrasing." [61] Jefferson could not have been more prescient.

With respect to themes of political philosophy, both the Declaration of Independence and the *Second Treatise* center around three: the nature of man, the nature of government, and the right of revolution. These themes are interrelated and, revealingly, are addressed in the same sequence in the two texts. [62] Although the details of the Lockean natural-rights political philosophy of the Declaration of Independence will be discussed in later sections, I do want to touch upon the essential elements of that political philosophy here in order to show the thematic congruence between the Declaration and the *Second Treatise*.

As the previously quoted passages suggest, the characterization of man's nature in the Declaration of Independence and in the *Second Treatise* is as a naturally free and equal individual possessing certain inherent, indefeasible rights by virtue of his humanity. This characterization leads directly to the concept of government in the two documents: that government is established by the consent of the people to secure each individual's natural rights from the transgressions of others. And if the government seriously fails in this responsibility, and more critically, if the government itself intentionally and repeatedly violates the people's natural rights, the people have a right (and duty) to abolish the existing governmental structure and institute a new one. Clearly, as with phraseology, there is a congruence between the themes of the Declaration of Independence and the *Second Treatise*.

Interestingly, Jefferson took offense at the observation of John Adams and others that the Declaration of Independence "contained no new ideas, that it is a commonplace compilation, its sentiments hackneyed in Congress two years before" and to Richard Henry Lee's charge that it was "copied from Locke's treatise on government." Jefferson's response was "I know only that I turned to neither book nor pamphlet while writing it. I did not consider it as any part of my charge to invent new ideas altogether and to offer no sentiment which had ever been expressed before."[63] But in a letter to Lee, Jefferson acknowledged that he relied on Locke's *Second Treatise*, a work he regarded as one of "the elementary books of public right."[64] In fairness to Jefferson, as I endeavor to demonstrate in a moment, "the harmonizing sentiments of the day" were those of Locke, and it is easy to understand how Jefferson could claim to have "turned to neither book nor pamphlet in writing" the Declaration. Jefferson's somewhat inconsistent statements notwithstanding, it is quite apparent that "Jefferson, having read Locke's treatise, was so taken with it that he read it again, and still again, so that afterwards its very phrases reappear in his own writing."[65]

Given the obvious similarity between the phraseology and themes of the Declaration of Independence and Locke's *Second Treatise*, the republican revisionists' neglect of the Declaration is certainly curious. This neglect is even more puzzling given the comprehensive examination the revisionists (Bailyn and Wood, in particular) conducted of seemingly everything else written and said during the revolutionary period. After all, it was through the Declaration of Independence, not the myriad pamphlets, letters, and speeches of the day, that the Founders were expressing to the "opinions of mankind"[66] the official political philosophy of the newly independent United States of America. As just described, that political philosophy is Lockean liberalism, not classical republicanism.[67]

A general analysis of the political thought of the intellectual leaders of the American Revolution—thought that culminated in the Declaration of Independence—sheds additional light on the dubiousness of the revisionists' reading of the period. In fact, such an analysis is indispensable, given that intellectual leadership played a crucial role in the movement toward independence, a point also curiously neglected by the revisionists.[68] Robert Webking gets to the heart of the matter. "Although Wood and Bailyn cite some authors and speakers more than others," Webking writes, "neither tends to treat the thought of the leaders of the Revolution as more important or more indicative of the thought of the period than that of the most obscure people."[69]*

The Intellectual Leaders of the American Revolution

The natural starting point for any discussion of the intellectual leadership of the American Revolution is Thomas Jefferson, author of the

* Donald Lutz criticizes what he considers the undue attention paid to the "political elites" of the American Founding. Lutz commends Wood for making an "unstated" methodological breakthrough about the role of the larger "political class" in the Founding. See Lutz, *A Preface to American Political Theory*, 99–112. Lutz's provocative argument suffers from at least three fatal flaws. First, if Wood, a sophisticated historiographer, were making the methodological breakthrough Lutz credits him with, he almost certainly would have been explicit about it. Second, Lutz's argument overlooks the obvious point—a point convincingly documented by historians time and time again—that the American Founding is the *classic* case of the power of intellectual leadership to shape political events, including the behavior of the larger political class and the nation as a whole. Third, Lutz's argument against intellectual leadership turns out to be nothing more than a rhetorical ploy in support of his ultimate, but unsuccessful, objective: to establish American political theory as an independent discipline. My criticism of Lutz's work should not be taken to mean that I do not respect what he has tried to do. Lutz's book on American political theory is one of the most impressive pieces of scholarship I have read, even though I disagree with it. (Here, I am echoing Lutz's concluding observation that scholars need to show more "humility" in evaluating their colleagues' work.)

Declaration of Independence. Two important caveats are necessary before proceeding, however. First, volumes could be, and in most cases have been, written on the political thought of each of the leaders I will discuss. Obviously, space constraints limit what I can hope to accomplish. Second, and making the first caveat less problematic, my objective is to elucidate the intellectual leaders' position on *the* fundamental question of political philosophy and the question that concerned them most: the basic purpose of government. To put it another way, the discussion that follows is not intended to suggest that the intellectual leaders of the Revolution were influenced solely by John Locke. They were too widely read and too sophisticated for that.[70] Indeed, the republican revisionists should be commended for dispelling the *Locke et praeterea nihil* of the Becker-Hartz thesis. But, as I endeavor to illustrate, on the issue of the basic purpose of government— the issue of preeminent concern to constitutional interpretation (see the Introduction), the subject of this volume—the intellectual leaders were Lockean liberals, not classical republicans. Here, perhaps as an ironic consequence of their admirable and impressive quest for comprehensiveness, the revisionists have missed the proverbial forest for the trees.

Thomas Jefferson was the quintessential man of the Enlightenment. His contributions to law, architecture, education, science, politics, and philosophy, to name but a few fields, are impressive enough when considered in isolation. When considered in totality, Jefferson's contributions truly make him the "person of the millennium," as one political commentator recently wrote.[71]

Jefferson's political philosophy has been much debated. The traditional interpretation emphasizes his liberal ideas.[72] Although the traditional interpretation neglects many subtleties,[73] Locke's influence on Jefferson's political philosophy during the revolutionary period is unmistakable even when those subtleties are taken into account—especially with respect to the basic purpose of government. When Jefferson expressed his views on the basic purpose of government, he invariably invoked the Lockean liberal concept of a limited state charged with protecting the natural rights of the governed. In addition to the Declaration of Independence, discussed earlier, which incorporates Locke's theory of government, there is Jefferson's *A Summary View of the Rights of British America*, written in 1774,[74] which anticipated many of the natural-rights arguments made in the Declaration, as well as some revealing letters authored by Jefferson. In a well-known 1790 letter to Thomas Mann Randolph, for example, explaining what books the young man should read to understand the American political system, Jefferson recommends the *Second Treatise* for the underlying principles of political philosophy, calling "Locke's little book on government, ... perfect as far as it goes."[75] Similarly, there is Jefferson writing in 1807 to John Norvell:

I think there does not exist a good elementary work on the organization of society into civil government: I mean a work which presents in one full and comprehensive view the system of principles on which such an organization should be founded, according to the rights of nature. For want of a single work of that character, I should recommend Locke on Government, Sidney, Priestley's Essay on the First Principles of Government, Chipman's Principles of Government, and the Federalist.[76]

The focus is once again on protecting natural rights, and the *Second Treatise* is at the head of Jefferson's list.

There are also the texts for government and law students at his beloved University of Virginia that Jefferson desired to assign. To understand the founding doctrine of the United States, Jefferson wanted the students to read Locke, Sidney,[77] and the Declaration of Independence itself.[78] Jefferson's profound interest in the curriculum for the University of Virginia's government and law students culminated in a resolution he helped pass while rector. The resolution speaks unequivocally to the essential principles underlying the American Revolution, and those principles are Lockean liberal:

Resolved, that it is the opinion of this Board that as to the general principles of liberty and the rights of man, in nature and in society, the doctrines of Locke, in his "Essay concerning the origins and extent of civil government," and of Sidney, in his "Discourses on government," may be considered those generally approved by our fellow citizens of this, and the United States.[79]

James Otis was the first great intellectual leader of the revolutionary period.[80] Otis's leading role in the initial stages of the road to independence makes his thought especially significant. The intellectual leaders who came after Otis were speaking to an audience that was generally familiar with the fundamental principles on which the dispute with England rested, but Otis, writing first, bore the considerable burden of explaining those principles in detail.[81] At bottom, Otis's arguments were based on a belief that the "*end* of government ... is above all to provide for the security, the quiet, and happy enjoyment of life, liberty, and property."[82] In other words, Otis's political writings were grounded in the tenets of Lockean liberalism. In fact, Otis, widely known for his daring, as well as his brilliance, was willing to invoke natural-rights arguments much earlier than were most of the other colonial leaders, who thought it wise to hold such arguments in reserve in order better to preserve the possibility of reconciling with England.

Otis's first great revolutionary pamphlet was *A Vindication of the Conduct of the House of Representatives of the Province of Massachu-setts-Bay*, written and published in 1762. There, Otis attacks the Royal Governor for expending public money without the approval of the Massachusetts House of Representatives. In so doing, Otis quotes approvingly at length from Locke's *Second Treatise*. Otis's reliance on Locke was so extensive that John Adams was led to comment years later that "this little fugitive pamphlet" contained the "solid substance" of the Declaration of Independence.[83]

In 1764 Otis wrote and published a pamphlet, *The Rights of the British Colonies Asserted and Proved*, in opposition to the Revenue Act of the same year. That pamphlet, which was a refined version of the earlier *Vindication*, finds Otis closing his discussion of political philosophy by reminding his audience that the primary end of government is the protection of the people's natural rights. Again Otis's authority is Locke, from whom Otis quotes freely on the right of the people to alter or abolish a government that has violated its trust to secure natural rights.[84] Otis's position on the fundamental purpose of government is unmistakable: government exists to secure the natural rights of the people.

Thomas Jefferson once remarked about Samuel Adams, "I always considered him as more than any other member the fountain of our important measures."[85] Although Adams, a leader in the Massachusetts House of Representatives from 1764 on, wrote no books or pamphlets, he did write scores of letters and state papers in which his acceptance of the then prevailing natural-rights doctrine is clear. In particular, Adams was a great admirer of Locke, as is illustrated by his 1770 letter to Lieutenant Governor Thomas Hutchinson opposing the Massachu-setts legislature's being summoned to meet in Cambridge instead of Boston. "We beg Leave to recite to your Honor," Adams writes, "what the Great Mr. Locke has advanced in his Treatise of civil Government, upon the like Prerogative of the Crown."[86]

In another important paper, a 1772 report adopted by the City of Boston in opposition to the Stamp Act of 1765, Adams invokes the same Lockean political principles later employed by Jefferson in the Declaration of Independence. Of particular interest is a passage asserting that the primary purpose of government is to secure the people's natural rights. Adams writes:

In short it is the greatest absurdity to suppose it in the power of one or any number of men at the entering into society, to renounce their essential natural rights, or the means of preserving those rights when the grand end of civil government from the very nature of its institution is for the support, protection, and defence of those very rights: the principal of which as is observed before, are life, liberty and property.[87]

The influence on this passage of Locke's argument that government exists to secure natural rights—a passage that made Adams famous throughout the colonies[88]—is undeniable.

Samuel Adams did occasionally reference the need for cultivating virtue. But, as the revisionists fail to appreciate,[89] Adams saw virtue as a means to help secure natural rights, not as an end in itself. For example, an often-quoted remark finds Adams alluding to virtue's supplementary role: "I once thought, that City would be the *Christian Sparta*. But Alas! Will men never be free! They will be free no longer than while they remain virtuous."[90] Elsewhere, there is Adams explaining that cultivating virtue should be a goal of public policy because "after all, virtue is the surest means of securing the public liberty."[91] Virtue is then a secondary rather than a primary concern for Adams. To put it another way, the objective for Adams was the protection of natural rights. The cultivation of virtue was but a way of accomplishing that objective, for virtue instilled in the people the necessity of restraining their selfish impulses—impulses that would otherwise render natural rights insecure.[92]

James Wilson, born and educated in Scotland, did not come to America until 1765. But Wilson's mastery of history and the philosophy of law brought him quickly to prominence in his new home. Given his Scottish upbringing and education, Wilson is often described as an adherent of the philosophical tenets of the Scottish Enlightenment.[93]

Although this may be true for matters of epistemology, Wilson's more general political philosophy was vintage Lockean liberalism.[94]

Wilson's great revolutionary pamphlet was *Considerations on the Nature and Extent of the Legislative Authority of the British Parliament*—written in 1770 and published in 1774—a pamphlet that Becker credits with helping to pave the way "for the general theory which Jefferson was later able to take for granted as the common sense of the matter."[95] Wilson's pamphlet is important for two reasons: (1) he, unlike even James Otis and Samuel Adams, denied the legislative authority of Parliament over the colonies "in every instance";[96] and (2) Wilson included a statement of political theory, brief though it is:

All men are, by nature, equal and free: no one has a right to any authority over another without his consent: all lawful government is founded in the consent of those who are subject to it: such consent was given with a view to ensure and to increase the happiness of the governed, above what they would enjoy in an independent and unconnected state of nature. The consequence is, that the happiness of the society is the *first* law of every government.[97]

A better summary of Lockean natural-rights political philosophy would be difficult to find. Here, Wilson is arguing, as both the *Second Treatise* and the Declaration of Independence do, that the basic purpose of government is to secure the natural rights of the people, what Wilson calls "the happiness of the society."

Born in the West Indies, Alexander Hamilton did not come to America until 1772, later than even James Wilson. Like Wilson, however, Hamilton's brilliance brought him quickly to the center of the American colonists' dispute with England. A mere seventeen years of age when he first started publishing pamphlets in 1774,[98] Hamilton was nonetheless one of the revolutionary period's most zealous and articulate proponents of natural-rights principles. Essentially, Hamilton applied natural-rights doctrine to find, as Wilson had, that the colonists were not subject to the legislative authority of Parliament. According to Hamilton, the only legitimate basis of government is a voluntary compact between the rulers and the ruled "for the security of the *absolute rights* of the latter."[99] And in the case of the colonists and Parliament, no such compact existed.

Hamilton's commitment to natural-rights principles is equally apparent in one of his most famous retorts to the loyalist Samuel Seabury, better known as "the Farmer," to whom Hamilton's pamphlets were typically addressed. Hamilton writes:

The fundamental source of all your [the Farmer's] errors, sophisms and false reasonings is a total ignorance of the natural rights of mankind. Were you at once to become acquainted with these, you could never entertain a thought, that all men are not, by nature, entitled to parity and privileges. You would be convinced that natural liberty is a gift of the beneficent Creator to the whole human race.[100]

Once again we find an intellectual leader of the American Revolution dedicated to natural-rights principles. Indeed, at one point in his reply Hamilton provided a list of natural-law theorists to whom the Farmer should refer for edification. Locke's name was prominently placed.[101]

John Adams has a central place in the intellectual leadership of the American Revolution. According to Wood, "no one read more and thought more about law and politics" during the period than Adams.[102] John Adams is also the intellectual leader who most fairly can be said to have been concerned with cultivating virtue. Here, however, John Adams, like his cousin Samuel before him, typically saw virtue as a means to help secure the people's natural rights.[103] On those occasions in which Adams seems to have envisioned the cultivation of virtue as an end in itself,[104] he nevertheless commended liberal theorists, including Locke, for explaining legitimate government forms well—a subject intimately connected in liberalism with the ends of government.[105]

John Adams's occasional allusions to virtue as an end in itself notwithstanding, his agreement with the principles articulated by Jefferson in the Declaration of Independence is clear. There is Adams's 1822 comment, for example, in which Adams sought to provide some perspective on Jefferson's role in writing the Declaration, a role that had by that time lifted Jefferson to near-mythical status.[106] "There is not an idea in it [the Declaration]," Adams writes,

but what had been hackneyed in Congress for two years before. The substance of it is contained in the declaration of rights and the violation of those rights, in the Journals of Congress, in 1774. Indeed, the essence of it is contained in a pamphlet, voted and printed by the town of Boston, before the first Congress met, composed by James Otis, as I suppose, in one of his lucid moments, and pruned and polished by Samuel Adams.[107]

One should also remember that Adams served on the committee appointed by the Continental Congress to draft the Declaration of Independence, and it would be strange indeed if he did not subscribe to the principles he played such a large part in articulating.[108]

Additional signs of Adams's support for the natural-rights principles embodied in the Declaration of Independence are found in many of his political writings of the revolutionary period. Adams's *Thoughts on Government*, written in 1776, contains praise for Locke, and his *Novanglus*, written in 1774, quotes Locke at length. A younger John Adams was equally committed to natural-rights principles. Like his older cousin Samuel, John wrote many pamphlets arguing in defense of the colonists' natural rights. In one of his most famous, *Dissertation on Canon and Feudal Law*, published in 1765, Adams sounds very much like the Declaration of Independence: There are "Rights . . . antecedent to all earthly government—*Rights*, that cannot be repealed or restrained by human laws—*Rights*, derived from the great Legislator of the Universe."[109]

Also worth noting is the leading role played by Adams in the passage of a set of resolutions by the first Continental Congress in 1774 proclaiming the colonies' total exemption from the regulatory power of Parliament. Adams later said, and this is the important point, that he sought to have included in the resolutions "an appeal to those general ideas of natural right so clearly and broadly laid down, not long afterwards, in the Declaration of Independence."[110] Like so many of the intellectual leaders of the American Revolution, John Adams was strongly committed to the natural-rights principles of the Declaration of Independence.[111]

Locke's presence in revolutionary America, especially in the Declaration of Independence and the writings and speeches of the intellectual leaders of the period, is too apparent for most scholars to deny. For those who seek to minimize Locke's influence the response always seems to be the same: the Founders employed Locke for his "rhetoric."[112] This characterization not only fails to explain why the Founders' use of Locke was any more "just rhetoric" than was their use of myriad other political theorists—including republican theorists—but also overlooks, as John Dunn notes in a famous essay on Locke's influence in eighteenth-century America and England, the Founders' agreement with Locke during the revolutionary period on the essential principles of political philosophy. In Dunn's words, "The Adamses and Jefferson, Dickinson and Franklin, Otis and Madison, had come to read the *Two Treatises* with gradually consolidated political intentions and they had come to it to gather moral support for these intentions."[113]

My discussion of the Founders' profound commitment to the natural-rights principles of the Declaration of Independence is not meant to deny that they read and were influenced by political theorists other than John Locke, including republican and Scottish theorists. As noted earlier, the revisionists should be commended for dispelling the *Locke et praeterea nihil* of the Becker-Hartz thesis. But the revisionists have gone too far in the other direction—to *omnia praeter Lockem*.[114] The revisionists are simply wrong in arguing that the American Revolution was motivated by concerns for virtue. As the Declaration of Independence states in no uncertain terms—terms well understood by the intellectual leaders of the Revolution—the *essential* political premise of the American regime is that government exists to secure natural rights, not to cultivate virtue. With respect to Locke specifically, although Locke was not the only liberal influence on the Founders, he was the most important influence, as well as representative of the basic liberal tenets that guided them.[115] In addition, Locke was the first thinker to put the leading themes of liberalism into a coherent whole.[116] The Founders' considerable reliance on Locke's writings, especially in the Declaration of Independence, is, therefore, understandable. The revisionists' neglect of the Declaration is not. It is now time to explore the Lockean natural-rights political philosophy of the Declaration of Independence. That discussion will be fairly abstract here but will become more concrete in chapter 5, when specific cases of constitutional interpretation are addressed.

The Political Philosophy of the Declaration of Independence

This section is in two parts. The first part discusses Locke's political philosophy. Although this is certainly not a treatise on Locke's thought—there are already many fine examples of that*—it is neces-

---

*The scholarship on John Locke is voluminous. In 1983 Roland Hall and Roger Wool-house published a 215-page bibliographic guide to the preceding eighty years of Locke scholarship. See Hall and Woolhouse, *80 Years of Locke Scholarship*. The years since 1983 have been equally active. See, for example, Ashcraft, *Revolutionary Politics and Locke's Two Treatises of Government;* Harpham, ed., *John Locke's Two Treatises of*

sary for me, given the understandably broad brush with which Jefferson was painting in the Declaration of Independence, to provide a conceptual analysis of the key components of Lockean liberalism.[117] The second part turns to the Declaration of Independence specifically. There, in light of the conceptual analysis of Lockean liberalism provided in the first part, the natural-rights principles of the Declaration are examined, principles largely neglected today, but which, as previously discussed, speak to our national heritage and mission.

John Locke

Four interrelated components of Locke's thought are of particular importance for understanding the political philosophy of the Declaration of Independence: the structure of Locke's moral theory, his concept of rights, his consent theory of political obligation, and his doctrine of revolution. I consider each in turn.

An essential foundation of Locke's moral theory is man's relationship with his Creator. Individuals ought to obey their Creator, Locke writes, because "they are his property whose workmanship they are, made to last during his, not one another's, pleasure." And the Creator's commands, discerned by reason, are what Locke means by natural law.[118] As Locke writes in his *Essays on the Law of Nature*, natural law is "the decree of the divine will discernible by the light of nature and indicating what is and what is not in conformity with rational nature."[119]

Government; Simmons, *The Lockean Theory of Rights.* What recent Locke scholarship has done (Simmons's work is a notable exception), due in large part to the path-breaking efforts of John Dunn, is to move away from the traditional analytical approach to the *Two Treatises* to a more historical approach. See generally Dunn, *The Political Thought of John Locke.* Although this new historical approach is certainly an important development in Locke scholarship, it has no role, in my judgment, in understanding the Lockean liberalism of the Declaration of Independence. Succinctly stated, the Declaration embodies an analytical approach to Lockean liberalism, and consequently, the new biographical information concerning Locke's activities and the general reassessment of the historical period in which Locke lived are irrelevant for discerning the essential principles of the American regime, the subject of this book. Therefore, in light of the analytic perspective on Locke's thought taken by the Declaration itself, the discussion in this section brackets the genealogical material on Locke's life in favor of emphasizing those rationally arrived at principles that the Founders believed people could know—even twentieth-century Americans.

Man's ability to understand natural law brings Locke's theory of knowledge to the fore. According to Lockean epistemology—an admittedly complex and sometimes confused theory—man discovers natural law intuitively. In Locke's words, "The mind perceives the agreement or disagreement of two ideas immediately by themselves, without the intervention of any other." In that instance of perceived agreement or disagreement, the mind does not try to prove or examine the particular natural law, but sees it "as the eye doth the light, only by being directed toward it."[120] To put it in the Declaration's terms, the natural law is "self-evident" to the interpreter.[121]

Significantly, only an elite few are able to discern the true dictates of natural law.[122] Locke writes:

Some people here raise an objection against the law of nature, namely that there is no such law in existence at all, since it can nowhere be found, for most people live as though there was no rational ground in life at all nor any law of such a kind that all men recognize it. ... If indeed natural law were discernable by the light of reason, why is it that not all people who possess reason have knowledge of it? ...

I admit that all people are by nature endowed with reason, and I say that natural law can be known by reason, but from this it does not necessarily follow that it is known to any and every one. For there are some who make no use of the light of reason but prefer darkness and would not wish to show themselves to themselves. ... There are others, brought up in vice, who scarcely distinguish between good and evil, because a bad way of life, becoming strong by lapse of time, has established barbarous habits, and evil customs have perverted even matters of principle. In others, again, through natural defect, the acumen of the mind is too dull to be able to bring to light those secret decrees of nature.[123]

In other words, the interpreter of natural law must be learned, uncorrupted, and unbiased. And because these qualities are rare, in seeking to understand natural law "not the majority of the people should be consulted but those who are more rational than the rest."[124] (This is a conclusion that has profound implications for part 2 of this study, an examination of the Supreme Court's role in identifying and applying natural-rights principles in constitutional interpretation.)

Man's relationship with his Creator in Locke's moral theory is evinced in Locke's repeated assertion that "the fundamental law of nature" is "the preservation of mankind."[125] Note that the emphasis is on the preservation of *mankind*, rather than on the preservation of *individual* persons. As such, there is a communitarian aspect to Locke's moral thought, an aspect ignored by many Locke scholars, including C. B. Macpherson and Leo Strauss.[126] This fundamental—and quite general—law of nature to preserve mankind is also the "basis" for the specific rules of natural law, including those pertaining to natural rights, the focus of the Declaration of Independence. Locke writes:

> By the basis of natural law we mean some sort of groundwork on which all other and less evident precepts of that law are built and from which in some way they can be derived, and thus they acquire from it all their binding force in that they are in accordance with that, as it were, primary and fundamental law which is the standard and measure of all the other laws depending on it.[127]

A sometimes overlooked aspect of Locke's moral thought is his belief that under the dictates of natural law an individual is entitled to a generous amount of moral freedom in those areas in which his actions do not harm himself or others. Locke makes the point eloquently when he writes that "in the greatest part of the actions of our lives ... I think God out of his infinite goodness considering our ignorance and frailty hath left us great liberty."[128] As a result, there is an individualistic aspect to Locke's moral thought, an aspect underestimated by such leading Locke scholars as John Dunn and James Tully.[129]

The structure of Locke's moral theory is thus neither exclusively duty-based, as Dunn and Tully suggest,[130] nor exclusively rights-based, as Macpherson and Strauss claim.[131] A more accurate assessment is to consider rights and duties as "roughly coextensive" in Locke's thought, with neither rights more fundamental than duties nor duties more fundamental than rights.[132] In fact, in much of the *Two Treatises* there is an overlap of rights and duties. For instance, Locke speaks of both the *right* of self-preservation and the preservation of mankind and a corresponding *duty*.[133] A similar correlation between rights and duties can be seen in Locke's discussions of charity[134] and natural equality,[135] among other places. Locke's discussion of charity is especially illuminating:

> As *Justice* gives every Man a Title to the product of his honest Industry, and the fair Acquisitions of his Ancestors descended to him; so *Charity* gives every Man a Title to so much out of another's Plenty, as will keep him from extream

want, where he has no means to subsist otherwise; and a Man can no more justly make use of another's necessity, to force him to become his Vassal, by withholding that Relief, God requires him to afford to the wants of his Brother, than he that has more strength can seize upon a weaker, master him to his Obedience, and with a Dagger at his Throat offer him Death or Slavery.[136]

In summary, Marxist, Straussian, and other readings that characterize Locke's moral thought as exclusively rights-based are mistaken. Equally mistaken are purely theological and communitarian duty-based interpretations. Locke recognizes, in roughly equal measure, both rights and duties.

With respect to Locke's theory of rights specifically, all individuals are equal. As Locke writes in one of the most well-known passages of the *Second Treatise:*

A state also of equality, wherein all the power and jurisdiction is reciprocal, no one having more than another; there being nothing more evident than that creatures of the same species and rank, promiscuously born to all the same advantages of nature and the use of the same faculties, should also be equal one amongst another without subordination or subjection; unless the lord and master of them all should, by any manifest declaration of his will, set one above another.[137]

Locke certainly does not deny that *physical* inequalities exist among individuals. For example, individuals differ in strength, appearance, and intelligence[138]—with intellectual inequality being particularly significant for Locke's epistemology, as previously discussed. What Locke is speaking of in his discussion of equality is the *moral* claim all persons have to equal rights, the sum of which Locke refers to as "natural freedom." It is only when a special situation or relationship among individuals exists—when they move beyond the bounds of natural law—that unequal rights may be recognized. Examples of such special situations or relationships include those based on consent, especially to political power (a topic I soon consider in detail), and serious misconduct, when an individual forfeits his rights.[139]

Perhaps the most misunderstood aspect of Locke's theory of rights is his concept of "property." Locke considers property to be more than just rights in materials goods. "Property," Locke writes, "must be understood . . . to mean that property which men have in their persons as well as goods."[140] And though Locke nowhere explicitly provides a definition of rights, his definition of property suggests that he considers *all* rights to be property. Because, for Locke, all rights are property, the *absoluteness* of rights with respect to one's fellow man is an aspect of Locke's thought that needs to be addressed.

Natural rights might be *nearly* absolute for Locke, but the communitarian aspect of his thought suggests that they are not *completely* so.[141] One need only recall the importance of charity in Locke's thought to appreciate this fact. A. John Simmons makes the point nicely when he says that "Locke recognizes both collective and individual goods, acknowledging that rights . . . are not all there is to morality."[142] Again, the fact that Locke identifies both rights and duties is evident.

Locke's discussion of the *inalienability* of natural rights is often considered to be the area in which he most influenced the Founders, especially because of the support Locke's discussion provides for the argument against political absolutism. As such, it is important to understand Locke's position on the matter. The key to understanding Locke's position on the inalienability of natural rights is to recall that man is the property of his Creator. An individual's life is his own only to use; ownership is with the Creator. Consequently, no individual "can give more power than he has himself."[143] To make the point another way, an individual cannot alienate what he does not own. Every individual is acting as a trustee of his Creator's property, with the purpose of the trust being the preservation of mankind. Importantly, however, an individual is free to use his life as he chooses, so long as he does so in a manner that is consistent with this fundamental law of preservation. As explained earlier, this zone of freedom is quite large.

The *Second Treatise* provides the classic statement of the consent theory of political obligation,[144] a theory plainly adopted in the Declaration of Independence, where it is stated that governments derive "their just powers from the consent of the governed." According to Locke, express consent to a political order clearly obligates an individual to obey the laws. "Nobody doubts," Locke writes, "but an express consent of any man entering into any society makes him a perfect member of that society, a subject of that government."[145] And, as Dunn points out, express consent is not as rare as one might think. Dunn writes:

Any express declaration is sufficient to commit a man to membership of the society and if some may be required to make such declarations on more ceremonial occasions and others may never be required to make them at all, there are enough occasions in any man's life in which he uses verbal formulae which imply a recognition of his membership in the national society to which he belongs for any adult to be held to have made some express declaration of such membership.[146]

Moreover, argues Locke, when express consent has not been given, tacit consent may have been:

The difficulty is, what ought to be looked upon as a tacit consent, and how far it binds—i.e., how far any one shall be looked upon to have consented and thereby submitted to any government, where he has made no expressions of it at all. And to this I say that every man that has any possessions or enjoyment of any part of the dominions of any government does thereby give his tacit consent and is as far forth obliged to obedience to the laws of that government, during such enjoyment, as anyone under it; whether this his possession be of land to him and his heirs for ever, or a lodging only for a week, or whether it be barely traveling freely on the highway; and, in effect, it reaches as far as the very being of anyone within the territories of that government.[147]

For Locke, tacit consent is therefore given by anyone who takes advantage of the resources of a society.

Locke's need for arguing that man has consented to government flows from his belief in man's natural freedom. Central to Locke's philosophy is the idea that man has natural rights that are prior to government and that an individual's obligation in the state of nature is simply to seek the preservation of mankind and himself (and the subsidiary rights and duties that flow from this fundamental law of nature). Because government exists to secure natural rights—indeed, the reason for leaving the state of nature is that rights are insecure in the absence of government protection—government can be legitimate, Locke maintains, only if consent has been personally given. And personal consent is not just *one* ground of political obligation for Locke; it is, because of man's natural freedom, the *sole* ground.[148]

A political society is formed only with "the consent of every individual,"[149] with the requirement of unanimity again stemming from man's natural freedom. Once unanimous consent is obtained,[150] and people leave the state of nature and enter political society, each person consents to give up *the exercise* of his "natural powers ... to do whatsoever he thinks fit for the preservation of himself and others within the permission of the law of nature" and "to punish the crimes committed against that law."[151] Simply put, an individual agrees to be bound by the decisions of the political structure on issues of economic and social power.[152] And each individual agrees to give up the exercise of these natural powers to *any form* of government the majority "think[s] good," provided that form is not absolutist in nature.[153]

The fact that an individual gives up only *the exercise* of his natural powers in political society is one of the most fundamental aspects of Locke's political thought. As is true with man's relationship with his Creator, the governors of society hold their powers in trust for the community (and, hence, for the Creator). "The legislative being only a fiduciary to act for certain ends [the protection of natural rights]," Locke writes, "there remains still in the people a supreme power to remove or alter the legislative when they find the legislative act contrary to the trust reposed in them."[154] If the governors do act contrary to the trust, "the power devolve[s] into the hands of those that gave it," and "the people have a right to act as supreme and continue the legislative in themselves, or erect a new form, or under the old form place it in new hands, as they think good."[155]

What Locke is speaking of here is, of course, the right of legitimate resistance to arbitrary government power, the most important aspect of his political philosophy and the aspect of most immediate significance to the Founders. According to Dunn, "The *Two Treatises* is a work principally designed to assert a right of resistance to unjust authority, a right, in the last resort, of revolution."[156]

Locke's doctrine of revolution is not a particularly radical one. The people are "slow and averse" to change,[157] will bear all but "great inconveniences,"[158] and, in sum, will rise up only if there has been "a long train of abuses, prevarications, and artifices."[159] Locke, in other words, is not arguing that the people have some "abstract right" to change an existing political order, no matter what its justice and wisdom. The right is simply to resist unjust power.[160] Moreover, anarchy will be avoided because a new government will be quickly formed, a government better designed to secure the people's natural rights.[161]

The conventional interpretation of Locke's right of resistance is that the right is held only by the community as a whole and can be exercised only upon the decision of the majority.[162] That interpretation is incorrect. A careful examination of the *Second Treatise* demonstrates that Locke argues for the right of resistance for both the community as a whole (by majority decision) and aggrieved individuals. As Locke states in no uncertain terms: "Where the body of the people, *or any single man*, is deprived of their right or is under the exercise of a power without right, and have no appeal on earth, there they have a liberty to appeal to heaven, whenever they judge the cause of sufficient moment."[163]

Indeed, an individual owes a duty to his Creator to resist any unjust and sustained[164] infringement of his natural rights and must, therefore, do so. Moreover, it is not just in the self-interest of the majority to assist the aggrieved individual in his resistance—because an attack on the one is likely a precursor of things to come for the many[165]—but it is also the majority's duty under the fundamental law of nature to preserve mankind (unless mankind would be better preserved by the unfortunate sacrifice of the one).[166]

Now that the basic tenets of Locke's philosophy—the structure of his moral theory, his concept of rights, his consent theory of political obligation, and his doctrine of revolution—have been examined, it is time to turn specifically to the political philosophy of the Declaration of Independence. Although my discussion of Locke's thought was not meant to be encyclopedic—that is a different book, one that others have written many times before—I hope the conceptual analysis of the key components of Locke's thought provided here will make the following discussion of the essential principles of the Declaration of Independence more meaningful.

The Declaration of Independence

In his classic study *The Declaration of Independence*, Carl Becker observes that "superficially, the Declaration seems chiefly concerned with the causes of the Revolution, with the specific grievances; but in reality it is chiefly, one might say solely concerned with a theory of government."[167] That theory of government is spelled out, in Thomas Jefferson's unforgettable words, in the second paragraph of the Declaration:

> We hold these Truths to be self-evident, that all Men are created equal, that they are endowed by their Creator with certain unalienable Rights; that among these are Life, Liberty and the Pursuit of Happiness—That to secure these Rights, Governments are instituted among Men, deriving their just Powers from the Consent of the Governed, that whenever any Form of Government becomes destructive of these Ends, it is the Right of the People to alter or to abolish it,

and to institute new Government, laying its Foundation on such Principles and organizing its Powers in such Form, as to them shall seem most likely to effect their Safety and Happiness.[168]

The argument of the Declaration of Independence is straightforward. First, "the laws of nature and of nature's God" govern the lives and relations of all people and all nations.[169] Second, these laws unmistakably evince that all individuals are created equal and that they are endowed by their Creator with "unalienable" rights. Third, and most important for our purposes, the basic purpose of government is to secure these rights. Fourth, individuals establish government through consent, and they consent only to the exercise of just governmental authority. Fifth, and last, the exercise of tyrannical government power violates the trust established in the government and entitles the people to alter or abolish the existing form of government and institute a new one.

Essential to understanding the political philosophy of the Declaration of Independence is the concept of "self-evident truths." In fact, the claim that the Declaration is a Lockean liberal document is buttressed by the unencumbered appeal there to self-evidence as the source of moral knowledge. Locke's rationalistic doctrine of self-evident principles was not the only theory of moral knowledge available to the Founders; the doctrine of "moral sense," as expressed by the Scottish Enlightenment thinkers was sometimes referenced in the writings of John Adams, James Wilson, and even Thomas Jefferson. Moral sense for these men meant that

when we engage in moral assessment we exercise a moral faculty which is different from reason ... because that moral faculty resembles the normal five senses. ... According to [moral sense] we are supposed to *sense* that a certain kind of action, such as telling the truth, is right, whereas lying is wrong; according to [moral rationalism] we are supposed to see this by the use of reason—the same reason that is employed in mathematics.[170]

Jefferson mentions both moral sense and reason in his *Summary View of the Rights of British America* (1774), a document that, as noted earlier, anticipates many of the natural-rights arguments that Jefferson employs in the Declaration of Independence. In his *Summary View* Jefferson writes that "not only the principles of common sense, but common feelings of human nature must be surrendered up, before his majesty's subjects here can be persuaded to believe that they hold their political existence at the will of a British parliament."[171] In the Declaration, however, all reference to moral sense is omitted. What this suggests is that the Declaration relies solely upon Locke's theory of knowledge, again illustrating the Declaration's great debt to Locke's philosophical teachings.[172]

The Founders also subscribed to Locke's view that only a select few are able to accurately discern the self-evident truths of natural law. Here, Jefferson's Bill for the More General Diffusion of Knowledge is illustrative. Through his bill Jefferson hoped to educate at public expense those "whom nature has endowed with genius and virtue" to become the guardians of liberty,[173] clearly illustrating his belief that there is a "natural aristocracy" of talent among individuals.[174] John Adams was in notable agreement with Jefferson on this issue of epistemology.[175]

The idea that only a select few can accurately discern self-evident truths—what Morton White calls "self-evidence to the learned"[176]—is not inconsistent with the claim made in the Declaration of Independence that "all men are created equal." What the Declaration, following Locke, means by this famous phrase is that all persons are created as members of the same species and, accordingly, that every individual has an "equal right ... to his natural freedom." No individual, in other words, has the right to exercise natural dominion over another. But this does not mean that individuals are equal in all respects, for example, with regard to abilities or capacities.[177]

Equality has been given a more egalitarian connotation in modern political discourse than the Declaration of Independence permits. The interpretation of equality consonant with the principles of the Declaration is that articulated by Abraham Lincoln:[178]

The authors of that notable instrument [the Declaration of Independence] ... did not intend to declare all men are equal *in all respects*. They did not mean to say all were equal in color, size, intellect, moral developments, or social capacity. They defined with tolerable distinctness, in what respects they did consider all men created equal—equal in "certain inalienable rights, among which are life, liberty, and the pursuit of happiness."[179]

Here, Lincoln recognizes that the Declaration of Independence requires equality of *opportunity*—"an equal chance"[180]—not equality of *result*. Under the Declaration, individuals are equally entitled to enjoy their natural freedom. They are not equally entitled to enjoy the same fruits that result from an exercise of that natural freedom.

Additionally, the contemporary demand for egalitarianism is inconsistent with the *Second Treatise*'s express statements on the matter. Originally, in the state of nature, it was against the law of nature for an individual to appropriate more property than he could use before it spoiled. To do so would violate the fundamental law of nature to preserve mankind, because what could spoil might be needed by others to live. However, the consensual introduction of money as a medium of exchange eliminated the spoilage problem. Because money does not spoil, it may be accumulated in unlimited quantity. Moreover, argues Locke, man's Creator gave the world "to the use of the industrious and rational—and labor was to be his title to it—not to the fancy or covetousness of the quarrelsome and contentious."[181] Plainly, Locke expects that individuals who work harder and more effectively than others will be rewarded with greater material wealth.

In fact, Locke emphasizes that a just government encourages equality of opportunity, but refrains from imposing equality of result:

The increase of lands and the right of employing them is the great art of government; and the prince who shall be so wise and godlike as by established laws of liberty to secure protection and encouragement to the honest industry of mankind, against the oppression of power and narrowness of party, will quickly be too hard for his neighbors.[182]

Lockean liberalism's commitment to an individual's natural right to take full advantage of his unique abilities and capacities so as to enjoy the fruits of his natural freedom does not mean, however, that an individual is never required to share his wealth. Indeed, natural law's emphasis on "the preservation of *mankind*,"[183] rather than on simply securing the liberties of *individual* persons, requires those who are better off to help those who cannot help themselves. Here, the right to and duty of charity in Lockean liberalism, mentioned earlier and discussed at length in chapter 5, comes into play. In addition to charity, there is also, as discussed at length in a moment, the related communitarian obligation to provide some assistance to others in their "pursuit of happiness," which the Declaration recognizes as a natural right.

The Declaration of Independence states that all individuals are "endowed by their Creator with certain unalienable rights." In this passage the Declaration pronounces that certain rights are given by man's Creator, rather than by civil authority. Those rights that are solely the product of positive law can be revoked by the same civil authority that instituted them: purely positive-law rights are thus defeasible. By contrast, natural rights, being inherent in the nature of man, rather than the creation of civil authority, are not. What government does not give it cannot justly take away. Government certainly has the power to take away natural rights. But such a government, as the Declaration of Independence repeatedly exclaims, is not a just government. And that is precisely why the Founders declared independence and fought the Revolutionary War.

"Among" the "unalienable" natural rights identified by the Declaration of Independence are "life, liberty, and the pursuit of happiness."[184] With respect to the natural right to "life," the fact that the fundamental law of nature is the preservation of mankind is of utmost importance. Briefly put, natural law decrees that an individual has duties to preserve his own life and not to take the life of another. If these duties conflict—in other words, if one life is threatened by another—the innocent party is entitled to defend himself. As Locke writes, I "have a right to destroy that which threatens me with destruction; for by the fundamental law of nature, man being to be preserved as much as possible when all cannot be preserved, the safety of the innocent is to be preferred."[185]

Additionally, one who takes the life of another, when not in self-defense, forfeits his right to life. This is because such an individual is not following the law of reason and is, therefore, acting like a wild animal, not a man. In Locke's colorful language:

One may destroy a man who makes war upon him, or has discovered an enmity to his being, for the same reason that he may kill a wolf or a lion, because such men are not under the ties of the common law of reason, have no other rule but that of force and violence, and so may be treated as beasts of prey, those dangerous and noxious creatures that will be sure to destroy him whenever he falls into their power.[186]

Moreover, the definition of "political power" is the right of making laws that impose the penalty of death and any lesser penalty necessary to best preserve mankind. (One of Locke's main arguments for civil society is the more effective mechanisms for the rightful punishment of criminals that exist therein.) Finally, "justice on an offender"—treating an offender with the dignity that comes from recognizing his free will and moral responsibility—may require that "mankind . . . take away [the offender's] life."[187]

In summary, the essence of the natural right to "life" is self-preservation and the preservation of mankind. An individual's right to life is not, however, absolute, because one individual may be required to kill another to ensure his own self-preservation, whereas that same individual may be said to forfeit his right to life if he kills when not in the act of self-defense.

The right to "liberty" is also fundamental to man's nature as endowed by his Creator. In the context of the American Founding, liberty should be largely understood in the classic liberal sense of "negative freedom"—an idea for which Locke was a chief spokesman.[188] That is to say, an individual is endowed with the natural right to be free from coercive interference when making choices as to how to control the course of his life.* Like the natural right to life, liberty is not absolute, because an individual owes a duty to his Creator to preserve himself and mankind, and because no individual is free to improperly interfere with the liberty of another. These principles flow from the natural equality of man. Every individual, writes Locke, has an "equal right . . . to his natural freedom," to be free from the "will or authority of any other man."[189]

Although Lockean liberalism accepts that man's natural right to liberty is not absolute, the scope of man's liberty is nevertheless quite extensive. This is because much of what an individual does is outside of his duty to preserve mankind.

The final natural right mentioned in the Declaration of Independence is "the pursuit of happiness." In writing in the Declaration that the pursuit of happiness is a natural right—because the desire for happiness is part of man's essence as endowed by his Creator—Jefferson was stating a central tenet of eighteenth-century political philosophy.[190]

---

* Under the negative conception of freedom, government is a "night watchman" charged with ensuring that individuals are free from interference in the exercise of their personal choices. The doctrine of "positive freedom," by contrast, charges the government with ensuring that individuals are using their freedom "in the right way," or virtuously, as Bailyn, Wood, and Pocock would put it. See generally Berlin, *Four Essays on Liberty*, 118–72.

For example, in his 1776 *Thoughts on Government*, John Adams asserts, "Upon this point all speculative politicians will agree, that the happiness of society is the end of government, as all divines and moral philosophers will agree that the happiness of the individual is the end of man."[191] Adams also mentioned the right of happiness five times in the Massachusetts Constitution.[192] Similarly, George Mason spoke of the natural right of happiness in the opening paragraph of the Virginia Declaration of Rights,[193] and happiness was a favorite theme of George Washington. As Washington writes in his justly acclaimed Circular Letter of 1783:

> The citizens of America ... are, from this period, to be considered as the actors on a most conspicuous theatre, which seems to be peculiarly designated by providence for the display of human greatness and felicity. Here, they are not only surrounded with every thing which can contribute to the completion of private and domestic enjoyment, but heaven has crowned all its other blessings, by giving a fairer opportunity for political happiness than any other nation has ever been favored with. ... The foundation of our empire was not laid in the gloomy age of ignorance and superstition, but at an epocha when the rights of mankind were better understood and more clearly defined, than at any former period; the researches of the human mind, after social happiness, have been carried to a greater extent, the treasures of knowledge, acquired by the labours of philosophers, sages and legislatures through a long succession of years, are laid open for our use, and their collective wisdom may be happily applied in the establishment of our forms of government; the free cultivation of letters, the unbounded extensions of commerce, the progressive refinement of manners, the growing liberality of sentiment, and above all, the pure and benign light of revelation, have had a meliorating influence on mankind and increased the blessings of society. At this auspicious period, the United States came into existence as a nation, and if their citizens should not be completely free and happy, the fault will be entirely their own.[194]

The right to "pursue" happiness entails claims one individual has on all others, and on organized society and government, to strive to attain his happiness.[195] These claims arise because the pursuit of happiness depends to some extent on external circumstances beyond an individual's control. Without such things as health and a minimum standard of living it is impossible for an individual to strive to attain a good and happy life. Henry Steele Commager, who makes the most detailed examination of the natural right to the pursuit of happiness in the literature, states well what the Founders meant by happiness. Happiness was the simple and just things of life. It was "material comfort, freedom, independence, and access to opportunity. Happiness meant milk for the children, and meat on the table, a well-built house and a well-filled barn, freedom from the tyranny of the state, the superstition of the church,[196] the authority of the military, and the malaise of ignorance."[197]

The Declaration of Independence, unlike George Mason's Virginia Declaration of Rights, does not provide that an individual has a natural right to *obtain* happiness. The word "obtain" was included in a rough draft but dropped in the final version. What its absence indicates is that the emphasis is on opportunity, not result, an emphasis that was also seen in the Declaration's definition of equality.

Another concept central to the political philosophy of the Declaration of Independence is that governments derive "their just powers from the consent of the governed." Here, the social contract theory is announced. Of course, what is at issue is the creation of legitimate government and the concomitant limits of legitimate governmental authority.

The doctrine of consent, like that of equality, has been misinterpreted in modern political discourse. The misinterpretation is that the Declaration *requires* majority-rule democracy. As Martin Diamond perceptively observes: "The Declaration does *not* say that consent is the means by which the government is to operate; it says that consent is necessary only to institute or establish government. It does not prescribe that the people establish a democratic form of government which operates by means of their consent."[198]

The Declaration of Independence is *neutral* about the form of government the people institute to secure their natural rights. The Declaration recognizes any form as legitimate, provided it secures natural rights and is created by popular consent.[199] It is the Constitution, not the Declaration of the Independence, that establishes the American form of government. And as discussed throughout this volume, the Constitution establishes a republican form of government, not a majority-rule democracy.[200]

The final concept in the political philosophy of the Declaration of Independence that needs to be addressed is that of "revolution." On revolution, the Declaration's reliance on Locke's *Second Treatise* is undeniable. The theory of revolution articulated in both the *Second Treatise* and the Declaration of Independence is an outgrowth of the social-contract theory just described. Specifically, because the principal purpose of government is to secure natural rights, the people have the "right . . . to alter or to abolish" the existing form of government when the "government becomes destructive of these ends." Caution and patience is urged in taking such action, but when the government exhibits a pattern of intentionally violating the natural rights of the governed, the Declaration asserts that the governed have a right and duty to resist. Once resistance has been successfully achieved, however, a new government will be quickly formed, because natural rights are at risk in the state of nature. As such, although the theory of revolution articulated in the Declaration of Independence may strike many today as radical, it is not anarchical.

This chapter has argued that the generally prevailing practice of rejecting the Lockean liberal basis of the American Revolution is mistaken. In essence, I attributed the rejection of Locke's substantive influence on the Revolution to a failure to recognize the significance of the Declaration of Independence to the character of that event.

After attempting to restore the Declaration to its rightful place as the embodiment of the political philosophy of the American Revolution, I examined the specifics of that philosophy. That discussion was fairly abstract.* When I turn to issues of constitutional interpretation, the discussion will become more concrete (see chapter 5). Before doing so, however, it is necessary to explain the relationship between the Declaration of Independence and the Constitution of the United States. Chapter 2 addresses that important subject.

---

* Many modern-day political philosophers reject the idea that there are natural rights. In fact, the anti-Lockean interpretation of the American Founding may be fairly characterized as part and parcel of this larger movement in political philosophy against natural rights. Proving, as a matter of first impression, that natural rights exist is well beyond the scope of my project. My objectives are more manageable than that. What I hope to do is show that the Founders dedicated this nation to identifiable principles and to explore the obligations to which those principles give rise.

2

The Constitution of the United States

Just as scholars have long been interested in discerning the character of the American Revolution, so too they have been captivated by the question of why the Constitution of the United States came to be. And as was true of the scholarship on the Revolution, the conclusions reached about the Constitution have varied dramatically. In perhaps the most controversial book ever written on the Constitution, Charles Beard argued at the beginning of this century that the Constitution was designed to protect the property interests of the Framers, especially their holdings of government securities[1]—an argument that was subjected to extensive criticism over the years.[2]

Even though Beard's hypothesis has been pretty much demolished,[3] the debate over the Constitution has continued unabated. For instance, in a wave of books published during the Constitution's bicentennial, scholars emphasized as the reason for the Constitution's passage the economic and foreign-policy failures of the Articles of Confederation,[4] the growing difficulties of governing an increasingly large territory under a decentralized form of government,[5] and the desire to promote a blend of economic and political theories,[6] to name but a few of the most well-received bicentennial theses.

While not intending to deny the various political, social, economic, legal, and other kinds of convictions and interests that went into the compromises that became the Constitution of the United States—convictions and interests thoughtfully described by scholars over the years—this chapter nevertheless offers an explanation for why the Constitution came to be that is different from those generally embraced, especially in these days of the self-proclaimed "republican revival" in constitutional theory.[7] After examining the preamble, the framing and ratification debates, the Bill of Rights, *The Federalist* papers, the writings and speeches of the intellectual leaders of the constitutional period, and early state constitutions, I conclude that the primary reason for the Constitution's passage was the desire to secure the natural rights of the American people in a more effective way than the Articles of Confederation were proving capable of doing.

As is evident from the list of historical texts and materials I consult, my methodology differs from traditional historiography, which focuses mainly on contexts at the expense of texts. In fact, it is this difference in methodology that has led historians to view with skepticism the possibility of discerning the original intent of the Framers (see the Introduction). As historian Peter Onuf aptly notes, however, historians' criticism of a largely text-centered methodology is often unfair and sometimes misleading. In Onuf's words, "skepticism about the historical record has not prevented historians from taking great interpretative leaps of their own. ... If lawyers and political theorists show lamentably little interest in contexts, historians—eager to get on with their own story—tend to discount and disregard texts."[8]

Although I discuss the context in which the texts and historical materials I consult were written,[9] and therefore attempt to avoid the "interpretative leaps" that Onuf justifiably criticizes, some metahistorical generalization is not only unavoidable but appropriate in constitutional interpretation—the subject of this volume. This is because the objective of constitutional interpretation should be to apply the fundamental moral and political principles on which this nation is based to issues of present-day concern (see the Introduction and chapter 5). To make the point somewhat differently, a constitution is not an end in itself. It is a means by which a political community's ideals—its ends—are ordered. In the words of Justice William Paterson, who wrote an early opinion on the subject:

What is a Constitution? It is the form of government, delineated by the mighty hand of the people, in which certain first principles of fundamental laws are established. The Constitution is certain and fixed; it contains the permanent will of the people, and is the supreme law of the land; it is paramount to the power of the Legislature, and can be revoked or altered only by the authority that made it. The life-giving principle and the death-doing stroke must proceed from the same hand.[10]

Chapter 1 demonstrated that for the political community that fought the American Revolutionary War and issued the Declaration of Independence, which established the "United States of America,"[11] the "first principle" of government was the protection of the people's natural rights. With respect to the Constitution specifically, this chapter aims to show that the primary goal of that document is to provide the institutional means to secure the natural-rights philosophical ends of the Declaration.[12] I maintain that there was a continuity of Lockean liberal ideas between the revolutionary period and the constitutional period with regard to the fundamental purpose of the state.[13] It is this interest in discerning the Founders' views on the *fundamental* purpose of the state that best explains my methodological differences with historians of the period.[14]

The position advanced in this chapter was succinctly expressed by James Wilson—who was "second to Madison and almost on par with him" in terms of contributions made to the Constitutional Convention of 1787[15]—during the debate over whether the Constitution should be ratified. Wilson quoted the second paragraph of the Declaration of Independence in the Pennsylvania ratifying convention and then proclaimed, "This is the broad basis on which our independence was placed; [and] on the same certain and solid foundation this system [the Constitution] is erected."[16] Summarily stated, although there may have been ideas competing with natural-rights doctrine during the framing and ratification of the Constitution, and although the Constitution is certainly concerned with matters other than protecting rights, it was natural-rights political philosophy that remained the guiding light in the adoption of the Constitution.

The Preamble

The preamble to the Constitution states the reasons for which the Constitution was written:

We, the People of the United States, in Order to form a more perfect Union, establish Justice, insure domestic Tranquility, provide for the common defence, promote the general Welfare, and secure the Blessings of Liberty to ourselves and our Posterity, do ordain and establish this Constitution for the United States of America.[17]

Many, including the Supreme Court,[18] fail to appreciate that the preamble has substantive significance. The preamble is not simply prefatory language. Rather, as Mortimer Adler nicely puts it, "The words of the Preamble, echoing in part the language of the Declaration, breathe spirit into the rest of the Constitution. To ignore the Preamble is to disregard the ideals of the Constitution and the fundamental ideas and principles that it derives from the Declaration."[19]

Several ideas are expressed in the preamble, but all relate to the basic purpose of government in the American regime: the protection of the people's natural rights. And while this is not explicitly stated in the preamble, Edmund Randolph's remarks during the federal Convention indicate it was certainly well understood:

A preamble seems proper not for the purposes of designating the ends of government and human polities—This . . . display of theory, howsoever proper in the first formation of state governments, . . . is unfit here; since we are not working on the natural rights of men not yet gathered into society, but upon those rights, modified by society, and . . . interwoven with what we call . . . the rights of states.[20]

The preamble's pronouncement that the Constitution is "ordain[ed] and establish[ed]" by "We, the People of the United States" expresses the Lockean liberal tenet—central to the Declaration of Independence—that political legitimacy flows only from the consent of the governed, because any legitimate political community must respect the natural rights of all persons subject to its power.

The proclamation that the Constitution is established "to form a more perfect union" reflects the Framers' unpleasant experience of living under the Articles of Confederation, and especially the fact that natural rights were being poorly protected by the decentralized form of government established therein. As explained at length throughout this chapter, James Madison, to name but the most notable example, was greatly concerned about the violations of natural rights occurring under the Articles, as his preconvention memorandum *Vices of the Political System of the United States* makes clear. Briefly stated, Madison argues in *Vices* that the Articles of Confederation had led to democracy run amok.[21]

The preamble's pledge to "establish justice" is a reflection of the Framers' underlying premise that the fundamental purpose of the Constitution is to secure natural rights. For the Framers, to establish justice meant instituting a form of government that would make individuals confident that their rights were secure. In other words, and contrary to the interpretive position of the proponents of a "living Constitution,"[22] justice is "*not* an 'ideal' to be progressively pursued or promoted by government; it is an arrangement established from the beginning. ... Accordingly, the most that can be 'established' is not justice itself but a government able to restrain injustice and unlikely to commit injustice."[23] Madison's response to Roger Sherman's claim that the sole objects of the union were better foreign relations and the prevention of disputes among the states nicely exemplifies the point that, for the Framers, to establish justice meant the Constitution was designed to protect natural rights. As Madison puts it, "The necessity of providing more effectually for the security of private rights, and the steady dispensation of Justice. Interferences with these were evils which had more perhaps than any thing else produced this convention."[24]

The preamble's pledge to establish justice is directly related to the Constitution's next objective, to "insure domestic tranquility." Here, the Constitution recognizes that without civil peace—the absence of civil disorders and disturbances—natural rights are insecure.

Next, the Constitution promises to "provide for the common defence." With this provision the preamble turns from a concern with domestic tranquility to a concern with international conflict. The covenant is that the national government will keep natural rights secure from foreign interference. While it was generally understood by the

Framers that national defense is the most important function of the national government for securing natural rights, they were cognizant of the threat that a standing army posed to those same rights. Madison's remarks during the ratification debate are illustrative:

A standing force, therefore, is a dangerous, at the same time that it may be a necessary, provision. On the smallest scale it has its inconveniences. On an extensive scale its consequences may be fatal. On any scale it is an object of laudable circumspection and precaution. A wise nation will combine all these considerations; and, whilst it does not rashly preclude itself from any resource which may become essential to its safety, will exert all its prudence in diminishing both the necessity and the danger of resorting to one which may be inauspicious to its liberties.[25]

The promise to "promote the general welfare" is the most ambiguous of the five phrases in the preamble that state the objectives of the Constitution. The "general welfare" is properly understood as the "public good" or "public happiness" of society, something that was frequently measured as "the permanent and aggregate interests of the community,"[26] rather than simply as the protection of the natural rights of individuals. Indeed, as Morton White rhetorically asks, "why would Madison have referred so often to the mischief of violating private rights *and* to that of acting in contravention to the public good if he had not distinguished between these two kinds of mischief?"[27]

While the Framers sometimes did distinguish between private rights on the one hand and the public good on the other, it must be remembered that the *principal* (i.e., the foremost, but not the sole) purpose of government in the American regime is to secure the people's natural rights[28] and that the violation of natural rights itself causes public unhappiness.[29] Moreover, as chapter 1 explained, according to the dictates of Lockean liberalism, the security of an individual's natural rights depends on the existence of political society, and the continuation of political society—the essence of the public good—therefore needs to be ensured.[30] Madison's observation in *The Federalist* no. 43 that "the great principle of self-preservation [and] ... the transcendent law of nature and of nature's God ... declares that the safety and happiness of society are the objects to which all political institutions aim and to which all such institutions must be sacrificed"[31] indicates that he well understood the connection between the protection of natural rights and the promotion of the public good.

The final clause of the preamble declares that one of the reasons for adopting the Constitution is to "secure the blessings of liberty to ourselves and our posterity." Here, the preamble is speaking of the liberty that exists when a government is established by consent and is indicating that the "blessings" previously enumerated are best secured by that liberty. In addition, the Constitution promises to preserve those blessings for the generations of Americans to come.[32]

In summary, the preamble to the Constitution is rich in meaning. It reflects the Framers' view that the Articles of Confederation, our nation's first effort at securing the philosophical ideals of the Declaration of Independence,[33] failed in its attempt. And the preamble manifests our nation's intention not to fail again.

The Framing and Ratification of the Constitution

Concern about the ineffectiveness of the Articles of Confederation, passed by the Continental Congress in 1777 and finally ratified by all thirteen states in 1781, had been expressed from the beginning. As long as the nation was still at war, however, the Articles seemed to work. But when the British surrendered in 1782, and the states' pressing need to work together seemingly disappeared, government quickly fell into disarray. As a result, after much soul searching, several intellectual and political leaders of the new nation—with James Madison and George Washington first among them—saw the need to rethink the form of government embodied in the Articles of Confederation, and the call for a national convention, originally empowered simply to amend the Articles, was made.

There was little philosophizing about the ultimate ends of government during the confederation period.[34] This dearth of philosophizing carried over to the Constitutional Convention of 1787 as well. The absence of much discussion about the ends of government was not, however, because the Framers were unconcerned about the matter. Rather, it was because the matter was so well settled by the Declaration of Independence: the fundamental purpose of government is to secure the natural rights of the people—a point reaffirmed repeatedly in the preamble to the Constitution.

The task facing the Framers of the Constitution was therefore different from that faced by those who issued the Declaration of Independence. For the revolutionary leaders the assignment was to articulate the ends of government; for the Framers of the Constitution it was to create a form of government that would best secure those ends.[35] Even the delegates who ultimately refused to sign the Constitution shared the Convention's underlying commitment to the ends articulated in the Declaration. Elbridge Gerry, for one, remarked at the Convention that he "wished we could be united in our ideas concerning a permanent Govt. All aim at the same end, but there are great differences as to the means."[36]

Although the subject of the philosophical ideals of government was taken largely for granted in Philadelphia in 1787, what was said demonstrates that the delegates remained committed to the natural-rights political philosophy of the Declaration of Independence. For example, George Mason responded to a statement by Gerry that the biggest problem with the Articles of Confederation was an "excess of democracy"[37] by admitting that the Articles were "too democratic." Mason, however, "was afraid that we should incautiously run into the opposite extreme. We ought to attend to the rights of every class of people." Elsewhere, Mason reminded the Convention that he had "for his primary object, for the pole star of his political conduct, the preservation of the rights of the people."[38]

James Madison, whose views on the relationship between the Declaration of Independence and the Constitution will be discussed throughout this volume, also stated during the Convention that his principal aim was to secure the "rights of the people." Indeed, in a June 6, 1787, speech to the Convention Madison previewed the famous argument on factions he was to make in *The Federalist* no. 10. "In all cases where a majority are united by a common interest or passion," Madison remarked, "the rights of the minority are in danger."[39] This concern with protecting rights also explains Madison's appeal just prior to the Convention to the Lockean notion of instituting a "disinterested and dispassionate umpire in disputes between different passions and interests in the States."[40]

Roger Sherman demonstrated that he well understood that the Constitutional Convention of 1787 was called to address a problem different from that confronting the Continental Congress in 1776. "The question [faced by the Convention] is not what rights naturally belong to men," Sherman declared, "but how they may be most equally and effectually guarded in society."[41] And recall Edmund Randolph's related observation about the time and place for philosophizing about the ideals of the state: "This ... display of theory, howsoever proper in the first formation of state governments, ... is unfit here; since we are not working on the natural rights of men not yet gathered into society, but upon those rights, modified by society, and ... interwoven with what we call ... the rights of states."[42]

On occasion the delegates were forced to confront proposals for the Constitution that were at odds with the natural-rights principles guiding their project. For example, Gouverneur Morris made a strong appeal to natural-rights doctrine when he opposed a proposal to count the slave population when apportioning representatives in Congress. Morris angrily exclaimed:

The inhabitant of Georgia and South Carolina who goes to the Coast of Africa, and in defiance of the most sacred laws of humanity tears away his fellow creatures from their dearest connections and damns them to the most cruel bondages, shall have more votes in a *Government instituted for protection of the rights of mankind*, than the Citizen of Pennsylvania or New Jersey who views with a laudable horror, so nefarious a practice. [This would be] a sacrifice of every right, of every impulse of humanity.[43]

Robert Yates was another delegate who strongly expressed his commitment to natural-rights principles. In fact, Yates characterized several natural-rights theorists—including Locke—as correctly explicating the fundamental purpose of government. "The first principle of government," Yates explained, "is founded on the natural rights of individuals, and in perfect equality. Locke, Vattel, Lord Somers, and Dr. Priestly, all confirm this principle."[44] As an examination of the records of the federal Convention indicates, when a delegate saw the occasional need to remind the Convention of the ends of government, those ends remained as articulated in the Declaration of Independence.

The debate over the ratification of the Constitution brought the doctrine of natural rights—assigned to the background of commonly accepted values during the Constitutional Convention—once again to the foreground of the political debate.[45] For instance, Mercy Otis Warren, one of the most strident opponents of the Constitution, opposed ratification because she believed that "the whole constitution with very few exceptions appears a perversion of the rights of particular states, and of private citizens." To Warren, "the rights of individuals ought to be the primary object of all government, and cannot be too securely guarded by the most explicit declarations in their favor."[46] Here, the chief objection of the "Antifederalists'"—those opposing ratification—to the Constitution is evinced: the absence of a bill of rights.*

Luther Martin shared Warren's concern about the absence of a bill of rights to secure the natural rights of the American people. Martin's position is well summarized in a March 21, 1788, letter to the citizens of Maryland explaining his opposition to ratification:

> Had the government been formed upon principles truly federal, as I wished it, legislating only in their collective or political capacity, and not on individuals, there would have been no need of a bill of rights, as far as related to the rights of individuals, but only as to the rights of states. But the proposed constitution being intended and empowered to act not only on states, but also on individuals, it renders a recognition and a stipulation in favour of the rights of both states and of men, not only proper, but in my opinion absolutely necessary.[47]

George Mason, author of the Virginia Declaration of Rights and one of the American Founding's most influential spokesmen on the natural rights of man, also opposed the Constitution because of the absence of a bill of rights. As Mason succinctly observed, "There is no declaration of rights: and the laws of the general government being paramount to the laws and constitutions of the several states, the declarations of rights in the separate states, are no security."[48] As the remarks of Warren, Martin, and Mason reveal, although Antifederalists throughout the country opposed the Constitution for a variety of reasons, the overriding concern of all Antifederalists was the absence of a bill of rights to protect the people's natural rights.[49]

Another notable advocate of the need to add a bill of rights to the Constitution was the author of the Declaration of Independence, Thomas Jefferson. Though Jefferson was in Paris during the framing

---

*Early in her *Observations on the New Constitution* Warren engages in an obvious exegesis on the political philosophy of the Declaration of Independence:

> All writers on government agree, and the feelings of the human mind witness the truth of these political axioms, that man is born free and possessed of certain unalienable rights—that government is instituted for the protection, safety, and happiness of the people, and not for the profit, honour, or private interest of any man, family, or class of men—That the origin of all power is in the people, and that they have an incontestible right to check the creatures of their own creation, vested with certain powers to guard the life, liberty and property of the community. (In Ford, ed., *Pamphlets on the Constitution of the United States*, 6)

and ratification of the Constitution, he nevertheless had tremendous influence on what transpired in the United States. The primary conduit through which Jefferson expressed his thoughts on the Constitution was an exchange of correspondence with James Madison. Jefferson was initially a reluctant supporter of the Constitution, and one of his most important letters to Madison tersely explains why. "A bill of rights," Jefferson writes, "is what the people are entitled to against every government on earth, general or particular, and what no just government should refuse, or rest on inference."[50] Indeed, it was only after Madison promised to secure the addition of the Bill of Rights that Jefferson became more supportive of the Constitution.

Not to be outdone in their dedication to the natural rights of man, the "Federalists"—those supporting the ratification of the Constitution—employed natural-rights doctrine to argue *against* the inclusion of a bill of rights in the proposed Constitution. The Federalists turned mainly to the nature of the federal Constitution. The federal Constitution is one of enumerated powers only, the Federalists argued, and the national government is not conferred power in the area of individual rights. As James Wilson stated in his State House speech of October 4, 1787, "It would have been superfluous and absurd, to have stipulated with a federal body of our own creation, that we should enjoy those privileges of which we are not divested either by intention or the act that has brought the body into existence."[51] Moreover, argued Wilson, a bill of rights would be dangerous to the natural rights of the American people because "it would imply that whatever is not expressed was given, which is not the principle of the proposed constitution."[52]

James Madison echoed Wilson's concerns when he initially spoke against the inclusion of a bill of rights in the Virginia ratifying convention. "Can the general government exercise any power not delegated? " Madison asked. "If an enumeration be made of our rights, will it not be implied that everything omitted, is given to the general government? "[53]

Alexander Hamilton brought Wilson's and Madison's argument to full flower in *The Federalist* no. 84:

> I go further and affirm that bills of rights, in the sense and to the extent in which they are contended for, are not only unnecessary in the proposed Constitution, but would even be dangerous. They would contain exceptions to powers not granted; and, on this very account, would afford a colorable pretext

to claim more than were granted. For why contend that things shall not be done which there is no power to do?[54]

Hamilton concludes no. 84 by reminding his audience that "the Constitution is itself ... A BILL OF RIGHTS. The several bills of rights in Great Britain form its constitution, and conversely the constitution of each state is its bill of rights. And the proposed Constitution, if adopted, will be the bill of rights of the Union."[55]

In the end, the Antifederalists prevailed in the debate over the Bill of Rights,[56] and the Constitution was ratified only because the Federalists promised to add a bill of rights at the first opportunity.* That promise soon was fulfilled by Madison in the first Congress, with Madison's change of heart being largely attributable to his recognition of the importance to the American people of securing their natural rights. Madison's closing remarks in his June 8, 1789, speech to the U.S. House of Representatives advocating the adoption of the Bill of Rights demonstrate the point. "I think we should obtain the confidence of our fellow-citizens," Madison argued, "in proportion as we fortify the rights of the people against the encroachments of the Government."[57]

The Bill of Rights

Although not included as part of the Constitution drafted in Philadelphia in 1787, the Bill of Rights, as the previous discussion suggests, is an important part of the Constitution as it was finally enacted. Herbert Storing, a leading authority on the American Founding, goes so far as to say that "it seems quite plausible today, when so much of constitutional law is connected with the Bill of Rights, to conclude that the Antifederalists, the apparent losers in the debate over the Constitution, were ultimately the winners."[58] While Storing's observation appears to overstate the difference of opinion that existed between the Federalists

---

* Although the Antifederalists were influenced by the classical republican tradition—especially in their concern about the size of the federal republic envisioned by the Federalists—the Antifederalists' insistence on a bill of rights shows they were liberals in the "decisive sense" of regarding the end of government as the protection of individual rights, not the cultivation of virtue or the promotion of some organic common good. Storing, *What the Anti-Federalists Were For*, 83. See also Sinopoli, *The Foundations of American Citizenship*, 7, 155; R. M. Smith, *Liberalism and American Constitutional Law*, 14.

and the Antifederalists on the necessity of securing the rights of the American people (the previous section described how the two camps differed about the best *means* to secure rights, but not about the *ends* of government itself), the observation nicely captures the significance of rights in the American regime. To make the point somewhat differently, the Constitution and the Bill of Rights had the same objective for the Framers—the latter merely declared the rights the former was designed to secure.*

The Bill of Rights does not seek to protect only natural rights— several provisions simply secure certain common-law rights[59]—but natural rights are what the Bill of Rights is most concerned with. An examination of the specific amendments comprising the Bill of Rights illustrates this fact. Obviously, a comprehensive analysis of the various clauses and provisions of the first ten amendments to the Constitution is beyond the scope of this section. It is possible, however, to discern the essential natural-rights principles embodied in the amendments. (A more detailed analysis of several of the amendments is available in chapter 5's discussion of constitutional interpretation.)

Before we turn to the specific amendments comprising the Bill of Rights, it should be recalled what the principal natural rights identified by the Declaration of Independence are and what they essentially mean. The natural rights identified are "life, liberty, and the pursuit of happiness," and they have been shown to mean, respectively, an individual's right (and duty) to protect his life, to freely control the course of his life, and to strive for a good and happy life.

In this light, the first amendment certainly embodies the idea of an individual's natural rights to liberty and the pursuit of happiness; guaranteeing as the amendment does freedom of religion, speech, press, assembly, and access to government by petition.

The second and third amendments, which guarantee, respectively,

---

*One should not interpret the fact that the Bill of Rights—or at least amendments 1 through 8 (see below)—did not originally apply to the states as a sign that the Federalists had abandoned their concern about the violations of natural rights occurring in the states. As explained above, the Bill of Rights was intended by the Federalists primarily to assuage the Antifederalists' fear that the national government would become too strong. As a result, there was no need to make the first eight amendments applicable to the states. The ninth and tenth amendments, discussed in detail below, illustrate the Federalists' continuing commitment to the Declaration of Independence's premise: no just government, federal or state, may violate natural rights.

an individual's right to keep and bear arms and to be free from government-imposed quartering of troops in his home, are designed to secure the natural rights of life and liberty.

The fourth amendment's prohibition against unreasonable or unwarranted government searches and seizures protects the natural right to liberty by proscribing government intimidation and coercion. The fifth and sixth amendments, by detailing a procedural floor to which the government must adhere when prosecuting an individual for offenses against the state, protect the natural rights of life and liberty. The natural right to property is likewise protected by the due process and just-compensation clauses of the fifth amendment.

The eighth-amendment* prohibitions against excessive bail and cruel and unusual punishment protect an individual's natural right to be free from inhuman treatment by the government.

Finally, there are the ninth and tenth amendments. Both provide that the rights not listed in the preceding eight amendments are still to be given government protection. The tenth amendment speaks to rights identified by state law (to be protected by state government), whereas the ninth amendment addresses all *unenumerated* rights (to be protected by both federal and state government).[60] Because, for natural-rights purposes, the ninth amendment is the most important, not to mention the most controversial, amendment to the Constitution, it warrants detailed consideration.

Though the ninth amendment lay dormant for most of the Constitution's history, it must have meant something to the Framers.[61] The ninth amendment means what it says: "The enumeration in the Constitution of certain rights shall not be construed to deny or disparage others retained by the people."[62] That the ninth amendment was intended to protect unenumerated rights seems clear from its text, as well as from James Madison's June 8, 1789, speech to the U.S. House of Representatives advocating the adoption of the Bill of Rights. In that speech Madison, who wrote the ninth amendment (as well as the other provisions of the Bill of Rights), made the following observation:

---

* The seventh amendment, which extends the right to trial by jury from criminal to civil matters and incorporates the common law into the law of the land, does not address issues of natural rights. See James Madison, Speech to the United States House of Representatives on Adopting the Bill of Rights, June 8, 1789, in Meyers, ed., *The Mind of the Founder*, 168.

It has been objected also against a bill of rights, that, by enumerating particular exceptions to the grant of power, it would disparage those rights which were not placed in that enumeration; and it might follow by implication, that those rights which are not singled out, were intended to be assigned into the hands of the General Government, and were consequently insecure. This is one of the most plausible arguments I have ever heard against the admission of a bill of rights into this system; but, I conceive, that it may be guarded against. I have attempted it, as gentlemen may see by turning to the last clause of the fourth resolution [the ninth amendment].[63]

In a well-known argument, Raoul Berger and Robert Bork, among others,[64] interpret Madison's remarks to mean that the ninth amendment was designed to ensure that rights already held by the people under state law would remain with the people and that the enumeration of rights in the federal Constitution did not change this fact.[65] The difficulty with this interpretation is that it accuses Madison of redundancy by characterizing the ninth amendment as just another way of stating the tenth amendment. Certainly, redundancy is a questionable accusation to make against a technician as skilled as the "father" of the Constitution and the Bill of Rights.

Moreover, Berger's and Bork's interpretation of the ninth amendment fails to recognize that enumerating rights in the Constitution was seen by the Framers as presenting *two* potential dangers, not one. Madison's just-quoted remarks identify these two potential dangers. The first was that an enumeration of rights could be used to justify an unwarranted enlargement of federal powers. The second was that any right excluded from an enumeration would be imperiled. The danger of interpreting federal powers too broadly was addressed by the tenth amendment, while the danger of jeopardizing unenumerated rights was handled by the ninth amendment.[66]

The fact that enumerating rights in the Constitution was seen by the Framers as presenting two potential dangers is further illustrated by letters written by Madison to Thomas Jefferson and George Washington. Madison's letter to Jefferson, one in a series between the two men written during the height of the debate over whether the Constitution should contain a bill of rights, shows Madison clearly separating the question of unenumerated powers from the question of unenumerated rights. Madison writes:

My own opinion has always been in favor of a bill of rights; provided it be so framed as not to imply powers not meant to be included in the enumeration.

... I have not viewed it in an important light—1. because I conceive that in a certain degree ... the rights in question are reserved by the manner in which the federal powers are granted. 2. because there is great reason to fear that a positive declaration of some of the most essential rights could not be obtained in the requisite latitude.[67]

Madison's letter to Washington—which is typically claimed *to support* Berger's and Bork's interpretation of the ninth amendment[68]— finds Madison explaining why Edmund Randolph's objection to the ninth amendment, on the ground that the amendment should have been stated "rather as a provision against extending the powers of Congress by their own authority, than a protection to rights reducible to no definite certainty,"[69] is without merit. According to Madison: "The distinction be, as it appears to me, altogether fanciful. If a line be drawn between the powers granted and the rights retained, it would seem to be the same thing, whether the latter to be secured by declaring that they shall not be abridged, or that the former shall not be extended."[70]

Reading Madison's letter in the context of Randolph's objection— which is usually not done—reveals that Madison is concerned in the ninth amendment with protecting unenumerated rights, rights he describes to Washington as "reducible to no definite certainty." To make the point directly, if Madison meant by the ninth amendment only that rights already held by the people under state law would remain with the people and that the enumeration of rights in the federal Constitution did not change this fact, those rights would *not* be "reducible to no definite certainty." The interpretation advanced by Berger and Bork cannot account for the possibility of an uncertainty in the enumeration of rights, because their view is that the ninth amendment is referring to rights already enumerated under state law. Here, one sees the importance of reading Madison's statement to Washington in context, something Berger and Bork fail to do.

Lastly, the fact that the ninth amendment is not just another way of stating the tenth amendment is demonstrated by considering the tenth amendment itself. The tenth amendment states: "The powers not delegated to the United States by the Constitution, nor prohibited by it to the States, are reserved to the States respectively, *or to the people.*"[71] The critical language is the italicized "or to the people." If the ninth amendment means what Berger and Bork say it means, then that language is unnecessary. Specifically, if "rights retained by the people" merely means "rights granted under state law," then it would have been sufficient for the tenth amendment to say that any power not granted to the federal government, nor withheld from the states, remains with the states. But the tenth amendment is not limited in that manner. And this is precisely because the Framers believed that there are certain rights—natural rights—beyond the power of any legitimate government, federal or state, to invade.[72] Simply put, the Framers were not positivists, despite the efforts of Berger and Bork to make them so.[73] Thomas Grey makes the point well in a famous article on natural rights and the Constitution, an article that emphasizes the significance of the ninth amendment. According to Grey:

For the generation that framed the Constitution, the concept of a "higher law," protecting "natural rights," and taking precedence over ordinary positive law as a matter of political obligation, was widely shared and deeply felt. An essential element of American constitutionalism was the reduction to written form—and hence to positive law—of some of the principles of natural rights. But at the same time, it was generally recognized that written constitutions could not completely codify the higher law. The ninth amendment is the textual expression of this idea in the federal Constitution.[74]

The ninth amendment's intended protection of both unenumerated *positive* rights and unenumerated *natural* rights is evident in Madison's differentiation in his June 8, 1789, speech between "the preexistent rights of nature," or "natural right[s]," and rights "resulting from a social compact," or "positive rights."[75] Madison's appreciation of the importance of protecting natural rights in the Bill of Rights is consistent with his writings in *The Federalist* and elsewhere (see the next two sections of this chapter), as well as with the view prevailing at the time he wrote the Bill of Rights.[76]

The unwillingness of Berger and Bork to recognize that the ninth amendment was designed to protect unenumerated natural rights is attributable to the fear they share with most contemporary conservatives about judicial activism and the encouragement of such activism that a substantive reading of the ninth amendment allegedly would provide.[77] Underlying the conservatives' position is a characterization of judicial review as a "deviant institution in the American democracy,"[78] because judicial review is outside of the processes of majoritarian politics. However, opposition to a robust judicial role in the American constitutional order mistakenly interprets the Declaration of

Independence as requiring that government operate by majority rule. As discussed in chapter 1, the Declaration is *neutral* about the form of government the people establish to secure their natural rights. The Declaration recognizes any form as legitimate, as long as the established form secures natural rights and is instituted by popular consent.

The Constitution, not the Declaration of Independence, addresses how the government is to operate. And the Constitution does not establish a majority-rule democracy. As described in the Introduction, virtually every component of the Constitution contains strong antimajoritarian features, because the Framers were concerned with majoritarian threats to the rights of individuals and minorities more than with anything else.[79] Indeed, James Madison's most important political writings are about the dangers of unchecked majorities and his suggested solutions for protecting against those dangers.[80] Following Madison's counsel, the Framers created a republican form of government, not a majority-rule democracy. The republican form of government they created, as part 2 discusses at length, gives the judiciary the chief role in protecting individual and minority rights. The interpretation of the ninth amendment advanced by so many contemporary conservatives—leaving unenumerated natural rights unprotected by the federal judiciary—is, therefore, influenced by an errant reading of the American constitutional order.*

The Federalist Papers

The Federalist papers are a series of newspaper essays written by Alexander Hamilton, James Madison, and John Jay under the pseudonym "Publius" to persuade the people of New York and, to a lesser

---

*An argument that seems to support the conservatives' position is the absence from early Supreme Court opinions of direct reference to the ninth amendment. As I show in chapter 3, however, early judges, including early Supreme Court justices, were not as explicitly textual in their approach to constitutional interpretation as the conservatives' argument requires. One commentator characterizes the issue of whether the Framers meant for the judiciary to enforce unwritten natural rights as "the critical issue—which has not been adequately answered by scholars" and the issue that separates the competing conceptions of the ninth amendment discussed in this section. See Mayer, "The Natural Rights Basis of the Ninth Amendment," 323. Part 2 of this volume attempts to fill that void in the literature.

degree, the other states, to ratify the Constitution. Notwithstanding their occasional polemical excesses, these brilliant essays are generally regarded as the best insight into the Framers' understanding of the Constitution.[81] As is true of the political philosophy of the Declaration of Independence, there is disagreement in the scholarly community about the influence of Lockean liberalism on *The Federalist*. For example, Garry Wills argues that the Scottish Enlightenment thinkers, not Locke, were Publius's guide.[82] David Epstein contends that *The Federalist* is a combination of Locke's theory of individual rights and classical republicanism.[83] Martin Diamond and Thomas Pangle claim that Locke was by far the predominant influence on the political philosophy of *The Federalist*, although, like most students of Leo Strauss, they tend to characterize Locke as just a sugar-coated version of the purely individualistic Hobbes.[84] Lastly, Morton White maintains that *The Federalist* is a hybrid of Locke's political philosophy and Hume's political science.[85]

White's interpretation of Locke's influence on *The Federalist* is consistent with Jefferson's observation that "Locke's little book on government, is perfect as far as it goes. ... Descending from theory to practice, there is no better book than *The Federalist*," as well as with Locke's distinction between political philosophy and "the art of governing men in society."[86] In other words, an examination of *The Federalist* provides additional evidence that the Constitution was intended by the Framers to provide the institutional means to secure the philosophical ends of the Declaration of Independence.

That *The Federalist* does not discuss political philosophy as directly as the Declaration of Independence does is not disputed. But this is because Publius—like the Framers of the Constitution generally—faced a task different from that faced by the revolutionary leaders. Publius was trying to persuade his audience that the Constitution represented the best *form of government* to secure the philosophical principles embodied in the Declaration of Independence; principles which, this chapter ultimately seeks to show, were widely understood and accepted. The authors of the Declaration, by contrast, were trying to articulate those first principles of American government in order to justify a revolution and establish a new nation. Although it was not, therefore, Publius's design in writing *The Federalist* to review the legitimacy and the wisdom of founding a nation on natural-rights principles, a close reading of *The Federalist* provides ample evidence that Publius remained committed to those principles.

Publius's commitment to the Declaration's philosophy of government is reaffirmed immediately. In *The Federalist* no. 2, John Jay restates the central tenet of the Declaration of Independence: that government is instituted to secure the people's natural rights. As Jay succinctly explains, "Nothing is more certain than the indispensable necessity of government; . . . [and that] the people must cede to [government] some of their natural rights, in order to vest [government] with requisite powers" to secure those rights.[87]

James Madison professes his commitment to the philosophical ideals of the Declaration of Independence in a number of *The Federalist* papers he wrote. In *The Federalist* no. 40, for example, Madison invokes the principles—and the words—of the Declaration to justify the admittedly extralegal efforts of the Convention in writing the Constitution:

In all great changes of established governments forms ought to give way to substance; . . . a rigid adherence in such cases to the former would render nominal and nugatory the transcendent and precious right of the people to "abolish or alter their governments as to them shall seem most likely to effect their safety and happiness," since it is impossible for the people spontaneously and universally to move in concert towards their object; and it is therefore essential that such changes be instituted by some informal and unauthorized propositions, made by some patriotic and respectable citizen or number of citizens.[88]

By the "safety and happiness" of the people, the Declaration—and Madison in *The Federalist*—means the security of natural rights.[89]

In *The Federalist* no. 37, Madison describes the tension that frequently exists between protecting the natural rights of individuals and promoting the more general public good, a classical republican concern. "Among the difficulties encountered by the convention," Madison writes, "a very important one must have lain in combining the requisite stability and energy in government with the inviolable attention due to liberty and the republican form." Unfortunately, Madison continues, "we must perceive at once the difficulty of mingling them together in their due proportions."[90]

In *The Federalist* no. 10—with which only no. 51[91] competes for significance in the annals of American political science—Madison decides that while it is important to protect both the general public good and the natural rights of individuals, if a choice has to be made, the choice should be in favor of first securing natural rights. Madison argues in his famous discussion of factions that self-interested groups bear the major responsibility for the problems facing the nation, but he emphasizes that this is true "*particularly*, for that prevailing and increasing distrust of public engagements and alarm for private rights which are echoed from one end of the continent to the other."[92] Once again Madison reaffirms his commitment to protecting rights.

The Federalist nos. 14, 39, 45, and 46 find Madison reminding his readers that the purpose of the Constitution is to fulfill the promise of the American Revolution. In no. 14, for instance, Madison appeals to the patriotism of the American people when explaining that the proposed Constitution is intended to secure the hard-won fruits of the Revolution. What is most significant about no. 14 is Madison's argument that the revolutionary patriots "erred" in the "structure of the Union"—that is, in the form of government established by the Articles of Confederation—but not in their desire to secure natural rights. In Madison's words:

Happily for America, happily we trust for the whole human race, [the revolutionary patriots] pursued a new and more noble course. They accomplished a revolution which has no parallel in the annals of human society. They reared the fabrics of governments which have no model on the face of the globe. They formed the design of a great Confederacy, which it is incumbent on their successors to improve and perpetuate. If their works betray imperfections, we wonder at the fewness of them. If they erred most in the structure of the Union, this was the work most difficult to be executed; this is the work which has been new modeled by the act of your convention, and it is that act on which you are now to deliberate and to decide.[93]

Similarly, in *The Federalist* no. 45, Madison criticizes those who emphasize the importance of maintaining state power by pointing to the objectives of the Revolution, objectives shared by the proposed Constitution:

If, in a word, the Union be essential to the happiness of the people of America, is it not preposterous to urge as an objection to a government, without which the objects of the Union cannot be attained, that such a government may derogate from the importance of the governments of the individual States? Was, then, the American Revolution effected, was the American Confederacy formed, was the precious blood of thousands spilt, and the hard-earned substance of millions lavished, not that the people of America should enjoy peace, liberty, and safety, but that the governments of the individual States, that particular municipal establishments, might enjoy a certain extent of power and be arrayed with certain dignities and attributes of sovereignty?[94]

Softening somewhat his criticism of the defenders of state power, Madison seeks in *The Federalist* no. 46 to assuage those who fear that the new Constitution would mean the elimination of the states. He does so by again drawing on the experiences and the principles of the Revolution:

Ambitious encroachments of the federal government would not excite the opposition of a single State, or of a few States only. They would be signals of general alarm. Every government would espouse the common cause. A correspondence would be opened. Plans of resistance would be concerted. One spirit would animate and conduct the whole. The same combinations, in short, would result from an apprehension of the federal, as was produced by the dread of a foreign, yoke; and unless the projected innovations should be voluntarily renounced, the same appeal to a trial of force would be made in the one case as was made in the other.[95]

Finally, but most importantly, there is *The Federalist* no. 43, wherein Madison invokes the very words of the Declaration of Independence to explain that a particular form of government is not an end in itself, but rather a means to secure the people's natural rights. In no. 43 Madison alludes to "the great principle of self-preservation; to the transcendent law of nature and of nature's God, which declares that the safety and happiness of society are the objects at which all political institutions aim and to which all such institutions must be sacrificed."[96]

Although Alexander Hamilton emphasizes the promotion of the public good in *The Federalist* more than James Madison does, *The Federalist* papers written by Hamilton show that he remained committed to the natural-rights principles he held as a young revolutionary pamphleteer. Hamilton best displays his commitment to natural law in *The Federalist* no. 31, where he speaks of epistemology. Hamilton writes: "In disquisitions of every kind there are certain primary truths, or first principles, upon which all subsequent reasonings must depend. These contain an internal evidence which, antecedent to all reflection or combination, commands the assent of the mind."[97] Hamilton seems to have understood well Locke's *Essay concerning Human Understand-*

ing, not to mention the associated doctrine of "self-evident truths" that is so fundamental to the philosophy of the Declaration of Independence.

In *The Federalist* no. 28, Hamilton demonstrates that he well learned another Lockean tenet of natural law, a tenet central to the Declaration of Independence: the natural right of revolution. If the government seriously fails the people in providing security for natural rights, Hamilton argues, "there is then no resource left but in the exertion of that original right of self-defense which is paramount to all positive forms of government."[98] And in *The Federalist* no. 26, Hamilton again speaks to the doctrine of revolution and the dictates of the Declaration of Independence when he observes that "security of private rights" was what the struggle against Great Britain was all about.[99]

Lastly, there is *The Federalist* no. 9, where Hamilton describes the totality of the Constitution as a "means" better to secure the natural rights of the American people. There, Hamilton provides a laundry list of structural devices proposed by the Convention to effectuate that end.[100]

In summary, although Publius typically took his audience's commitment to the natural-rights principles of the Declaration of Independence for granted, a careful reading of *The Federalist* reveals that he did, on more than one occasion, and whether speaking through the pen of John Jay, James Madison, or Alexander Hamilton, reaffirm his commitment to those principles. An investigation of the political thought of several of the intellectual leaders of the constitutional period likewise shows that the Framers intended the Constitution to secure the philosophical ideals of the American Revolution.

The Intellectual Leaders of the Constitutional Period

Chapter 1 described how crucial intellectual leadership was in the drive toward American independence. Intellectual leadership was also indispensable in the effort to frame and ratify the Constitution. The natural starting point for the discussion of the intellectual leadership of the revolutionary period was Thomas Jefferson, author of the Declaration of Independence. The natural starting point for a discussion of the intellectual leadership of the constitutional period is James Madison, "father" of the Constitution.[101] As was the case in chapter 1, two important caveats are necessary before turning to Madison's political thought. First, volumes could be, and in most cases have been, written on the political thought of each of the leaders I will discuss. Clearly, space constraints limit what I can accomplish. Second, and making the first caveat less troublesome, my objective here, as it was in the discussion of the revolutionary period, is to elucidate the intellectual leaders' position on the *basic* purpose of the state. More precisely, I hope to show that the intellectual leaders of the constitutional period remained dedicated to the central tenet of the Declaration of Independence: that government exists to secure natural rights.

Though James Madison's views on the relationship between the Constitution and the Declaration of Independence were previously discussed in the analyses of the framing and ratification of the Constitution, the Bill of Rights, and *The Federalist* papers, Madison's role as the chief architect of the Constitution warrants additional consideration of his views. That Madison framed the Constitution in order to provide better security for natural rights than the Articles of Confederation were providing is seen in the preface to his notes on the debates of the Federal Convention of 1787 that he wrote near the end of his life. Madison explained:

I feel it a duty to express my profound and solemn conviction of observing and appreciating the views of the Convention, collectively and individually, that there never was an assembly of men, charged with a great and arduous trust, who were more pure in their motives, or more exclusively or anxiously devoted to the object committed to them, than were the members of the Federal Convention of 1787, to *the object of devising and proposing a constitutional system which should best supply the defects of that which it was to replace, and best secure the permanent liberty and happiness of their country.*[102]

Madison's desire to replace the Articles of Confederation in order better to protect the natural rights of the American people was repeatedly emphasized in letters he wrote to Jefferson. One of the most illuminating of the letters finds Madison poignantly describing the oppression being imposed by majority factions under the Articles. In Madison's words:

The injustice of them has been so frequent and so flagrant as to alarm the most stedfast friends of Republicanism. I am persuaded I do not err in saying that the evils issuing from these sources contributed more to that uneasiness which produced the Convention, and prepared the public mind for a general reform, than those which accrued to our national character and interest from the inadequacy of the Confederation to its immediate objects.[103]

Madison's alarm about the infringements on natural rights occurring at the state level under the Articles led him to advocate a national veto over state laws. In a letter to George Washington just prior to the Convention, Madison writes that "a negative *in all cases whatsoever* on the Legislative acts of the States, as heretofore exercised by the Kingly prerogative, appears to me to be absolutely necessary." A national veto, Madison argues, would not only protect necessary national power, but "would ... control ... the aggressions of interested majorities on the rights of minorities and individuals."[104] Indeed, the failure of the Convention to adopt Madison's proposed national veto made Madison doubt that natural rights would be adequately protected by the new form of government.[105]

Madison's most comprehensive exegesis on the need for government to protect the people's natural rights is his preconvention memorandum *Vices of the Political System of the United States*. There, Madison previews the concern about factions he was to raise during the Convention and in *The Federalist* no. 10 when he identifies an urgent need to safeguard "the rights and interests of the minority, or of individuals" against oppression by self-interested majorities. Also previewed—and also illustrating Madison's commitment to protecting natural rights—is Madison's most original contribution to political science: that "the enlargement of the sphere is found to lessen the insecurity of private rights."[106]

As discussed above, Madison was required to seek passage of the Bill of Rights in order to ensure the Constitution's ratification. Madison's first proposal for the Bill of Rights displays his commitment to the natural-rights principles of the Declaration of Independence. In fact, Madison's proposal is a virtual paraphrase of Jefferson's masterpiece:

That all power is originally vested in, and consequently derived from the people.

That government is instituted, and ought to be exercised for the benefit of the people; which consists in the enjoyment of life and liberty, with the right of acquiring and using property, and generally of pursuing and obtaining happiness and safety.

That the people have an indubitable, unalienable, and indefeasible right to reform or change their government, whenever it be found adverse or inadequate to the purpose of its institution.[107]

Madison displays his dedication to natural-rights principles elsewhere as well, most notably in a 1792 essay in the *National Gazette*, "Property." In that essay Madison provides a comprehensive analysis of property, one that could have been written by Locke himself. According to Madison, "property"

in its particular application, means "that dominion which one man claims and exercises over the external things of the world, in exclusion of every individual." In its larger and juster meaning, it embraces everything to which a man may attach a value and have a right, and *which leaves to every one else the like advantage.* In the former sense, a man has a property in his opinions and the free communication of them. He has a property of peculiar value in his religious opinions, and in the profession and practice dictated by them. He has a property, very dear to him in the safety and liberty of his person. He has an equal property in the free use of his faculties, and free choice of the objects on which to employ them. In a word, as a man is said to have a right to his property, he may be equally said to have a property in his rights.[108]

Most importantly, and also in the best tradition of Lockean liberalism, Madison asserts in his essay that government "is instituted to protect property of every sort: as well that which lies in the various rights of individuals, as that which the term particularly expresses. This being the end of government, that alone is a *just* government which *impartially* secures to every man whatever is his *own.*"[109]

Lastly, if government fails adequately to protect natural rights, Madison accepted the Lockean consequences of that failure: the people's right of revolution. As Madison put it late in life, a "resort to the original rights of the parties to the system" is justified.[110] As was evident in the discussion of the framing and ratification of the Constitution and the Bill of Rights and in the discussion of *The Federalist* papers, Madison's personal writings confirm his dedication to the essential tenet of the Declaration of Independence: that government exists to secure natural rights.

James Wilson ranks second to James Madison in terms of contributions made to the framing and ratification of the Constitution, as earlier noted. Although Wilson rejected Locke's rationalistic epistemology, and even considered it dangerous,[111] he was committed during the constitutional period to natural-rights political philosophy—especially to the central premise that government exists to secure the natural rights of individuals. This was a position Wilson also held during the revolutionary period.

Wilson's commitment to natural-rights doctrine during the constitutional period is revealed in a host of statements he made on political philosophy. In one of his Pennsylvania ratifying-convention speeches, for example, Wilson specifically refers to the Constitution as a "means" to secure the philosophical "ends" of the Declaration of Independence.[112] In another ratifying-convention speech, discussed at the beginning of this chapter, Wilson went so far as to quote the Declaration of Independence at length and then state, "This is the broad basis on which our independence was placed; [and] on the same certain and solid foundation this system [the Constitution] is erected."[113]

Wilson's view that government exists to secure the natural rights of individuals is most systematically expressed in his famous *Lectures on Law* given at the College of Philadelphia in 1790–92, while Wilson was a law professor. (Wilson was also serving on the U.S. Supreme Court at the time.) One of the main reasons why Wilson gave those lectures was to provide an American answer to the jurisprudence of William Blackstone, as well as to the position staked out by Edmund Burke in his recently published *Reflections on the Revolution in France.* Specifically, Wilson was responding to Blackstone's and Burke's position—a position shared by those who today approach the American Founding from a Straussian perspective[114]—that all natural rights are ceded to government in exchange for a secure enjoyment of certain civil rights. Under the Blackstonean and Burkean conception of rights, rights are communal property to be conferred upon individuals as society sees fit, and individuals are, as Wilson puts it, "nothing but what society frames." The British conception of rights is in stark contrast to that embodied in the Declaration of Independence, and Wilson expressly rejects it. "Government, in my humble opinion," Wilson declares, "should be formed to secure and to enlarge the exercise of the natural rights of its members; and every government, which has not this in view, as its principal object, is not a government of the legitimate kind."[115] Nor is the conception of rights of mere academic concern to Wilson. In Wilson's words:

I go farther; and now proceed to show, that in peculiar instances, in which those rights can receive neither protection nor reparation from the civil government, they are, notwithstanding its institution, entitled still to that defence, and to those methods of recovery, which are justified and demanded in a state of nature.

The defence of one's self, justly called the primary law of nature, is not, nor can it be abrogated by any regulation of municipal law.[116]

Here, Wilson is advancing the same Lockean conception of rights and purpose of government embodied in the Declaration of Independence. For Wilson, as for the Declaration of Independence, the fundamental purpose of government is to secure the natural rights of individuals. If government fails in this assignment, individuals have the right and duty to protect themselves.[117]

Although some argue that the postrevolutionary Alexander Hamilton "ceased to have much sympathy with the doctrine of natural rights,"[118] concerned as he is said to have been during the constitutional period and thereafter with so-called "state-centered theories of power and sovereignty,"[119] at bottom, Hamilton remained dedicated to the natural-rights principles of the Declaration of Independence. Certainly, Hamilton was less committed than Madison and Wilson in the desire for a *limited* government to secure the people's natural rights, but Hamilton nevertheless considered the basic purpose of government to be securing rights. For instance, in *The Federalist* no. 26 Hamilton makes the claim that the purpose of "energy in government" is to ensure "the security of private rights."[120] And recall Hamilton's observation in *The Federalist* no. 84 that "the Constitution is itself ... A BILL OF RIGHTS."[121]

In order to press for his preferred strong national government, Hamilton did sometimes employ what can only be described as a strained interpretation of Lockean liberalism. Hamilton's June 29, 1787, remarks in the Constitutional Convention arguing for representation in the new Congress strictly on the basis of population are illustrative. Hamilton states:

Men are naturally equal—societies or Nations are equal when independent— it is reasonable that States shd. inter into a League departing from the Equality of States, as that men shd. inter into the Social Compact and agree to depart from the natural Equality of man. ... We propose that the people shd. be reprented [*sic*] in proportion to yr. numbers, the people then will be free ... — yet it is said the States will be destroyed & therefore the people will be slaves—

The Consequence is not true. The people are free, at the expense of a mere ideal & artificial being.[122]

While some may question the sincerity with which Hamilton employed the Lockean social-contract theory on the issue of state sovereignty, the fact that Hamilton felt obligated to invoke the argument demonstrates that for Hamilton, as for the Framers in general, Lockean liberalism remained the benchmark of political legitimacy.

Thomas Jefferson's continued commitment during the postrevolutionary period to the natural-rights political philosophy he so majestically expressed in the Declaration of Independence was seen in the earlier discussion of the Bill of Rights.[123] Indeed, in response to Madison's primary concern about the Bill of Rights, "that a positive declaration of some of the most essential rights could not be obtained in the requisite latitude,"[124] Jefferson argued that "half a loaf is better than no bread. If we cannot secure all our rights, let's secure what we can."[125]

The best way to characterize Jefferson's understanding of the American regime is that he believed Locke's *Second Treatise* correctly stated the ends of government, whereas *The Federalist* papers well explain how the Constitution is to serve as a means to secure those ends. This characterization is pointedly seen in a 1790 letter, noted earlier, on what books students should read to understand the American political order. Jefferson writes: "Locke's little book on government, is perfect as far as it goes, ... [d]escending from theory to practice, there is no better book than the Federalist."[126]

Most of Jefferson's postrevolutionary writings on specific rights are steeped in Lockean natural-rights theory. For example, Jefferson had a Lockean conception of the relations between church and state. Jefferson writes in his *Notes on the State of Virginia* (1782):

The error seems not sufficiently eradicated, that the operations of the mind, as well as the acts of the body, are subject to the coercion of the laws. But our rulers can have authority over such natural rights only as we have submitted to them. The rights of conscience we never submitted, we could not submit. We are answerable for them to our God. The legitimate powers of government extend to such acts only as are injurious to others. But it does me no injury for my neighbour to say there are twenty gods, or no god. It neither picks my pocket nor breaks my leg.[127]

Jefferson's agreement with Locke's views on the natural right to toleration is also seen in the text of Jefferson's celebrated Virginia Bill for Establishing Religious Freedom. Jefferson considered this statute, his authorship of the Declaration of Independence, and his founding of the University of Virginia, his greatest achievements. The statute concludes as follows:

And though we well know this assembly, elected by the people for the ordinary purposes of legislation only, have no power to restrain the acts of succeeding Assemblies, constituted with the powers equal to our own, and that therefore to declare this act irrevocable, would be of no effect in law, yet we are free to declare, and do declare, that the rights hereby asserted are of the natural rights of mankind, and that if any act shall be hereafter passed to repeal the present or to narrow its operation, such act will be an infringement of natural right.[128]

Jefferson's Lockean approach to toleration carried over to the subject of the natural limits of positive law generally. Here, Jefferson's debt to Locke is unmistakable, as is his agreement with James Wilson in rejecting the Blackstonean and Burkean notion that individuals cede all natural rights to government in exchange for the secure enjoyment of specified civil rights. In Jefferson's words:

Our legislators are not sufficiently apprized of the rightful limits of their power; that their true office is to declare and enforce only our natural rights and duties, and to take none of them from us. No man has a natural right to commit aggression on the equal rights of another; and this is all from which the laws ought to restrain him; every man is under the natural duty of contributing to the necessities of the society; and this is all the laws should enforce on him; and, no man having a natural right to be the judge between himself and another, it is his natural duty to submit to the umpirage of an impartial third. When the laws have declared and enforced all this, they have fulfilled their functions, and the idea is quite unfounded, that on entering into society we give up any natural right.[129]

The right of revolution, so central to the Declaration of Independence, always remained an essential tenet of Jefferson's political philosophy. "What country can preserve its liberties," Jefferson writes in 1787, "if its rulers are not warned from time to time that this people preserve the spirit of resistance? Let them take arms."[130]

As this sampling of Jefferson's political writings reveals, Jefferson remained committed throughout his life to the natural-rights principles he played such a key role in articulating during the American Revolution. Indeed, Jefferson's fervent commitment to the natural rights of man is evinced by the last letter he was ever to write. In a June 24,

1826, letter to Roger Weightman regretfully declining an invitation, because of poor health, to take part in the fiftieth-anniversary celebration of the Declaration of Independence, Jefferson reaffirms his lifelong dedication to the natural-rights principles of the Declaration:

May it be to the world, what I believe it will be, (to some parts sooner, to others later, but finally to all,) the signal of arousing men to burst the chains under which monkish ignorance and superstition had persuaded them to bind themselves, and to assume the blessings and security of self-government. That form which we have substituted, restores the free right to the unbounded exercise of reason and freedom of opinion. All eyes are opened, or opening to the rights of man. The general spread of the light of science has already laid open to every view the palpable truth, that the mass of mankind has not been born with saddles on their backs, nor a favored few booted and spurred, ready to ride them legitimately, by the grace of God. These are grounds of hope for others. For ourselves, let the annual return of this day forever refresh our recollections of these rights, and an undiminished devotion to them.[131]*

Eerily, Jefferson, as well as John Adams, died ten days after writing this letter, fifty years to the day after the passage of the Declaration of Independence.

John Adams was in England working out a commercial treaty with the English during the framing and ratification of the Constitution. Adams's influence was, however, felt from England, as was Jefferson's from France. The first volume of Adams's great work of political science during the constitutional period, *A Defence of the Constitutions of Government of the United States of America* (1787),[132] a work that Madison called "a powerful engine in forming the public opinion,"[133] was made available to the Federal Convention of 1787, and his innovation in the Massachusetts Constitution—defended at length in *A Defence*—of an independently elected executive with veto power was incorporated into the federal Constitution itself. As will be seen, Adams's vigorous defense of the doctrine of separation of powers was also influential.

---

*This passage also reveals the importance in Jefferson's thought of the distinction between the ends of government and the means by which those ends are effectuated. In Jefferson's view, periodic revision of the constitutional structure, reflecting "the progress of the human mind," would provide better security for natural rights than would staying the course with an existing constitution. See Letter from Thomas Jefferson to Samuel Kercheval, July 12, 1816, in *The Portable Thomas Jefferson*, 559. As the Introduction described, Madison disagreed with Jefferson on this question of institutional design. See *The Federalist* no. 49, 314; Letter from James Madison to Thomas Jefferson, February 4, 1790, in *The Papers of Thomas Jefferson*, vol. 16, 148.

For years, the standard interpretation of Adams's political thought was that "as a young man he was a disciple of Locke and the natural-rights school, but as he grew older he abandoned the natural-rights theory." During the constitutional period Adams was characterized as being virtually obsessed with protecting private property and wealth. Progressive historian Vernon Parrington provided a typical description of Adams: "During the revolutionary struggle he had been a member of the left wing; during the early struggles under the Constitution he was a member of the right wing. The young man had been a stalwart defender of human rights, the old man was a stalwart defender of property rights; and this shift of position was fatal to his reputation." [134]

Such an unfavorable characterization of Adams is unfair and inaccurate. In fact, Adams's *Defence*, like his works of the revolutionary period, particularly *Dissertation on Canon and Feudal Law* (1765) and *Novanglus* (1774), is based on the premise that the fundamental purpose of government is to protect natural rights. Adams writes in *A Defence:*

> The United States of America have exhibited, perhaps, the first example of governments erected on the simple principles of nature; and if men are now sufficiently enlightened to disabuse themselves of artifice, imposture, hypocrisy, and superstition, they will consider this event an era in their history. ... Thirteen governments thus founded on the natural authority of the people alone, without a pretence of miracle or mystery, and which are destined to spread over the northern part of that whole quarter of the globe, are a great point in favor of the rights of mankind. [135]

Adams's conception of equality could not be more Lockean. As discussed in chapter 1, equality in Lockean liberalism means equality of opportunity, not equality of result. "Though I have said," Locke writes, "that all men are by nature equal, I cannot be supposed to understand all sorts of equality. Age or virtue may give men a just precedence; excellence of parts and merit may place others above the common level." [136] Likewise, for Adams, equality means that all men have one common nature and, from that, equal rights and duties. "But," Adams writes, "equal ranks and equal property never can be inferred from it, any more than equal understanding, agility, vigor or beauty. Equal laws are all that ever can be derived from human equality." [137]

Much of Adams's approach to political science was motivated by his desire to protect the natural rights of individuals. For example, Adams's argument for a separation of powers was the traditional one, most notably articulated by Montesquieu, that such a doctrine would best secure natural rights. In fact, as one scholar aptly points out, this was the "essential argument" of *A Defence:*

Adams's book is long, turgidly burdened with long extracts from all the writers Adams deemed pertinent, and often carelessly expressed in ways that obscured for Americans his essential argument, namely, that an upper house and independent executive were necessary to prevent aristocratic domination, which would be inconsistent with a Lockean respect for equal rights.[138]

Also worth noting is an innovation made by Adams in the Massachusetts Constitution of 1780. At Adams's behest, the Massachusetts Constitution was popularly ratified, the first fundamental instrument of a state to be so. Popular ratification is a Lockean liberal feature employed by the Framers of the federal Constitution as well.

As in his revolutionary writings, Adams sometimes seems to argue in *A Defence* that the cultivation of virtue is an end in itself. For example, at one point Adams approvingly quotes Aristotle's conclusion "that a happy life must arise from a course of virtue."[139] But Adams's major argument in *A Defence* is that the basic objective of government is the protection of natural rights, with the cultivation of virtue being valued principally as a way to accomplish that objective.[140] In Adams's words:

It is not true, in fact, that any people ever existed who loved the public better than themselves, their private friends, neighbors, & c., and therefore this kind of virtue, this sort of love, is as precarious a foundation for liberty as honor or fear; it is the laws alone that really love the country, the public, the whole better than any part; and that form of government which unites all the virtue, honor and fear of the citizens, in a reverence and obedience to the laws, is the only in which liberty can be secure.[141]

As an examination of Adams's great work of political science during the constitutional period reveals, Adams did not abandon the ideals of natural-rights political philosophy after independence had been successfully won. Indeed, sounding very much like Jefferson's Declaration of Independence, Adams concludes in *A Defence* that "the end of all government is the good and ease of the people, in a secure enjoyment of their rights, without oppression."[142]

In summary, an analysis of the political thought of several of the most influential intellectual leaders of the constitutional period demonstrates that the Founders remained as dedicated to natural-rights principles during the period of the framing and ratification of the Constitution as they had been during the heyday of the American Revolution. Some may have been more explicit about this than others, but they all shared an essential commitment to the view that the fundamental purpose of the Constitution is to secure the natural rights of the American people. An investigation of early state constitutions provides additional evidence of this fact.

Early State Constitutions

In his 1888 essay *The American Commonwealth,* Lord James Bryce observes that the federal Constitution is largely an outgrowth of the early state constitutions.[143] Like the federal Constitution that followed, the early state constitutions were greatly influenced by natural-rights political philosophy. As Allan Nevins, a leading authority on the early state constitutions, puts it, "not only upon the practice of a century and a half, but upon the political theorizing of the same period . . . were the new American constitutions built."[144]

Nearly all of the state constitutions framed and ratified during the founding period made express reference to the basic purpose of government's being to protect the people's natural rights. The reference was usually in the form of a separate bill of rights or, in those state constitutions not containing a bill of rights, in a section, typically the preamble, reaffirming an allegiance to the natural-rights principles of the Declaration of Independence.[145]

The most famous and influential restatement of natural-rights principles found in the early state constitutions is the Virginia Declaration of Rights, written by George Mason just prior to the passage of the Declaration of Independence.[146] The first three articles of the Virginia Declaration of Rights are plainly a summary of natural-rights political philosophy.[147] Not surprisingly, those articles sound very much like the Declaration of Independence, albeit without Jefferson's unparalleled literary flair:

1. That all men are by nature equally free and independent, and have certain inherent rights, of which, when they enter into society, they cannot by any compact deprive or divest their posterity; namely, the enjoyment of life and

liberty, with the means of acquiring and possessing property, and pursuing and obtaining happiness and safety.

2. That all power is vested in, and consequently derived from, the people; that magistrates are their trustees and servants, and at all times amenable to them.

3. That government is, or ought to be instituted for the common benefit, protection, and security of the people, nation, or community; of all the various modes and forms of government, that is best which is capable of producing the greatest degree of happiness and safety, and is most effectually secured against the danger of maladministration; and that when any government shall be found inadequate or contrary to these purposes, a majority of the community hath an indubitable, unalienable and indefeasible right to reform, alter or abolish it, in such manner as shall be judged most conducive to the public weal.[148]

Following Virginia's lead, other states expressed similar commitment to natural-rights principles. Georgia's preamble to its constitution, brief though it is, is illustrative:

Whereas the conduct of the legislature of Great Britain for many years past has been so oppressive on the people of America ... which conduct, being repugnant to the common rights of mankind, hath obliged the Americans, as freemen, to oppose such oppressive measures, and to assert the rights, and privileges they are entitled to by the laws of nature and reason.[149]

Likewise illustrative is the New York Constitution, with its straightforward approach of incorporating the Declaration of Independence as its preamble.[150]

Many of the early state constitutions alluded to the importance of a virtuous citizenry. But, as in the writings of those intellectual leaders of the American Founding who spoke of virtue, the state constitutions appealed to virtue as a way to help secure natural rights. Again, the Virginia Declaration of Rights served as the model.[151] Section 15 reads: "That no free government, or the blessings of liberty, can be preserved to any people, but by a firm adherence to justice, moderation, temperance, frugality, and virtue, and by frequent recurrence to fundamental principles."[152]

Succinctly stated, the early state constitutions recognized that if excessive selfishness was controlled, rights would be more generally secured. The ultimate objective was, then, the protection of natural rights, not the cultivation of virtue. Nowhere is this more forcefully stated than in the preamble to the Massachusetts Constitution of 1780, written by John Adams:

The end of the institution, maintenance, and administration of government is to secure the existence of the body-politic, to protect it, and to furnish the individuals who comprise it with the power of enjoying, in safety and tranquility, their natural rights and blessings of life; and whenever these great objects are not obtained the people have a right to alter the government, and to take measures for their safety, prosperity, and happiness.[153]

The early state constitutions were many times revised. The frequency of the revisions, however, provides more, not less, evidence of the Founders' commitment to natural rights. That is to say, the constitutions were plagued by structural problems, problems that led to an inadequate protection of rights.

According to Jefferson, revisions were so quickly necessary because the American people had been so focused on the abuses of the British system when the state constitutions were initially framed. "The abuses of monarchy had so filled the speeches of political men," Jefferson writes, "that we imagined everything republican that was not monarchical. We had not yet penetrated to the mother principle that governments are republican only in proportion as they embody the will of the people and execute it."[154] In effect, what the revisions to the early state constitutions attempted to do was to eliminate the structural problems in order better to protect the people's natural rights. The idea that a constitution is a means to an end, and not an end itself, is once again evident. And as has been argued throughout this volume, the end that the Founders invariably sought to achieve was the protection of the natural rights of the American people.[155]

Part 1 of this volume identified the essential tenet of the American regime to be that government exists to secure the people's natural rights. This fact was shown through history and political philosophy. Part 2 now explains that it is ultimately the role and duty of the Supreme Court to identify and apply the natural-rights principles of the Declaration of Independence in American life.

II

Natural Rights and
the Role of the Court

Part 2 addresses the Supreme Court's role in the American constitutional order. Given that part 1 explained that the Constitution was enacted chiefly to provide the institutional framework through which the natural-rights principles of the Declaration of Independence can be effectuated; the question considered here concerns the Court's role in protecting the natural rights of the American people. As in part 1, I approach this question through history and political philosophy, as well as through law.

Chapter 3 explains that the Framers commissioned the Court as the principal guardian of the people's natural rights. The originalist context of my thesis requires that I examine cases and historical materials that have been examined many times before. Indeed, few—if any—

questions have received more attention from commentators on the Court than the origins and scope of judicial review. Whether it be the classic exchange on the legitimacy of judicial review between Louis Boudin and Charles Beard early in this century or the flood of books on the subject in the present day, the debate over judicial review has always been an active one. What I attempt to do in chapter 3 is to provide a revised reading of that debate, a reading that is in keeping with the American Founding's commitment to natural rights.

The theory of constitutional interpretation advanced in this volume affords the Supreme Court tremendous authority. Chapter 4 discusses ways in which the Court can be prevented from abusing that authority. There, I explain that the impeachment and appointment powers, among others, are available to keep the members of the Court from substituting their own personal moral and political views on the Constitution for the natural-rights principles to which the Constitution is dedicated.

Chapter 5 turns from theory to practice. I endeavor to demonstrate that, contrary to the position of many critics of natural-law jurisprudence, a natural-rights–based theory of judicial review can resolve disputes that come before the Court. To that end, the natural-rights political philosophy of the Declaration of Independence is applied to some of the leading cases in constitutional law and history.

3

The Court

This chapter enters the debate over the origins and scope of judicial review in America. While I hesitate to add to the seemingly endless literature on the subject, the importance of history to my theory of constitutional interpretation—what I call "liberal originalism" (see the Introduction)—requires that I do so. In other words, it is not enough for me simply to assume or assert that the Supreme Court is to play a specified role in my theory: I must substantiate that role historically.*

* Michael Perry maintains that an originalist argument for an originalist approach to judicial review is "question-begging." Perry, *The Constitution in the Courts*, 50. The issue is more subtle than Perry implies. (Perry, a talented lawyer, simply appears reluctant to do history, as his frequent statements about the "indeterminacy of history" illustrate.) Political theory instructs that it is only through a dedication to history that commentators on the Court can avoid imposing their own opinions on the rest of us. That is to say, a commitment to the rule of law—a cornerstone of Anglo-American political theory—requires a commitment to history.

Obviously, an extensive treatment of the roots of judicial review is a volume unto itself, as the fact that many fine books have been written on the subject suggests. I am not, however, interested in recalculating the "Beard tally"; that has been done enough.[1] Instead, my approach to the origins of judicial review is in terms of constitutional theory. I examine the historical materials in order to assess what they have to say about the Supreme Court's role in advancing the natural-rights principles of the Declaration of Independence, principles to which the Constitution is dedicated.

After examining the historical record on judicial review, I conclude that the Supreme Court is the institution of American government that should be ultimately responsible for identifying and applying the natural-rights political philosophy of the Declaration of Independence in constitutional interpretation. Given the conviction with which opinions about judicial review are held, those opposing a "significant"* role for the Court in the American constitutional order are likely to view this conclusion with skepticism. With respect to these skeptics, I hope that the discussion in this chapter at least gives them something to think about, for what I attempt to do is to approach the debate over judicial review from a new perspective, one that takes seriously the Founders' commitment to protecting the American people's natural rights.

From Legislative Supremacy to Judicial Review

Judicial protection of individual rights is one of the great American contributions to constitutional theory. This contribution did not, however, arise out of thin air; it is the product of history. That is to say, the American people's ability to turn to the courts for the protection of their rights[2] is traceable to the Founders' unpleasant experience with

---

*I purposely avoid saying an "active" role for the Court, because the word "active" has become caricatured in public law. With respect to natural law, this is because commentators on the Court typically conflate two questions: (1) whether natural law exists (or is sufficiently determinate), and (2), assuming there is natural law, who has the authority to interpret it. Hittinger, "Natural Law in Positive Laws," 24. Part 1 demonstrated that the United States of America is based on the assumption that natural law exists. This chapter examines who, as a matter of institutional design, is ultimately charged with interpreting that law.

seeking to protect rights through representation, which, in colonial and revolutionary America, was the orthodox approach.[3] This section examines the movement from legislative to judicial protection of individual rights in early American constitutional history. Following that discussion, I turn to the role of natural-rights doctrine in judicial review and then to the authoritativeness of the Supreme Court's interpretation of that doctrine.

The central tenet of the British theory of government is legislative supremacy, a doctrine that came about because of the Glorious Revolution of 1688 and the efforts therein to limit the power and authority of the crown. As a result of the successful culmination of the Glorious Revolution, Parliament, or more formerly the-crown-in-Parliament, is supreme over any other governmental body, including the crown or the crown's appointed officials. With respect to judges, they are largely limited to the ministerial task of ensuring that the procedures mandated by particular legislative acts have been properly followed in specific cases. As Sir William Blackstone's classic statement on the matter makes clear, under the British doctrine of legislative supremacy judges do not enjoy the power of judicial review in the American sense of striking down legislation they deem in conflict with the Constitution. In Blackstone's famous language:

If the parliament will positively enact a thing to be done which is unreasonable, I know of no power that can control it: and the examples usually alleged in support of this sense of the rule do none of them prove, that where the main object of a statute is unreasonable the judges are at liberty to reject it; for that were to set the judicial power above the legislative, which would be subversive of all government.[4]

The notion that judges are without significant authority has not gone unchallenged in British history. In fact, the first claim by a court to enjoy the power of judicial review is usually said to be the 1610 opinion of Sir Edward Coke, then the Lord Chief Justice, in *Dr. Bonham's Case.* At issue in the case was Parliament's claim of an exclusive right to control the licensing of physicians. Coke considered the claim contrary to the common law. And in now legendary language, he planted the seed for the American doctrine of judicial review: "When an act of Parliament is against common right and reason, or repugnant, or impossible to be performed, the common law will controul it and adjudge such an act to be void."[5] However, by promptly reenacting the disputed statute, Parliament rejected Coke's claim of judicial review for British courts. Indeed, Coke's decision in *Dr. Bonham's Case* played no small part in his subsequent removal from the bench,[6] and the idea that British judges are without authority to set aside acts of Parliament—a matter definitively settled by the Glorious Revolution—has continued ever since.[7]

Given that the Founders were originally British subjects, it was natural that they initially subscribed to British ideas about government. As just described, foremost among those ideas was that the legislature was supreme. The Founders' commitment to the principle of legislative supremacy is well illustrated by the strength of their resentment of the royal governors' consistent attempts to frustrate this principle in practice. As Allan Nevins aptly remarks, "The beginnings of the Revolution were first discerned in a clash between the [colonial] legislature[s] and the royal officers."[8] With respect to the courts specifically, a key source of friction during the dawn of the Revolution was the dispute between the colonial legislatures and the royal governors over who should control the courts, since the idea of an independent judiciary had yet to take hold. This was a point included in the Declaration of Independence's list of grievances against the king: "He has made Judges dependent on his Will alone, for the tenure of their offices, and the amount and payment of their salaries."

The first state constitutions adopted after the Declaration of Independence were organized around the doctrine of legislative supremacy. Although a few of the early constitutions contained an explicit declaration of the separation of powers,[9] none provided for judicial review, and all made the elected legislature the dominant branch of government. This was a point not lost on judges of the day. In typically Blackstonean fashion, Judge Daniel Chipman of Vermont wrote:

When [the first state constitutions] constituted the legislature, they considered that its power was necessarily supreme and uncontrollable, and that all constitutional restrictions upon their power were merely directory. No idea was entertained that an act of the legislature, however repugnant to the constitution, could be adjudged void and set aside by the judiciary, which was considered by all a subordinate department of government.[10]

The Founders' initial commitment to the doctrine of legislative supremacy did not mean that they were unconcerned about protecting individual rights. Rather, it reflected the conventional wisdom that the security of rights depended on the power of the legislature to check the power of the executive—an idea that the Founders' disputes with the royal governors had brought directly home. In fact, the chief task of the legislative branch was not to legislate, it was to protect rights.[11]

Although the idea that the legislature was charged, above all else, with protecting individual rights will undoubtedly strike modern Americans strangely, accustomed as we are to a powerful judicial check on the legislative and executive branches alike in the realm of individual rights, it was an idea to which the Founders were initially strongly committed. Indeed, the cry "no taxation without representation" symbolized not only the Founders' dispute with the British, generally, but their belief that the protection of rights depended on representative government, specifically. The first state constitutions reflected this faith in the power of representation to protect rights, attempting as they did to limit as much as possible the distance between constituents and representatives through structural devices like annual elections, rotation in office, the right of instruction, equitable apportionment, and a broad franchise.

In time, however, the Founders came to realize that even a reformed system of representation provided inadequate security for private rights—a sentiment well reflected in Thomas Jefferson's famous remark, "An *elective despotism* was not the government we fought for."[12] Mobilization for the War of Independence and reorganization of society and government after the war required that the new American state legislatures govern actively, something to which the newly independent American people were unaccustomed. Most notably affected by the increased legislative activity were private property rights. Fighting a war and rebuilding a society in its aftermath are expensive propositions, and the Founders were not spared from this fact. As a result, the state legislatures imposed a host of taxes and other economic restraints. The specific impact of those measures on private property rights was certainly resented. More importantly, though, the measures and the overall increased legislative activity caused the Founders to rethink their position on the broader question of the power of representation to protect individual rights. After all, the scope of the legislative function had changed, and the Founders realized that their faith in representation must change as well.

As a consequence of their diminishing faith in representation to protect individual rights, the Founders attempted more and more to limit legislative power. The proliferation of written constitutions during the early days of the American republic was directly attributable to this perceived need to limit the legislature. And in those written constitutions, not only were the grants of power to the legislature becoming more specific, but formal exemption of certain rights from the legislature's reach through a bill of rights was becoming commonplace. Virginia, for example, adopted a bill of rights in 1776, and most other states soon followed suit.[13]

Emerging concurrently with the attempts to limit the legislative branch through the enumeration of particular legislative powers and the constitutional exemption of specific rights was one of the most significant American contributions to constitutional theory: the idea that judges had the authority to protect individual rights from infringement by the forces of representation through the power of judicial review.* Before judicial review took root, however, one last attempt was made to reform representation, this time at the national level.

Chapter 2 explained that for the delegates who met in Philadelphia during the summer of 1787, the ultimate objective was to establish a form of government that would provide better security for natural rights than was then provided under the Articles of Confederation. In the words of James Madison, "The necessity of providing more effectually for the security of private rights, and the steady dispensation of Justice. Interferences with these were evils which had more perhaps than any thing else produced this convention."[14] And Madison was far from alone in this view, as chapter 2 documented.

What was the cause of the insecurity of rights under the Articles of Confederation? In the minds of most of the delegates to the Constitutional Convention, the answer lay in the failure of representation in the state assemblies. As John Mercer succinctly explained, "What led to the appointment of this Convention? The corruption and mutability of the Legislative Councils of the States."[15]

While those who met in Philadelphia agreed that a new constitution was to better secure rights, considerable disagreement arose over how to accomplish this. As Mercer's remarks reflect, most of the delegates

*Prior to the Constitutional Convention, several state courts declared acts of their respective state legislative assemblies unconstitutional. The next section discusses those state cases.

had lost faith in representation at the *state* level.[16] However, several in attendance thought that a reformed system of representation at the *national* level could provide the requisite security for the people's rights. James Madison was the foremost proponent of this view.

Madison arrived in Philadelphia well prepared to set the terms of the debate. Before the Convention began, he drafted a plan of government that went far beyond simply revising the Articles of Confederation. Under Madison's plan, commonly known as the "Virginia plan" because it was introduced by Virginia Governor Edmund Randolph on behalf of the Virginia delegation, a strong national government with sweeping powers to check state legislative assemblies was envisioned. Significantly, those sweeping national powers were lodged principally in the national legislature by way of a veto power over laws passed in the state assemblies. For Madison, all faith in representation was not lost. But his faith depended upon having in the national assembly a different kind of legislator from those then serving in the state assemblies. In short, legislators in Congress had to be far more resistant to the pressures of self-interest than their counterparts in the states. Here, Madison's vision of an extended federal republic came to the fore.

An extended federal republic was important to Madison for several reasons. The most widely recognized reasons were that majority factions would be less likely to exist in a large territory and that they would find it more difficult to organize if they did.[17] An often overlooked reason was that an expanded pool of potential representatives would be created, thereby making it more probable that meritorious representatives would emerge.[18]

When all was said and done, however, even the Virginia plan showed only modest faith in the power of representation to secure rights. Most notable in this regard was Madison's call for a council of revision, consisting of the national executive and several federal judges, that would have the authority to veto acts of the national legislature.[19] Clearly, the reason Madison wanted a national veto over state laws was that he distrusted representation at the state level.[20] But the reason he wanted a council of revision was that he did not have full confidence in representation at the national level. As Madison advised the Convention:

[The council of revision] would ... be useful to the Community at large as an additional check agst. a pursuit of those unwise & unjust measures which constituted so great a portion of our calamities [under the Articles of Confederation]. ... Experience in all the States had evinced a powerful tendency in the Legislature to absorb all power into its vortex. This was the real source of danger to American Constitutions; & suggested the necessity of giving every defensive authority to the other departments that was consistent with republican principles.[21]

Despite Madison's repeated efforts to convince the Convention of the need for both a national veto over state laws and a council of revision, he could obtain passage of neither. The national veto failed primarily because of the potent political argument that the states would not accept such an arrangement; the council of revision was rejected chiefly because it would give the Supreme Court a double negative over laws passed by Congress. Luther Martin's remarks typified this latter concern: "As to the Constitutionality of laws, that point will come before the Judges in their proper official character. In this character they have a negative on the laws. Join them with the Executive in the Revision and they will have a double negative."[22]

If not by representation at the national level, how then were rights to be protected? Ultimately, by the courts.[23] In place of the congressional veto over state laws emerged the supremacy clause, under which state courts are required to strike down state laws that violate the federal Constitution.[24] With respect to the council of revision, that proposal was rejected because, as just noted, many of the delegates did not want to involve the Supreme Court in reviewing congressional acts twice.[25] Although my objective is not to recalculate the Beard tally, the evidence from Philadelphia, especially that surrounding the council of revision, supports the prevailing scholarly view that the Constitution commissions the Court with the power to void unconstitutional federal and state legislation alike. Admittedly, the evidence is not unambiguous. Indeed, the text of the Constitution the Framers finally agreed upon does not expressly provide for judicial review at all.[26] However, any doubt about the Supreme Court's authority to exercise a broad power of judicial review is, in my judgment, dispelled when one turns to the ratification debates. For example, there are James Wilson's remarks to the Pennsylvania ratifying convention:

If a law should be made inconsistent with those powers vested by this instrument in Congress, the judges, as a consequence of their independence, and the particular powers of government being defined, will declare such law to be null and void. For the power of the Constitution predominates. Anything therefore that shall be enacted by Congress contrary thereto will not have the force of law.[27]

There are also the observations of John Marshall in the Virginia ratifying convention. Marshall's observations are particularly interesting, given the role he was to play in *Marbury v. Madison* (1803), the landmark Supreme Court case on judicial review:

Has the government of the United States power to make laws on every subject?
. . . Can they make laws affecting the mode of transferring property, or contracts, or claims between citizens of the same state? Can they go beyond the delegated power? If they were to make a law not warranted by any of the powers enumerated it would be considered by the judges as an infringement of the Constitution which they are to guard. They would consider such a law as coming under their jurisdiction. They would declare it void.[28]

Finally, there is Alexander Hamilton in *The Federalist* no. 78:

The interpretation of the laws is the proper and peculiar province of the courts. A constitution is, in fact, and must be, regarded by the judges as fundamental law. It must, therefore, belong to them to ascertain its meaning, as well as the meaning of a particular act proceeding from the legislative body. If there should happen to be an irreconcilable variance between the two, that which has the superior obligation and validity ought, of course, to be preferred, or in other words, the Constitution ought to be preferred to the statute, the intention of the people to the intention of their agents.[29]

This is but a sampling of the historical evidence in support of a strong judicial check on the forces of representation—evidence that reveals how far the Founders had moved from their original faith in the power of representation to secure private rights. Indeed, some opposed ratification precisely because the Constitution had, in their judgment, moved too far from the doctrine of legislative supremacy. Most notable in this regard was Robert Yates, better known as "Brutus," who feared that the Supreme Court's broad power of judicial review and its independent status under the Constitution would make the Court despotic.[30] As the discussion in this section suggests, however, Brutus's continued faith in representation was a minority view.

Natural Rights and Judicial Review

The previous section chronicled the movement from legislative to judicial protection of individual rights in early American constitutional
history. This section examines the more specific question of the role of
natural-rights doctrine in judicial review. I conclude that the Founders
expected judges to decide cases involving individual rights in light of
natural-rights principles.* Like the political leaders involved in the
more general attempts to curb the legislature, early American judges
and lawyers[31] turned to natural-rights doctrine gradually and somewhat hesitantly, for they, too, were steeped in the tradition of legislative supremacy, in the belief that representation was the vehicle
through which to secure individual rights. This is a subtle, but critical,
as well as previously overlooked, point. In fact, it is the failure to
recognize the gradual and somewhat hesitant turn to judicial protection
of *individual* rights that has led scholars to characterize the existence
of *natural*-rights–based judicial review in such unnecessarily all-or-
nothing terms.[32]

This conclusion about the use of natural-rights doctrine in judicial
review is undoubtedly a controversial one, because it runs counter to
two powerful trends in the literature: an increasing skepticism about
natural rights and a growing mistrust of judicial power.† Nevertheless,
given that during the American Founding the fundamental objective of
government was to safeguard natural rights (see part 1), and that
representation was proving incapable of accomplishing that objective
(see the previous section), it should be expected that early American
judges would come to appeal to natural-rights doctrine when deciding

---

* As the discussion in this section will reveal, the Founders were not as explicitly textual
in their approach to constitutional interpretation as many modern conservatives claim
they were. When I say the Founders expected judges to decide individual rights cases "in
light of" natural-rights principles, I am referring to an interpretive attitude of viewing
the Constitution as the institutional framework through which natural rights are to
be secured.

† The increasing skepticism in the public-law community about natural rights is traceable
to the larger movement in political philosophy against natural rights, whereas the growing mistrust of judicial power is primarily a result of the conservative backlash against
the liberal jurisprudence of the Warren Court.

individual-rights cases. In short, the reading advanced in this section is grounded in common sense, and the failure of modern skeptics to acknowledge a role for natural-rights doctrine in early American judicial practice is attributable to the modern tendency to interpret historical materials in light of modern predilections.[33]* Although the reporting of judicial decisions during the American Founding was far from the science it is today, sufficient documentation exists to reveal that natural-rights doctrine came to play an important role in judicial review.

Pre–Federal-Constitution Precedents

The first recorded statement in America of the power of judicial review is an argument by James Otis before the Massachusetts Superior Court in 1761 in the famous writs of assistance case, *Paxton v. Gray.*[34] According to a young John Adams, who chronicled the case, in dispute was a request by the royal customs office that the court issue general search warrants, or writs of assistance, because particular search warrants had proved ineffective in the customs office's efforts to curb smuggling.[35] Nothing was more repugnant to the colonists' conception of liberty than general searches, violating as they did the cherished maxim that "a man's house is his castle."[36] Otis was so strongly opposed to the idea of general search warrants that he not only refused to argue the case on behalf of the customs office, as was his charge as the king's advocate in the province, but he decided to represent the local merchants instead. Significantly, Otis's argument against the general search warrants—an argument heavily reliant upon Coke's opinion in *Dr. Bonham's Case*—centered around the power of a court to void legislation that conflicts with the constitution and natural rights. In Otis's words: "As to acts of Parliament. An act against the Constitution is void; an act against natural equity is void; and if the act of Parliament should be made, in the very words of the Petition, it

---

*Charles Grove Haines expressed a similar concern some three-quarters of a century ago. Haines wrote: "It is the practice to insist that while references to these [natural-law and rights] phrases are somewhat frequent the utterances are almost invariably in the form of dicta, the decision resting on other grounds, and involving specific provisions of the written constitution." Haines, "The Law of Nature in State and Federal Judicial Decisions," 625. Haines strongly disagreed with the tendency to discount the role of natural-law and rights doctrine in judicial review.

would be void. The executive Courts must pass such acts into disuse."[37]

When Otis argued the writs of assistance case, the doctrine of legislative supremacy held sway. It should therefore come as no surprise that Otis lost the case. This fact notwithstanding, Otis's argument for judicial review—and for a natural-rights–based theory of judicial review at that—was a milestone in American history, portending as it did events to come.* According to John Adams, Otis's argument about the unenforceability of legislative acts that contravene natural rights was so influential that with it "the child of independence was born."[38]

Another noteworthy case in the development of judicial review is *Robin v. Hardaway* (1772). In that case, George Mason argued that a 1682 Virginia law giving slave traders the right to sell the descendants of Indians as slaves violated the Indians' natural rights and was, therefore, void. In Mason's words:

All acts of the legislature apparently contrary to natural right and justice, are, in our laws, and must be in the nature of things, considered as void. The laws of nature are the laws of God; whose authority can be superseded by no power on earth. A legislature must not obstruct our obedience to him from those whose punishments they cannot protect us. All human constitutions which contradict his laws, we are in conscience bound to disobey. Such have been the adjudications of our courts of justice.[39]

A forceful advocate, Mason no doubt overstated the frequency with which judges in 1772 were striking down legislation they deemed violative of natural rights. In fact, the judges in *Robin v. Hardaway* worked hard to avoid passing on the legitimacy of the statute in question. In a maneuver reflective of the still-widespread commitment to legislative supremacy,[40] the judges concluded that the statute had been repealed in 1705.[41] They were not, therefore, required to assess the statute's constitutionality in light of natural-rights principles, as Mason had requested. Nevertheless, Mason's argument, like Otis's before it, is representative of a growing willingness on the part of the bar to challenge legislative power by invoking natural-rights doctrine in the

---

*Modern students of political philosophy and jurisprudence often draw distinctions between terms like "natural equity," "natural justice," "natural law," and "natural rights." See, for example, Strauss, "On Natural Law." An examination of the early cases reveals that early American judges and lawyers typically did not make such distinctions.

courts.* This trend continued after the colonists declared independence.

More has been written, with less consensus achieved, about a handful of state cases decided before the Constitution went into effect than one would think possible. With respect to the status of those cases as precedent for judicial review, the range of scholarly opinion is from all to none.[42] As I now explain, not only do those cases serve as precedent for judicial review, but they illustrate the judiciary's emerging role as the special guardian of the people's natural rights.

Commonwealth v. Caton (Va., 1782)[43] is the first reported case in the United States in which a court openly exercised judicial review.[44] At issue was the constitutionality of a 1776 Virginia statute that moved the pardon power from the executive to the legislature. The statute was before the Virginia Court of Appeals, the state's highest tribunal, because a dispute arose when the lower legislative house pardoned three men condemned to death for treason, and the upper house refused to concur. The attorney general, seeking to enforce the death sentences, insisted that the pardons were ineffective because the statute required the assent of both legislative houses. The condemned men disagreed, arguing that either the statute granted the pardoning power to the lower house alone or it was unconstitutional.

The judges agreed unanimously with the attorney general. More

---

*In a widely cited study of the treatment of slavery in the judicial process prior to the Civil War, Robert Cover reaches the opposite conclusion about the representativeness of Mason's argument in *Robin v. Hardaway*. According to Cover, appeals like Mason's to natural-rights principles in court "were not all that common" among early lawyers and judges. Cover, *Justice Accused*, 19. Positivists who seek refuge in Cover's work are missing a critical point: the unrepresentativeness of the slavery cases as evidence of the general jurisprudential climate of the times. That is to say, those judges who upheld slavery did so primarily because to do otherwise would likely lead to disunion. Indeed, the authors of both the Declaration of Independence and the Constitution of the United States faced the same pressure and dealt with that pressure in a similar, though less explicit, fashion. (Judges were forced to write opinions about slavery, whereas the authors of the Declaration could ignore it and the Framers of the Constitution could dance around it.) Cover's failure to afford due weight to the pressure of disunion is curious, especially since most of his analysis focuses on post-1850 cases—when that pressure was enormous. For a superb discussion of the pressure of disunion facing judges of the day, see Levy, *The Law of the Commonwealth*, chaps. 5–6. In addition, some judges avoided the obvious implications of natural-rights doctrine for the institution of slavery by characterizing Blacks as inferior to Whites, a point also surprisingly neglected by Cover.

significantly, though, they held that they had the power to strike down laws that violated the constitution.[45] Although individual rights were at stake, *Caton* was chiefly about the allocation of governmental power, specifically, about where the pardon power resided. As such, natural-rights doctrine did not figure in the court's decision, because that doctrine has little to say about government structure.[46] Judge George Wythe's opinion nevertheless offers a revealing glimpse into the developing conception of the judicial function, and it is a conception that is consistent with the focus in natural-rights doctrine on the individual. Of particular interest are Judge Wythe's observations about the threat of legislative power to the rights of individuals and about the responsibility of judges to protect against that threat:

> If the whole legislature, an event to be deprecated, should attempt to overleap the bounds, prescribed to them by the people, I, in administering the public justice of this country, will meet the united powers, at my seat in this tribunal; and, pointing to the constitution, will say to them, here is the limit of your authority; and hither, shall you go, but no further.[47]

One of the most intriguing of the early state cases is *Rutgers v. Waddington* (N.Y., 1784), argued by Alexander Hamilton.[48] At issue was whether Hamilton's client, a British citizen named Joshua Waddington, committed a trespass by occupying plaintiff Elizabeth Rutgers's property during the American Revolution. Rutgers sued Waddington pursuant to a New York statute that entitled any person who vacated his or her property under threat of the war to recover in trespass against any person who occupied or destroyed the property.

Formally, Hamilton challenged the statute on the grounds that finding Waddington liable for trespass would violate the law of nations and the peace treaty between the United States and Great Britain. In point of fact, however, Hamilton, like Otis and Mason before him, emphasized natural-law and rights doctrine in his argument to the court. "The enemy having a right to the use of the Plaintiffs property & having exercised their right through the Defendant & for valuable consideration he cannot be made answerable to another without injustice and a violation of the law of Universal society," Hamilton insisted.[49]

The court was fully aware of the importance of natural-law and rights arguments to Hamilton's challenge to the statute. Indeed, the court noted that Hamilton's defense centered on the claim that "statutes against law and reason are void." And the court appeared to accept Hamilton's defense:

> We profess to revere the rights of human nature; at every hazard and expence we have vindicated, and successfully established them in our land! and we cannot but reverence a law which is their chief guardian—a law which inculcates as a first principle—that the amiable precepts of the law of nature, are as obligatory on nations in their mutual intercourse, as they are on individuals in their conduct towards each other; and that every nation is bound to contribute all in its powers to the happiness and perfection of others![50]

Despite this strong language about natural law and rights, the court upheld the statute, explicitly acknowledging the supremacy of the legislature.[51] The court did, however, deny the plaintiff relief. What the court's inconsistent actions suggest is that the judges were torn between their increasing awareness of the need for judges to protect natural rights and their lingering commitment to the doctrine of legislative supremacy. In a Connecticut decision the following year such inconsistency was conspicuously absent.

The *Symsbury Case* (Conn., 1785) involved a land dispute between two neighboring Connecticut towns. Originally, title to the land was held by the town of Symsbury. Subsequently, the town of New Hartford surveyed the land and found that the land was located within the New Hartford town limits. The state legislature agreed and granted title to New Hartford. The proprietors of the town of Symsbury sued, demanding that title to the land be returned to them. The court ruled in favor of Symsbury. In the court's judgment, the act of the state legislature granting title to New Hartford "could not legally operate to curtail the land before granted to the proprietors of the town of Symsbury, without their consent."[52]

Brief though it is, the court's decision in the *Symsbury Case* is important for two related reasons. The first reason is that the decision is plainly an early example of judicial review. The second reason is that the decision is further evidence of a growing awareness among judges that they must serve as a check against legislative power when natural rights are at stake, such as the natural right to property involved in the dispute before the court.

Another landmark case in the development of judicial review is *Trevett v. Weeden* (R.I., 1786). As is so often true of cases from the early days of the American republic, the opinion of the court has not been found. A widely read account of the case by James Varnum, the lead defense attorney, is available, however.[53] At issue was a controversial Rhode Island statute that required local merchants to accept paper money as legal tender, a requirement that, given the inflationary pressures of the day, the merchants did not wish to submit to. Merchants who refused to accept paper money were subject to arrest and to trial without the benefit of a jury. Varnum's client was one such merchant.

Varnum made a variety of arguments in defense of his client, but according to Varnum himself, "by far the most important" was a direct challenge to the statute's constitutionality.[54] In no uncertain terms Varnum claimed both that the statute was unconstitutional and that the judges must declare it so. "The true distinction lies in this," Varnum contended, "that the legislative have the uncontrollable power of making laws not repugnant to the constitution; the judiciary have the sole power of judging of those laws, and are bound to execute them; but cannot admit any act of the legislative as law, which is against the constitution."[55]

Even more interesting than Varnum's discussion of the *existence* of the power of judicial review is his argument about *how* that power should be exercised: in light of natural-rights doctrine. In essence, Varnum's substantive attack on the statute was that trial by jury is an "unalienable right" that the legislature cannot justly infringe.[56] Indeed, Varnum's argument is replete with references to natural rights and to the fact that the American regime was founded to secure them.

Unfortunately, because the court's opinion has not been found, the court's reaction to Varnum's argument is somewhat unclear. Newspaper reports suggest that most of the judges were receptive to Varnum's position. Resolutions passed by the Rhode Island legislature condemning the judges' handling of the case provide additional evidence of this fact.[57]

The most famous of the early state precedents for judicial review is *Bayard v. Singleton* (N.C., 1787). Like most states during the American Revolution, North Carolina confiscated property held by persons who remained loyal to the British. At issue in the case was a statute that required judges to dismiss, without regard to merit, any action brought by persons seeking to recover title to confiscated property. In a short opinion, the Supreme Court of North Carolina unanimously declared the statute unconstitutional on the ground that persons seeking to recover title to confiscated property were entitled to a jury trial on the merits of their claim.[58]

The court was undoubtedly influenced by a widely discussed letter "To the Public" published in a local newspaper prior to the outcome of the litigation.[59] The letter was written by James Iredell, the plaintiff's cocounsel and later a leading member of the North Carolina ratifying convention and one of the first justices of the U.S. Supreme Court. In the letter Iredell emphasized the need to curb the legislature. He did so by drawing on the lessons of the American Revolution:

It was, of course, to be considered how to impose restrictions on the legislature, that might still leave it free to all useful purposes but at the same time guard against the abuse of unlimited power, which was not to be trusted, without the most imminent danger, to any man or body of men on earth. We had not only been sickened and disgusted for years with the high and almost impious language of Great Britain, of the omnipotent power of the British Parliament, but had severely smarted under its effects. We felt in all its rigor the mischiefs of an absolute and unbounded authority, claimed by so weak a creature as man, and should have been guilty of the basest breach of trust, as well as the grossest folly, if the moment when we spurned at the insolent despotism of Great Britain, we had established a despotic power among ourselves.[60]

After the court's decision declaring the confiscation statute unconstitutional, Richard Dobbs Spaight, then serving as a North Carolina delegate to the Constitutional Convention in Philadelphia, wrote a letter to Iredell severely criticizing him for encouraging the court to engage in such a "usurpation" of power. Spaight's letter is interesting both because of the commitment he displays to the notion that representation is the vehicle through which to protect rights and because of the thoroughly modern attack he makes on judicial review. On the latter point, Spaight writes that allowing the court to declare legislative acts unconstitutional means that the people, "instead of being governed by the representatives in the general assembly, would be subject to the will of three individuals, who united in their own persons the legislative and judiciary powers, which no monarch in Europe enjoys, and which would be more despotic than the Roman decemvirate, and equally insufferable."[61]

Iredell responded to Spaight in a letter that expanded on his earlier letter "To the Public." In his second letter, Iredell makes an interesting allusion to the role of natural-rights doctrine in judicial review. Al-

though the focus of Iredell's argument for rejecting the notion of legislative supremacy is the written status of the North Carolina Constitution, he states that even if the constitution were not written, the courts
would have the power to reject legislative enactments that violate
principles of "natural justice."[62] Curiously, Iredell later, as a U.S. Supreme Court justice, rejected this position in a famous decision, *Calder
v. Bull* (1798).[63] But at the time of the framing of the U.S. Constitution,
he recognized both the power of judicial review and a role for natural-
rights doctrine in the exercise of that power.

Constitutional-Period Precedents

Spaight's letter to Iredell illustrates that the delegates who met in
Philadelphia in 1787 were well aware of the state precedents for judicial review.[64] As noted earlier, however, the Constitution does not
expressly provide for judicial review, let alone specify how that document should be interpreted by the Court. Because the Founders' primary reason for writing the Constitution was to protect natural rights
more effectively than the Articles of Confederation were proving capable of doing, it seems reasonable to suggest that the Founders simply
took for granted that Court would interpret the Constitution in light of
natural-rights doctrine when deciding cases involving individual rights.
Fortunately, this suggestion need not rest on inference, no matter how
strong that inference may be. The debates surrounding the ratification
of the Constitution provide tangible evidence of the fact that the
Founders expected the Court to interpret the Constitution in light of
natural-rights principles.

The logical starting point for any discussion of the Founders' position on judicial review during the ratification debate is *The Federalist*
no. 78. In that famous essay Alexander Hamilton clearly states that the
Constitution commissions the Court with the power of judicial review.
What is often overlooked about no. 78, however, is Hamilton's explanation about the primary reason judicial review is necessary: to help
protect the natural rights of the American people. Hamilton writes, for
example, that "the complete independence of the courts of Justice is
particularly essential in a limited Constitution. ... Without this, all the
reservations of particular rights or privileges would amount to
nothing."[65]

Other notable references to the role of natural-rights doctrine in judicial review are available from the debates in the state ratifying conventions. For instance, James Wilson, later an original member of the U.S. Supreme Court, justified the Constitution's judicial tenure provisions to the Pennsylvania convention in natural-rights terms. In Wilson's words, "Personal liberty, and private property, depend essentially upon the able and upright determinations of independent judges." Wilson added, with judicial independence "private property and personal liberty ... will be guarded with firmness and watchfulness."[66]

The central role of natural-rights doctrine in judicial review was emphasized by less prominent delegates to the ratifying conventions as well. William Grayson, for one, closed the discussion on judicial review in the Virginia convention by observing that judges "are the best check we have; they secure us from encroachments on our privileges" and that "if the Congress cannot make a law against the Constitution, I apprehend that they cannot make a law to abridge it. The judges are to defend it."[67]

Perhaps the clearest sign that judges were expected to appeal to natural-rights philosophy in constitutional interpretation is that they did in fact do so after the Constitution went into effect. Indeed, in his influential book, *The Revival of Natural Law Concepts*, Charles Grove Haines concludes that but for natural-rights doctrine, "judicial review ... would have had relatively slight influence on the American government and politics, just as is the case in most foreign countries which have adopted this practice."[68]

Turning first to the state courts, there are myriad examples available to illustrate that judges frequently decided individual rights cases in light of natural-rights principles. One of the best is a 1789 South Carolina case, *Ham v. M'Claws*. At issue was the claim of several recently arrived South Carolina residents that their slaves were improperly seized by a South Carolina revenue officer. Although the claimants acknowledged that the revenue officer had properly seized the slaves under an existing South Carolina import law, they maintained that they were unfamiliar with that law when they decided to move to South Carolina from Honduras. The claimants argued that they were induced to move to South Carolina because of an earlier, less restrictive law. (The claimants were en route to South Carolina when the law was changed.) The court directed the jury to decide the case in light of natural-rights principles:

It is clear, that statutes passed against the plain and obvious principles of common right, and common reason, are absolutely void, as far as they are calculated to operate against those principles. ... We are, therefore, bound to give such a construction to this enacting clause of the act of 1788, as will be consistent with justice, and the dictates of natural reason, though contrary to the strict letter of the law; and this construction is, that the legislature never had it in their contemplation to make the forfeiture of the negroes in question.[69]*

Another instance of natural-rights–based judicial review in the state courts is *Page v. Pendleton* (Va., 1793). In that case Judge Wythe held that the rights of British creditors were not extinguished by the American Revolution. To hold otherwise, Wythe maintained, would violate the "law of nature," because the British creditors had not consented to Virginia law.[70]

The early nineteenth century found state judges continuing to employ natural-rights–based judicial review. In *Currie's Administrator v. Mutual Assurance Society* (Va., 1809), the Virginia legislature had enacted a law that retroactively changed the status of certain insured parties. The affected parties sued, claiming the retroactive change was unconstitutional. Defense counsel John Wickham urged the court to reject the claim, and he did so by stressing the *inappropriateness* of natural-rights–based judicial review. Wickham argued: "No doubt every government ought to keep in view the great principles of justice and moral right, but no authority is expressly given to the judiciary by the Constitution of *Virginia*, to declare a law void as being morally wrong or in violation of a contract."[71]

Judge Spencer Roane, whom Jefferson was reportedly planning to make Chief Justice of the United States had Adams not named Marshall, explicitly rejected Wickham's argument. Roane dismissed out of hand the idea that natural rights are adequately protected by the legislature (which was the essence of Wickham's defense):

It was argued by a respectable member of the bar, that the legislature had a right to pass any law, however just, or unjust, reasonable, or unreasonable.

---

*Although slaves were involved, *Ham v. M'Claws* was not about the *institution* of slavery. *Ham*, unlike the cases directly challenging the institution of slavery discussed in Cover's book, is, therefore, evidence of the general jurisprudential climate of the times.

This is a position which even the courtly Judge *Blackstone* was scarcely hardy enough to contend for, under the doctrine of boasted *omnipotence* of parliament. What is this, but to lay prostrate, at the footstool of the legislature, all our rights of person and property, and abandon those great objects, for the protection of which, alone, all free governments have been instituted.[72]

Other early-nineteenth-century state judges employed similar natural-rights analysis. For example, New York Chancellor James Kent, one of the leading legal scholars of the day, interpreted a statute in *Gardner v. Newburgh* (1816) so that it would conform to the "clear principle of natural equity, that the individual whose property is thus sacrificed, must be indemnified."[73] And though, in *Trustees of Dartmouth College v. Woodward* (1817), the Supreme Court of New Hampshire upheld a series of state statutes that significantly affected the way Dartmouth College was governed, as well as the right of the former trustees to reclaim corporate books from an officer appointed under the new laws, Chief Justice William Richardson voted to do so only after interpreting the statutes in light of natural-rights principles. Chief Justice Richardson wrote:

A complaint that private rights protected by the constitution have been invaded, will at all times deserve and receive the most deliberate consideration of this court. ... [But] [t]he legislative power of this state extends to every proper object of legislation, and is limited only by our constitutions and by the fundamental principles of all government and the inalienable rights of mankind.[74]

Early Supreme Court Practice

The federal courts in general, and the Supreme Court in particular, were in their formative stage during the early days of government under the Constitution. Under the Articles of Confederation, the national judiciary was virtually nonexistent, its business limited almost exclusively to admiralty cases. The reason for this was that the newly independent states jealously guarded their sovereignty, and the judicature power was considered an essential component of that sovereignty. The debate over the judiciary at the Constitutional Convention reflected the tensions between creating a strong national judicial system and maintaining some degree of state sovereignty.[75] As in most decisions involving institutional matters that came out of Philadelphia in

1787, a compromise on the issue was reached. In essence, the compromise was this: a national Supreme Court was created, it was left to Congress to establish lower federal courts (something Congress did in the Judiciary Act of 1789), and the states maintained their own judicial systems, but their courts were obligated by the supremacy clause to invalidate state laws that conflicted with the federal Constitution.

Given that national courts of any significance were an innovation in the Constitution, as well as the product of compromise, it should be expected that it would take some time before their role in the American constitutional order would take root. Indeed, during the twelve-year period before John Marshall became chief justice, the Supreme Court heard few cases. According to legal historian David Currie, this was because of "the relative paucity of early federal legislation, the absence of a general grant of original jurisdiction over cases arising under federal law, and the fact that the Court's jurisdiction was largely appellate."[76] It is, therefore, misleading to criticize natural-law and rights jurisprudence, as many scholars do,[77] on the basis that the early Court did not interpret the Constitution in light of those principles that often. In fact, in relative terms, appeal to natural law and rights in constitutional interpretation during the 1789–1801 period was the rule, not the exception. Of the three full-scale decisions construing the Constitution before 1801,[78] two relied on natural-rights principles.[79] When a significant circuit opinion of Justice William Paterson is added, the ratio rises to three out of four.[80] An examination of those early cases provides strong evidence that the Court was expected to interpret the Constitution in light of natural-rights principles, because the justices did in fact do so, with only one notable objector.*

The first constitutional-law case decided by the Supreme Court was *Chisholm v. Georgia* (1793).[81] At issue was whether a citizen of one state, South Carolina, could bring suit in federal court against another state, Georgia. The official report is silent as to the basis of the action,

---

*A careful review of the U.S. Supreme Court Reports reveals how frequently both justices and lawyers invoked natural-rights arguments in nonconstitutional law individual-rights cases during the early days of the American republic. A perusal of the justices' early grand jury charges is likewise illuminating. See Marcus, ed., *The Documentary History of the Supreme Court of the United States, 1789–1800*, vols. 2–3. These sources show how dedicated the early bench and bar were to natural-rights principles. It should therefore not be surprising that the Court would appeal to those principles in constitutional interpretation as well.

though constitutional historians describe it as a dispute over private property.[82] The justices' opinions support the historians' characterization.

As was the custom at the time, each justice delivered his own opinion. The vote was four to one in favor of permitting the South Carolina citizen to sue the state of Georgia.[83] In a brief opinion, Justice John Blair concluded that the citizen's suit was authorized by the plain words of the Constitution.[84] In their respective opinions, Chief Justice John Jay and Justices William Cushing and James Wilson invoked natural-rights principles to find for the individual. Chief Justice Jay's opinion emphasized the need to let the individual bring suit against the state because the purpose of the Constitution is to protect an individual's natural rights, no matter who violates them. According to the chief justice, this point was so obvious that it required little discussion. In Jay's words:

[It is unnecessary] to show that the sentiments of the best writers on government and the rights of men, harmonize with the principles which direct my judgment in the present question. The acts of the former Congresses, and the acts of many of the state conventions are replete with similar ideas; and to the honor of the United States, it may be observed, that in no other country are subjects of this kind better, if so well, understood. The attention and attachment of the Constitution to the equal rights of the people are discernible in almost every sentence of it.[85]

Justice Cushing wrote an opinion similar to Chief Justice Jay's: "The rights of individuals and the justice due them, are as dear and precious as those of the states. Indeed the latter are founded upon the former; and the great end and object of them must be to secure and support the rights of individuals, or else vain is government."[86]

Justice Wilson's opinion was the longest and most complex of the majority opinions. Like the others, however, he emphasized that the purpose of government is to protect the natural rights of individuals and that a state that violates those rights is subject to suit.[87]

The second of the four full-scale constitutional decisions decided during the Court's opening years was *Van Horne's Lessee v. Dorrance* (1795). In that case Justice William Paterson, on circuit, forbade the state of Pennsylvania to take property from an individual without just compensation. While Pennsylvania maintained that the fifth amendment applied only to the national government, Justice Paterson appealed to natural-rights doctrine and ruled that the just-compensation principle behind the amendment was binding on the states. In Justice Paterson's words:

It is evident that the right of acquiring and possessing property and having it protected, is one of the natural, inherent and inalienable rights of man. ... The preservation of property then is a primary object of the social compact. ... The legislature, therefore, had no authority to make an act divesting one citizen of his freehold, and vesting it in another, without just compensation. It is inconsistent with the principles of reason, justice and moral rectitude; it is incompatible with the comfort, peace, and happiness of mankind; it is contrary to the principles of social alliance in every free government; and lastly, it is contrary to both the letter and spirit of the constitution.[88]

The Supreme Court's most famous appeal to natural-law and rights principles during the early years—indeed, ever—came in *Calder v. Bull* (1798).[89] At issue was a Connecticut statute that set aside a probate court decree that refused to validate a will. The Court unanimously upheld the statute, primarily on the ground that the invalidation of the will by the probate court had not created any vested rights in the heirs. Opinions were written by Justices Cushing, Paterson, Samuel Chase, and Iredell. Justice Cushing's opinion consisted of two unilluminating sentences.[90] Although Justice Paterson alluded to "the fundamental principles of the social compact" in his opinion,[91] it was Justice Chase who most forcefully invoked natural-rights principles in deciding the case. His opinion is worth quoting at length:

I cannot subscribe to the omnipotence of a state Legislature, or that it is absolute and without control; although its authority should not be expressly restrained by the constitution, or fundamental law, of the state. The people of the United States erected their constitutions, or terms of government, to establish justice, to promote the general welfare, to secure the blessings of liberty, and to protect their persons and property from violence. The purposes for which men enter into society will determine the nature and terms of the social compact; and as they are the foundation of the legislative power, they will decide what are the proper objects of it: The nature, and ends of legislative power will limit the exercise of it. ... There are certain vital principles in our free Republican governments, which will determine and overrule an apparent and flagrant abuse of legislative power; as to authorize manifest injustice by positive law; or to take away that security for personal liberty, or private property, for the protection whereof the government was established. An act of the Legislature (for I cannot call it a law) contrary to the first great principles of the social compact, cannot be considered a rightful exercise of legislative authority. . . . The genius, the nature, and the spirit, of our state governments, amount to a prohibition of such acts of legislation; and the general principles of law and reason forbid them.[92]

Because, in his view, the Connecticut legislature's action impaired no vested right, Justice Chase judged the statute consistent with natural-rights doctrine. However, what is significant is that Justice Chase, like Chief Justice Jay and Justices Cushing and Wilson in *Chisholm v. Georgia*, and Justice Paterson in *Van Horne's Lessee v. Dorrance*, unambiguously appealed to that doctrine when interpreting the Constitution.

During the confederation period, James Iredell recognized a role for natural-rights doctrine in judicial review, as a letter explaining his position in *Bayard v. Singleton* (N.C., 1787) indicates.[93] In *Calder v. Bull*, however, Justice Iredell responded directly to Justice Chase's natural-rights approach and firmly rejected it.* In Justice Iredell's words:

> If . . . the legislature of the union, or the legislature of any member of the union, shall pass a law, within the general scope of their constitutional power, the court cannot pronounce it to be void, merely because it is, in their judgment, contrary to the principles of natural justice. The ideas of natural justice are regulated by no fixed standard; the ablest and the purest men have differed upon the subject.[94]

Like Robert Bork of the present day, Justice Iredell rejected natural-rights–based judicial review because people can disagree on the meaning of natural law.[95] The reason for Justice Iredell's change of heart is unclear. Nevertheless, his position in *Calder v. Bull* is inconsistent with the epistemology of the American Founding. The Founders acknowledged that the "self-evident truths" of natural law are not discernible to everyone. But, they believed, natural law is discernible to some, as the opinions of the members of the early Supreme Court, other than Justice Iredell, reveal.[96]

With the notable exception of *Marbury v. Madison* (1803),[97] the first

---

* Currie aptly characterizes the Chase-Iredell exchange as "the opening salvo in a running battle [over the role of natural-law and rights doctrine in judicial review] that never has simmered down completely." Currie, *The Constitution in the Supreme Court*, 47–48. The word "opening" is the most significant part of Currie's statement. That is to say, Justice Iredell's rejection of natural-rights–based judicial review marked the *first* time (I have found) that was done by a sitting judge in a nonslavery context. I have more to say below about this important, but previously overlooked, point.

decade of John Marshall's lengthy chief justiceship was devoted largely to jurisdictional matters,[98] as was the period between 1789 and 1801. In fact, *Marbury* itself concerned the authority of the federal courts, specifically the authority of the federal courts to declare acts of Congress unconstitutional. In 1810, however, the Marshall Court began to issue major decisions on substantive questions of constitutional law.[99]

The first major substantive decision of the Marshall era, *Fletcher v. Peck* (1810),[100] found the Court once again invoking natural-law and rights principles in constitutional interpretation. Speaking, as the early Marshall Court typically did, through the chief justice,[101] the Court struck down the Georgia legislature's attempt to revoke a huge, fraudulent land grant made by a previous legislature. Chief Justice Marshall opened his opinion for the Court with a discussion of "certain great principles of justice, whose authority is universally acknowledged" to restrict legislative power. Marshall spent three pages examining these "great principles of justice" before turning to the contract clause of the Constitution. The chief justice concluded his opinion for the Court in a manner that suggests the holding was influenced by natural-law and rights principles. In Marshall's words: "The state of Georgia was restrained, either by general principles, which are common to our free institutions, or by the particular provisions of the constitution of the United States, from passing a law whereby the estate of the plaintiff ... could be constitutionally and legally impaired and rendered null and void." [102]

Interestingly, just prior to the quoted passage, Marshall made a statement that intimates that he would have found the act in question unconstitutional even if the contract clause had not forbade it. The chief justice remarked:

Would it have been a defense in such a suit to say that a state had passed a law absolving itself from the contract? It is scarcely to be conceived that such a defense could be set up. And yet, *if* a state is *neither* restrained by the general principles of our political institutions, *nor* by the words of the constitution, from impairing the obligation of its own contracts, such a defense would be a valid one.[103]

Justice William Johnson, who was one of the few members of the early Marshall Court occasionally to write separately, concurred in an opinion clearly reliant upon natural-law and rights doctrine. Justice Johnson wrote: "I do not hesitate to declare that a state does not possess the power of revoking its own grants. But I do it on a general principle, on the reason and nature of things: a principle which will impose laws even on the Deity." Justice Johnson turned to *The Federalist* for support for his position that the Constitution exists to secure natural rights and should be interpreted accordingly. "There is reason to believe, from the letters of Plubius *[sic]*, which are well known to be entitled to the highest respect," Justice Johnson maintained, "that the object of the convention was to afford a general protection to individual rights against the acts of the state legislatures." [104]

The Marshall Court decided several other significant contract clause cases. [105] The next notable case in terms of interpretive methodology was *Terrett v. Taylor* (1815). [106] At issue was an attempt by the Virginia legislature to claim land originally acquired by the Episcopal Church before the American Revolution. The legislature, which had earlier both confirmed the Church's title to the land and incorporated the Church, maintained that the statutes by which that was done were inconsistent with religious liberty. In his first opinion for the Court, Justice Joseph Story strongly disagreed—and he did so by interpreting the Constitution in light of natural-rights principles. In Justice Story's words:

That the legislature can repeal statutes creating private corporations, or confirming to them property already acquired under the faith of previous laws, and by which such repeal can vest the property of such corporations exclusively in the state ... we are not prepared to admit; and we think ourselves standing upon the principles of natural justice, upon the fundamental laws of every free government, upon the spirit and letter of the constitution of the United States, and upon the decisions of most respectable judicial tribunals, in resisting such a doctrine. [107]

The final significant contract clause case of the Marshall era is *Ogden v. Saunders* (1827). [108] That case would have been an otherwise insignificant application of the contract clause to the bankruptcy context [109] had it not been for a dissent filed by Chief Justice Marshall from the Court's decision that a state was free to discharge obligations incurred to its own citizens after an insolvency law was passed. Marshall's dissent is chock-full of natural-law and rights references. Although some seek to dismiss those references as "nothing but a distraction,"[110] they were determinative of Marshall's opinion in the case. Indeed, the chief justice chastised the majority for failing to understand a basic tenet of natural-rights philosophy, namely, that it is not the state that gives validity and force to a contract, but a contract that gives validity and force to the state.* According to Marshall, "Individuals do not derive from government their right to contract, but bring that right with them into society; that obligation is not conferred on contracts by positive law, but is intrinsic, and is conferred by the act of the parties." Although the state may regulate contracts, it may not go so far as to impair their obligation, as was done, in Marshall's judgment, in the case at bar. Importantly, the chief justice closed his dissenting opinion by emphasizing the foundational place of natural-rights philosophy in the Constitution. As Marshall stated in no uncertain terms:

When we advert to the course of reading pursued by American statesmen in early life, we must suppose that the framers of our constitution were intimately acquainted with the writings of those wise and learned men, whose treatises on the law of nature and nations have guided public opinion. ... We must suppose that the framers of our constitution took the same view on the subject and the language they have used confirms this opinion.[111]

The Marshall Court decided substantive constitutional questions in non–contract clause cases as well. The great majority of those cases, including the most famous, *McCulloch v. Maryland* (1819)[112] and *Gibbons v. Ogden* (1824),[113] involved the power of the national government vis-à-vis the states. As is well known, the Marshall Court offered an expansive reading of national power. More significant for present purposes than the specific holdings of those cases is that the Court did *not* employ natural-rights doctrine to arrive at them. As most critics of natural-law and rights jurisprudence fail to appreciate, however, there is a dichotomy between individual-rights cases and allocation-of-powers cases. In allocation-of-powers cases like *McCulloch v. Maryland* and *Gibbons v. Ogden* natural-rights doctrine has little to say, since that doctrine is concerned with normative questions about the origins

---

* One commentator on the *Ogden* case attributes the majority's failure to grasp the significance of Marshall's natural-rights arguments to the fact that those justices were from "the second generation of interpreters of the Constitution," once removed from the Framers. Isaacs, "John Marshall on Contracts," 425. This point could be applied even more forcefully to modern critics of natural-rights jurisprudence.

of society and the rise and extent of political power. But when it comes to questions of individual rights, natural-rights doctrine has much to say, and the early Court's constitutional jurisprudence reflects this fact.

Unfortunately, the Marshall Court did not adhere consistently to the dichotomy between individual-rights cases and allocation-of-powers cases. The clearest example of this inconsistency is *Barron v. Baltimore* (1833).[114] At issue was a fifth-amendment claim by an individual that the city of Baltimore had taken his property without just compensation by destroying the navigability of a stream and rendering his wharf useless. In a similar case, *Van Horne's Lessee v. Dorrance*, discussed above, Justice Paterson had ruled that, although a state might have a plausible argument that the fifth amendment was intended by the Framers to apply only to the national government, natural-rights doctrine required that the basic just-compensation principle behind the amendment be applied to the states as well. In *Barron v. Baltimore*, however, Chief Justice Marshall dismissed the individual's claim. Nowhere in his brief opinion did Marshall consider the possibility that the city's action had violated the individual's natural rights. Instead, the chief justice concluded that the Bill of Rights guarantees were not binding on the states and localities.

How can the Marshall Court's failure to interpret the Constitution in light of natural-rights philosophy in *Barron v. Baltimore* be explained when the case so clearly involved individual rights? Chiefly by the fact that when the Court decided *Barron* in 1833, belief in higher law had given way to a view of the written Constitution as the sole source of fundamental principles. Although the declining role of natural-rights philosophy in mid–nineteenth-century American politics is generally attributed to a growing belief, epitomized by the rise of Jacksonian democracy, in the right of the people to rule in any way they see fit, unencumbered by the concern for protecting individual rights that is at the heart of natural-rights teaching,[115] the Court turned away from natural rights with apparent reluctance.

Several of Chief Justice Marshall's opinions illustrate this reluctance to abandon natural-rights doctrine. In *The Antelope Case* (1825),[116] for example, Marshall strongly condemned slavery and the slave trade on natural-rights grounds. However, when faced with an explicit positive law permitting the slave trade, the chief justice proved unwilling to interfere.[117] Undoubtedly, as one commentator has aptly remarked,

Marshall was "a mind in transition" during the later stages of his chief justiceship.[118]*

Assessing the Natural-Rights Precedents

I have endeavored to show in this section that the Framers expected judges to interpret the Constitution in light of natural-rights philosophy when deciding individual-rights cases.† This required careful attention to the context in which the various arguments and court opinions concerning judicial review were made. That context revealed that, whereas the practice of interpreting the Constitution in light of natural-rights philosophy in individual rights cases had become the norm for the early Supreme Court, pre–federal Constitution American lawyers and judges turned to natural-rights–based judicial review gradually and somewhat hesitantly: only after they became convinced the legislature had proved incapable of protecting natural rights. This is a point overlooked by both sides of the modern debate over the role of natural-law and rights doctrine in judicial review. As a result, the modern debate tends to be framed in unnecessarily all-or-nothing terms.

Because my conclusion about natural-rights–based judicial review runs counter to two powerful trends in the literature—an increasing skepticism about natural rights and a growing mistrust of judicial power—many readers will likely resist what I have had to say. Indeed, the force of these trends necessitated that my analysis be detailed. In

---

*Justice William Johnson's dissenting opinion in the otherwise uneventful *Shanks v. Dupont* (1830) shows that other members of the Court were also "minds in transition." (Recall Justice Johnson's strong natural-law and rights references in *Fletcher v. Peck.*) "I had this question [about partitioning land] submitted to me on my circuit some years since, and I then leaned in favor of this right of election," Justice Johnson wrote. "But more mature reflection has satisfied me that I then gave too much weight to natural law and the suggestions of reason and justice in a case which ought to be disposed upon the principles of political and positive law." *Shanks v. Dupont,* 28 U.S. (3 Pet.) 239, 250, 258 (1830) (Johnson, J., dissenting).

† Maybe Robert Bork—the prototype modern legal positivist—will now become a natural lawyer! Bork did say he would convert if the requisite historical proof was made. In Bork's words:

If there was evidence that the framers and ratifiers intended judges to apply natural law, I would accept that judges had to proceed in that fashion. When an institution is intended and designed to operate in a particular way, when its members take an oath to operate in that way, it seems appropriate that the institution and its members should do so. (Bork, "Natural Law and the Law," 52)

my judgment, however, the "burden of proof" should be on those who reject the role of natural-rights doctrine in constitutional interpretation.[119] After all, the United States of America was founded to secure natural rights (see part 1).[120] My examination of the historical record discloses that this will be a difficult burden of proof to meet. In fact, Justice Iredell's rejection of natural-rights–based judicial review was the *only* such rejection issued by a sitting judge in a nonslavery context during the pre-Jacksonian years.[121] Except for Iredell's position and an *unsuccessful* lawyer's argument in *Currie's Administrator v. Mutual Assurance Society* (Va., 1809),[122] *no* direct evidence has been brought forward suggesting that, once the Founders recognized that judges needed to protect individual rights against the overreaching forces of representation, resort to natural-rights principles to do so was inappropriate. A careful reading of the modern debate reveals that opponents of natural-rights–based judicial review rely almost exclusively on rhetorical techniques; specifically, on attempts to "distinguish" the direct evidence proffered by proponents. Frankly, given their failure to offer direct evidence, I am amazed that the positivists are winning the debate.

In addition to the historical point—and one that has also been overlooked in the modern debate on judicial review—rejecting a role for the natural-rights political philosophy of the Declaration of Independence in constitutional interpretation ignores the obvious fact that the modern Court frequently appeals to natural-law–like concepts, most notably through the doctrine of substantive due process. And what is so troubling about the modern Court's approach is that evolving natural-law–like concepts such as substantive due process have served largely as a vehicle through which the justices write their own personal moral and political beliefs into the Constitution. Clearly, a nation based on the rule of law demands more than this: it demands a return to first principles.

Judicial Finality

The authoritativeness of the Supreme Court's interpretation of the Constitution is an issue that has received considerable attention over the years. Many scholars, as well as several of this nation's most prominent chief executives, have argued for a more egalitarian approach to constitutional interpretation than the Court's authoritarian conception of its role permits.[123]

This section rejects the egalitarian approach to constitutional interpretation, an approach that, in its most attractive form, views the Constitution as a communally interpreted document in which the Supreme Court plays an important, but not predominant, role.[124] Briefly put, the fact that the Constitution should be interpreted in accordance with the natural-rights political philosophy of the Declaration of Independence suggests that the Court is the institution of American government that should have the final say in constitutional interpretation. As just noted, this is an argument that many will reject. Indeed, Harry Jaffa—the foremost contemporary proponent of the view that the Constitution should be interpreted in light of the Declaration of Independence[125]—expressly denies a role for the Court in identifying and applying that philosophy in American life. According to Jaffa, the Founders held that it is through the legislative process, not through the judicial process, that the ideals of natural justice are to be achieved. Jaffa bases his argument on the right of self-government in and through the consent of the governed. In Jaffa's words:

The "arbitrary will of another man" is not less arbitrary for being the will of a judge. It is no less arbitrary when intrinsically or naturally right, if it is imposed without that process—the legislative process—whereby the consent of the governed enters into the making of the laws that the governed are to live under.[126]

Jaffa's position on the role of the Court in the American constitutional order is similar to that advanced by Edwin Meese, Robert Bork, Chief Justice William Rehnquist, and myriad other conservative proponents of a jurisprudence of original intention (see the Introduction).[127] Importantly, Jaffa, like the conservative originalists, misinterprets what the Declaration of Independence means by "the consent of the governed." The Declaration's famous phrase speaks to how a legitimate government is *established,* not to how government is to *operate* once it is established. It is the *Constitution* that addresses how government is to operate once established. And, as this section explains, the Constitution commissions the Court as the principal interpreter of the natural-rights political philosophy of the American regime. That is to say, unless and until the people reverse the Court's interpretation of the Constitution's underlying political philosophy by constitutional amendment or revolution, the Court's interpretation should be controlling.

Although modern-day constitutional commentators have written and spoken in considerable detail about the authoritativeness of the Supreme Court's interpretation of the Constitution, the Founders said very little—at least explicitly.[128] What little they did say does support the notion of judicial finality. For instance, Alexander Hamilton comments in *The Federalist* no. 81 on the "absurdity in subjecting the decisions of men, selected for their knowledge of the laws, acquired by long and laborious study, to the revision and control of men who, for want of the same advantage, cannot but be deficient in that knowledge,"[129] and Melancton Smith writes in his "Letters of a Federal Farmer" that "it is proper that the federal judiciary should have ... the power of deciding finally on the laws of the union."[130] And who can forget Brutus's famous charge, "From this court there is no appeal? "[131]

James Madison is another of the relatively few Founders who made express statements about judicial finality. Madison is often cited for support by proponents of egalitarian constitutional jurisprudence.[132] This interpretation of Madison's views fails to appreciate that Madison's position on judicial finality evolved during the course of his life, not to mention that he *lost* the original debate on the role of the Court. Because Madison was so important to the framing and ratification of the Constitution, it is necessary to consider his views on judicial finality in some detail. By so doing, one may see the evolving nature of his thoughts on the subject.

In *The Federalist* no. 49 Madison writes that "the several departments being perfectly co-ordinate by the terms of their commission, neither of them, it is evident, can pretend to an exclusive or superior right of settling the boundaries between their respective powers."[133] Similarly, in remarks made in the first Congress Madison noted that "in the ordinary course of Government, ... the exposition of the laws and the Constitution devolves upon the Judiciary," but he wondered "upon what principle it can be contended, that any one department draws from the Constitution greater powers than another, in marking out the limits of the powers of the several departments." "Nothing," he argued, "has yet been offered to invalidate the doctrine, that the meaning of the Constitution may as well be ascertained by the legislative as by the judicial authority."[134] But later in life, though still contending that because the Court, the president, and Congress "are co-ordinate, and each equally bound to support the Constitution, ... each must ... be guided by the text of the Constitution according to its own interpretations of it," Madison acknowledged that the Court "most familiarizes itself to the public attention as the expositor, by the *order* of its functions in relation to the other departments." As a result, he concluded, the "ultimate discussion and operative decision" on the meaning of the Constitution belonged to the Court because the Court was the final avenue of appeal within the government itself. What these remarks suggest is that Madison came to accept that the Court, "when happily filled," was the "surest expositor of the Constitution" in disputes "concerning the boundaries between the several departments of Government as in those between the Union and its members."[135]

In addition to the handful of statements described above, the Founders' acceptance of judicial finality is evident in the structure of government they embodied in the Constitution,[136]* specifically in the complementary mechanisms of separation of powers and checks and balances, which were designed to ensure that the three branches of the national government were equal to and independent of each other so the government would not become despotic.[137] What this means in practical terms is that, in the words of *The Federalist*, each branch must own "a constitutional control over the others."[138]

The president has, among other checks, a veto over congressional acts and the power to nominate federal judges. Congress has, among other checks, the power to override presidential vetoes and to control the size and jurisdiction of the federal courts (within the limits to be discussed in chapter 4), as well as the power to impeach all federal officials. Without the power of definitive judicial review what check—what "constitutional control"—would the Court have on the president and Congress? The answer is "none" and, as a consequence, the com-

---

*In the absence of explicit statements by the Founders, structural reasoning provides the best implicit evidence of their views. In other words, structural reasoning should be considered a subset of originalist methodology. Interestingly, some leading conservative originalists have invoked structural reasoning to *reject* the notion that the Founders intended for the Supreme Court to be the principal institutional protector of individual rights. See, for example, McDowell, "Postscript," 108; Rehnquist, *The Supreme Court*, 318. As this section shows, I strongly disagree with the conservatives' reading of the structure of the Constitution.

plementary mechanisms of separation of powers and checks and balances strongly imply that the Founders commissioned the Court as the ultimate interpreter of the Constitution.

The Constitution's principal objective of protecting natural rights also intimates that the Founders intended for the Court to have the final say in constitutional interpretation, because the Court is the branch of government most immune from majoritarian pressures. In the thoughtful words of Justice Brennan:

> It is the very purpose of a Constitution—and particularly of the Bill of Rights— to declare certain values transcendent, beyond the reach of temporary political majorities. The majoritarian process cannot be expected to rectify claims of minority right that arise as a response to the outcomes of that very majoritarian process.[139]

Hence, the need for the judiciary—the lone branch of the national government that is not directly accountable to majoritarian processes—to safeguard individual and minority rights through the definitive exercise of judicial review. Madison's June 8, 1789, speech to the U.S. House of Representatives upon introducing his proposal for a Bill of Rights illustrates that the Founders were well aware of this fact:

> If they are incorporated into the constitution, independent tribunals of justice will consider themselves in a peculiar manner the guardians of those rights; they will be an impenetrable bulwark against every assumption of power in the legislative or executive; they will be naturally led to resist every encroachment upon rights expressly stipulated for in the constitution by the declaration of rights.[140]

Many conservative originalists maintain that the political process adequately protects the rights of the entire American political community.[141] As Brennan's and Madison's remarks make clear,[142] however, this view fails to account for the self-interested nature of political majorities. This chapter has described how the Founders came to view the Court as an indispensable check on the machinations of the political process in the area of individual rights. The conservative originalists' emphasis on representation as the vehicle through which rights are to be protected therefore turns the Founders' position on its head.

Closely related to the Court's role in the Constitution's system of separation of powers and checks and balances are considerations of institutional competence. These considerations suggest that the Found-

ers empowered the Court with the final say in constitutional interpretation. The most obvious of these considerations relates to one just
discussed: the Court is more insulated from majoritarian pressures
than the other institutions of American government are. The Constitution provides federal judges with life tenure, unless impeached, a salary
that cannot be decreased, and, most importantly, the benefit of not
having to run for election. Given these unique institutional safeguards,
judges are relatively free to make decisions without worrying about the
personal political ramifications.[143]

The Court's relative freedom from political pressure also enables it
to work in an environment conducive to discerning the meaning of the
Constitution, including the often abstract nature of the Constitution's
underlying natural-rights political philosophy. In Alexander Bickel's
well-known language, "Courts have certain capacities for dealing with
matters of principle that legislatures and executives do not possess.
Judges have, or should have, the leisure, the training, and the insulation
to follow the ways of the scholar in pursuing the ends of government."[144] And as part 1 described, the "end of government" according
to the principles of the American regime is the protection of the natural
rights of the American people.

The advantages the Court *potentially* enjoys in matters of epistemology should not be overlooked. (Suggestions for helping to actualize
this potential will be offered in chapter 4.) Locke's discussion in his
Essays on the Law of Nature of the epistemological difficulties of
discerning natural law bears repeating:

> Some people here raise an objection against the law of nature, namely that
> there is no such law in existence at all, since it can nowhere be found, for most
> people live as though there was no rational ground in life at all nor any law of
> such a kind that all men recognize it. ... If indeed natural law were discernible
> by the light of reason, why is it that not all people who possess reason have
> knowledge of it? ...
> I admit that all people are by nature endowed with reason, and I say that
> natural law can be known by reason, but from this it does not necessarily
> follow that it is known to any and every one. For there are some who make no
> use of the light of reason but prefer darkness and would not wish to show
> themselves to themselves.
> ... There are others, brought up in vice, who scarcely distinguish between good
> and evil, because a bad way of life, becoming strong by lapse of time, has
> established barbarous habits, and evil customs have perverted even matters of

principle. In others, again, through natural defect, the acumen of the mind is too dull to be able to bring to light those secret decrees of nature.[145]

Many of the Founders agreed with Locke's claim that only a select few are able to discern the self-evident truths of natural law. Jefferson, through his Bill for the More General Diffusion of Knowledge, was addressing the point (see chapter 1). Jefferson's views on the existence and role of the so-called "natural aristocracy" are clearly stated in an 1813 letter to John Adams (who was in agreement with Jefferson on the subject):[146]

For I agree there is a natural aristocracy among men. The grounds of this are virtue and talents. ... The natural aristocracy I consider as the most precious gift of nature, for the instruction, the trusts, and government of society. ... May we not even say, that that form of government is best, which provides most effectually for a pure selection of these natural aristoi into the offices of government?[147]

Although it is frequently argued that Jefferson distrusted the judiciary, it is more appropriate to say he distrusted John Marshall and other like-minded Federalist-party judges.[148] Jefferson's questioning of the authoritativeness of judicial interpretations of the Constitution came only *after* the Federalists showed their political colors on the Court. Jefferson's earlier favorable opinion about the potential of the judiciary is evident in a 1789 letter trying to convince Madison of the necessity of adding a bill of rights to the Constitution:

Your thoughts on the subject of the Declaration of rights in the letter of Oct. 17 I have weighed with satisfaction. Some of them had not occurred to me before, but were acknowledged just in the moment they were presented to my mind. In the arguments in favor of a declaration of rights, you omit one which has great weight with me, the legal check which it puts into the hands of the judiciary. This is a body, which if rendered independent, and kept strictly to their own department merits great confidence for their learning and integrity. In fact what degree of confidence would be too much for a body composed of such men as Wythe, Blair, and Pendleton?[149]

Madison, like Jefferson and Adams, subscribed to the ideal of government by natural aristocracy.[150] Though he initially rejected the argument that the Court should have the final say in constitutional interpretation, Madison came to appreciate, as earlier noted, that the Court, "when happily filled," would be the "surest expositor" of all matters of constitutional interpretation.[151] And what Madison undoubtedly had in mind when he referred to a Court "happily filled," and what Jefferson surely meant when he mentioned the names of "Wythe, Blair, and Pendleton," was the necessity of selecting judges of extraordinary ability—members of the "natural aristocracy," as they phrased it. A subject to be discussed at length in chapter 4, it is worth emphasizing here that the role of the Court prescribed in this volume *requires* that any person appointed to the Supreme Court be of exceptional ability. Charles Pinckney captured this point succinctly when he remarked at the federal Convention that "the importance of the Judiciary will require men of first talents."[152]

Finally, the Court should have the final say in constitutional interpretation because there are no feasible alternatives. This chapter has suggested why neither the president nor Congress should have the final say: because of the resulting threat of majoritarian tyranny.[153] The only other alternative is an egalitarian approach to constitutional interpretation, an approach once embraced by Madison himself.

There are certainly compelling reasons for adopting an egalitarian approach to constitutional interpretation. First is the danger of "judicial supremacy"—a danger identified by Presidents Jefferson, Jackson, Lincoln, Franklin Roosevelt, Nixon, and Reagan—wherein unelected judges are said to possess unchecked governmental power. Given their experience with the tyranny of the British crown, it is barely imaginable that the Founders intended judicial supremacy.

Another argument in favor of an egalitarian approach to constitutional interpretation is that it recognizes the value of a constitutional dialogue. As Sanford Levinson explains, egalitarian constitutional jurisprudence identifies "the Constitution as a public source of social understanding and the concomitant ability of all citizens to share in the debates about the meaning of our tenuously shared life."[154] In other words, all segments of the American polity should play an active role in discerning the meaning of the Constitution. In practice, to achieve a constitutional dialogue the American people, speaking primarily through their elected representatives, would be required to ignore what they consider to be an incorrect judicial interpretation of the Constitution—at least until that interpretation is "well settled,"[155] whatever that means.

There are even more compelling reasons for *rejecting* an egalitarian approach to constitutional interpretation. For one, that approach, at least in its Jeffersonian manifestation, leads to executive supremacy by permitting the president to refuse to execute laws passed by Congress and decisions issued by the Court with which he disagrees.[156] Clearly, the Founders, who pointedly condemned the tyranny of the king in the Declaration of Independence, opposed that state of affairs.

An egalitarian approach to constitutional interpretation should be rejected also because, without a final interpreter of the Constitution, constitutional gridlock would likely result. For this nation's (indeed, *any* nation's) government to work, some branch must have the final say. Otherwise, nothing will be settled, and no one's rights will be secure—a situation patently at odds with the Founders' conception of government.

But the most important reasons for rejecting an egalitarian approach to constitutional interpretation are those discussed in this section: because the Founders committed this nation to protecting individuals from majoritarian tyranny, because the Court is, at least potentially, more of a meritocracy than the political branches, and because the Court operates in an environment conducive to discerning the dictates of an often abstract natural-rights political philosophy.

This chapter has endeavored to show that the Founders commissioned the Court as the principal guardian of the American people's natural rights. To that end, I examined cases and historical materials that have been examined many times before. But what I sought to do is to provide a revised reading of those cases and materials, a reading that is in keeping with the American Founding's commitment to natural rights. Admittedly, the historical record on the origins and scope of judicial review is not unambiguous (especially when interpreted in light of *modern* predilections). If it were, scholars would not have disagreed about these issues for so long. In essence, however, what I have tried to explain is that a definitive power of judicial review is an indispensable feature of any government dedicated to securing natural rights, a conclusion to which the Founders were *gradually* led, given their increasingly unpleasant experiences with representation.

To ensure that the Founders' vision of the Court as the principal guardian of the American people's natural rights is respected by the Court today, appropriate checks must be placed on the Court. Chapter 4 discusses these checks.

4

Checks on the Court

The theory of constitutional interpretation advanced in this volume affords the Supreme Court immense authority. To prevent the Court's role as the ultimate interpreter of the Constitution from devolving into the unacceptable state of government by judiciary, checks on the Court are essential—a point surprisingly neglected in virtually all of the volumes on constitutional interpretation.[1] And what those checks must ensure is that the Court interprets the Constitution in light of its underlying natural-rights philosophy, instead of on the basis of the personal moral and political preferences of individual justices.

This chapter considers five potential checks on the Supreme Court's interpretive authority: restricting the Court's appellate jurisdiction, the Article 5 amendment process, impeachment, judicial self-restraint, and the appointment process. Although other constraints on the Court exist—for example, the force of public opinion, the press, and scholarship—the five discussed here are the most significant *constitutional* constraints. I begin by examining the appropriateness of limiting the Court's appellate jurisdiction.

Limiting the Court's Appellate Jurisdiction

With the possible, albeit significant, exceptions of Justice Joseph Story's opinion in *Martin v. Hunter's Lessee* (1816)[2] and the views of one or two constitutional scholars,[3] it has long been agreed that the Constitution does not require the existence of the lower federal courts. Two points support this nearly unanimous view: the unambiguous language of Article 3 and the records of the Constitutional Convention of 1787.

Article 3 provides in pertinent part that "the judicial Power of the United States, shall be vested in one supreme Court, *and in such inferior Courts as the Congress may from time to time ordain and establish.*"[4] The language is clear: Although the Supreme Court must exist, the lower federal courts may not. Indeed, much debate took place in the Constitutional Convention about whether the state courts or the lower federal courts should serve as the initial forum for resolving disputes involving federal law. A compromise was reached, and that compromise, reflected in Article 3, leaves the establishment and jurisdiction of the lower federal courts to the discretion of Congress.

The status of the Supreme Court's jurisdiction is not as clear. Although Article 3 requires that the Supreme Court have "original Jurisdiction ... in all Cases affecting Ambassadors, other public Ministers and Consuls, and those in which a State shall be Party," in all other cases arising under federal law "the supreme Court shall have appellate Jurisdiction, both as to Law and Fact, *with such Exceptions, and under such Regulations as the Congress shall make.*"[5] The question to be addressed here is the meaning of the so-called "exceptions clause." Unfortunately, the records of the Constitutional Convention on the meaning of the exceptions clause are meager and uninformative.[6] It is therefore necessary to turn to the decisions of the Supreme Court.

The congressional proposals to limit the appellate jurisdiction of the Supreme Court have arisen from dissatisfaction with specific decisions made by the Court, those concerning school prayer, abortion, and busing, for example. The modern Court, however, has not had to address the constitutionality of the proposals because none have been passed by Congress. In fact, the Court has directly ruled on the meaning of the exceptions clause on only two occasions in its history.[7] Unfortunately, those two occasions provide little guidance, because they point in opposite directions.

The first case in which the Supreme Court directly ruled on the meaning of the exceptions clause is *Ex Parte McCardle* (1868).[8] In that case the Court refused to decide the constitutionality of Congress's post–Civil War Reconstruction policy because the challenge was brought by way of a writ of habeas corpus and—this is the important point—Congress had repealed the habeas corpus statute through which the appeal was filed—an action that the Court ruled Congress had the constitutional authority to take. Although *Ex Parte McCardle* might appear to be a precedent for broad congressional power to withdraw the Court's appellate jurisdiction, most constitutional scholars recognize that there were alternative avenues of habeas corpus review available to the petitioner in that case and, hence, the case should not be construed as sanctioning wide-ranging congressional power over the Court's appellate jurisdiction.[9] The Court itself so implied in the very next term in *Ex Parte Yerger* (1869).[10]

The other Supreme Court case of note is *United States v. Klein* (1872).[11] There, the Court struck down a statute enacted under the exceptions clause because the statute was nothing more than a thinly-veiled attempt by Congress to dictate the outcome of the case. Although some scholars argue that *Klein* nevertheless accepted the authority of Congress to withdraw the Court's appellate jurisdiction on all but such result-oriented occasions,[12] that argument overlooks the fact that attempts by Congress to exercise the exceptions clause power have been, and are likely to continue to be, motivated by concerns with how the Court has decided or might decide a specific question.

Although the Founders and the Supreme Court may have said little about the meaning of the exceptions clause, constitutional scholars have said a lot. Many scholars, looking primarily at the language of the exceptions clause, contend that Congress has the constitutional power to abolish *all* of the Court's appellate jurisdiction (though most of these same scholars believe that such an exercise of congressional power would be unwise).[13] This broad reading of the exceptions clause fails to recognize "that in a legal context neither an exception nor a regulation can destroy the essential characteristics of the subject to which it applies."[14] In other words, the term "exceptions" implies that *some* appellate jurisdiction is retained; indeed, it suggests that the *major* portion of appellate jurisdiction is retained, because otherwise the "exception" would trump the "rule."

Moreover, those scholars who argue that Congress has unlimited authority to restrict the Supreme Court's appellate jurisdiction disregard the "internal" and "external" restraints on Congress's power. "Internal" restraints are those implied by Article 3. "External" restraints are those flowing from the other provisions of the Constitution.[15]

The idea that there are restraints in Article 3 on Congress's authority to limit the Supreme Court's appellate jurisdiction originated with a 1953 law review article by Henry Hart. In that article Hart argues that any exercise of the exceptions clause by Congress "must not be such as will destroy the essential role of the Supreme Court in the constitutional plan."[16] Hart's position certainly has common-sense appeal. After all, if the argument that Congress can withdraw *all* of the Court's appellate jurisdiction is coupled with Congress's authority to abolish the lower federal courts, the federal judiciary could be reduced to one court, the Supreme Court, exercising original jurisdiction when a state or a ranking foreign diplomat is a party.[17] As chapter 3 explained, such a limited role for the Court is not what the Founders' Constitution envisions.

While Hart did not define the scope of what has become known as the "essential functions" thesis,[18] other legal scholars have, most notably Leonard Ratner, who disagrees with those who believe that the "'essential functions' thesis is little more than constitutional wishful thinking."[19] According to Ratner, the essential functions of the Supreme Court are "to maintain the supremacy and uniformity of federal law." Following Hart's lead, Ratner concludes that Congress cannot limit the Court's appellate jurisdiction if those essential functions would be jeopardized, because to do so would be "[in]consistent with the constitutional plan."[20]

Surprisingly, Ratner fails to identify the protection of individual and minority rights from majoritarian excesses as an essential function of the Supreme Court, a function that this volume has repeatedly emphasized. In fact, in the context of the debate over limiting the Court's appellate jurisdiction, this function has been largely forgotten. The Court's indispensable role in checking the political branches has not, however, been lost on Raoul Berger. In Berger's words:

The Founders were deeply concerned with, and in no little part designed judicial review as a restraint on, *Congressional* excesses. If the Court was intended to curb Congressional excesses in appropriately presented "cases or controversies," and if an attempt to exercise that power might be blocked by Congress as a judicial "excess," then the Convention was aimlessly going in circles.[21]

Briefly stated, *the* essential function of the Supreme Court is to protect the natural rights of the American people (see chapter 3). Any effort by Congress to "except" this function from the Court's appellate jurisdiction would therefore be illegitimate.[22]

There are also constitutional restraints "external" to Article 3 on Congress's authority to limit the Supreme Court's appellate jurisdiction. The most important is the Bill of Rights. Even assuming that the Article 3 exceptions clause did initially provide Congress with unlimited authority to withdraw the Court's appellate jurisdiction, that authority was revoked when the Bill of Rights was added to the Constitution. By definition, if an amendment to the Constitution is inconsistent with a provision in the body of the Constitution, the amendment takes precedence. And when the Bill of Rights was added to the Constitution to help safeguard individual and minority rights from the excesses of the political process, Congress lost any power it may have arguably had to restrict the Court's appellate jurisdiction over those rights. To put it another way, the basic message of the Bill of Rights is that fundamental rights are off limits to majoritarian abuse. Hence the need for providing the Supreme Court with wide-ranging appellate jurisdiction, for the Court is the lone branch of the American government not strictly accountable to majoritarian pressures (see chapter 3).

Even scholars who believe that Congress has plenary authority over the jurisdiction of the federal courts agree that the implicit equal protection guarantee of the fifth amendment[23] prohibits Congress from employing its authority to deny groups like Blacks or aliens the right of Supreme Court appellate review.[24] But why should the fifth amendment be any more important than the other amendments to the Constitution that seek to protect individual and minority rights? No persuasive answer to this question has been, or can be, provided.

The complementary mechanisms of separation of powers and checks and balances impose an additional external restraint on Congress's authority to limit the Supreme Court's appellate jurisdiction. One of the most articulate statements of this view comes from William French Smith, President Ronald Reagan's first attorney general. In 1982, then attorney general Smith responded to an inquiry from the chairman of the Senate Judiciary Committee about the constitutionality of a bill sponsored by North Carolina Senator Jesse Helms to withdraw the Court's appellate jurisdiction in cases relating to "voluntary" prayer in the public schools. Smith informed the chairman that Congress may *not* constitutionally make

"exceptions" to Supreme Court jurisdiction which would intrude upon the core functions of the Supreme Court as an independent and equal branch in our system of separation of powers [and that] Congress can limit the Supreme Court's appellate jurisdiction only up to the point where it impairs the Court's core functions in the constitutional scheme.[25]

As Smith's remarks suggest, one of the essential principles of the Constitution is that each branch of the national government must have the means to defend itself against the unwarranted actions of the other branches of the government. Plenary congressional control over the Court's appellate jurisdiction would violate this principle because it would render the Court defenseless. As chapter 3 pointed out, without the power of judicial review, the Court would have no check on the actions of Congress and the president, a state of affairs that the complementary mechanisms of separation of powers and checks and balances will not permit. Senator Barry Goldwater got to the heart of the matter when he came out in 1982 against the flurry of court-stripping bills sponsored by Senator Helms, among others, because such bills are, in effect, efforts "to override constitutional decisions of the Supreme Court by a simple bill."[26] If the decisions of the Court are thought to be in error there is a more constitutionally appropriate means of redress: the Article 5 amendment process.

The Article 5 Amendment Process

"The idea of amending the organic instrument of a state is peculiarly American," writes Lester Bernhardt Orfield in his 1942 study on amending the federal Constitution, the first comprehensive examination of the subject.[27] The notion that a constitution may be amended flows from another "peculiarly American" idea: popular sovereignty. Under the doctrine of popular sovereignty, the people may make a constitution. And if they may make a constitution, it follows that they may also revise and amend that constitution.

The fact that so little had been written on the amendment process as late as 1942—and not much more today[28]—is surprising, given the importance of the process. The amendment process is perhaps the most important part of a constitution, because a formal mechanism for change is essential for the very survival of the state. Renowned political scientist John Burgess made the point well many years ago:

> A complete constitution may be said to consist of three fundamental parts. The first is the organization of the state for the accomplishment of future changes in the constitution. This is usually called the amending clause, and the power which it describes and regulates is called the amending power. This is the most important part of a constitution. Upon its existence and truthfulness, i.e., its correspondence with real and natural conditions, depends the question as to whether the state shall develop with peaceful continuity or shall suffer alternations of stagnation, retrogression and revolution. A constitution, which may be imperfect and erroneous in its other parts, can be easily supplemented and corrected, if only the state be truthfully organized in the constitution; but if this be not accomplished, error will accumulate until nothing short of revolution can save the life of a state.[29]

The amending process of the United States Constitution is enumerated in Article 5, which provides essentially two ways in which the Constitution may be amended.[30] The first way is upon the proposal of two-thirds of both houses of Congress, if the proposed amendment is subsequently ratified by three-fourths of the states, whether that ratification is by the state legislatures or by special state conventions called for the purpose of ratification. The second way the Constitution may be amended is by a special convention called by two-thirds of the states, if, again, the proposed amendment is subsequently ratified by three-fourths of the states. To date, only the first alternative has been utilized.

The Founders intended the Article 5 amendment process to be a peaceful substitute for revolution. George Mason made the point directly when he remarked at the Constitutional Convention of 1787 that amendments to the Constitution would occasionally be necessary and that it would "be better to provide for them, in an easy, regular and Constitutional way than to trust to chance and violence."[31] Abraham Lincoln, who understood the philosophical underpinnings of the Constitution better than any statesman since the Founding,[32] demonstrated an appreciation of the relationship between the Article 5 amendment process and revolution in his first inaugural address. "This country, with its institutions, belongs to the people who inhabit it," Lincoln exclaimed. "Whenever they shall grow weary of the existing Government, they can exercise their *constitutional* right of amending it or their *revolutionary* right to dismember or overthrow it."[33]

The Article 5 amendment process is difficult,[34] as is illustrated by the fact that the process has been successfully employed on only twenty-seven[35] occasions in the more-than-two-hundred-year history of the Constitution. Many critics emphasize the difficulty of the formal amendment process and make two related claims; first, that Article 5 is an ineffective check on the Court and second, that Article 5 is an unworkable mechanism for coping with modern circumstances unforeseen by the Founders and, thus, should not be used as a check on the Court.

The problem with criticizing the difficulty of the Article 5 amendment process is that this criticism overlooks the fact that the Founders intended to make the process difficult. If the amendment process was easy, James Madison explains in *The Federalist* no. 49, the Constitution would be deprived "of that veneration" that is so essential to political stability.[36] And, as seen in part 1, the Founders thought political stability essential to the security of natural rights.

Turning specifically to the effectiveness of Article 5 as a check on the Court, Stephen Carter, for one, argues that today "article V is very nearly a dead letter. The contention that it provides a realistic check on judicial activity is at best wishful thinking, certainly somewhat naive, and at worst disingenuous."[37] Here, it must be recalled that Article 5 has been successfully employed as a check on the Court. Six of the twenty-seven amendments to the Constitution were direct responses to Supreme Court decisions the nation thought were in error. The eleventh amendment reversed *Chisholm v. Georgia* (1793),[38] which decided that a state could be sued in federal court by a plaintiff from another state. The thirteenth, fourteenth, and fifteenth amendments reversed *Dred Scott v. Sandford* (1857),[39] a decision that relegated Blacks to the status of property. The sixteenth amendment over-ruled *Pollack v. Farmers' Loan and Trust Company* (1895),[40] which struck down a federal income tax. Finally, the twenty-sixth amendment was ratified in 1971 to reverse *Oregon v. Mitchell* (1970),[41] a decision that voided a congressional attempt to lower the minimum voting age in state and local elections to eighteen. Any argument that the Article 5 amendment process is incapable of providing a check on judicial activity is, therefore, historically inaccurate. The process may be difficult, but that is because the Founders intended it to be. Moreover, the quick passage of the twenty-sixth amendment shows that the process can work expeditiously if the nation strongly disagrees with a ruling issued by the Court.

Next, it is necessary to consider the criticism that the Article 5 amendment process cannot effectively deal with modern problems unforeseen by the Founders—and the consequences of that alleged ineffectiveness for the Court. Walter Murphy raises this criticism in particularly dramatic fashion: "If the United States had to undergo the delay and uncertainty of the amending process every time a problem arose that the framers had not foreseen or had foreseen in such a different context as to distort their vision of later problems, the practical effects would destroy the nation."[42]

For Murphy, the Article 5 amendment process should not be used as a check on the Court. Murphy shares Justice Brennan's position, discussed at length in the Introduction, that the Court must amend the Constitution when unforeseen circumstances so demand. In addition, in a well-known essay, Murphy goes so far as to contend that on some occasions the Court should strike down amendments enacted through the Article 5 process![43] According to Murphy, certain provisions in the Constitution are so fundamental and so essential to "human dignity" that an amendment repealing them should be declared unconstitutional by the Court. (Murphy's example is an amendment endorsing racial discrimination.)

Besides failing to recognize that the natural-rights political philosophy of the Declaration of Independence is flexible enough to address today's circumstances (see the next chapter), the problem with substituting the judicial process for the Article 5 amendment process is that doing so is an exercise of "force and will" by the Court, rather than "judgment,"[44] and is therefore at odds with the way the Constitution mandates that fundamental change take place. Concomitantly, it is a threat to the stability of the Constitution itself. President George Washington made this point forcefully in his legendary farewell address:

If, in the opinion of the people, the distribution of the Constitutional powers be in any particular wrong, let it be corrected by an amendment in the way, which the Constitution designates. But let there be no change by usurpation; for, though this, in one instance, may be the instrument of good, it is the customary weapon by which free governments are destroyed. The precedent must always greatly overbalance in permanent evil any partial or transient benefit, which the use can at any time yield.[45]*

The seriousness with which the Founders took the Article 5 amendment process is likewise illustrated by Elbridge Gerry's observation in the first Congress that "an attempt to amend" the Constitution in "any other way" than by Article 5 "may be a high crime or misdemeanor," impeachable under Article 1,[46] a subject I consider in detail below. Further, Article 5's supermajority requirements—two-thirds for proposing and three-fourths for ratifying an amendment—make it unlikely that a "dignity-denying" scenario like that hypothesized by Murphy would ever arise.†

In summary, the Article 5 amendment process provides a workable, albeit arduous, mechanism for reversing Supreme Court decisions that the nation deems to be in error, including those concerning the Constitution's underlying natural-rights political philosophy. The difficulty of utilizing the formal amendment process for checking the Court is actu-

---

*The danger of substituting the judicial process for the Article 5 amendment process is illustrated by Justice Brennan's actions during the formative stages of *Frontiero v. Richardson*, 411 U.S. 677 (1973), an important gender discrimination case. Although he was well aware the equal rights amendment had already passed Congress and was being acted upon by the states, Brennan nevertheless circulated a draft opinion that declared classification by gender constitutionally impermissible. Brennan argued privately that there "was no reason to wait several years for the states to ratify the amendment" and proposed instead to author an opinion for the Court that "would have made the Equal Rights Amendment unnecessary." Quoted in Woodward and Armstrong, *The Brethren*, 254. See generally Berns, *Taking the Constitution Seriously*, 229–31.

† If a dignity-denying scenario did arise, the political philosophy of the American regime provides a means of redress for the aggrieved individual or group: revolution. Although revolution may initially seem a draconian remedy, such is not the case for the theory of revolution embodied in the Declaration of Independence. According to the Declaration, revolution is resorted to cautiously and, if successfully employed, leads to the prompt formation of a new government. See chapter 1 and the Conclusion.

ally a beneficial aspect of the process, given the institutional advantages enjoyed by the Court in discerning the often abstract nature of the political philosophy of the Declaration of Independence.

Impeachment

Impeachment is the most direct constitutional check on the Court. It has, however, been rarely employed in practice, and even more rarely does it result in conviction. Samuel Chase is the only member of the Supreme Court to have faced impeachment proceedings—he was impeached by the House of Representatives in 1804, but acquitted by the Senate—and only ten lower federal court judges (as of July 1994) have suffered through the process (seven were actually removed).[47]

The limited use of impeachment in history has led the vast majority of Court watchers to conclude that impeachment is too difficult to be an effective check on the Court. Thomas Jefferson, for one, frequently criticized Congress's use of its impeachment power over the Court, calling impeachment "not even a scare-crow," "nugatory," and "inefficient."[48]

Turning from practice to theory, some commentators consider impeachment to be too blunt a check on the Court. Indeed, they argue that it is good that impeachment has been rarely used in practice. John Agresto's remarks are illustrative of this view:

Impeachment not only verges on the politically impossible, as Jefferson soon found out when he tried it against the Federalist-dominated judiciary; it also, in a liberal society, has awkward moral-philosophical implications. In fact, the reason impeachment is impossible politically is in large measure that it seems extremely inappropriate morally. Impeachment of sitting justices for criminal activity or manifest incompetence is surely supportable. But impeachment to remedy judicial decisions smacks too much of a punishment imposed for the expression of an opinion, for the exercise of a duty laid upon one by force of oath and office, for the statement of a thoughtful judgment.[49]

Chief Justice William Rehnquist echoes Agresto's sentiment. "The impeachment power conferred on Congress by the Constitution," the chief justice writes in a 1991 article, "was sort of a 'wild card' which could have upset the checks and balances established in the Constitution, and on two occasions almost did so."[50] Like Agresto, Rehnquist believes the nation is fortunate that impeachment has not been more widely utilized by Congress to curb the Court.[51] Before directly addressing the criticisms of impeachment, it is necessary to consider the specific constitutional clauses relating to the process.

The constitutional provisions bearing on impeachment are strewn throughout the document. Although the Founders focused most of their discussions of impeachment on the president, Article 2, section 4, clearly contemplates the impeachability of federal judges in its coverage of "all civil Officers of the United States."[52] Article 1, section 2, states that the House "shall ... have the sole Power of Impeachment," and Article 1, section 3, gives the Senate "the sole Power to try all Impeachments" and also requires for conviction a two-thirds vote of those senators present.

Article 2, section 4, states that impeachable offenses are "Treason, Bribery, or other high Crimes and Misdemeanors," whereas Article 3, section 1, provides that federal judges "shall hold their Offices during good Behaviour." The punishments imposable upon conviction are "removal from Office, and disqualification to hold and enjoy any Office of honor, Trust or Profit under the United States,"[53] and the president cannot grant reprieves or pardons for the impeachment itself.[54]

A host of questions are raised by the various impeachment provisions, but the most important for present purposes—given my thesis that the Constitution should be interpreted in accordance with the natural-rights philosophy of the Declaration of Independence, rather than in light of the moral and political preferences of individual justices—is: For what kinds of offenses may a justice be impeached?[55]

The Constitution lists "Treason, Bribery, or other high Crimes and Misdemeanors" as impeachable offenses.[56] It is easy to understand what the Constitution means by "treason," because that offense is specifically and narrowly defined in Article 3, section 3: "Treason against the United States shall consist only in levying War against them, or in adhering to their Enemies, giving them Aid and Comfort." Likewise, although not defined in the Constitution, the offense of "bribery" is readily understandable, since the Founders used the term in the traditional common-law sense of the giving or taking of something of value in exchange for a political favor.[57] It is more difficult to know what the Constitution means by the catchall phrase "other high Crimes and Misdemeanors." A careful examination of the evolution of the phrase sheds light on its meaning.

The delegates to the Constitutional Convention of 1787 early agreed that officials of the new government would not enjoy immunity from prosecution for common-law crimes. The Founders foresaw an overlapping body of offenses for which federal officials could be impeached. Initially, they felt that neglect of duty, maladministration and corrupt administration, and misconduct in office should be the only impeachable offenses, with common-law crimes such as treason, bribery, and felony left to the courts to address. On August 20, 1787, the Committee of Detail presented a proposal that would make federal officials "liable to impeachment and removal from office for neglect of duty, malversation, or corruption." On September 8, 1787, however, the delegates debated a proposal that would make "Treason & bribery" the sole grounds of impeachment.[58] George Mason objected, and the brief colloquy that ensued marked the first and only discussion during the Convention of the phrase "other high Crimes and Misdemeanors." Mason began:

Why is the provision restrained to Treason & bribery only? Treason as defined in the Constitution will not reach many great and dangerous offences. Hastings is not guilty of Treason. Attempts to subvert the Constitution may not be Treason as above defined—As bills of attainder which have saved the British Constitution are forbidden, it is the more necessary to extend: the power of impeachments. He movd. to add after "bribery" "or maladministration."[59]

Mason's motion was seconded by Elbridge Gerry,[60] but James Madison objected on the ground of vagueness. "So vague a term will be equivalent to a tenure during pleasure of the Senate," Madison argued.[61] Mason then "withdrew 'maladministration' & substituted 'other high crimes & misdemeanors,'"[62] and the impeachment provision as it now appears in the Constitution was born.

The phrase "other high Crimes and Misdemeanors" has been subject to much debate. The most frequent dispute is whether criminality is required for impeachment. Most scholars who have addressed the issue have concluded that impeachment is not limited to criminal offenses,[63] but a few have argued otherwise.[64]

By far the most interesting—and contentious—interpretation of the impeachment clause was that offered by former president Gerald Ford, when Ford, a Republican, was serving as minority leader of the U.S.

House of Representatives. In proposing the impeachment of Justice William Douglas, a liberal Democrat, in April 1970, Ford asserted that an "impeachable offense" is whatever the House and Senate "consider it to be at a given moment in history."[65] The problem with Ford's interpretation is that it gives Congress too much power over the Court (and the president). As Raoul Berger succinctly points out, Ford "laid claim to an illimitable power that rings strangely in American ears."[66] After all, the Founders designed a system of checks and balances and separation of powers precisely because they sought to avoid too much power in one set of hands.[67]

The meaning of "high Crimes and Misdemeanors" is discernible if it is recognized that the Founders considered impeachment to be a *political* punishment for a *political* offense against the state, with "political" being conceived of in the noble sense of the word, rather than in the crassly partisan terms proposed by Ford. (In seeking to impeach Justice Douglas, Ford was reacting to the rejection of two of President Nixon's nominees to the Supreme Court and to Warren Court liberalism generally.) *The Federalist* no. 79 expressly rejects the notion of partisan impeachments. There, Hamilton declares that "inability" is not in and of itself an impeachable offense because "an attempt to fix the boundary between the regions of ability and inability would much oftener give scope to personal and party attachments and enmities than advance the interests of justice or the public good."[68]

The political nature of impeachment is central to the English tradition on which the Founders based their understanding of the process.[69] According to English practice, a "high" crime or misdemeanor was distinguishable from an ordinary crime or misdemeanor on the ground that the former required proof of an "injury to the commonwealth— that is, to the state and to its constitution."[70]

The Constitutional Convention debates reflect the Founders' understanding of the political nature of impeachment. In complaining that the proposal limiting impeachment to "Treason & bribery" was too narrow, Mason alluded to the contemporary British impeachment of Warren Hastings (the governor-general of India) as being not for treason, but for an attempt to "subvert the Constitution."[71] Although Mason's proposal to add the term "maladministration" to the list of impeachable offenses was withdrawn upon Madison's vagueness objection,[72] the accepted alternative—"other high Crimes and Misdemeanors"—was understood to encompass attempts to "subvert the Constitution" and other serious offenses, both civil and criminal, against the state.[73]

The Federalist plainly indicates that impeachment was designed to address political offenses against the state. In *The Federalist* no. 65, Hamilton writes:

> A well-constituted court for the trial of impeachments is an object not more to be desired than difficult to be obtained in a government wholly elective. The subjects of its jurisdiction are those offenses which proceed from the misconduct of public men, or, in other words, from the abuse or violation of some public trust. They are of a nature which may with peculiar propriety be denominated POLITICAL, as they relate chiefly to injuries done immediately to the society itself.[74]

An examination of the ratification debates likewise illustrates the generally understood political nature of impeachment. For example, James Iredell remarked in the North Carolina ratifying convention that impeachment "will arise from acts of great injury to the community,"[75] and in Massachusetts a delegate observed that impeachment would lie against any federal official who "dare to abuse the powers vested in him by the people."[76]

Finally, remarks by James Wilson and Thomas Jefferson during the early years of government under the Constitution manifest the political nature of the impeachment power. Wilson made the point unambiguously in his *Lectures on Law* of 1790–92: "In the United States ... impeachments are confined to political characters, to political crimes and misdemeanors, and to political punishments."[77] With respect to President Jefferson, although he likely sought to impeach Justice Samuel Chase for overridingly partisan reasons, the justification Jefferson used for his action was put in more noble, philosophical terms: Chase had allegedly engaged in a "seditious official attack upon the principles of our Constitution."[78] (Chase, a Federalist, had been using his grand jury charges as occasions to criticize several Jeffersonian policies.)[79]

The political nature of the impeachment power suggests that a Supreme Court justice willfully substituting his or her own personal political philosophy for the political philosophy of the Constitution should be impeached.[80] Indeed, as earlier noted, Elbridge Gerry remarked in the first Congress that "an attempt to amend" the Constitution in "any other way" than by the Article 5 amendment process "may be a high crime or misdemeanor" impeachable under Article 1.[81] After all, nothing goes more to the heart of the Constitution than the natural-rights political philosophy upon which the Constitution and this nation are based (see part 1). To make the point in the Founders' terms, nothing could more "subvert the Constitution"[82] than intentionally disregarding the philosophical principles upon which the Constitution is erected.

Although Jefferson may be correct in arguing that *in practice* impeachment has "not even [been] a scare-crow,"[83] that does not mean it should remain so.[84] The *theory* of the Constitution *requires* that Congress exercise the political courage necessary to perform its constitutional duty of impeaching those justices who seek to "rewrite" the Constitution rather than "interpret" it.[85] Hamilton writes in *The Federalist* no. 81 that impeachment is a "complete security" against the "deliberate usurpations" of the Court,[86] a clear indication that the Founders expected the impeachment power to be more frequently invoked than it actually has been.

With respect to the charge that impeachment is too blunt a check on the Court to be desirably used,[87] this charge, like that concerning how impeachment has actually been employed in practice, ignores the theory of the Constitution. As Charles Black aptly notes, "the Framers of our Constitution very clearly envisaged the occasional necessity of this awful step, and laid down a procedure and standards for its being taken."[88] (The intentionally arduous nature of the impeachment procedures and standards also protects against impeachment being an unnecessarily blunt check on the Court.)[89] As unsettling as the impeachment process may sometimes seem, the Constitution requires that it be sometimes used. President William Howard Taft, himself a great admirer of the Court and later its chief justice, made the point well in some remarks about the perceived shortcomings of the judiciary of his day: "Make your judges responsible. Impeach them. Impeachment of a judge would be a very healthful thing in these times."[90] And in these present times of justices reading their own values into the Constitution and imposing them on the rest of us, Taft's remarks deserve special heed, for it is only if the impeachment power is taken more seriously that the natural-rights principles upon which this nation is based can be reaffirmed.

Judicial Self-Restraint

In theory, judicial self-restraint—when a judge interprets the Constitution as written, rather than as he or she wishes it were written—would seem to be the easiest and most commonsensical check on the Court. Felix Frankfurter, likely the most consciously committed proponent of judicial self-restraint ever to sit on the Supreme Court, got to the heart of the matter in a passionate 1943 dissent from the Court's decision striking down West Virginia's compulsory public school flag salute policy. Justice Frankfurter exclaimed:

> One who belongs to the most vilified and persecuted minority in history [the Jews] is not likely to be insensible to the freedoms guaranteed by our Constitution. Were my purely personal attitude relevant I should wholeheartedly associate myself with the general libertarian views in the Court's opinion, representing as they do the thought and action of a lifetime. But as judges we are neither Jew nor Gentile, neither Catholic nor agnostic. We owe equal attachment to the Constitution and are equally bound by our judicial obligations whether we derive our citizenship from the earliest or the latest immigrants to these shores. *As a member of this Court I am not justified in writing my private notions of policy into the Constitution, no matter how mischievous I may deem their disregard.* ... Most unwillingly, therefore, I must differ from my brethren with regard to legislation like this. I cannot bring my mind to believe that the word "liberty" secured by the Due Process Clause gives this Court authority to deny to the State of West Virginia the attainment of that which we all recognize as a legitimate legislative end, namely the promotion of good citizenship, by employment of the means here chosen.[91]

Whether the debate is framed in terms of "judicial activism" and "judicial restraint," or "judicial legislating" and "judicial judging," or "lawmaking" and "lawfinding," or "noninterpretivism" and "interpretivism," or the notion of a "living Constitution" and a "jurisprudence of original intention,"[92] most observers of the judicial process recognize that judicial self-restraint does not occur in practice. They often argue that judicial self-restraint is impossible. Judges are human beings, the argument goes, and they cannot help but read their personal views into the Constitution they are interpreting. In the inimitable words of Benjamin Cardozo, "The great tides and currents which engulf the rest of men do not turn aside in their course and pass the judges by."[93] Or, as Justice John Clarke once pithily observed, "I have never known any judges, no matter how austere of manner, who discharged their judicial duties in an atmosphere of pure, unadulterated reason. Alas! We are all 'the common growth of Mother Earth,'—even those of us who wear the long robe."[94]

The problem with arguments like those made by Cardozo and Clarke is that they confuse practice with theory, explanation with justification. Henry Abraham makes the point especially well:

> These are honest, eloquent, realistic assessments *cum* explanations of the facts of life of the judicial role. But they are *explanations*—not justifications per se for a conscious or, for that matter, subconscious failure to observe that elusive line between judicial activism and restraint or lawmaking and lawfinding or judicial judging and judicial legislating. There is, quite naturally, an explanation for everything we do. Yet an explanation is by no means a justification. Certainly an explanation does not absolve us from the quest for *the* line—or at least *a* line—in our search for a full measure of freedom and equal justice under law.[95]

Fortunately, for years many of this nation's most preeminent constitutional scholars have been lending their considerable talents to attempting to articulate the proper "line" between judicial restraint and judicial activism.[96] In addition to the debate, discussed in the Introduction, between the conservative proponents of a jurisprudence of original intention (for example, Edwin Meese, Robert Bork, and Chief Justice William Rehnquist) and those specifically rejecting the conservatives' call and asserting the need for a "living Constitution" that adapts to meet contemporary circumstances by way of judicial interpretation (for example, Justice William Brennan, Walter Murphy, and Laurence Tribe), there has been a cottage industry of literature on the subject of judicial restraint. While an examination of these many provocative "line-drawing" works is beyond the scope of the present volume,[97] a brief analysis of three of the leading and most representative treatments—one prescribing an extremely limited amount of judicial discretion, another accepting a moderate degree, and the third calling for virtually unbounded judicial activism—will shed light on this difficult, yet essential, check of judicial self-restraint.

The first great work on the meaning of judicial self-restraint, and the most restrictive of the three discussed here, is James Bradley Thayer's classic 1893 *Harvard Law Review* essay, "The Origin and Scope of the American Doctrine of Constitutional Review."[98] In that essay—called by Felix Frankfurter "the most important single essay" ever written on American constitutional law[99]—Thayer articulates what has come to be known as the "reasonable-doubt test."[100] The reasonable-doubt test maintains that the Court should not strike down a law when the executive or the legislature has "merely made a mistake," but only when one or the other has made "a very clear one—so clear that it is not open to rational question . . . not merely their own judgment as to constitutionality, but their conclusion as to what judgment is permissible to another department which the Constitution has charged with the duty of making it."[101]

The deferential nature of the reasonable-doubt test reflects Thayer's belief that the Constitution is amenable to a variety of legitimate interpretations. As a consequence, Thayer maintains that the unelected judiciary should be hesitant to step in and interfere with the choices made by the democratic branches of the government, whom Thayer insists have a constitutional duty to make a determination of the constitutional propriety of their own actions before they take them.

Despite the conviction with which Thayer articulates his vision of judicial restraint, his theory suffers from a fatal flaw: an underestimation of the dangers posed by political majorities. Simply put, Thayer prescribes a role for the Court that is so deferential to the political branches that the Court cannot possibly safeguard the rights of individuals and minorities from majoritarian excesses, which, as chapter 3 explained, is the Court's principal charge under the Constitution.[102]

An example of a middle-ground approach to the meaning of judicial restraint, as well as the leading contemporary work on the subject, is John Hart Ely's *Democracy and Distrust: A Theory of Judicial Review* (1980).[103] There, Ely criticizes both those who advocate a jurisprudence of original intention (Ely calls them "interpretivists") and those who support the notion of a living Constitution ("noninterpretivists" to Ely). To Ely, interpretivists are inappropriately focused on the past and also confront constitutional provisions that cannot be construed by simply reading the text of the Constitution or seeking the history of its meaning. "Noninterpretivists," on the other hand—whether they look to tradition, "neutral principles," perceptions of popular consensus, natural law,* or the like—are, at bottom, Ely believes, simply reading their own personal values into the Constitution.

What Ely argues for is a *process*-oriented jurisprudence. Under Ely's approach, the Court would actively concern itself with ensuring that the political process is free from systemic biases. In nonpolitical process matters, however, the Court would refrain from substituting its judgment for the legislature's. The choice of substantive policy values, Ely contends, should be largely left to the political process.

A major problem with Ely's argument is that process is not as easily distinguishable from substance as he would have his readers believe. In reality, it is not unfair to characterize Ely's work as an attempt to legitimate the Warren Court's liberal *substantive* results by ingeniously describing them as correctly policing the political *process* or, in some cases, as an articulate rationalization of the leading "can't help" decisions made by that Court (for example, *Brown v. Board of Education*). Moreover, by claiming that value choices should be made in the political process, Ely overlooks the fact that those choices have already been made by the Founders in the Declaration of Independence. To reiterate, the Founders dedicated this nation to equality, life, liberty, and the pursuit of happiness.

By far the most supportive of judicial activism of the contemporary literature on the subject is Arthur Miller's *Toward Increased Judicial Activism: The Political Role of the Supreme Court* (1982). There, Miller unabashedly calls for the appointment of nine Platonic philosopher-kings who will lead the nation to a more "just" society, no matter what the Declaration and the Constitution have to say. In Miller's words, "more judicial activism is both necessary and desirable . . . if it furthers the attainment of human dignity."[104]

The problems with Miller's approach—which is really just an extremely impassioned version of the notion of a living Constitution—are many, but two merit singling out. First, by arguing that the Court should "update" the Constitution, Miller disregards the Constitution's specified mechanism for change: the Article 5 amendment process. Second, and even more troubling, is Miller's failure to appreciate that the Constitution is a limit on all governmental power, including judicial

---

* As the Introduction explained, I consider natural law to be an interpretivist category.

power. By not recognizing that judges unbounded by constitutional limits can become despotic just as easily as any other political official, Miller proposes a formula for the destruction of the polity he so desperately seeks to save.

The vastly different degrees of judicial discretion prescribed in these three leading treatments of judicial review illustrate the complicated nature of the seemingly straightforward check of judicial self-restraint. With respect to the theory of constitutional interpretation advanced in this volume, judicial self-restraint would center on a proper knowledge and application of the natural-rights political philosophy of the Declaration of Independence. The admittedly difficult nature of this task puts a premium on the thoughtful exercise of the appointment power, a subject to which I now turn.

The Appointment Process

Perhaps the most important potential check on the Court is the appointment process. If this process were employed thoughtfully, the other checks on the Court—limiting appellate jurisdiction, the Article 5 amendment process, impeachment, and judicial self-restraint—would become less a cause for concern.

The appointment process has received considerable attention following the controversies surrounding the confirmation battles over Robert Bork and Clarence Thomas. (Bork's nomination to the Supreme Court was defeated in October 1987, whereas Thomas's was confirmed—albeit by the narrowest margin in modern history—in October 1991.) As a result, literature on the appointment process is seemingly unending[105] and, in the cases of Bork and Thomas, the process even came to prime-time television.

There are essentially three components to the appointment process: (1) the proper respective roles of the president and the Senate, (2) the qualifications of the nominees, and (3) the methodology of selection.[106] This section considers each in turn.

Article 2, section 2, of the Constitution provides that the president, "by and with the Advice and Consent of the Senate, shall appoint ... Judges of the supreme Court." The appointment process as it exists in the Constitution is the product of a compromise reached at the Convention of 1787.[107] One group of delegates, including Roger Sherman, Oliver Ellsworth, Elbridge Gerry, Benjamin Franklin, Gunning Bedford, George Mason, and John Rutledge, was opposed to giving the appointment power to the executive because it could lead to monarchy.[108] Another group, consisting of Gouverneur Morris, James Wilson, Nathaniel Gorham, Alexander Hamilton, and James Madison—those favoring the creation of a strong executive—believed that vesting the appointment power in a large legislative body would not only lead to lesser quality appointments, but also to deals and intrigues.[109] Given these diametrically opposed positions, compromise was not easily reached. The appointment power was debated extensively, and despite the best efforts of Gorham and Madison to reach an early compromise on the issue by giving both the executive and the Senate roles in the process,[110] the debate continued into the last days of the Convention. Then, almost mysteriously,[111] the provision as it now exists, in which the president nominates and the Senate confirms or rejects, was adopted.

The uncertain nature of the Constitutional Convention debates on the appointment power makes it somewhat difficult to discern what exactly the Founders intended the nature of the Senate's "advice and consent" role to be. *The Federalist* envisions a limited role for the Senate. Hamilton argues in no. 76 that there is "no difference between nominating and appointing" and he also expresses doubt that the president's "nomination would often be overruled" by the Senate.[112] This limited view of the Senate's role was not, however, shared by all of those who were asked to pass on the Constitution. In his "Letters of a Federal Farmer," Melancton Smith claimed that "the president is connected with or to the senate; he may always act with the senate, but he can never effectually counteract its views: The president can appoint no officer, civil or military, who shall not be agreeable to the senate."[113] And Samuel Spencer informed the North Carolina ratifying convention that "the President may nominate, but they [the Senate] have a negative on his nomination, till he has exhausted the number of those he wishes to be appointed. He will be obliged, finally, to acquiesce in the appointment of those whom the Senate shall nominate, or else no appointment will take place."[114]

The proper respective roles of the president and the Senate in the appointment process are still subject to much debate. Even leading members of the Senate Judiciary Committee—the standing committee in the Senate assigned the task of conducting judicial confirmation hearings—disagree on the matter. Senator Patrick Leahy contends that the president and the Senate are "equal partners" in the appointment process,[115] but Senator Orrin Hatch believes that the president is to have the dominant role.[116]* A careful reading of the Convention debates suggests that those favoring an equal role for the Senate have better discerned the Founders' intent. The evidence is subtle, but not inconclusive. Charles Black ties the evidence together with uncommon clarity:

> In the Constitutional Convention, there was much support for appointment of judges *by the Senate alone*—a mode which was approved on July 21, 1787, and was carried through into the draft of the Committee of Detail. The change to the present mode came on September 4th, in the report of the Committee of Eleven and was agreed to *nem. con.* on September 7th. This last vote must have meant that those who wanted appointment by the Senate alone—and in some cases by the whole Congress—were satisfied that a compromise had been reached, and did not think the legislative part in the process had been reduced to the minimum. The whole process, to me, suggests the very reverse of the idea that the Senate is to have a confined role.[117]

Concluding that both the president and the Senate should play major roles in the appointment process[118] answers only half the question. Next, it must be decided what qualifications a nominee should possess.

History suggests four reasons why a president has nominated a particular person to the Supreme Court: (1) merit, (2) friendship, (3) representativeness (for example, geographic, racial, sexual, and religious), and (4) political and ideological compatibility.[119] History also intimates seven reasons why the Senate has rejected certain nominees to the Court:

(1) opposition to the nominating president, not necessarily to the nominee; (2) the nominee's involvement with one or more contentious issues of public policy or, simply, opposition to the nominee's perceived jurisprudential or sociopolitical philosophy (i.e., politics); (3) opposition to the record of the

*The position senators take on this fundamental question of the respective roles of the president and the Senate in the appointment process seems to depend largely on their political relationship with the president. If the president is *not* of a particular senator's party—as in the case of Senator Leahy when he made his remark quoted in the text—that senator is likely to insist that the Senate is an equal partner in the appointment process. But if the president *is* of a particular senator's party—as was the case at the time of Senator Hatch's remark—the senator will usually maintain that the president is to have the dominant role. See Walker and Epstein, *The Supreme Court of the United States*, 41.

incumbent Court, which, rightly or wrongly, the nominee presumably supported; (4) senatorial courtesy (closely linked to the consultative nominating process); (5) a nominee's perceived political unreliability on the part of the party in power; (6) the evident lack of qualification or limited ability of the nominee; (7) concerted, sustained opposition by interest or pressure groups; and (8) fear that the nominee would dramatically alter the Court's jurisprudential lineup.[120]

In other words, the selection of Supreme Court justices has typically been, in practice, "political," in the partisan sense of the term.[121] As chapter 3 pointed out, however, partisan usage of the appointment power is not what the Founders sought. Instead, the Founders hoped for "a bench happily filled"[122] with the esteemed likes of "Wythe, Blair, and Pendleton."[123] The Convention debates are silent on the criteria for appointment precisely because the delegates assumed that the basis of selection would be merit.[124] Even Hamilton, who saw a limited role for the Senate in the appointment process, believed that the Senate would—and should—reject a nominee who was lacking in objective merit. "Thus it could hardly happen," Hamilton writes in *The Federalist* no. 66, "that the majority of the Senate would feel any other complacency toward the object of an appointment than such as the appearances of merit might inspire and the proofs of the want of it destroy."[125]

Although some scholars believe that a merit-based appointment process is "not realistic," given the realities of constitutional politics,[126] others disagree, including Henry Abraham, the leading authority on the appointment process. According to Abraham, "merit need not, indeed it does not, 'lie in the eye of the beholder.' It is eminently identifiable and attainable." Abraham identifies nine factors to consider when making a merit-based evaluation of a candidate for the Supreme Court:

(1) demonstrated judicial temperament; (2) professional expertise and competence; (3) absolute personal as well as professional integrity; (4) an able, agile, lucid mind; (5) appropriate professional educational background or training; (6) the ability to communicate clearly, both orally and in writing, and especially the latter; (7) resolute fair-mindedness; (8) a solid understanding of the proper judicial role of judges under our Constitution; and (9) ascertainable good health.[127]

To this wise list, given my claim that the Court should interpret the Constitution in light of the philosophy of the Declaration of Independence, I would add a thorough understanding of legal and political philosophy.

The necessity for judges to have a firm grasp of legal and political philosophy was identified by two of the most powerful minds ever to sit on the federal bench: Felix Frankfurter and Learned Hand. In a 1957 essay calling for the appointment of Supreme Court justices "wholly on the basis of functional fitness," Frankfurter argues that a Supreme Court justice must be a philosopher, historian, and prophet. Other factors, such as prior judicial experience, he believes, should have no place in the appointment decision. "One is entitled to say without qualification that the correlation between prior judicial experience and fitness for the Supreme Court is zero," Frankfurter writes. "The significance of the greatest among the Justices who had such experience, Holmes and Cardozo, derived not from that judicial experience but from the fact that they were Holmes and Cardozo. They were thinkers, and more particularly, legal philosophers."[128]

Hand agreed with Frankfurter on the relationship between philosophy and constitutional interpretation:

It is as important to a judge called upon to pass on a question of constitutional law, to have a bowing acquaintance with Acton and Maitland, with Thucydides, Gibbon and Carlyle, with Homer, Dante, Shakespeare and Milton, with Machiavelli, Montaigne, and Rabelais, with Plato, Bacon, Hume, and Kant as with books which have been specifically written on the subject. For in such matters everything turns upon the spirit in which he approaches the questions before him.[129]

While I certainly quarrel with Locke's absence from Hand's list(!), the idea that judges cannot interpret the Constitution without recourse to political philosophy, and the concomitant need for judges to have a firm grasp of such philosophy, is keenly stated.

A merit-based appointment process obviously requires Senate inquiry into a nominee's judicial philosophy, something the Senate has been doing since the first days of the Republic.[130] Yet some scholars oppose such an inquiry by the Senate. Bruce Fein, for one, contends that "the Senate . . . is ill-suited intellectually, morally, and politically to pass on anything more substantive than a nominee's professional fitness for the office of Supreme Court Justice. Because senators tend to be intellectually shallow and result-oriented, their ostensible inquiries into 'judicial philosophy' will almost invariably degenerate into partisan posturing."[131]

Bork, himself allegedly a victim of precisely the process Fein describes, warns of the chilling effects of Senate inquiry into the judicial philosophy of a nominee. According to Bork:

A president who wants to avoid a battle like mine, and most presidents would prefer to, is likely to nominate men and women who have not written much, and certainly nothing that could be regarded as controversial by left-leaning senators and groups. ... It is quite conceivable that some lower court judges may be affected in the decisions they make and the opinions they write. ... Lawyers and professors have been encouraged to think twice or three times about what they write.[132]

Because the appointment process is, by definition, essential to deciding who is empowered to have the final say on the meaning of the fundamental law of the land, an inquiry by the Senate into a nominee's approach to constitutional interpretation is *required*. After all, the role of the Court in the American constitutional order is to "'defend the Constitution,' not to revise it."[133] In addition, it is precisely the Senate's role in the appointment process to make such determinations. As Charles Black remarks in his important essay on the subject:

To me, there is just no reason at all for a Senator's not voting, in regard to confirmation of a Supreme Court nominee, on the basis of a full and unrestricted review, not embarrassed by any presumption, of the nominee's fitness for office. In a world that knows a man's social philosophy shapes his judicial behavior, that philosophy is a factor in his fitness. If it is a philosophy the Senator thinks will make a judge whose service on the Bench will hurt the country, then the Senator can do right only by treating this judgment of his, unencumbered by deference to the President's, as a satisfactory basis in itself for a negative vote. I have as yet seen nothing textual, nothing structural, nothing prudential, nothing historical, that tells against this view.[134]

In short, a failure to inquire—by the Senate and the president alike—into a nominee's judicial philosophy is nothing short of reckless, for it is only through an examination of a nominee's judicial philosophy that a commitment to the jurisprudence of the American regime can be ascertained and the natural rights of the American people thereby better secured. The fact that the Senate and the president are thought to be ill equipped to evaluate a nominee's judicial philosophy brings the third aspect of the appointment process to the fore, the methodology of selection.

There are certainly a wide variety of resources available to the president and the Senate to help them make judicial appointments based on merit. Besides the respective staffs of the White House and the Senate Judiciary Committee, these resources include the traditional voices of public and private leaders with interests in the nomination, the American Bar Association's Standing Committee on Federal Judiciary, and sitting and retired members of the bench.[135] Other resources are available and have been occasionally employed. Most notably, these resources are academe, as President Franklin Roosevelt recognized (especially with his use of then Harvard Law professor Felix Frankfurter), and "merit" commissions, as President Carter appreciated (though, in practice, the Carter commissions were far more partisan than merit-based).[136]

With access to all of this information and expertise the president and the Senate certainly have the ability to identify individuals of demonstrable merit to serve on the Supreme Court—they must simply be willing to stop playing politics with the appointment process.[137] As Abraham eloquently puts it, "Mr. Madison's plea for 'a bench happily filled' would appear to be readily attainable—given the necessary resolve to select on the basis of merit. It is *not* an 'impossible dream.' "[138] Although some commentators on the selection process are skeptical about the possibility of the political branches exercising such resolve,[139] it has been done in the past; for example, with the appointment of Benjamin Cardozo, a Democrat appointed by a Republican president and for whose appointment both Democrats and Republicans worked tirelessly.[140] Given what is at stake—the natural rights of the American people—the Constitution demands no less.

The vast majority of constitutional theorists do not discuss the subject of checks on the Court, choosing instead to focus exclusively on their particular normative agendas. I believe this is a mistake. By ignoring checks on the Court, not only do constitutional theorists perpetuate the myth of judicial supremacy, but they fail to give "teeth" to their constitutional theories. If a constitutional theorist believes that the Court should interpret the Constitution in a certain way, he or she should at least provide suggestions for getting the Court to comply. I have therefore endeavored to afford the subject of checks on the Court suitable attention. I explained in this chapter that there are checks available to prevent the Supreme Court's role as the ultimate interpreter of the Constitution from devolving into the unacceptable state of government by judiciary. And those checks—the Article 5 amendment process, impeachment, judicial self-restraint, and the appointment process (though not the "exceptions clause" to the Court's appellate jurisdiction)—if properly used, can help ensure that the Court interprets the Constitution in accordance with the natural-rights philosophy of the Declaration of Independence, rather than in light of the moral and political convictions of particular justices. Next, it is necessary to demonstrate that the seemingly abstract natural-rights–based theory of judicial review prescribed in this volume can adjudicate constitutional cases.

5

Constitutional Interpretation

Up to this point I have attempted to show that the Constitution of the United States should be interpreted in light of the natural-rights political philosophy of the Declaration of Independence and that the Supreme Court is the institution of American government that should be primarily responsible for identifying and applying that philosophy in American life. Even if this thesis is accepted, however, the potentially disabling criticism that a natural-rights–based theory of judicial review is unworkable must be addressed. Simply stated, it must be shown here that the political philosophy of the Declaration of Independence is sufficiently determinate to be a practical guide to judgment in individual cases that come before the Court. Otherwise, the Declaration will remain largely relegated to antiquarian interest, and a judge seeking to interpret the Constitution will be able to continue doing so in light of his or her own moral and political preferences. As a result, the fundamental purpose of judicial review—the safeguarding of the natural rights of the American people (see chapter 3)—will remain unfulfilled.

In 1798 Justice James Iredell issued one of the most famous criticisms of natural-rights–based judicial review in an opinion in *Calder v. Bull* rejecting Justice Samuel Chase's natural-rights approach to the case. "The ideas of natural justice are regulated by no fixed standard," Justice Iredell exclaimed. "The ablest and the purest men have differed upon the subject."[1] Nearly two centuries later Robert Bork expresses a similar reservation. "There may be a natural law," Bork contends, "but we are not agreed upon what it is, and there is no such law that gives definitive answers to a judge trying to decide a case."[2]

This chapter endeavors to rebut the criticism voiced by Iredell, Bork, and others[3] by applying the natural-rights political philosophy of the Declaration of Independence to some of the leading cases in American constitutional law and history. Three caveats are necessary before proceeding to the initial area of inquiry. First, it is not the purpose of this chapter to resolve most—let alone all—questions of constitutional-rights adjudication. What is intended here is a discussion of some of the most significant questions in order to demonstrate that the proposed natural-rights–based theory of judicial review is workable. My method for doing that—through themes of equality, life, liberty, and the pursuit of happiness—will also, I hope, make the fairly abstract Lockean natural-rights doctrine of the Declaration of Independence, discussed in chapter 1, easier to understand.*

Second, I have tried to approach this project in an objective fashion. Not only will some of the results discerned both please and upset contemporary liberals and conservatives alike, but perhaps me as well. (For what it is worth, I *personally* oppose the death penalty. Natural-rights philosophy does not.) In short, what I hope to avoid is the standard criticism that natural-law approaches merely mask the biases of those who employ them.

Third, as the Introduction discussed, the results discerned are not necessarily equivalent to what the Founders may have decided about

---

*Part 1 explained that the Founders were Lockean liberals on the basic purpose of government, which is the controlling question in constitutional interpretation. Therefore, I frequently refer to Locke's philosophical writings in this chapter to flush out the Lockean liberal principles of the Declaration of Independence. Reference to "Locke" means Locke's theory, not Locke's personal practices.

specific rights. The Founders' intentions are controlling at the level of natural-rights principle because, as part 1 described, that principle speaks to our origins, purposes, and ideals as a nation. However, the Founders' views at the level of specific outcomes are merely suggestive.[4] This is because the Founders occasionally ignored the dictates of natural law for practical reasons (for instance, on slavery, as I discuss below) and because they could not possibly have foreseen many of the complexities involved in applying natural-rights doctrine in the modern world. With these caveats made, I now turn to the subject of equality.

Equality

Chapter 1 explained that the concept "all men are created equal" is central to the political philosophy of the Declaration of Independence. What the Declaration means by equality is that all people are created as members of the same species and each person has, as Locke puts it, an "equal right ... to his natural freedom, without being subjected to the will or authority of any other man." Every person, in other words, has an equal moral claim to freedom. This moral claim does not mean, however, that all people are entitled to the same material benefits upon exercising their freedom, because individuals differ in abilities and capacities. "Age or virtue may give men a just precedence," Locke writes. "Excellence of parts and merit may place others above the common level."[5]

The most profound issue in American constitutional law and history to consider in a discussion of equality is slavery. Clearly, slavery is in direct contradiction with the Declaration's concept of equality as a moral claim shared by all people to natural freedom. The fact that race has always been the "American dilemma"[6] is underscored by the inconsistency between the philosophical condemnation of slavery by many of the Founders—among them John Adams, Benjamin Franklin, Alexander Hamilton, John Jay, Thomas Jefferson, James Madison, and George Washington—and the reality that many of these same men owned slaves.[7] To their credit, Jefferson sought to include a denunciation of slavery in the Declaration of Independence,[8] and the Framers struggled in Philadelphia with the issue.[9] But powerful economic pressures prevailed, and slavery continued as an uneasy compromise in a regime dedicated to the natural rights of man until the passage of the thirteenth amendment in 1865.[10] Indeed, in an impassioned 1987 speech, then justice Thurgood Marshall—the first Black appointed to the Supreme Court and one of the most famous and influential civil rights lawyers in the history of the United States—attacked the original Constitution because it permitted slavery. Justice Marshall thundered:

> I do not believe that the meaning of the Constitution was forever "fixed" at the Philadelphia Convention. Nor do I find the wisdom, foresight, and sense of justice exhibited by the Framers particularly profound. To the contrary, the government they devised was defective from the start, requiring several amendments, a civil war, and momentous social transformation to attain the system of constitutional government, and its respect for the individual freedoms and human rights, we hold fundamental today. When contemporary Americans cite "the Constitution," they invoke a concept that is vastly different from what the Framers barely began to construct two centuries ago.[11]

The tension between slavery and the Declaration's concept of equality was highlighted in *Dred Scott v. Sandford* (1857),[12] the Supreme Court's "self-inflicted wound"[13] that not only greatly damaged the Court's reputation, but helped bring on the Civil War. Civil war, the end result of the tension between slavery and the natural-rights principles of the Declaration of Independence, was predicted by Jefferson in his *Notes on the State of Virginia* (1782):

> I tremble for my country when I reflect that God is just: that his justice cannot sleep forever: that considering numbers, nature and natural means only, a revolution of the wheel of fortune, an exchange of situation, is among possible events: that it may become probable by supernatural interference! The Almighty has no attribute which can take side with us in such a contest.[14]

Dred Scott involved a claim by a Black man, born into slavery, that his subsequent residence in a state and a territory that prohibited slavery made him free. By a seven-to-two vote the Supreme Court, speaking through Chief Justice Roger Taney, disagreed and went so far as to strike down the Missouri Compromise, a set of federal laws adopted in 1820 to maintain the balance between slave and nonslave states, on the ground that the Compromise violated the fifth-amendment property rights of slave owners. While the Court conceded that the Declaration's assertion that "'all men are created equal' ... would seem to embrace the whole of the human family," the fact that many of the Founders themselves owned slaves led the Court to conclude otherwise. As Chief Justice Taney phrased it, Blacks "had for more than a century been regarded as beings ... so far inferior, that they had no rights which the white man was bound to respect. ... Accordingly, a negro of the African race was regarded ... as an article of property" and was not entitled to an equal enjoyment of the natural rights of man.[15]

What such events as the omission of Jefferson's condemnation of slavery in the Declaration of Independence, the reluctant recognition of slavery in the Constitution, and the disastrous *Dred Scott* decision suggest is that the United States was not yet ready as a nation to rid itself of an institution it knew was contrary to natural law.[16] The Declaration's avowal that "all men are created equal" did, however, provide the framework for slavery's eventual demise, something which Abraham Lincoln understood clearly. Lincoln's famous speech on the *Dred Scott* decision is worth quoting at length:

> Chief Justice Taney, in his opinion in the Dred Scott case, admits that the language of the Declaration is broad enough to include the whole human family, but he and Judge Douglas argue that the authors of that instrument did not intend to include negroes, by the fact that they did not at once, actually place them on an equality with the whites. Now this grave argument comes to just nothing at all, by the other fact, that they did not at once, *or ever afterwards*, actually place all white people on an equality with one another. ... They did not mean to assert the obvious untruth, that all were then actually enjoying that equality, nor yet, that they were about to confer it immediately upon them. In fact they had no power to confer such a boon. **They meant simply to declare the *right*, so that the *enforcement* of it might follow as circumstances should permit.** They meant to set up a standard maxim for free society, which could be familiar to all, and revered by all, constantly looked to, constantly labored for, and even though never perfectly attained, constantly approximated, and thereby constantly spreading and deepening its influence and augmenting the happiness and value of life to all people of all colors everywhere.[17]

As Lincoln's remarks intimate, omitting Jefferson's condemnation of slavery in the Declaration of Independence and including guarantees to slavery in the original Constitution were unfortunate political compromises that had to be made if the United States of America was to come into being in 1776 and create a strong central government in 1787— both of which were necessary if slavery was one day to be abolished.

The necessity for political compromise aside, the inhumane treatment of slaves and the long and bloody Civil War that resulted from slavery are indelible proof of the pain that departing from the Declaration's natural-rights principles has engendered in the United States.

As is all too clear from American history, the unequal treatment of Blacks continued well past the successful conclusion of the Civil War. Slavery may have been formally abolished by the Civil War, the Emancipation Proclamation, and the thirteenth amendment, but racial prejudice was not. The Black Codes of 1865, passed in almost all of the southern states, were meant to replace the formally forbidden institution of slavery with a caste system and to preserve as much as possible the prewar way of life. Although the Reconstruction Congress enacted several measures to deal with the racial injustice in the South, most notably a strong Civil Rights Act (1866) and the fourteenth and fifteenth amendments (ratified in 1868 and 1870, respectively), these measures had little lasting effect as the North—itself seduced by racism—soon lost interest in Black welfare. As a consequence, slavery was replaced by a system of legal and social apartheid.[18]

The Supreme Court continued its abysmal record on racial equality when it constitutionalized this system of apartheid. That fateful decision came in *Plessy v. Ferguson* (1896),[19] with the ground being set in earlier decisions such as *Hall v. DeCuir* (1878),[20] which struck down as an unconstitutional burden on interstate commerce a state statute that outlawed discrimination on account of race in common carriers, and the *Civil Rights Cases* (1883),[21] in which the Court declared the Civil Rights Act of 1875—a law that prohibited discrimination in the furnishing of transportation and accommodations to Blacks—unconstitutional on the basis that the fourteenth amendment forbade only discrimination by state governments and state officials, not by private parties.[22]

Plessy was an especially unfortunate decision, because the state statute at issue spoke directly to equality when it required "equal but separate accommodation for the white and colored races" in railway carriages. The statute was challenged on equal protection grounds, principally on the basis that the "separate but equal" concept it embodied was intended to "stamp the colored race with a badge of inferiority." The Supreme Court, in a seven-to-one decision, disagreed and declared that the "badge of inferiority ... [was] not by reason of anything found in the act, but solely because the colored race chooses to put that construction upon it." The Court added that "if one race be inferior to another socially, the Constitution of the United States cannot put them on the same plane."[23] The segregationist statute was thus upheld and apartheid became the constitutional law of the land.

In a powerful and prophetic dissent, the first Justice John Marshall Harlan, the sole dissenting member of the Court in *Plessy*, maintained that "the arbitrary separation of citizens on the basis of race, while they are on a public highway, is a badge of servitude wholly inconsistent with the civil freedom and the equality of the law established by the Constitution. It cannot be justified upon any legal grounds." Justice Harlan explained why this was so in one of the most famous passages in Supreme Court history:

In view of the Constitution, in the eye of the law, there is in this country no superior, dominant, ruling class of citizens. There is no caste here. Our constitution is color-blind, and neither knows nor tolerates classes among citizens. In respect of civil rights all citizens are equal before the law. The humblest is the peer of the most powerful. The law regards man as man, and takes no account of his surroundings or of his color when his civil rights as guaranteed by the supreme law of the land are involved.[24]

Justice Harlan's dissent—which was to carry the day six decades later in *Brown v. Board of Education* (1954),[25] the Supreme Court's unanimous, landmark decision outlawing segregation in the public schools—correctly identified the meaning of equality in the American regime.* Justice Harlan recognized, as the Warren Court was to reiterate, that segregation was the product of racist hatred and degradation and had no connection whatsoever to any relevant differences among the races. According to the political philosophy of the Declaration of Independence, only relevant differences, such as talent and effort,[26] may affect an individual's enjoyment of natural freedom. Segregation is therefore inconsistent with every person's equal moral claim to natural freedom, because it represents a denial of that very claim to moral equality by stigmatizing Blacks as inferior to Whites. To put it plainly, the point of segregation was *not* to keep both Whites and Blacks from using each other's facilities, but to make sure that Blacks would not

---

*As the discussion of preferential treatment later in this section reveals, the modern Court's acceptance of Justice Harlan's color-blind interpretation of the Constitution was short lived. See Kull, *The Color-Blind Constitution*, 151–224.

"contaminate" facilities used by Whites[27]—a badge of inferiority the Declaration will not tolerate.

As the discussion of racial segregation intimates, the equal protection clause of the fourteenth amendment and the implicit equal protection guarantee of the fifth amendment[28] are the Constitution's vehicles through which the Declaration's concept of equality should be implemented. The scope of the equal protection guarantee has been subject to much debate.* For example, in a controversial study of the fourteenth amendment, Raoul Berger contends that the equal protection clause forbids only state-sanctioned racial discrimination in a specific and narrow range of civil rights (such as equal access to government protection of life and property).[29] Chief Justice William Rehnquist, on the other hand, extends the coverage of the equal protection clause to all areas of civil rights but, like Berger, claims that equal protection disallows only discrimination on account of race.[30]

Many scholars disagree with Berger's and Rehnquist's narrow reading of the fourteenth amendment. While I have neither the space nor the inclination to add to the crowded literature yet another lengthy discussion of the debates surrounding the framing and ratification of the fourteenth amendment, my reading of those debates confirms the position thoughtfully advanced by Judith Baer, Howard Jay Graham, Alfred Kelly, and Jacobus ten Broek, to name but the most well known, that the fourteenth amendment was intended to embody the broad principles of equality and natural rights articulated in the Declaration of Independence.[31]

Further support for a broad reading of the equal protection clause is found in William Nelson's examination of the fourteenth amendment. Although Nelson does not speak explicitly of natural rights, he does maintain that the fourteenth amendment was designed to reaffirm our

---

*The separate question of whether the thirty-ninth Congress meant to make the Bill of Rights applicable to the states through the fourteenth amendment has been addressed in a vast and often contradictory literature. As the discussion of the Bill of Rights in chapter 2 suggests, however, the incorporation debate is misdirected, given that the Founders rejected the authority of *any* government, federal and state alike, to violate the people's natural rights. What the thirty-ninth Congress essentially did with the fourteenth amendment was to try to *restore* the principles of the Declaration of Independence to the American regime, principles the South had been resisting by demanding that the institution of slavery be continued. See Farber and Muench, "The Ideological Origins of the Fourteenth Amendment," 272; Richards, *Conscience and the Constitution*, chap. 4.

nation's long-standing commitment to general principles of equality and individual rights.[32] Additionally, even Alexander Bickel, who has a fairly modest reading of the fourteenth amendment, acknowledges that the language of the amendment is "sufficiently elastic" to permit the broader interpretation advanced in this volume.[33] Specifically, section 1 of the fourteenth amendment says that no "person" may be denied the equal protection of the laws, whereas section 2 speaks of depriving "male citizens" of the right to vote as a ground for penalizing states in House apportionment, and the fifteenth amendment outlaws discrimination in voting on account of "race." What this language suggests is that when the Reconstruction Congress intended to limit the reach of a provision to specific groups, they knew how to do so. The equal protection clause is not so limited. *All* "persons," regardless of race, sex,[34] or any other involuntary, immutable, and irrelevant characteristic, are therefore entitled to the equal enjoyment of their natural freedom.

What the Declaration of Independence's broad concept of equality means for constitutional interpretation is that *all* class-based differentiation through law that is not based on a *universally* true and relevant characteristic is unconstitutional. For example, with respect to sex— the classification that is second only to race in historical significance[35]—unless the difference is one that is characteristic of *all* women and *no* men, or *all* men and *no* women, it is not the sex factor but the individual factor that should be determinative.[36] This is a principle that was central to the unsuccessful equal rights amendment.[37] In practical terms, sex is an impermissible characteristic by which to determine such things as the custody of children, working hours, wages and conditions, the obligation to register for the military draft, and the opportunity to serve in military combat, but would be an acceptable distinguishing classification in situations like state payments of medical costs of childbearing (because men cannot bear children). Briefly stated, sex is *almost* never a constitutionally permissible class-based distinction. Women and men should be treated as individuals, not as members of a group. Everyone deserves, under the political philosophy of the Declaration of Independence, to have his or her situation evaluated on an individualized basis. The costs of administering the case-by-case determinations necessary to conform to the Declaration's mandate may be high, but our nation's commitment to the equal right of all people to enjoy their natural freedom requires that we bear the cost.

More difficult classifications exist; most notably, age and disability.* Distinctions in the law based on age have been less controversial than most. After all, the argument goes, age-based distinctions simply reflect significant differences in abilities and capacities. The issue is, however, more complicated than that. In fact, legal distinctions based on sex were once accepted because of similar alleged differences in abilities and capacities—a notion that most Americans have come to reject.[38]

The leading Supreme Court decisions on age discrimination are *Massachusetts Board of Retirement v. Murgia* (1976),[39] in which the Court upheld a state law requiring uniformed police officers to retire at fifty, and *Vance v. Bradley* (1979),[40] in which the Court sustained a federal law requiring foreign service officers to retire at sixty. Both cases depended on generalizations about the abilities and capacities of older age groups. As in questions of sex discrimination, however, generalizations of this sort are frequently wrong and, more importantly, are based on insulting stereotypes—the Court's observation in *Murgia* to the contrary notwithstanding.[41] Under the Declaration of Independence's concept of equality, mandatory retirement laws are unconstitutional, because they violate every individual's moral right to be judged on the basis of his or her individual merits.

With respect to the young, laws affecting them are usually not thought to raise issues of equality at all. For example, in *Re Gault* (1967), a case involving a juvenile accused of a crime, the Supreme Court made the following observation:

A child, unlike an adult, has a right "not to liberty but to custody." He can be made to attorn to his parents, to go to school, etc. If his parents default in effectively performing their custodial functions—that is, if the child is "delin-

*Alienage, poverty, illegitimacy, and sexual preference are, like race, easy cases: class-based differentiation on these grounds is *never* constitutionally permissible, because these characteristics have no relevance to one's ability to perform a function or enjoy a liberty. As history shows, differentiation on account of alienage, poverty, illegitimacy, and sexual preference is based on fear, ignorance, and hatred, none of which is consistent with the Declaration's concept of equality. The Supreme Court's record in these areas is mixed. See generally O'Brien, *Constitutional Law and Politics*, vol. 2, 1456–96. I have more to say about sexual preference and poverty later in this chapter.

quent" the state may intervene. In doing so, it does not deprive the child of any rights, for he has none.[42]

According to the Court, a child has no rights, only duties. This is a conclusion that many scholars attribute to Lockean liberalism as well.[43] More precisely, because the Lockean account of persons and rights emphasizes rationality and autonomy, and because these are traits that the very young seem to lack, and which children acquire only gradually, children are not deemed to be persons or to possess rights. As A. John Simmons convincingly argues, however, children do have the *capacity* for rationality and autonomy; they simply often lack the maturity to exercise it. But given children's capacity for rationality and autonomy, they are "persons now" and, therefore, do possess rights,[44] something that Locke seems to appreciate when he remarks that a child must be allowed "the privilege of his nature to be free."[45]

What the Lockean account of children means for constitutional interpretation is that children must be deemed to have rights. The fact that children have rights was emphasized by Justice William Douglas in a famous dissenting opinion in *Wisconsin v. Yoder* (1972),[46] a case in which the Supreme Court upheld the right of Amish *parents* to withdraw their children from compulsory school attendance on religious grounds. Justice Douglas's dissent is worth quoting at length, because it perceptively and eloquently identifies the importance of recognizing that children have rights:

On this important and vital matter of education, I think the children should be entitled to be heard. While the parents, absent dissent, normally speak for the entire family, the education of the child is a matter on which the child will often have decided views. He may want to be a pianist or an astronaut or an ocean geographer. To do so he will have to break from the Amish tradition.

It is the future of the student, not the future of the parents, that is imperilled in today's decision. If a parent keeps his child out of school beyond the grade school, then the child will be forever barred from entry into the new and amazing world of the preferred course, or he may rebel. It is the student's judgment, not his parents', that is essential if we are to give full meaning to what we have said about the Bill of Rights and of the right of students to be masters of their own destiny. If he is harnessed to the Amish way of life by those in authority over him and if his education is truncated, his entire life may be stunted and deformed. The child, therefore, should be given an opportunity to be heard before the State gives the exemption which we honor today.[47]

It is important to note what Justice Douglas did *not* say in his dissenting opinion. Justice Douglas did *not* say that the wishes of a child must always control. Many children are simply not mature enough to understand the implications of their desires. But some children are, and as Justice Douglas pointed out, all children have the right to be heard so that their individual levels of maturity can be discerned. Otherwise, a child's moral right to be treated as an individual is violated.

Turning to cases involving disability, some class-based distinctions are constitutionally acceptable, as they sometimes are in cases involving sex, because there are inherent physical limitations involved. To take an obvious example, laws prohibiting blind persons from driving are not unconstitutional, because blind persons are not physically capable of driving. Of course, any such class-based restrictions should be kept to a minimum, because the physically challenged share a moral claim to natural freedom equal to that of the rest of us.

The most controversial issue facing modern America relating to equality is preferential treatment. Those who favor preferential treatment typically argue that class preferences in employment and education are necessary to overcome America's long history of discrimination against minorities and women. In the words of Justice Lewis Powell—the Supreme Court's decisive voice on the divisive issue of preferential treatment during his fifteen-year tenure (1972–1987)[48]— "In order to remedy the effects of prior discrimination, it may be necessary to take race [and sex, etc.] into account," even if "innocent persons may be called upon to bear some of the burdens of the remedy."[49] In other words, the Constitution may need to be color and gender conscious in order to be color and gender blind.[50]

The problems with preferential treatment are many, but two stand out when applying the Declaration of Independence's concept of equality. First, as Justice Powell acknowledges, the practice itself discriminates—and almost always against innocent individuals—to overcome the vestiges of class-based discrimination, something critics refer to as "reverse discrimination."[51]

Second, preferential treatment stigmatizes minorities and women by implying that they are less capable of succeeding on the basis of individual merit than are White males. Preferential treatment therefore represents a denial of moral equality to minorities and women. Interestingly, Baer argues that preferential treatment passes constitutional muster because it does not stigmatize *White males* as inferior.[52] Baer has it backwards, however. She fails to appreciate that preferential treatment stigmatizes *minorities and women*. Justice Clarence Thomas, who argues in some of his speeches and writings that the Constitution should be interpreted in light of the Declaration of Independence,[53] makes the point well: "I think that preferential hiring on the basis of race or gender will increase racial divisiveness, disempower women and minorities by fostering the notion that they are permanently disabled and in need of handouts, and delay the day when skin color and gender are truly the least important things about a person."[54]

Although Justice Thomas may be a controversial figure to whom to refer for support on preferential treatment,[55] he correctly recognizes that preferential treatment impermissibly implies that minorities and women are morally inferior to White males. Justice Thomas also discerns an equally serious problem with the practice: by focusing on groups instead of on individuals, preferential treatment is inconsistent with the Declaration's mandate that an individual be treated as an individual, a point emphasized throughout this section. In Justice Thomas's words, it is an "error" to focus on groups instead of on individuals in civil rights adjudication, "for it is above all the protection of *individual* rights that America, in its best moments, has in its heart and mind."[56] In short, the United States of America is a liberal regime (see part 1). Here, rights are possessed by individuals, not by groups. Preferential treatment violates this fundamental tenet of liberal political theory by focusing on groups instead of on individuals.

The fact that equality in the political philosophy of the Declaration of Independence relates to equality of *opportunity*, rather than to equality of *result*, provides further evidence of the unconstitutionality of class preferences. The modern association of equality with equal results took root in the writings of a group of radical theorists in the early 1960s, led by Michael Harrington.[57] Governmentally, the foremost example of this egalitarian mind-set was President Lyndon Johnson's Great Society program of the 1960s, through which the president sought "not just ... equality as a right and a theory but equality as a fact and equality as a result."[58] As chapter 1 explained, however, in

Lockean liberalism unequal results may be the legitimate manifestation of unequal individual talent and effort. In fact, Locke emphasizes that a just government encourages equality of opportunity, but avoids imposing equality of result.[59] The modern egalitarian approach to preferential treatment is inconsistent with the Lockean concept of equality, because the redistributive nature of that approach denies a talented and hardworking individual his or her natural right to enjoy the benefits of his or her superior ability and effort.

My discussion of equality has emphasized the need under the political philosophy of the Declaration of Independence to treat individuals as individuals. What this means for constitutional interpretation is that the Supreme Court's awkward multitier approach to questions of equality, wherein some classifications (for example, race) are handled in one way ("strict scrutiny" review), others (for example, sex) in another way ("strict rationality" review), and still others (for example, indigency) in yet a third way ("rational basis" review), should be discarded. Under the Declaration, classifications are treated in a single way: *all* class-based differentiation through law that is not based on a *universally* true and relevant characteristic is unconstitutional. Not only is this standard easier to apply than the Court's present multitier approach, but it speaks directly to the equal moral status of all individuals, a principle to which the Founders dedicated this nation.

Life

No issues in modern American constitutional law are more emotionally charged than those concerning the natural right to "life." The three most controversial issues relating to life are considered in this section: the death penalty (which was briefly discussed in the Introduction), the "right to die," and abortion. Welfare is also addressed. Before proceeding to the discussion of constitutional interpretation it should be recalled that, in natural-rights doctrine, "the fundamental law of nature" is "the preservation of mankind."[60] Note that the emphasis is on the preservation of *mankind,* rather than on the preservation of *individual* persons. As will be seen, this distinction has profound implications for constitutional interpretation.

The importance of preserving life in natural-rights doctrine flows from man's relationship with his Creator, a point clearly recognized in the Declaration of Independence's claim that "all men ... are endowed by their Creator with certain unalienable rights." Locke discusses the status and implications of man's relationship with his Creator in one of the most famous passages in the *Second Treatise:*

No one ought to harm another in his life, health, liberty, or possessions; for men being all the workmanship of one omnipotent and infinitely wise Maker— all servants of one sovereign master, sent into the world by his order, and about his business—they are his property whose workmanship they are, made to last during his, not one another's pleasure.[61]

Given that man is the "property" of his Creator and, as a result, that he holds his life in trust for his Creator, the constitutional issues relating to life are of utmost significance. With this brief review of the philosophical meaning of the natural right to life in mind (for more, see chapter 1), I now turn to constitutional interpretation.

The death penalty is confronted in the Constitution by the eighth amendment, which forbids "cruel and unusual punishments," as applied to the states through the fourteenth amendment.[62] Additionally, the fifth amendment speaks to capital punishment in the double jeopardy clause, and the fifth and fourteenth amendments address it in their respective due process clauses.[63] Under the letter of the Constitution, a person may be deprived of life with due process, and life may be jeopardized once.

Those who argue that the death penalty is unconstitutional typically do so on the basis of the so-called "*evolving* standards of decency that mark the progress of a maturing society."[64] There are two problems with the evolving-standards-of-decency test. First, as Christopher Wolfe points out, the proponents of an evolving standard assume that evolution is "upward," when in actuality "'evolving' standards can cut both ways."[65] In other words, evolving standards need not always progress to a more humanitarian result. Second, as discussed in the Introduction in the context of Justice Brennan's unyielding opposition to the death penalty, in application the evolving-standards-of-decency test is likely based on nothing other than a particular justice's own conception of morality. This problem is well illustrated by Justice Thurgood Marshall's dissenting opinion in *Gregg v. Georgia* (1976), the case in which the Supreme Court first ruled that the death penalty, if properly administered, is constitutional.[66]

In his *Gregg* dissent, Justice Marshall rejected the argument that the passage of death penalty statutes by many states in recent times was evidence of modern America's acceptance of the moral legitimacy of capital punishment. According to Justice Marshall, who, like Justice Brennan, considered the death penalty to be unconstitutional under all circumstances,

> if the constitutionality of the death penalty turns, as I have urged, on the opinion of an informed citizenry, then even the enactment of new death statutes cannot be viewed as conclusive. In *Furman*, I observed that the American people are largely unaware of the information critical to a judgment on the morality of the death penalty, and concluded that if they were better informed they would consider it shocking, unjust and unacceptable. ... The opinions of an informed public would differ significantly from those of a public unaware of the consequences and effects of the death penalty.[67]

What Justice Marshall is suggesting is that *he* will tell the American people what they really think, a suggestion that is as subject to abuse by a justice claiming to speak for an "unaware" public as it is inconsistent with the political philosophy of the American Founding on the fundamental natural right to life.

A natural-rights interpretation of the Constitution supports the current Supreme Court position that the death penalty is constitutional.[68] As discussed in chapter 1, an individual owes a duty to his Creator to preserve his own life and not to take the life of another. An individual who takes the life of another, when not acting in self-defense, forfeits his right to life, because that individual is not acting rationally in violating the fundamental law of nature to preserve mankind. Here, it is necessary to recall that acting rationally is a condition in Locke's moral theory for being subject to natural law and the possessor of natural rights under that law.[69]

Additionally, the death penalty is a necessary component of the political authority of a regime, such as ours, dedicated to the preservation of the *whole* of the political community. On this point, the fact that the fundamental law of nature is the preservation of *mankind*, not the preservation of *individual* persons, is dispositive.

"Justice on an offender"[70]—treating an offender with the dignity that comes from recognizing his free will and moral responsibility— also sanctions the imposition of the death penalty in egregious cases like the intentional taking of the life of another. As a result, the argument, most notably advanced by Justice Brennan, that the death penalty is never morally or constitutionally acceptable because it violates the "human dignity" of the offender[71] must be rejected, because this view equates biological existence with human dignity. As Locke's call for the need to do "justice on an offender" intimates, the essence of human dignity is not just *that* we live, but *how* we live.

As with most questions of constitutional interpretation, there are situations involving capital punishment that require separate consideration; namely, applying the death penalty to the young and to the mentally impaired. With respect to young people who kill, the Supreme Court has established fifteen years old as the age at which one is too young to be sentenced to death.[72] Unfortunately, the Court's decisions pertaining to youth and capital punishment are based on generalizations about the maturity of specific age groups. The Declaration of Independence's charge that individuals be treated as individuals requires that an individualized assessment of a juvenile killer's maturity and moral responsibility be conducted[73]—a requirement that is consistent with the Court's own recognition of the need for individualized sentencing of adults.[74]

If the individualized hearing determines that the juvenile killer *was* of sufficient maturity at the time of his crime to understand the wrongfulness of his actions, then the juvenile *may* be executed because, as in the case of an adult, the juvenile is not acting rationally when he violates the fundamental law of nature to preserve mankind. In that case, the juvenile killer, like the adult, forfeits his right to life because to possess rights under Locke's moral theory one must be acting rationally. If the individualized hearing determines that the juvenile killer was *not* mature enough to understand the moral implications of his crime, the juvenile may *not* be executed. Although, at first blush, it might appear that a juvenile killer lacking maturity is also lacking rationality, and thus not possessing rights, I explained earlier how the juvenile's *capacity* for rationality makes him a person now and, therefore, a possessor of rights—especially of the right to life, the preservation of which is the fundamental law of nature.

Curiously, the generalization problem that exists with respect to juveniles is not present in the Court's treatment of capital punishment and the mentally impaired. In the case of the mentally impaired, the Court rightly requires an individualized assessment of whether the death penalty is appropriate.[75] If, under the natural-rights theory advanced in this volume, that assessment determines that the mentally impaired killer *has* the capacity to act rationally in the future, that individual may *not* be executed. Again, the fact that *capacity* for rationality exists now means that the mentally impaired killer has rights now, including the fundamental natural right to life. On the other hand, if the individualized assessment concludes that the mentally impaired killer does *not* have the capacity to act rationally in the future, the offender *may* be executed. This is because the mentally impaired killer is operating outside of the laws of nature—which are discerned by reason[76]—and is, therefore, a threat to the preservation of mankind.

In *Cruzan v. Director of the Missouri Department of Health* (1990),[77] the Supreme Court entered into the vexing legal-medical-ethical debate over the "right to die."[78] When Nancy Cruzan was twenty-five years old she was involved in a terrible car accident. By the time medical help arrived her brain had been deprived of oxygen for twelve to fourteen minutes. Cruzan's heart and lungs were restarted, but she never regained consciousness. Initially, Cruzan's parents approved the surgical insertion of feeding tubes into their daughter's body to keep her alive. However, after learning that there was no possibility that their daughter's condition would improve and that she would likely remain in a vegetative state for another thirty years, Cruzan's parents decided to seek permission to have the feeding tubes removed. The state of Missouri denied the parents' request and the case ended up in the Supreme Court of the United States.

Although the majority of the Court upheld the state's refusal to permit Cruzan's parents to remove the life-sustaining devices, all but one of the justices (Justice Antonin Scalia) recognized a constitutional-liberty right to refuse or terminate unwanted medical treatment if the individual is able to express that desire at the time of treatment or, in the event of incompetence at the time of treatment, if the individual had previously expressed the desire clearly. In Cruzan's case, the necessary "clear and convincing" evidence of her desire to terminate the medical treatment was deemed lacking. For our purposes, however, what is important is that the Court identified a constitutional right to die in the fourteenth amendment if the requisite proof that this is what the incompetent person wishes is available.

The fact that the fundamental law of nature is the preservation of mankind seems to suggest that there is *no* right to die under a natural-rights interpretation of the Constitution. Locke writes in the *Second Treatise* that "every one . . . is bound to preserve himself and not to quit his station wilfully."[79] Upon closer examination, Locke's prohibition on the right to die is not as absolute as it first appears.[80]

For example, in the same section in which Locke seems absolutely to forbid suicide,[81] he states that there are "nobler" uses of life than "bare preservation."[82] Locke likely has in mind situations like fighting a just war or a parent sacrificing his or her life for that of his or her child. What is significant for determining whether there is a constitutional right to die is that Locke recognizes that the duty of preservation is not absolute, a position also seen in the discussion of capital punishment.

Moreover, although Locke seems to forbid suicide in section 6 of the *Second Treatise*, he permits it in section 23. In section 23, Locke condones suicide for a slave who finds that the hardships of his slavery "outweigh the value of his life."[83] Clearly, an equally strong case can be made for someone suffering unbearably or existing in a vegetative state. That is to say, the Lockean duty of self-preservation requires that an individual refrain from killing himself or endangering his life frivolously or arbitrarily;[84] it does *not* require that an individual continue to exist when that person has no opportunity to enjoy life, as in Nancy Cruzan's case, or in the case of an individual who is suffering great pain. There is, in other words, a difference between being biologically *alive* and *living*. A natural-rights interpretation of the Constitution therefore supports the Supreme Court's position that there is a right to die in some circumstances.*

The most emotionally explosive and politically divisive decision issued by the Supreme Court in recent times is *Roe v. Wade* (1973),[85] the case in which the Burger Court ruled that there is a constitutional right to abortion. The *Roe* decision created a "political firestorm"[86] that has since affected political campaigns and Supreme Court nominations. For example, all of the Republican presidential platforms since 1980 have called for a constitutional amendment banning abortion, and Robert Bork's harsh criticism of *Roe* played no small part in the defeat of

---

*The fact that the fundamental law of nature is the preservation of life suggests that the *Cruzan* majority was also correct in requiring a clear evidentiary showing that one wishes to die. Justice Brennan's dissent, ranking autonomy above the sanctity of life, is therefore flawed. See 110 S.Ct., 2863–92 (Brennan, J., dissenting).

his nomination to the Supreme Court. Subsequent nominees to the Court have been likewise barraged by questions, though only Ruth Bader Ginsburg and Stephen Breyer have provided answers, about whether they believe there is a constitutional right to abortion. (Both Ginsburg and Breyer stated in their confirmation hearings that they believe there is a constitutional right to abortion.)

In *Roe v. Wade* the Supreme Court, in a seven-to-two vote, struck down a Texas antiabortion statute on the ground that a woman has a fundamental right of personal autonomy in childbearing decisions. In its decision the Court, speaking through Justice Harry Blackmun, promulgated a trimester approach to abortion. During the first three months of pregnancy the abortion decision is left to the woman and her doctor. In the second trimester, the state may regulate abortions in the interest of women's health because, the Court found, abortions are less safe than childbirth. In the third trimester, states may regulate and even ban abortions—unless the life of the woman is jeopardized—because it is here, the Court decided, that a fetus becomes "viable."[87]

In subsequent cases the Court issued a series of opinions both reaffirming *Roe* and applying *Roe* to specific situations.[88] Those cases reveal that as the composition of the Court became more conservative, support for *Roe* among the justices declined. Notable among *Roe*'s progeny is *Webster v. Reproductive Health Services* (1989),[89] in which the Rehnquist Court upheld a restrictive state statute requiring fetal viability testing. Perhaps more important than the decision itself, *Webster* signaled that the increasingly conservative Rehnquist Court might soon overrule *Roe*, a decision the Reagan and Bush administrations had long been urging. However, due largely to the cautious approach of the Court's then-lone female justice, Sandra Day O'Connor, the justices, with the exception of Justice Scalia, declined in *Webster* to say that *Roe* should be reversed.

After the retirement of the Rehnquist Court's most liberal justices, William Brennan and Thurgood Marshall, and their respective replacement by the more conservative David Souter and Clarence Thomas, many Court watchers expected that *Roe* would be overruled. *Planned Parenthood of Southeastern Pennsylvania v. Casey* (1992) shows how unpredictable the Court can be. In *Casey*, five members of the Court— Justices Blackmun, John Paul Stevens, O'Connor, Anthony Kennedy, and Souter—voted to reaffirm what the unusual O'Connor-Kennedy-

Souter joint opinion called the "essential holding" of *Roe v. Wade:* that a woman has a constitutional right to an abortion before the fetus attains viability. The O'Connor-Kennedy-Souter opinion did, however, adopt a more lenient standard for evaluating abortion restrictions, with that standard—the "undue burden" standard—replacing *Roe*'s stringent "compelling" state-interest test and its accompanying trimester framework. An "undue burden" is one placing a "substantial obstacle" in the path of a woman seeking an abortion.[90] Chief Justice Rehnquist and Justices Byron White, Scalia, and Thomas voted to overturn *Roe*, marking the first time four members of the Court had expressly done so.

Abortion, to borrow Oliver Wendell Holmes's phrase, is a "hard case."[91] This is because there is so much uncertainty about when life begins. In *Roe v. Wade* the Court expressly refused to "resolve the difficult question of when life begins,"[92] a position to which the Court has consistently adhered ever since. The title of Laurence Tribe's book on abortion, *Abortion: The Clash of Absolutes,*[93] well describes the Court's dilemma, given that abortion directly impacts two fundamental rights, life and liberty.

The natural-rights political philosophy of the Declaration of Independence *cannot* determine whether a woman has a constitutional right to choose whether to have an abortion, *until it is established when life begins.* If the unborn child *is* a "life," then there is *not* a natural right to an abortion because "the fundamental law of nature" is the preservation of life and "when all cannot be preserved, the safety of the *innocent* is to be preferred."[94] There certainly can be no more innocent a life than that of an unborn child. But if the unborn child is *not* a "life," then there *is* a natural right to an abortion because a woman's natural right to "liberty"—to freely direct the course of her life—surely includes the childbearing decision. Abortion is, therefore, an issue for which, at present, the natural-rights political philosophy of the Declaration of Independence cannot provide the rule of decision. However, the Declaration enumerates the relevant considerations— especially the primacy of the natural right to life—and will be able to provide the rule of decision when it is established when life begins.

Here, it is necessary to reject conservative activist Lewis Lehrman's controversial article, "The Declaration of Independence and the Right to Life: One Leads Unmistakably from the Other,"[95] an article that burst onto the national political scene during the Clarence Thomas Supreme Court confirmation hearing.[96] Lehrman argues that *Roe v. Wade* was a "coup" against the Constitution. Equating the current struggle to ban abortion with Abraham Lincoln's struggle to ban slavery, Lehrman characterizes the Court's unwillingness to protect a "child-about-to-be-born (a person)" as a "holocaust" that is fundamentally inconsistent with the "expressly stipulated right to life, as set forth in the Declaration and the Constitution."[97]

Lehrman asserts as an article of religious faith that life begins at conception.[98] He fails to appreciate, however, that under the Constitution the question of when life begins is a scientific one, not a religious one, because the first amendment codifies the strict wall of separation between church and state that was so fundamental to the Founders, as well as to Locke.[99]* Unfortunately, scientists still disagree on when life begins.[100] The political philosophy of the Declaration of Independence therefore cannot decide the abortion question at the present time.

Before proceeding to the next area of inquiry I need to say a few words about the implications for my project of the inability of the political philosophy of the Declaration of Independence to presently resolve the abortion question. In my judgment, an interpretive methodology need not be able to resolve *all* questions to be workable. As long as the methodology can resolve the vast majority of questions, as well as provide guidance for the remainder, the methodology works. This is especially true if those unanswered questions will one day be resolved. Such is the case for the natural-rights methodology proposed in this volume. As will be apparent from this chapter, abortion is the only issue of constitutional-rights adjudication that the proposed interpretive methodology cannot at present resolve.

The last issue concerning the natural right to life considered in this section is welfare, or what Locke calls "charity." There is an intimate

---

*The Founders' reference in the Declaration of Independence to individuals' being "endowed by their Creator with certain unalienable rights" is not inconsistent with the strict wall of separation between church and state they later wrote into the first amendment. In other words, the Declaration—and Locke, for that matter—need not be read theistically. Jefferson himself was making the point in the Declaration with his use of the phrase "the Laws of Nature and of Nature's God."

connection between charity and life in natural-rights doctrine: the right to and duty of charity flows from the fundamental law of nature to preserve mankind. As one leading Locke scholar puts it:

Beneath the flexible and diversified structure of social convention, there remains the rigid and unitary order of nature and its demands have none of the permissive delicacy of human complaisance, for they are the demands of [the Creator]. All men have a duty to preserve their fellow men to the best of their ability. It is the duty of charity. ... Charity [is] a right on the part of the needy and a duty on the part of the wealthy.[101]

The purely individualistic interpretation of Lockean liberalism, most notably advanced by C. B. Macpherson and Leo Strauss, rejects a duty of charity.[102] However, a careful reading of Locke reveals how central charity is to Lockean liberalism, given that the fundamental law of nature is the preservation of mankind. For instance, Locke states in the *First Treatise* that "*Charity* gives every Man a Title to so much out of another's Plenty, as will keep him from extream want, where he has no means to subsist otherwise."[103] Locke also speaks of charity in the *Second Treatise*, explaining that "when his own preservation comes not in competition, [an individual ought], as much as he can, to preserve the rest of mankind" and that an individual owes "relief and support to the distressed."[104] Finally, in "Venditio," an essay that constitutes Locke's most extensive discussion of charity, he goes so far as to declare that if anyone dies as a result of another's denial of charity, the person denying charity "is no doubt guilty of murder."[105]

While Locke's statements about the duty of charity are made largely in the context of his analysis of the state of nature, and hence speak to a *private* duty under natural law, a central tenet of Locke's theory of government is that individuals cede to government the power to enforce fundamental private duties in political society—especially those duties relating to the preservation of mankind (see chapter 1). As a result, the private duty of charity can be enforced by government through public law. Although the Founders subscribed to this view, using local taxes to provide relief to the indigent,[106] the Supreme Court has never held that there is a constitutional right to public assistance.

In several noteworthy cases the Supreme Court has acknowledged, in seemingly Lockean terms, the significance of welfare benefits. For example, in *Shapiro v. Thompson* (1969), the Court struck down, on a six-to-three vote, a durational residency condition on the availability of

Aid to Families with Dependent Children benefits on "right to travel" grounds. The Court noted in passing that the challenged requirement operated to "[deny] welfare aid upon which may depend the ability of families to obtain the very means to subsist—food, shelter, and other necessities of life,"[107] a statement Locke himself could have made.

In *Goldberg v. Kelly* (1970),[108] a five-person majority held that due process requires a trial-type hearing prior to the termination of previously provided welfare benefits. As in *Shapiro*, the Court stopped short in *Goldberg* of holding that there is a constitutional right to welfare. And as the Court has become more conservative, it has backed away from its earlier statements suggesting that there may be such a constitutional right.

DeShaney v. Winnebago County Department of Social Services (1989) illustrates the Court's departure from its earlier statements suggesting that there may be a constitutional right to welfare. In *DeShaney*, the Rehnquist Court rejected the claim of a mother that welfare workers were liable for the repeated beatings, and accompanying brain damage, levied on her son by the young boy's natural father. The Court justified its decision by noting that "our cases have recognized that the Due Process Clauses generally confer no affirmative right to governmental aid, even where such aid may be necessary to secure life, liberty, or property interests of which the government itself may not deprive the individual."[109]

Given the right to and duty of charity in natural-rights doctrine there is, contrary to the Supreme Court's most recent pronouncements, as well as to the position advanced by many modern-day conservatives,[110] a constitutional right to welfare. It is essential, however, to appreciate the extent of this right. A careful reading of Locke advises that only those who cannot help themselves are entitled to welfare.[111] An able-bodied individual must fend for himself or herself, unless conditions are such that, despite the individual's best efforts, he or she cannot. Additionally, as I explain more fully in the next sections, natural-rights doctrine rejects, under the guise of public assistance, egalitarian claims for the redistribution of wealth. Under a natural-rights interpretation of the Constitution, only the basic needs of the poor must be met to satisfy the natural right to life. But, as explained below, the natural right to the pursuit of happiness that is so central to the political philosophy of the Declaration of Independence affords an individual who cannot help himself or herself more than simply the means to stay alive. In other words, there is more to public assistance than that involved with protecting the natural right to life.

Liberty

"Liberty," an individual's natural right to freely direct the course of his or her life (see chapter 1), is a concept integral to the political philosophy of the American regime. Indeed, "the United States of America" stands for liberty perhaps more than for anything else. From the Founders' long and bloody struggle for the freedom to govern themselves, to immigrants streaming through New York harbor in search of a better life and being welcomed by the Statue of Liberty, to foreign peoples overthrowing oppressive governments and turning to the United States as a model, liberty has always been at the heart of the American way of life.

The privacy cases provide an excellent vehicle through which to illustrate how the Declaration of Independence's concept of liberty can be applied in constitutional interpretation. The Supreme Court first recognized privacy interests in the 1886 search and seizure/self-incrimination case of *Boyd v. United States*. There, the Court declared unconstitutional a statute allowing the government to order individuals to produce private papers and invoices as evidence of illegally imported goods. The Court emphasized the privacy interests involved and held that the fourth and fifth amendments apply

to all invasions on the part of the government and its employees of the sanctity of a man's home and privacies of life. It is not the breaking of his doors, and the rummaging of his drawers, that constitutes the essence of the offense; but it is the invasion of his indefeasible right of personal security, personal liberty and private property.[112]

Four years later, in a widely read *Harvard Law Review* article, Samuel Warren and Louis Brandeis developed a theory of privacy that went beyond *Boyd*'s property and criminal procedure context. According to Warren and Brandeis, there should be a broad privacy right in the law because what is at stake is "man's spiritual nature," his "inviolate personalty."[113] Although particular members of the Court continued to recognize privacy interests in specific provisions of the

Bill of Rights,[114] it was not until the 1965 case of *Griswold v. Connecticut*[115] that the potential for a *general* constitutional right of privacy was identified by a majority of the Court.

At issue in *Griswold* was a Connecticut statute barring distribution and use of contraceptive devices. The Court, in a seven-to-two vote, declared the statute an unconstitutional infringement on marital privacy. Writing for the majority, Justice William Douglas argued that while there is no "right of privacy" mentioned in Constitution, such a right can be inferred from the existence of "penumbras" that are formed by "emanations" from other provisions of the Bill of Rights which recognize "zones of privacy."[116]

Justice Douglas's opinion for the Court instantly became one of the most controversial in the Court's history.[117] In addition to the stinging dissents of Justices Hugo Black and Potter Stewart in *Griswold* itself,[118] Robert Bork writes that "the protection of marriage was not the point of *Griswold*. The creation of a new device for judicial power to remake the Constitution was the point."[119] In fact, the Court's decision in *Griswold* that there is a right of privacy in the Constitution was a principal cause of the call, by Bork and others, for a jurisprudence of original intention (see the Introduction).

Albeit perhaps even more controversially than Justice Douglas's opinion for the Court, Justice Arthur Goldberg's concurring opinion in *Griswold*[120] demonstrates that the Court did not need to stretch as far as Justice Douglas did—to the "penumbras" of the Bill of Rights—to find a right of privacy in the Constitution. Justice Goldberg turned directly to the ninth amendment. He contended that the language and history of the ninth amendment reveal that "the Framers believed that there are additional fundamental rights, protected from governmental infringement, which exist alongside those fundamental rights specifically mentioned in the first eight amendments." According to Justice Goldberg, the unenumerated rights protected in the ninth amendment are not identified "in light of [a justice's] personal and private notions." Rather, they are identified by looking "to the 'traditions and [collective] conscience of our people.'"[121]

As part 1 explained, the tradition and collective conscience to which the Supreme Court should refer when interpreting the ninth amendment is the natural-rights political philosophy of the Declaration of Independence. David O'Brien makes the point well in his thoughtful book on privacy. "The Ninth Amendment's provision for 'rights retained by the people,'" O'Brien writes, "registered in part the authors' acceptance of natural law teachings and the inherent rights of individuals."[122] In other words, the Founders did not believe that the Bill of Rights *conferred* rights upon individuals. Rather, the Bill of Rights *reaffirmed preexisting* rights possessed by individuals. And the Founders included the ninth amendment to make clear that individuals have more rights under natural law than those enumerated in amendments 1 through 8.

Although *Griswold* has been widely criticized for, among other things, failing to "stick close to the text and the history" of the Constitution,[123] interpreting the Constitution in light of the natural-rights political philosophy of the Declaration of Independence reveals that a *general* right of personal privacy is *central* to the Constitution. Recall, for instance, Locke's observation that "in the greatest part of the action of our lives ... I think God out of his infinite goodness ... hath left us great liberty."[124] This is a conclusion that illustrates, perhaps better than any other, the difference between liberal originalism and conservative originalism.[125] As part 1 described, the Constitution establishes a *limited* government whose principal purpose is to secure individual rights. In so doing, the Constitution certainly protects an individual's "right to be let alone," which is the essence of the right of privacy.[126] The fundamental place of personal privacy in the Constitution was well appreciated by Justice Louis Brandeis in a justly acclaimed dissenting opinion in the 1928 wiretap case, *Olmstead v. United States*. According to Justice Brandeis, who made a similar argument some four decades earlier in his path-breaking article with Samuel Warren:

The makers of our Constitution undertook to secure conditions favorable to the pursuit of happiness. They recognized the significance of man's spiritual nature, of his feelings and of his intellect. They knew that only part of the pain, pleasure, and satisfactions of life are to be found in material things. They sought to protect Americans in their beliefs, their thoughts, their emotions and their sensations. They conferred as against the Government, the right to be let alone—the most comprehensive of rights and the right most valued by civilized man.[127]

In the twenty years after *Griswold* the Supreme Court extended the right to be free from unwarranted government interference to the use of contraceptives by unmarried persons,[128] including adolescents,[129] the decision to marry,[130] cohabitation with one's extended family,[131] parental control over the education and upbringing of children,[132] and abortion,[133] to name the most well-known decisions. On the issue of gay rights, however, the Court backed away from the generous right of privacy identified in *Griswold.*

In *Bowers v. Hardwick* (1986), the Supreme Court confronted the challenge of a gay man who claimed that a state statute making it a crime to engage in adult, consensual, private homosexual sodomy was unconstitutional.[134] In a five-to-four vote, the Court upheld the statute. The majority opinion was written by Justice Byron White, who appealed to history and reasoned that

proscriptions against that conduct [consensual sodomy] have ancient roots. . . . Sodomy was a criminal offense at common law and was forbidden by the laws of the original thirteen States when they ratified the Bill of Rights. In 1868, when the Fourteenth Amendment was ratified, all but 5 of the 37 states in the Union had criminal sodomy laws. In fact, until 1961, all 50 States outlawed sodomy, and today, 24 States and the District of Columbia continue to provide criminal penalties for sodomy performed in private and between consenting adults. . . . Against this background, to claim that a right to engage in such conduct is "deeply rooted in this Nation's history and tradition" or "implicit in the concept of ordered liberty" is, at best, facetious.[135]

Justice White's history is certainly impressive. In fact, in 1779 Thomas Jefferson—the author of the Declaration of Independence— drafted A Bill for Proportioning Crimes and Punishments that included severe penalties for engaging in sodomy.[136] In addition, Harry Jaffa, who, like this author, argues that the Constitution should be interpreted in accordance with the natural-rights political philosophy of the Declaration of Independence,[137] contends that homosexual acts are inconsistent with that philosophy because they run counter to regeneration. Homosexual acts "are unnatural acts," Jaffa writes, "and, being unnatural, the very negation of anything that could be called a right according to nature. The very root of nature is generation."[138] Unfortunately, by requiring that sex be procreational Jaffa is advancing an unnecessarily rigid and formalistic approach to homosexuality.

Although a strictly historical approach to the issue of homosexual sodomy, à la Justice White's opinion, as well as the perspective promoted by the conservative proponents of a jurisprudence of original intention, does seem to support the Court's decision in *Bowers*, examining the issue at a more general level of natural-rights principle—the approach advanced in this volume—does not. Specifically, because the preservation of mankind does not appear to be seriously threatened by adult, consensual, private homosexual acts, a natural-rights interpretation of the Constitution recognizes a constitutional privacy right to engage in such acts. (AIDS is certainly a threat to the preservation of mankind. But that dreaded disease is not, contrary to popular mythology, unique to homosexuals.) It is difficult to imagine a more fundamental privacy interest than that concerning sexual activity—homosexual as well as heterosexual.[139] To make the point another way, laws against homosexual sodomy represent nothing more than the majority's attempt to enforce its morality on the minority,[140] something that is flatly incompatible with the concept of liberty embodied in the Declaration of Independence and the Constitution. In the American regime, an individual is supposed to enjoy the natural right to freely direct the course of his or her life, including his or her sex life.

The final subject to be discussed in this section is "economic liberty." Ever since the Supreme Court began upholding President Franklin Roosevelt's New Deal legislation in 1937,[141] the Court has been employing a "double standard," whereby noneconomic rights are provided greater judicial protection than economic rights.[142] Because economic rights are said not to fall within the rubric of "preferred freedoms"[143]—which include such "personal" rights as freedom of religion, of speech, and of the press—they no longer enjoy the protection they did during the heyday of the Fuller, White, and Taft Courts. But the question that must be asked is: freedoms preferred by whom? As Learned Hand once remarked, "Just why property itself was not a 'personal right,' nobody took the time to explain."[144] Clearly, the subordination of economic rights to noneconomic rights in the hierarchy of judicial protection can be explained by nothing other than the personal political preferences of a majority of the justices who have served on the post-1937 Supreme Court.*

Under the double standard the Supreme Court employs a highly

---

*Henry Abraham suggests three justifications for the double standard: (1) "the crucial nature of basic freedoms," (2) "the explicit language of the Bill of Rights," and (3) "the appropriate expertise of the judiciary." Abraham, *Freedom and the Court*, 28–37. As will be evident below, a natural-rights–based theory of judicial review rejects all alleged justifications for the double standard, including those thoughtfully presented, although not necessarily embraced, by Abraham.

permissive test in judging the constitutionality of economic regulations. The Constitution is violated only if the economic regulation at issue is not rationally related to a legitimate government purpose. Only twice since 1937 have economic regulations failed to pass this test.[145] By contrast, regulation of fundamental noneconomic rights is frequently deemed unconstitutional on the basis of a highly protective test: there must be a compelling state interest for the regulation.

Arguing that the double standard has improperly sacrificed the individual right of economic liberty, some scholars—most notably Richard Epstein, Leonard Levy, Stephen Macedo, Richard Posner, and Bernard Siegan[146]—maintain that the Court should abandon the double standard because economic rights are as deserving of protection as noneconomic rights. According to Macedo:

> The modern Court's double standard, which neglects economic liberties and protects other "personal" liberties, like privacy, is incoherent and untenable. It flies in the face of the plain words of the Constitution, ignores important aspects of our legal and political traditions, and fails to recognize that economic and other "favored" liberties are mutually interdependent and commonly grounded on an even more basic, implicit constitutional principle: the dignity of persons who are bearers of broad rights and capable of responsible self-government.[147]

Siegan is even more blunt than Macedo in his criticism of the double standard. "The judiciary lacks legitimacy to discriminate against certain liberties," Siegan writes. "Judicial withdrawal from the protection of economic activity violates Article III."[148]

The modern Supreme Court has occasionally cast doubt on the wisdom of the double standard. In *Lynch v. Household Finance Corporation* (1972), the Court held that wages deposited in a savings account were subject to certain civil rights statutes. Writing for a unanimous Court—and invoking Locke's *Second Treatise* as evidence of the profound American commitment to private property rights—Justice Stewart described the problems of selectivity and objectivity caused by the double standard:

> The dichotomy between personal liberties and property rights is a false one. Property does not have rights. People have rights. The right to enjoy property without unlawful deprivation, no less than the right to speak out or the right to travel, is, in truth, a "personal" right, whether the "property" in question be a welfare check, a home, or a savings account. In fact, a fundamental interdepen-

dence exists between the personal right to liberty and the personal right in property. Neither could have meaning without the other. That rights in property are basic civil rights has long been recognized. J. Locke, of Civil Government . . . ; J. Adams, A Defence of the Constitutions of Government of the United States of America . . . ; 1. W. Blackstone, Commentaries.[149]

As Justice Stewart's opinion suggests, the double standard is inconsistent with the natural-rights principles on which this nation is based.[150] The political philosophy of the American Founding recognizes the importance of individual economic rights just as much as it does the importance of individual noneconomic rights. For instance, James Madison writes in *The Federalist* no. 10 that "the first object of government" is "the protection of different and unequal faculties of acquiring property,"[151] and John Adams argues in *Discourses on Davila* that "property must be secured, or liberty cannot exist."[152] In addition, the Lockean trinity of "life, liberty, and property" is written into the fifth and fourteenth amendments of the Constitution itself.

Finally, as I explained earlier, the Lockean liberal concept of equality is closely linked to a generous amount of economic liberty. While many treatments of Locke's political philosophy do focus too narrowly on the discussion of private property in chapter 5 of the *Second Treatise*,[153] it is impossible to deny that a major purpose of government in Locke's theory is to protect private property—a purpose the Founders understood well. For example, in words echoed by Madison in *The Federalist* no. 10, Locke writes that

the increase of lands and the right of employing them is the great art of government; and the prince who shall be so wise and godlike as by established laws of liberty to secure protection and encouragement to the honest industry of mankind, against the oppression of power and narrowness of party, will quickly be too hard for his neighbors.[154]

Under a natural-rights interpretation of the Constitution the double standard is, therefore, illegitimate. Every individual has a natural right to economic liberty, just as every individual has a natural right to, among other things, practice the religion of his or her choice and speak his or her mind.

It should be noted here, however, that although natural-rights political philosophy is largely, with respect to economics, a philosophy of laissez-faire, it is not the "simplistic version of laissez faire" represented by Herbert Spencer's social Darwinism and written into the

Constitution by the Supreme Court in the late nineteenth and early twentieth centuries.[155] As described above, natural-rights doctrine recognizes a right to and a duty of charity. In Locke's words, "Common charity teaches, that those shall be most taken care of by the law, who are least capable of taking care for themselves."[156] Moreover, the preservation of mankind—the fundamental law of nature—requires some degree of public-health regulation of the economy, especially in these times of environmental crisis. Lastly, as I now discuss, the natural right of all Americans to "the pursuit of happiness" sometimes requires a minimal level of government encroachment on an otherwise generous right of individual economic liberty.

The Pursuit of Happiness

An individual's natural right to "the pursuit of happiness"—to strive to attain a good and happy life—is a key component of the political philosophy of the Declaration of Independence (see chapter 1). Indeed, Henry Steele Commager argues that the eighteenth century was dominated by concerns with the pursuit of happiness.[157] And Thomas Jefferson once wrote that "the freedom and happiness of man . . . are the sole objects of all legitimate government."[158]

The Declaration of Independence, unlike George Mason's Virginia Declaration of Rights, does not speak of the natural right of *obtaining* happiness. But the assistance of others—including the government—is nevertheless sometimes required, because without the minimum necessities of life an individual is forced to struggle for daily survival and therefore has no opportunity to pursue his or her happiness. To put it bluntly, "life" and "liberty" are not the only natural rights mentioned in the Declaration of Independence. The "pursuit of happiness" must mean something. What it means is that all individuals who are unable to fend for themselves must be furnished with the material conditions indispensable to the *pursuit* of happiness, facilitating but not ensuring its attainment.[159]

As noted above, a majority on the Supreme Court has never held that there is a constitutional right to the minimum material conditions of life (despite the profound impact of Charles Reich's 1964 article, "The New Property," which argued to the contrary on the basis of economic due process).[160] Interpreting the Constitution in accordance with the natural-rights political philosophy of the Declaration of Independence suggests, however, that there is a constitutional right to basic education, health care, food, housing, and clothing, for without these things an individual is denied an opportunity to pursue a good and happy life. Justice Brennan made the point well in his opinion for the Court in *Goldberg v. Kelly*, when he observed that "welfare provides the means to obtain essential food, clothing, housing, and medical care," that "from its founding the Nation's basic commitment has been to foster the dignity and well-being of all persons within its borders," that "welfare ... can help bring within the reach of the poor the same opportunities that are available to others to participate meaningfully in the life of the community," and that "public assistance, then, is not mere charity, but a means to 'procure the Blessings of Liberty to ourselves and our Posterity.'"[161]

Despite this reasoning, the Court stopped short of holding that there is a constitutional right to the essential material conditions of life. The natural right to the pursuit of happiness requires that the Court take this step forward, rather than continue to step backward as it has done in cases like *DeShaney v. Winnebago County Department of Social Services* (1989),[162] discussed earlier, and *San Antonio v. Rodriguez* (1973),[163] which held that education is not a fundamental right. Although the political philosophy of the American Founding does not envision an egalitarian welfare state—indeed, the Declaration's concepts of "equality" and "liberty" forbid it—that philosophy does require some public assistance programs so that every individual has an opportunity to pursue his or her happiness. In effect, and contrary to opposing modern liberal and conservative schools of thought, public assistance need not be an all-or-nothing proposition.

While, at times, the discussion in this chapter seemed to focus more on explaining key components of natural-rights doctrine than on describing particular provisions of the Constitution, that was unavoidable. As explained in the Introduction, and as is readily apparent from myriad books and articles on constitutional interpretation, it is exceedingly difficult, if not impossible, to divorce constitutional interpretation from political philosophy—especially when interpreting provisions of the

Constitution that are phrased in general terms, as are the individual-rights provisions addressed in this chapter.

What I have endeavored to show in this chapter is that, though a natural-rights–based theory of judicial review is inevitably abstract, the theory is not so abstract as to be unworkable. To that end, I applied the natural-rights political philosophy of the Declaration of Independence to some of the leading—and most controversial—cases in constitutional law and history in order to demonstrate that the proposed theory of judicial review can resolve constitutional disputes that come before the Court. Significantly, the results discerned from the application of the natural-rights theory are neither consistently "liberal," nor consistently "conservative," in the modern conception of those terms. (Readers who are simply looking for post-hoc rationalizations for preconceived political results are therefore likely to be disappointed.) Instead, the results are "liberal" in the classic seventeenth- and eighteenth-century sense, an outcome that, given the jurisprudence of the American Founding, should be expected.

Conclusion:
A New American Revolution?

From the discussion in chapter 1 of the character of the American Revolution to the analysis in chapter 5 of the constitutional status of welfare, this book has addressed a host of important subjects. As I stated in the Preface, however, the book is as much a methodological statement as it is a substantive statement. I have tried to show that scholars from different disciplines need to talk *to* each other, rather than *past* each other—especially where the Constitution is concerned. In fact, my underlying theme is that the Constitution cannot be properly understood without recourse to history, political philosophy, and law—all three. The book is therefore broad in scope, and many of the issues I have addressed have themselves been the subject of a vast and varied independent literature.

Of course, interdisciplinary approaches run the risk of failing to meet the justifiably demanding standards of particular disciplines. This risk is magnified when the interdisciplinary approach leads to conclusions in a particular area that go against the conventional wisdom in that area—such as my conclusion about the character of the American Revolution, for instance. That said, what I have attempted to do is to identify the core components of some largely isolated debates and integrate them into the specific framework of constitutional interpretation. To that end, I have considered two essential questions. First, *how* should the Constitution of the United States be interpreted? Second, *who* should be primarily responsible for making that interpretation?

The conclusions reached are that the Constitution should be interpreted in light of the natural-rights political philosophy of the Declaration of Independence and that the Supreme Court is the institution of American government that should be primarily responsible for identifying and applying that philosophy in American life. These conclusions are no doubt controversial, because they run counter to two powerful trends in the literature: an increasing skepticism about natural rights and a growing mistrust of judicial power.

In effect, I advance a largely conservative methodology—a jurisprudence of original intention—but arrive at liberal results, as "liberal" is understood in the classic sense of seventeenth- and eighteenth-century political philosophy. The proposed jurisprudence of original intention—what I call "liberal originalism"—is, therefore, far different from that promoted by modern political and jurisprudential conservatives such as former attorney general Edwin Meese, Robert Bork, and Chief Justice William Rehnquist. (My theory will likely be resisted by *both* conservatives, because the theory is "liberal," *and* liberals, because I call for "originalism.") An originalism that takes history and political philosophy seriously, as this volume has tried to do, reveals that the political and jurisprudential conservatives are simply substituting conservative result-oriented jurisprudence for modern liberal result-oriented jurisprudence. The conservative originalists also mischaracterize the Constitution as establishing a majority-rule democracy, a mischaracterization that is also made by many modern constitutional theorists of so-called "moderate" and "liberal" political views. This has led to an unfortunate portrayal of the Court as a "deviant institution in the

American democracy"[1] and to an unnecessary preoccupation with trying to reconcile judicial review and democracy.

Because I advance a jurisprudence of original intention, I addressed,
in an introductory section, the prevailing criticisms of that interpretive
methodology: that modern Americans cannot understand what the
Founders intended because our language is different from theirs, that
there is no single entity that can be called "the Founders," and that the
existing documentary record of the Founders' intentions is unreliable.
These criticisms were found to be misplaced at the level of the natural-
rights principle proposed here. Found equally wanting is the criticism
offered by proponents of the notion of a "living Constitution," such as
retired associate justice William Brennan, that the Founders' intentions
cannot address modern circumstances and problems and that the Constitution must, therefore, "evolve" through judicial interpretation. The
notion of a living Constitution was rejected because it permits unelected and life-tenured judges to read their own moral and political
preferences into the Constitution and impose them on the rest of us
and because a jurisprudence of original intention at the level of natural-
rights principle can meet modern exigencies.

Related to my defense of originalist methodology was a discussion
of the connection between the Founders' background attitudes on
the basic purpose of government (articulated in the Declaration of
Independence) and the interpretation of the particular provisions of
the Constitution, especially the open-ended provisions concerning individual rights (the subject of this volume). To restate my point directly,
lawyers like Ronald Dworkin who write on constitutional interpretation correctly recognize that political philosophy is essential for understanding the Constitution. But, unless constitutional theorists immerse
themselves in the history of why the Constitution came to be, they
cannot understand what that political philosophy is: a classical liberal
philosophy of individual rights and limited government. A constitutional theorist without a proper historical foundation for his or her
political philosophy is therefore left arguing that, *in his or her opinion*,
the Constitution should stand for "this or that." And under that scenario, constitutional values are inevitably established by those with the
best argumentation skills. No wonder lawyers have a virtual monopoly
on normative constitutional scholarship! Indeed, my ultimate aim in
this book is to suggest that political scientists and historians should do

more normative constitutional scholarship, given their sensitivity to American political history.

Turning to the major points in support of the above conclusions, part 1, "The Jurisprudence of the American Founding," explicated the political philosophy of the Declaration of Independence and the jurisprudence of the Constitution of the United States. It revealed that the Declaration articulates the philosophical *ends* of our nation and that the Constitution embodies the *means* to effectuate those ends.

Chapter 1, "The Declaration of Independence," embraced the traditional—though currently unpopular—view that the character of the American Revolution was Lockean liberal. The Lockean liberal reading of the American Revolution was derived by examining the influence of Lockean liberalism on the Founders generally and on the Declaration of Independence specifically. Revisionist characterizations of the Revolution, especially the largely successful republican revisionism of Bernard Bailyn, J. G. A. Pocock, and Gordon Wood, were discussed and rejected.*

The Lockean natural-rights political philosophy of the Declaration of Independence was then systematically explored and analyzed. To that end, the key concepts "all men are created equal," "the consent of the governed," and, of course, the "unalienable" natural rights of "life, liberty, and the pursuit of happiness" were examined. What resulted is a political philosophy that is predominantly individualistic, but not exclusively so. The political philosophy of the Declaration of Independence was shown to recognize some communitarian obligations, both in its acceptance of the duty of charity and in its concept of the pursuit of happiness.

The most important substantive objective of this book was to identify the fundamental purpose of the Constitution. Chapter 2, "The Constitution of the United States," addressed that issue. Several sources proved invaluable for illuminating the fundamental purpose of the Constitution to be securing the natural rights identified in the Declaration of Independence. As Thomas Jefferson wrote in the Declaration

---

*I am *not* arguing that the Founders were influenced solely by John Locke. They were too widely read and too sophisticated for that. My point is that the Founders were Lockean liberals on the *basic* purpose of government—the controlling question in constitutional interpretation.

itself, "to secure these rights governments are instituted among men" (hence, the title of this volume).*

The preamble to the Constitution states the reasons for which the Constitution was written. Although the preamble has been dismissed by many as simply prefatory language, the preamble is more than that, and it merited careful consideration. The debates surrounding the framing and ratification of the Constitution provided an excellent source of information about the fundamental purpose of the Constitution. *The Federalist* papers, generally regarded as the best insight into the Founders' understanding of the Constitution, were also examined at length, as were the personal letters, writings, and speeches of leading Founders and statesmen such as James Madison, Thomas Jefferson, James Wilson, Alexander Hamilton, and John Adams. All of these sources revealed the fundamental purpose of the Constitution to be protecting the natural rights of the American people.

Additionally, chapter 2 found the Bill of Rights to be a central part of the Constitution enacted by the Founders. Consequently, the reasons for the Bill of Rights' adoption and the specific meanings of the first ten amendments were studied. The ninth amendment, with its protection of "unenumerated" rights, was particularly significant. That amendment, perhaps more than any other, evinced the importance to the Constitution of protecting natural rights. The primacy of protecting natural rights was also apparent from an examination of early state constitutions.

Part 2, "Natural Rights and the Role of the Court," explained that the Supreme Court is the institution of American government that should be primarily responsible for identifying and applying the natural-rights political philosophy of the Declaration of Independence in constitutional interpretation. Chapter 3, "The Court," is likely the most controversial part of this book. There I described, as a matter of original intent, that the Constitution commissions the Court as the chief guardian of the American people's natural rights. In effect, chapter 3 entered the long-standing debate over the origins and scope of judicial review. That required examining cases and historical materials that have been

---

* As was true of my interpretation of the character of the American Revolution, I am *not* advancing a monistic interpretation of the character of the Constitution. In other words, I am not saying that the Constitution is concerned only about protecting rights. But protecting rights is what the Constitution is concerned most about.

examined many times before. But what I aspired to do in chapter 3 was to provide a revised reading of the debate over judicial review, a reading that takes seriously the American Founding's commitment to natural rights.

Chapter 3's analysis of judicial review was in three separate, but related, parts. I began by explaining how the Founders, consistent with their British heritage, initially attempted to protect individual rights through representation. In time, however, the Founders came to realize that representation, even a reformed system of representation, provided inadequate security for rights. Hence, the inevitable emergence of one of the most significant American contributions to constitutional theory: the idea that judges have the authority to protect individual rights through the power of judicial review.

I followed my analysis of the movement from legislative to judicial protection of individual rights with an examination of the more specific question of the role of natural-rights doctrine in judicial review. Given the strength of the two previously mentioned trends in the literature— an increasing skepticism about natural rights and a growing mistrust of judicial power—my conclusion that the Court was expected to appeal to natural-rights doctrine when deciding individual-rights cases no doubt will be resisted by many. Nevertheless, the conclusion is supported by a detailed analysis of early judicial theory and practice, including that of the early Supreme Court. In fact, Justice James Iredell's famous opinion in *Calder v. Bull* (1798) and a virtually identical opinion he wrote on circuit the same year are the *only* opinions uncovered to date in a pre–Jacksonian era nonslavery context* in which a judge rejected natural-rights–based judicial review after the Constitution went into effect. Modern opponents of natural-rights–based judicial review have therefore been forced to rely almost exclusively on rhetorical techniques, most notably on attempts to belittle the evidence, overwhelming in my judgment, proffered by proponents of such review.

Modern opponents of natural-rights–based judicial review are not the only ones to blame for the unfortunately vitriolic character of the debate over the role of natural law in constitutional interpretation. I

---

*Chapter 2 explained why the slavery cases are not representative of the general jurisprudential climate of the times.

suggested in chapter 3 that it has been the failure of *both sides* of the debate to recognize the *gradual* and somewhat *hesitant* turn to judicial protection of *individual* rights that has led scholars to characterize the existence of *natural*-rights–based judicial review in such unnecessarily all-or-nothing terms. This is a subtle, but critical, as well as previously overlooked, point.

Finally, chapter 3 addressed the authoritativeness of the Supreme Court's interpretation of the Constitution. My conclusion is that, apart from the people's power of amendment and right of revolution, the Court should have the final say in constitutional interpretation. I therefore rejected egalitarian approaches to constitutional interpretation.

The theory of constitutional interpretation advanced in this volume affords the Supreme Court immense authority. To prevent the Court's role as the ultimate interpreter of the Constitution from devolving into the unacceptable state of government by judiciary, chapter 4, "Checks on the Court," provided recommendations on how to best ensure that the Court interprets the Constitution in light of its underlying natural-rights philosophy, rather than in accordance with the personal moral and political views of individual justices. (Surprisingly, most works on constitutional interpretation do not pay much attention to checks on the Court.) Chapter 4 emphasized that we should not forget that the Article 5 amendment process is available to correct judicial misinterpretations of the Constitution and that Congress has the constitutional power—and duty—to impeach any member of the Court who clearly exceeds his or her authority by reading his or her own values into the Constitution at the expense of natural-rights principles. The related safeguards of selecting meritorious court personnel and of judicial self-restraint were also discussed. In particular, chapter 4 underscored the need to employ a merit-based judicial selection process—one that recognizes the importance of a nominee's being well versed in legal and political philosophy—because by so doing the other checks on the Court would become less a cause for concern.

Chapter 5, "Constitutional Interpretation," endeavored to illustrate that, contrary to the position of many critics of natural-law jurisprudence, a natural-rights–based theory of judicial review can resolve constitutional disputes that come before the Court. With this objective in mind, I applied the natural-rights political philosophy of the Declaration of Independence to some of the most important—and controversial—areas of constitutional law, including slavery, discrimination, preferential treatment, capital punishment, the "right to die," abortion, privacy, economic liberty, and welfare. With the notable exception of the abortion issue, the proposed natural-rights–based theory of judicial review was shown to provide consistent and concrete answers for constitutional-rights adjudication (and will be able to resolve the abortion question once it is established when life begins). Significantly, the results discerned were neither consistently "liberal" nor consistently "conservative" in the modern conception of those terms. Although perhaps disappointing to those who are simply interested in political results, the "inconsistency" should come as no surprise. After all, the Founders were *classical* liberals, not modern liberals or modern conservatives.

The doctrine of revolution is, of course, central to the natural-rights political philosophy of the Declaration of Independence.[2] Because this volume maintains that the Constitution should be interpreted in accordance with the political philosophy of the Declaration, the issue of revolution cannot be ignored.

While mention of revolution may strike many today as radical, the theory of revolution embraced in the Declaration of Independence is not opposed to political authority; it is simply opposed to tyranny. That is to say, because the basic purpose of government is to secure natural rights, the Declaration recognizes that once a tyrant is removed a new government will be quickly formed. This is because natural rights are at risk in the absence of government protection. In fact, when the Founders revolted against British oppression they immediately established a new and uniquely American form of government to secure their natural rights, a form of government that, after much thought and experimentation, became that embodied in the Constitution of United States. The jurisprudence of the American Founding therefore represents that a particular form of government—including that established by the Constitution—is not an end in itself. Thomas Jefferson, for one, writes in a famous letter "that we have not yet so far perfected our constitutions as to venture them unchangeable,"[3] and James Madison—though certainly more reluctant than Jefferson to engage in constitutional change[4]—acknowledges in *The Federalist* no. 43 that the Constitution must be altered if it fails to protect the natural rights of the American people.[5]

What of the current state of the American people's natural rights? Has the situation in the American regime devolved again to the point necessitating revolution and the establishment of a new form of government? These are, of course, momentous questions. The answer suggested by this volume is that a new form of government is not necessarily required. Indeed, it is difficult to image a better form of government for securing natural rights than that devised, through "reflection and choice,"[6] by the Founders. What is required, however, is a more principled approach to government under the existing Constitution, an approach that recognizes the necessity of protecting the natural rights of the entire American political community—including individuals and minorities—not just the power of political majorities.[7] If a more principled approach to government is not adopted, the political philosophy on which the Constitution and this nation are based decrees that revolution and the establishment of a new form of government may be necessary. As it was for the Founders, the choice is ours to make.

Notes

Note to the Preface

1. Scholars are beginning to see the value of asking additional questions as well. See Graber, "Asking Better Questions," 216–22. See generally Murphy, Fleming, and Harris, *American Constitutional Interpretation* (arguing that constitutional theory needs to be reconceptualized). As I hope my book shows, however, there is still much to be learned from the *how* and the *who* inquiries.

Notes to the Introduction

1. 2 U.S. (2 Dall.) 419 (1793).
2. U.S. Constitution, amend. 11 (1795).
3. See Story, *Commentaries on the Constitution of the United States*, vi.
4. Blackstone, *Commentaries on the Laws of England*, vol. 1, 69–70.

5. M. White, *Social Thought in America*.
6. Ronald Dworkin's major contribution to jurisprudence is his candid recognition of the marriage, both unavoidable and desirable in his view, of legal interpretation and political philosophy. I have more to say below about Dworkin's jurisprudence. To their credit, constitutional theorists are beginning to appreciate the significance of what Dworkin has been arguing publicly since the 1960s. See, for example, Sunstein, *The Partial Constitution*, 8 ("The meaning of any text, including the Constitution, is inevitably and always a function of interpretive principles, and these are inevitably and always a product of substantive commitments"). The slow pace by which constitutional theorists are coming to appreciate the significance of political philosophy to constitutional interpretation is likely attributable to the facts that American law schools focus on the mechanics of legal argument and that most theories of constitutional interpretation are advanced by lawyers. (My ultimate aim in this book is to suggest that political scientists and historians should do more normative constitutional scholarship.) As my discussion of originalism evinces, there is still some notable resistance to the unavoidable marriage of constitutional interpretation and political philosophy.
7. Frankfurter, "The Zeitgeist and the Judiciary," 6.
8. The Declaration of Independence, par. 2. Hereafter, quotations from the Declaration of Independence will follow modern capitalization.
9. See, for example, Berns, *Taking the Constitution Seriously*; Diamond, "The Declaration and the Constitution"; Jaffa, "What Were the 'Original Intentions' of the Framers of the Constitution of the United States?"; Murphy, "The Art of Constitutional Interpretation."
10. Wood, *The Fundamentalists and the Constitution*, 1. See generally Tarcov and Pangle, "Epilogue," 932 (arguing that the "primary concern [of Strauss's students], as political scientists, should be the study of our own regime").
11. Although Straussians argue with each other—for example, Jaffa believes equality is the central value of the Declaration of Independence, while Diamond claims it is liberty—they all share their teacher's commitment to transcending historical understanding and recovering the "eternal truth" of classical political philosophy, what Strauss called "natural right." See Wood, *The Fundamentalists and the Constitution*. See generally Strauss, *Natural Right and History*. In stark contrast to the philosophical conservatism of the Straussians, Murphy sees the Declaration of Independence as primarily an egalitarian statement of the "human dignity" of every individual, a value he believes the Court should advance through constitutional interpretation. Murphy thus arrives at largely the same place as retired associate justice William Brennan.
12. Jaffa, for one, unequivocally rejects a role for the Court in identifying and applying the political philosophy of the Declaration of Independence in constitutional interpretation, whereas Murphy wants the Court to amend

the Constitution in pursuit of an evolving conception of human dignity. See, for example, Jaffa, "Judicial Conscience and Natural Rights," 237–45; Murphy, "Constitutional Interpretation," 1768–69.

13. See, for example, Rakove, Review of *Taking the Constitution Seriously,* by Walter Berns, 120 ("That the ... commitments of the Declaration offer the ... true perspective from which to view the Constitution is primarily a statement of faith. ... Berns can only assert, but not prove, that the Constitution 'constitutionalizes' ... the theory of the Declaration").

14. Thomas, "The Higher Law Background of the Privileges or Immunities Clause of the Fourteenth Amendment," 64, 68 (emphasis in original). See also Thomas, "Toward a 'Plain Reading' of the Constitution." See generally Gerber, "The Jurisprudence of Clarence Thomas."

15. Thomas testified that he saw no "role for the application of natural rights to constitutional adjudication." Senate Committee on the Judiciary, *Nomination of Clarence Thomas to Be Associate Justice of the Supreme Court of the United States,* 114. True to his testimony, Justice Thomas has not, to date, invoked the Declaration of Independence in constitutional interpretation. See Gerber, "Justice Clarence Thomas."

16. Schwartz, *The New Right and the Constitution,* 93.

17. See, for example, Ely, *Democracy and Distrust,* 48–54; O'Brien, *Constitutional Law and Politics,* vol. 1, 85.

18. But see Arkes, *Beyond the Constitution* (arguing that it is necessary to go "beyond the Constitution" to recover the principles of natural justice that precede our constitutional government).

19. For example, Meese, "Address before the American Bar Association"; Bork, *The Tempting of America;* Rehnquist, "The Notion of a Living Constitution."

20. Bassham, *Original Intent and the Constitution,* 127, 73. See generally Dworkin, *Law's Empire,* 348–50, 388. I frequently employ Dworkin's useful distinction between the Framers' specific "conceptions" and the abstract "concepts" they wrote into the Constitution. Dworkin first advanced this distinction, which has roots in philosophy, in a brilliant essay in the *New York Review of Books* criticizing "strict constructionists," the precursors of conservative originalists. See Dworkin, "The Jurisprudence of Richard Nixon." As I explain below, however, my interpretation of the abstract concepts embodied in the Constitution is far less open-ended than Dworkin's.

21. Bork, *The Tempting of America,* 153.

22. Bork, "Original Intent and the Constitution," 26.

23. Bork, "Neutral Principles and Some First Amendment Problems," 2.

24. Senator Arlen Specter of Pennsylvania made this point convincingly in his lengthy questioning of Robert Bork during Bork's unsuccessful Supreme Court confirmation hearing. See Senate Committee on the Judiciary, *Nomination of Robert H. Bork to Be Associate Justice of the Supreme Court of the United States,* 277–88, 427–38, 713–22, 815–42.

25. 472 U.S. 38, 91–114 (1985) (Rehnquist, J., dissenting). See generally Davis, *Original Intent.*
26. Meese, "Toward a Jurisprudence of Original Intention," 586.
27. Some agree with Rehnquist's reading of history (that the first amendment prohibits only governmental preference of one religion over another, not an accommodation of religion by the state). For example, there is John Baker, the losing counsel in *Wallace v. Jaffree* and the author of the argument Rehnquist articulated in dissent. See Baker, "The Establishment Clause as Intended." See also Cord, *Separation of Church and State.*
28. Thomas Jefferson, Address to the Danbury Baptist Association, January 1, 1802, in *The Writings of Thomas Jefferson*, vol. 16, 281. See generally Levy, *The Establishment Clause.*
29. See, for example, Thomas Jefferson, Bill for Establishing Religious Freedom, in *The Portable Thomas Jefferson*, 251–53; James Madison, *Memorial and Remonstrance against Religious Assessments*, in *The Writings of James Madison*, vol. 2, 183–91. See generally Locke, *A Letter on Toleration*, 65 (explaining that it is "necessary above all to distinguish between the business of civil government and that of religion, and to mark the true bounds between the church and the commonwealth").
30. See, for example, Agresto, *The Supreme Court and Constitutional Democracy*; Choper, *Judicial Review and the National Political Process*; Ely, *Democracy and Distrust.*
31. Bickel, *The Least Dangerous Branch*, 18.
32. Chemerinsky, "The Vanishing Constitution," 74–75. See also O'Brien, "The Framers' Muse on Republicanism, the Supreme Court, and Pragmatic Constitutional Interpretivism," 119–31.
33. *West Virginia Board of Education v. Barnette*, 319 U.S. 624, 638 (1943).
34. Farrand, ed., *The Records of the Federal Convention*, vol. 1, 48 (remarks of Elbridge Gerry). See generally Billias, *Elbridge Gerry*, 160 (explaining that "what Gerry meant by 'an excess of democracy' was that the mixed constitution, at the time, was weighted too much in favor of the democratic branch of government").
35. *The Federalist* no. 10, 82 (James Madison). A republican form of government is defined by Madison in *The Federalist* no. 39. Madison writes: "We may define a republic to be . . . a government which derives all its powers directly or indirectly from the great body of the people, and is administered by persons holding their offices during pleasure for a limited period, or during good behavior." Ibid., no. 39, 241 (emphasis omitted).
36. Invoking Proverbs 25:11, Abraham Lincoln characterized the Constitution as the "picture of silver" around the "apple of gold" of the Declaration of Independence. Abraham Lincoln, "Fragment on the Constitution and the Union," 1861? in *The Collected Works of Abraham Lincoln*, vol. 4, 169. Lincoln, more than any other statesman since the American Founding, valued the Declaration of Independence in constitutional interpretation. See generally Jaffa, *Crisis of the House Divided.* But see Wills, *Lincoln*

at Gettysburg (arguing that Lincoln changed conclusively the bearing of Jefferson's Declaration).

37. O'Brien, *Constitutional Law and Politics*, vol. 1, 89.

38. For a useful collection of and commentary on many of the most well-known theories of constitutional interpretation, see Gerhardt and Rowe, *Constitutional Theory.* See also Barber, *The Constitution of Judicial Power.*

39. Dworkin, *Life's Dominion*, 145.

40. In essence, Dworkin's goal is "to cultivate in us an *argumentative* attitude toward law." Guest, *Ronald Dworkin*, 8 (emphasis in original). And in the end, as others have frequently pointed out, Dworkin's "Hercules," his ideal judge who has the ability to decide the "hard" interpretive questions, is Dworkin himself.

41. Brennan, "The Constitution of the United States," 171.

42. Justice Brennan is certainly not alone in his approach to constitutional interpretation. Most modern liberals employ a similar approach. In addition, the most famous case in modern American constitutional law, *Brown v. Board of Education* (1954), explicitly invoked the notion of a living Constitution. There, Chief Justice Earl Warren wrote for a unanimous Court, "In approaching this problem, we cannot turn the clock back to 1868 when the Amendment was adopted, or even to 1896 when *Plessy v. Ferguson* was written." 347 U.S. 483, 492 (1954).

43. Jaffa, "What Were the 'Original Intentions' of the Framers of the Constitution of the United States?," 356.

44. Brennan, "The Constitution of the United States," 173, 179.

45. "No person shall be … twice put in jeopardy of life or limb, … nor be deprived of life … without due process of law." U.S. Constitution, amend. 5. "No state shall … deprive any person of life … without due process of law." Ibid., amend. 14.

46. See, for example, Dworkin, *Life's Dominion*, 135–36 (discussing only the eighth amendment); Brest, "The Misconceived Quest for the Original Understanding," 257 n. 59 (focusing on the eighth amendment and characterizing the fifth amendment's reference to capital punishment as simply "casual").

47. Locke, *Second Treatise*, sec. 16.

48. Hughes, *Addresses and Papers of Charles Evans Hughes*, 139.

49. 17 U.S. (4 Wheat.) 316, 407, 415 (1819).

50. Berns, *Taking the Constitution Seriously*, 207.

51. 5 U.S. (1 Cr.) 137, 176–77 (1803).

52. See *Trop v. Dulles*, 356 U.S. 86, 101 (1958) (arguing that the death penalty must be measured by the Court against the "evolving standards of decency that mark the progress of a maturing society").

53. Chemerinsky, *Interpreting the Constitution*, 59.

54. For example, Brest, "The Misconceived Quest for the Original Understanding," 252; Carter, "Constitutional Adjudication and the Indeterminate Text," 843; Murphy, "Constitutional Interpretation," 1768–69.

55. *The Federalist* no. 49, 314 (James Madison). See also Letter from James Madison to Thomas Jefferson, February 4, 1790, in *The Papers of Thomas Jefferson*, vol. 16, 147–50.
56. In Schwartz, *The Unpublished Opinions of the Warren Court*, 274–75.
57. Ball and Pocock, Introduction, 11. See generally Pocock, *Politics, Language, and Time*.
58. The classic statement of the problem of changing meaning, that offered by William Crosskey, illustrates that the problem is not irremediable. After all, Crosskey was able to discern what the Framers meant by a particular provision—Article 1, section 8's grant of power to Congress to regulate "commerce among the several states"—even though the word "among," the operative word of that provision, had a different meaning for the Framers than it has for us. See Crosskey, *Politics and the Constitution in the History of the United States*, vol. 1, chap. 3 (describing how the word "among" was used by the Framers as a synonym for "within" rather than for "between two or more").
59. As Paul Brest points out, during the "tough times," when we do run into interpretive difficulties, "the defense that 'We are doing the best we can' is no less available to constitutional interpreters than to anyone else"—not to mention that interpretive difficulties are no justification for those with political power (including Supreme Court justices) simply reading their own values into the Constitution. See Brest, "The Misconceived Quest for the Original Understanding," 241. Chapter 4 explains how a merit-based appointment process can reduce the interpretive difficulties sometimes posed by a natural-rights–based theory of judicial review.
60. Levy, *Original Intent and the Framers' Constitution*, 294.
61. For example, Lofgren, "The Original Understanding of Original Intent?" 118. This argument can be extended one step further by alleging that the *people* of the United States—those citizens or voters whose agents, the Framers and the ratifiers, proposed and adopted the Constitution—are the true source of original intent. See Bassham, *Original Intent and the Constitution*, 35.
62. *Annals of Congress*, vol. 5, 776 (remarks of Rep. James Madison).
63. Hutson, "The Creation of the Constitution," 158.
64. Brest, "The Misconceived Quest for the Original Understanding," 235. Although Brest personally prefers the open-ended notion of a living Constitution, he considers moderate originalism to be a "coherent and workable" method of constitutional interpretation. Ibid., 228.
65. There is some discussion in the literature about whether conservative originalists like Meese, Bork, and Rehnquist have become moderate originalists. See, for example, Bassham, *Original Intent and the Constitution*, 56. Addressing this question at the level of the conservatives' resolution of cases—which is, after all, what originalism is ultimately about—reveals, as Senator Arlen Specter's questioning of Robert Bork during Bork's unsuccessful confirmation hearing made clear, that the conservatives are moder-

ate originalists only when strict originalism cannot support politically sac-
rosanct decisions like *Brown v. Board of Education* (1954). In all other
cases, as Rehnquist's analysis in *Wallace v. Jaffree* (1985), also suggests,
they are strict originalists, their statements to the contrary notwithstanding. See, for example, Bork, *The Tempting of America*, 218–19 (dismissing
Leonard Levy's attack on the conservatives' strict originalism).

66. Hutson, "The Creation of the Constitution," 152.
67. See Powell, "The Original Understanding of Original Intent"; Levy, *Original Intent and the Framers' Constitution*, 1–29, 284–321.
68. Levy, *Original Intent and the Framers' Constitution*, 2.
69. Some constitutional historians disagree. See, for example, Berger, "'Original Intent' in Historical Perspective"; R. N. Clinton, "Original Understanding, Legal Realism, and the Interpretation of 'This Constitution,'" 1186–1220; Lofgren, "The Original Understanding of Original Intent?"
70. Levy, *Original Intent and the Framers' Constitution*, 284.
71. See Gerber, "Original Intent and Its Obligations."
72. Chesterton, *What I Saw in America*, 7.
73. Ralph Ketcham likewise maintains that the Framers dedicated our nation to certain "enduring" principles in the Constitution; specifically, to republi-canism, liberty, the public good, and federalism. See Ketcham, *Framed for Posterity*. As my discussion in part 1 suggests, Ketcham, a leading figure in the republican revisionism of the American Founding, underestimates the Framers' commitment to Lockean liberalism.

Notes to Chapter 1

1. The classic collection of colonial responses is Bailyn, ed., *Pamphlets of the American Revolution*.
2. Becker, *The Declaration of Independence*, 80. As shown below, some colo-nists turned to natural-rights doctrine earlier than others. James Otis, for one, invoked natural-rights arguments from the beginning.
3. Dumbauld, *The Declaration of Independence*, 52.
4. In Commager, ed., *Documents of American History*, 100.
5. Becker, *The Declaration of Independence*, 194.
6. Letter from John Adams to Timothy Pickering, August 6, 1822, in *The Works of John Adams*, vol. 2, 513–14.
7. Garry Wills disagrees with this assessment in his controversial work on the Declaration of Independence. See Wills, *Inventing America*. Wills claims there are three Declarations: the philosophical discourse written by Jeffer-son, the symbol of nationhood adopted by the Continental Congress, and the reinterpretation by Lincoln that the American people have come to revere. See also Wills, *Lincoln at Gettysburg*. It will become obvious that I disagree strongly with Wills's argument.
8. The legislative history of the Declaration of Independence is comprehen-

sively examined in Hazelton, *The Declaration of Independence.* See also Boyd, *The Declaration of Independence.*

9. Letter from John Adams to Timothy Pickering, August 6, 1822, in *The Works of John Adams,* vol. 2, 514.

10. In *The Works of Thomas Jefferson,* vol. 1, 33.

11. Letter from Thomas Jefferson to Robert Walsh, December 4, 1818, in ibid., vol. 12, 109–10 n.

12. But see Wills, *Inventing America.* Wills argues that the Declaration of Independence is grounded in Scottish moral philosophy, not natural-rights doctrine. Wills's argument is addressed in the next section.

13. Becker, *The Declaration of Independence,* 27.

14. Letter from John Adams to Timothy Pickering, August 6, 1822, in *The Works of John Adams,* vol. 2, 514.

15. Letter from Thomas Jefferson to Richard Henry Lee, May 8, 1825, in *The Writings of Thomas Jefferson,* vol. 16, 118–19.

16. See, for example, Ramsey, *History of the American Revolution.* Ramsey was a preeminent historian of the revolutionary generation. See P. Smith, "David Ramsey and the Causes of the American Revolution."

17. See, for example, Bancroft, *History of the United States,* vols. 4–7; Trevelyan, *The American Revolution.*

18. M. White, *Social Thought in America.*

19. See, for example, Becker, *History of Political Parties in the Province of New York;* Beard, *An Economic Interpretation of the Constitution;* Parrington, *Main Currents in American Thought,* vol. 1; Schlesinger, *The Colonial Merchants and the American Revolution.*

20. The progressives were not without their critics, even during the height of their influence. For example, the "imperial" school criticized them for focusing too narrowly on life within the colonies. Instead, these critics maintained, the Revolution could be understood only within the context of the empire as a whole. See, for example, Namier, *England in the Age of the American Revolution.*

21. See, for example, Hartz, *The Liberal Tradition in America;* E. S. Morgan and H. M. Morgan, *The Stamp Act Crisis.*

22. The progressives also emphasized Locke's influence. They, however, focused solely on Locke's discussions of private property and conflicting material interests, a focus that, I argue below, is too narrow.

23. See, for example, Bailyn, *The Ideological Origins of the American Revolution;* Pocock, *The Machiavellian Moment;* Wood, *The Creation of the American Republic.* Although Bailyn, Pocock, and Wood are generally credited with beginning the revisionism in early American historiography, Clinton Rossiter actually initiated the movement against the hegemonic influence of Lockean liberalism. See Rossiter, *Seedtime of the Republic* (noting the additional influences of Hebraic, Christian, and classical traditions).

24. By referring to Bailyn, Pocock, and Wood as "revisionists" I do not mean to

be disparaging in any way. I use the term simply for ease of expression and because it is so widely employed in the literature.

25. Dworetz, *The Unvarnished Doctrine*, 12.

26. Becker, *The Declaration of Independence*, 27.

27. Hartz, *The Liberal Tradition in America*, 140. Many other scholars reached a similar conclusion. Merle Curti, for instance, contended, "It is scarcely too much to say, even when the importance of other thinkers is taken into account, that Locke was America's philosopher during the Revolutionary period." Curti, *Probing Our Past*, 69–70. Locke's influence on the Founding is still emphasized in basic textbooks on American government. See, for example, J. Q. Wilson, *American Government*, 26.

28. Shalhope, "Toward a Republican Synthesis," 51.

29. Wood, *The Radicalism of the American Revolution*, 96.

30. Kramnick, *Republicanism and Bourgeois Radicalism*, 35. Some scholars are beginning to reconsider the revisionist historiography. In addition to Kramnick, see, for example, Diggins, *The Lost Soul of American Politics;* Dworetz, *The Unvarnished Doctrine;* Pangle, *The Spirit of Modern Republicanism.*

31. Bailyn, *The Origins of American Politics*, ix–x, 41.

32. Wood, *The Creation of the American Republic*, 53, 58. In *The Radicalism of the American Revolution*, Wood sometimes refers to this concept as "the general will," an antiliberal concept if there ever was one. See, for example, Wood, *The Radicalism of the American Revolution*, 189. The "general will" is, of course, a term made famous by Rousseau. See generally Rousseau, *The Social Contract and Discourses.*

33. Wood, *The Creation of the American Republic*, 54. Recently, Wood appears to be attempting to "rewrite" his original work in the face of growing criticism of the revisionists' rejection of the substantive influence of Lockean liberalism on the American Revolution. See, for example, Wood, Afterword (arguing that the revolutionary period is best characterized as "liberal-republican," rather than as simply "republican" or "liberal"). Although the next logical step for the literature to take is to claim that the dichotomy between republicanism and liberalism in the political thought of the American Revolution is false, it is extremely difficult to argue that the masterworks of Bailyn, Pocock, and Wood make this claim. See Banning, "The Republican Interpretation." Moreover, Wood's most recent book on the Revolution reaffirms his original republican thesis. See Wood, *The Radicalism of the American Revolution.* Lastly, and most importantly, the larger question remains: Whatever happened to the Declaration of Independence? As this section shows, neglecting the Declaration is a curious oversight, to say the least.

34. Letter from Samuel Adams for the Massachusetts House of Representatives to Lieutenant Governor Hutchinson, August 3, 1770, in *The Writings of Samuel Adams*, vol. 2, 22.

35. See, for example, Bailyn, ed., *Pamphlets of the American Revolution*, 23.

36. Pocock, "Virtue and Commerce in the Eighteenth Century," 134.
37. Pocock, *The Machiavellian Moment*, 424, 506, 509, 545.
38. Pocock, *Politics, Language, and Time*, 144. Like Wood, Pocock appears to be backing away from his strong anti-Lockean statements about the character of the American Revolution. See, for example, Pocock, *"The Machiavellian Moment* Revisited," 53 (maintaining that *The Machiavellian Moment* was a "tunnel history" pursuing a "single theme" to the "partial exclusion of parallel phenomena"). As noted earlier, Pocock's seminal work does not support his more recent characterizations of it.
39. In a persuasive essay, Ronald Hamoway argues that the revisionists' extensive reliance on *Cato's Letters* to make their case that the Founders were republicans is seriously flawed, because those letters are themselves Lockean on the essential principles of government. See Hamoway, *"Cato's Letters,* John Locke, and the Republican Paradigm."
40. See Wills, *Inventing America.* There are other non-Lockean interpretations of the American Revolution, albeit less widely followed than the republican and Scottish interpretations. See, for example, Reid, *Constitutional History of the American Revolution* (reducing everything to common-law ideas).
41. Pangle, *The Spirit of Modern Republicanism*, 37.
42. Horwitz, "Republicanism and Liberalism in American Constitutional Thought," 70 (characterizing the republicans as more hierarchial than the Scots).
43. Wills, *Inventing America*, 175, 189. In *The Radicalism of the American Revolution*, published twenty-three years after *The Creation of the American Republic*, Wood appears to move to a more Scottish conception of virtue—a "modern virtue" as Wood calls it—based on "love and benevolence." See Wood, *The Radicalism of the American Revolution*, 213–25. Wood claims that classical virtue, with its emphasis on educating the people to sacrifice their private interests for those of the public good, proved too difficult for the Founders.
44. Wills, *Inventing America*, 239.
45. See, for example, Pocock, *Virtue, Commerce, and History*, chap. 4; Pocock, *Politics, Language, and Time*, chaps. 3, 4.
46. See Bailyn, *The Ideological Origins of the American Revolution*, 155 ("The enumeration of conspiratorial efforts . . . forms the substance of the Declaration of Independence"). See also Bailyn, *The Origins of American Politics*, 12. John Phillip Reid likewise focuses on the list of grievances against the king. Reid characterizes the Declaration's preceding statement of political philosophy as "rhetoric." Reid, *Constitutional History of the American Revolution*, 5, 91.
47. Diggins, *The Lost Soul of American Politics*, 37. In an appendix, Diggins cleverly rewrites the Declaration of Independence using republican concepts and language. See ibid., 364–65. This device shows the seriousness of the revisionists' neglect of Jefferson's Declaration.

48. Letter from Thomas Jefferson to James Madison, August 30, 1823, in *The Works of Thomas Jefferson*, vol. 12, 307. See also Becker, *The Declaration of Independence*, 27 ("The Declaration, in its form, in its phraseology, follows closely certain sentences in Locke's second treatise on government").
49. Locke, *Second Treatise*, secs. 95, 87.
50. See Wills, *Inventing America*, 240–55.
51. See Locke, *An Essay concerning Human Understanding*, vol. 1, bk. 1, 342, 345, 348, 355.
52. Levy, "Property as a Human Right," 174–75.
53. Locke, *Second Treatise*, secs. 173, 123.
54. Ibid., sec. 6.
55. See Adler and Gorman, *The American Testament*, 38.
56. The emphasis here, and to follow, is mine.
57. Locke, *Second Treatise*, sec. 104.
58. Ibid., sec. 222.
59. Ibid., sec. 230.
60. Ibid., sec. 225.
61. Becker, *The Declaration of Independence*, 198.
62. Sheldon, *The Political Philosophy of Thomas Jefferson*, 42.
63. Letter from Thomas Jefferson to James Madison, August 30, 1823, in *The Works of Thomas Jefferson*, vol. 12, 307.
64. Letter from Thomas Jefferson to Richard Henry Lee, May 8, 1825, in *The Writings of Thomas Jefferson*, vol. 16, 118–19. Jefferson considered Locke one of the three greatest men who ever lived (the other two were Isaac Newton and Francis Bacon). See Letter from Thomas Jefferson to John Trumbull, February 15, 1789, in *The Portable Thomas Jefferson*, 434–35. In addition, the *Second Treatise* occupied a principal place in all of the libraries Jefferson owned throughout the course of his life, from his first as a student to his last in retirement, and all of those in between. Hamoway, "Jefferson and the Scottish Enlightenment," 511–14.
65. Becker, *The Declaration of Independence*, 7.
66. The Declaration of Independence, par. 1.
67. Wood himself acknowledges that "no phrase except 'liberty' was invoked more often by the Revolutionaries than 'the public good,'" yet he somehow manages to conclude that the public good was the goal of the American Revolution—a conclusion that seems inconsistent with his own characterization of the evidence. See Wood, *The Creation of the American Republic*, 55.
68. Reid also fails to appreciate the importance of intellectual leadership in the movement toward independence. See Reid, *Constitutional History of the American Revolution*.
69. Webking, *The American Revolution and the Politics of Liberty*, xi, 13.
70. See, for example, Lutz, "The Relative Influence of European Writers on Late Eighteenth-Century American Political Thought" (employing a citation count to show how widely read the Founders were).

71. Will, "Person of the Millennium."
72. See, for example, Boorstin, *The Lost World of Thomas Jefferson*; Chinard, *Thomas Jefferson*; Koch, *The Philosophy of Thomas Jefferson*.
73. See Sheldon, *The Political Philosophy of Thomas Jefferson*, 2 (arguing that "Jefferson's political philosophy was a rich constellation of theoretical qualities from several traditions").
74. In *The Portable Thomas Jefferson*, 1–21.
75. Letter from Thomas Jefferson to Thomas Mann Randolph, May 30, 1790, in *The Writings of Thomas Jefferson*, vol. 8, 31.
76. Letter from Thomas Jefferson to John Norvell, June 11, 1807, in ibid., vol. 11, 222–23.
77. Although Sidney often alluded to the importance of virtue in his writings, it was always in the context of helping to secure natural rights. See, for example, Sidney, *Discourses concerning Government*, 23, 112, 151, 242. I have more to say about the connection between cultivating virtue and securing natural rights in my discussions of the political thought of Samuel Adams and John Adams.
78. See, for example, Hellenbrand, *The Unfinished Revolution*, 164; Meyers, ed., *The Mind of the Founder*, 347–50 (discussing February 1825 correspondence between Jefferson and Madison on the University of Virginia's curriculum).
79. Transcript of the Minutes of the Board of Visitors of the University of Virginia, during the Rectorship of Thomas Jefferson, March 4, 1825, in *The Writings of Thomas Jefferson*, vol. 19, 460–61.
80. See, for example, Letter from John Adams to William Tudor, June 1, 1818, in *The Works of John Adams*, vol. 10, 317 ("I sincerely believe Mr. Otis to have been the earliest and the principal founder of one of the greatest political revolutions that ever occurred among men").
81. See Webking, *The American Revolution and the Politics of Liberty*, 20.
82. James Otis, *The Rights of the British Colonies Asserted and Proved* (1764), in Bailyn, ed., *Pamphlets of the American Revolution*, 419, 425 (emphasis in original).
83. Letter from John Adams to William Tudor, April 5, 1818, in *The Works of John Adams*, vol. 10, 310–11.
84. In Bailyn, ed., *Pamphlets of the American Revolution*, 435.
85. Letter from Thomas Jefferson to Waterhouse, 1819, in *Democracy by Thomas Jefferson*, 267.
86. Letter from Samuel Adams for the Massachusetts House of Representatives to Lieutenant Governor Hutchinson, August 3, 1770, in *The Writings of Samuel Adams*, vol. 2, 22.
87. Samuel Adams, *The Rights of the Colonists, a List of Violations of Rights and a Letter of Correspondence*, adopted by the Town of Boston on November 20, 1772, in *The Writings of Samuel Adams*, vol. 2, 354–55.
88. Lewis, *The Grand Incendiary*, 139.
89. See, for example, Wood, *The Creation of the American Republic*, 118.

90. Letter from Samuel Adams to John Scollay, December 30, 1780, in *The Writings of Samuel Adams*, vol. 4, 238 (emphasis in original).
91. Letter from Samuel Adams to Elbridge Gerry, October 29, 1775, in ibid., vol. 3, 231.
92. See Webking, *The American Revolution and the Politics of Liberty*, 75–76.
93. See, for example, Stimson, *The American Revolution in Law*, 128.
94. Scholars like Shannon Stimson and Garry Wills who try to show the influence of the Scottish Enlightenment on the American Founding fail to recognize the Scots' agreement with Locke on the essential principles of political philosophy, especially on the legitimacy of government and the right of resistance. Where the Scots departed from Locke was on epistemology and anthropology. See, for example, Hamoway, "Jefferson and the Scottish Enlightenment," 506–9; Sinopoli, *The Foundations of American Citizenship*, 53–82.
95. Becker, *The Declaration of Independence*, 105–6.
96. In McCloskey, ed., *The Works of James Wilson*, vol. 2, 735. This was an argument first advanced by Benjamin Franklin. See Letter from Benjamin Franklin to William Franklin, March 13, 1768, in *The Life and Writings of Benjamin Franklin*, vol. 5, 115.
97. In McCloskey, ed., *The Works of James Wilson*, vol. 2, 723 (emphasis in original).
98. See Alexander Hamilton, *A Full Vindication of the Measures of Congress* (1774), in *The Papers of Alexander Hamilton*, vol. 1, 47–78.
99. Alexander Hamilton, *The Farmer Refuted* (1775), in ibid., 87–88 (emphasis in original).
100. Ibid., 104.
101. Ibid., 86 ("Apply yourself, without delay, to the study of the law of nature. I would recommend to your perusal Grotius, Pufendorf, Locke, Montesquieu, and Burlamaqui").
102. Wood, *The Creation of the American Republic*, 568.
103. See Webking, *The American Revolution and the Politics of Liberty*, 131.
104. "The happiness of society is the end of government. ... All sober inquirers after truth, ancient and modern, pagan and Christian, have declared that the happiness of man, as well as his dignity, consists in virtue." John Adams, *Thoughts on Government* (1776), in *The Works of John Adams*, vol. 4, 193.
105. See ibid., 194.
106. See Becker, *The Declaration of Independence*, 24.
107. Letter from John Adams to Timothy Pickering, August 6, 1822, in *The Works of John Adams*, vol. 2, 514.
108. The close connection Adams had with the formulation of the political principles articulated in the Declaration of Independence is evinced by Jefferson's submitting his draft to Adams (and Franklin) for approval before submitting it to anyone else. See Letter from Thomas Jefferson to

James Madison, August 30, 1823, in *The Writings of Thomas Jefferson,* vol. 15, 461.

109. In *The Works of John Adams,* vol. 3, 449 (emphasis in original).
110. In ibid., vol. 1, 160.
111. There is certainly room for disagreement about whom to consider an intellectual leader of the American Revolution. Bailyn lists the two Adamses, John Dickinson, and Jefferson. See Bailyn, *The Origins of American Politics,* 12. Webking discusses Otis, Patrick Henry, Dickinson, the two Adamses, and Jefferson. See Webking, *The American Revolution and the Politics of Liberty.* I agree with Webking on the importance of Otis. While not wishing to minimize the importance of Dickinson and Henry, I nevertheless include James Wilson and Alexander Hamilton at the expense of Dickinson and Henry because of the leading role Wilson and Hamilton were to play during the framing and ratification of the Constitution, a connection that is important to my argument that the Framers of the Constitution remained committed to the natural-rights principles of the Declaration of Independence (see chapter 2), and because their significance during the revolutionary period is often overlooked. In any event, Webking competently shows Dickinson's and Henry's dedication to natural-rights principles. See Webking, *The American Revolution and the Politics of Liberty,* 30–60. Indeed, who can forget Henry's cry "Give me liberty, or give me death!" or Dickinson's retort "We . . . are animated by a just love of our invaded rights." Patrick Henry, Speech in the Virginia Convention, March 23, 1775, in McCants, *Patrick Henry, The Orator,* 125; John Dickinson, Address to the Congress of the Inhabitants of Quebec, October 26, 1774, in *The Political Writings of John Dickinson,* vol. 2, 14.
112. See, for example, Bailyn, ed., *Pamphlets of the American Revolution,* 23. See also Reid, *Constitutional History of the American Revolution,* 5, 88, 91. For an attempted demonstration, intriguing, albeit unconvincing, that the *Second Treatise* was itself the propaganda of a "hard-line radical," rather than a systematic study of political philosophy, see Ashcraft, *Revolutionary Politics and Locke's Two Treatises of Government.*
113. See Dunn, "The Politics of Locke in England and America in the Eighteenth Century," 77. Dunn's widely read essay is also widely misunderstood. Contrary to the contention of many revisionists, Dunn does not deny, as the quoted passage suggests, that the *Second Treatise* was of profound relevance to the intellectual leaders of the American Revolution. He simply argues that Locke was expressing a position about the fundamental purpose of government—a position shared by many liberal theorists of the seventeenth and eighteenth centuries—to which the revolutionary leaders had independently arrived. See Dunn, ibid., 79–80.
114. Dworetz, *The Unvarnished Doctrine,* 7. Concluding that Bailyn, Pocock, and Wood have gone too far with their dismissal of Locke's substantive

influence on the American Revolution, some scholars, as noted above, are now arguing for a "liberal-republican" interpretation of the period. Although an improvement over the purely republican interpretation, the emerging liberal-republican reading likewise undervalues the Declaration of Independence. This liberal-republican trend in the literature on the American Revolution is discussed in Klein, Brown, and Hench, eds., *The Republican Synthesis Revisited.* See also Appleby, *Liberalism and Republicanism in the Historical Imagination.*

115. See, for example, Rahe, *Republics Ancient and Modern,* 543–72; R. M. Smith, *Liberalism and American Constitutional Law,* 16.

116. Germino, *Machiavelli to Marx,* 116.

117. My reading of Locke's thought was assisted greatly by A. John Simmons's superb book, *The Lockean Theory of Rights,* which I had the pleasure of reading in both manuscript and final form.

118. Locke, *Second Treatise,* sec. 6.

119. Locke, *Essays on the Law of Nature,* 111.

120. Locke, *An Essay concerning Human Understanding,* vol. 1, bk. 1, chap. 2, sec. 1.

121. Locke was certainly not the only philosopher to employ the notion of self-evident truths. That notion has roots in the ancients. But Locke did contribute markedly to the development of the doctrine, and he was the philosopher to whom the Founders generally deferred on the subject. See M. White, *The Philosophy of the American Revolution,* 11.

122. Simmons disagrees. See Simmons, *The Lockean Theory of Rights,* 55 n. 99. Simmons's interpretation is aimed at overcoming the elitism in Locke's theory.

123. Locke, *Essays on the Law of Nature,* 113–14.

124. Ibid.

125. Locke, *Second Treatise,* secs. 7, 16, 134, 135, 149, 159, 171, 183.

126. See Macpherson, *The Political Theory of Possessive Individualism;* Strauss, *Natural Right and History.* Macpherson provides a Marxist reading of Locke, whereas Strauss characterizes Locke as a sugar-coated version of the purely individualistic Hobbes.

127. Locke, *Essays on the Law of Nature,* 205.

128. Letter from John Locke to Denis Grenville, quoted in Simmons, *The Lockean Theory of Rights,* 53. As Simmons nicely puts it:

> Locke believes that our conduct in a large part of our lives is "up to us," or outside of the realm of required and forbidden actions. ... Doing our duty [to preserve mankind] does not occupy the whole of our lives, but only occasionally limits our conduct. We enjoy a significant sphere of moral liberty within which we can pursue our own (harmless) goals and desires. (Ibid.)

129. See Dunn, *The Political Thought of John Locke;* Tully, *A Discourse on Property.*

130. Other Locke scholars who subscribe to the duty-centered interpretation

include Willmore Kendall. See Kendall, *John Locke and the Doctrine of Majority-Rule.*

131. Richard Cox is among those who agree with the rights-centered reading of Locke's moral philosophy. See Cox, *Locke on War and Peace.*

132. See, for example, Simmons, *The Lockean Theory of Rights,* 69; M. White, *The Philosophy of the American Revolution,* 145–50.

133. Locke, *Second Treatise,* secs. 11, 6.

134. Locke, *Two Treatises of Government, First Treatise,* sec. 42; Locke, *Second Treatise,* secs. 5, 6, 70, 93.

135. Locke, *Second Treatise,* secs. 4–6.

136. Locke, *Two Treatises of Government, First Treatise,* sec. 42 (emphasis in original). See also Locke, *Second Treatise,* secs. 5, 6, 70, 93.

137. Locke, *Second Treatise,* sec. 4.

138. "Though I have said ... that all men are by nature equal, I cannot be supposed to understand all sorts of equality. Age or virtue may give men a just precedence; excellence of parts and merit may place others above the common level." Ibid., sec. 54.

139. Ibid., secs. 54, 2, 16.

140. Ibid., sec. 173. Locke adds elsewhere that property involves individuals "united for the general preservation of their lives, liberties, and estates." Ibid., sec. 123. See also sec. 87.

141. Not to mention that rights often conflict, which also shows they cannot be absolute. See ibid., sec. 183.

142. Simmons, *The Lockean Theory of Rights,* 101.

143. Locke, *Second Treatise,* sec. 23.

144. Locke's doctrine of consent has been much criticized. See, for example, Hume, *Moral and Political Philosophy,* 363; Simmons, *Moral Principles and Political Obligations,* 75–101. Modern political theorists have spent considerable time and energy arguing about whether it is ever possible to say an individual has an obligation to obey the state. Resolution of that debate is beyond the scope of this book. The Founders believed consent was possible, as the Declaration of Independence makes clear.

145. Locke, *Second Treatise,* sec. 119. See also secs. 121–22.

146. Dunn, *The Political Thought of John Locke,* 140–41.

147. Locke, *Second Treatise,* sec. 119.

148. Ibid., secs. 87, 95.

149. Ibid., sec. 96.

150. Locke is, of course, speaking hypothetically.

151. Ibid., sec. 128.

152. See Tully, *A Discourse on Property,* 158.

153. See Locke, *Second Treatise,* secs. 131–32. The flexibility as to the *form* of government that may be established will be of especial importance in part 2, an examination of the Court's role in the American constitutional order.

154. Ibid., sec. 149. See also sec. 222.

155. Ibid., secs. 149, 243.

156. Dunn, *The Political Thought of John Locke*, 28. Note that Locke does not refer to legitimate resistance as "rebellion," an act he views in negative terms. For Locke, it is the government, acting arbitrarily, that has rebelled. Locke, *Second Treatise*, sec. 226. See generally Germino, *Machiavelli to Marx*, 145.
157. Locke, *Second Treatise*, sec. 223. See also sec. 230.
158. Ibid., sec. 168.
159. Ibid., sec. 225. See also secs. 208–10. Mere accidental government incompetence is not grounds for resistance. Ibid., sec. 225.
160. Richards, *Foundations of American Constitutionalism*, 136.
161. Locke, *Second Treatise*, secs. 222, 243.
162. See, for example, M. White, *The Philosophy of the American Revolution*, 229.
163. Locke, *Second Treatise*, sec. 168 (emphasis supplied). See also secs. 208, 228, 230, 241.
164. An individual, like the community as a whole, will be slow to resist.
165. Ibid., sec. 209.
166. Ibid., sec. 205 ("It being safer for the body that some few should be sometimes in danger to suffer than that the head of the republic should be easily and upon slight occasions exposed").
167. Becker, *The Declaration of Independence*, 18.
168. The Declaration of Independence, par. 2.
169. The "laws of nature and of nature's God" is actually a *philosophical* concept found in the preamble of the Declaration of Independence, rather than in the section that addresses issues of *political* philosophy (the second paragraph). As it does for Locke, this natural-law philosophy provides the foundation—the "basis"—for the Founders' natural-rights political philosophy.
170. M. White, *The Philosophy of the American Revolution*, 98 (emphasis in original).
171. In *The Portable Thomas Jefferson*, 10. Several of Jefferson's postrevolutionary writings likewise reference moral sense as a source of moral knowledge. See, for example, Letter from Thomas Jefferson to Maria Cosway, October 12, 1786, in ibid., 400–412; Letter from Thomas Jefferson to Peter Carr, August 10, 1787, in ibid., 423–28.
172. Accordingly, Garry Wills's claim that, in the Declaration of Independence, Jefferson relied upon the moral-sense theory of the Scottish Enlightenment, rather than upon Locke's theory of moral rationalism, must be rejected. See Wills, *Inventing America*, 167–258. It was earlier pointed out that James Wilson was an adherent of the moral-sense epistemology of the Scottish Enlightenment. However, the Declaration of Independence, a document signed by Wilson, is not. See generally M. White, *The Philosophy of the American Revolution*, 11 (arguing that the Declaration of Independence incorporates Locke's theory of knowledge).
173. In *The Papers of Thomas Jefferson*, vol. 2, 526–27.

174. See, for example, Letter from Thomas Jefferson to John Adams, 1813, in *Democracy by Thomas Jefferson*, 126–27.
175. See *The Works of John Adams*, vol. 1, 195, vol. 3, 457, vol. 4, 259.
176. M. White, *The Philosophy of the American Revolution*, 48. White concludes that "whatever the admirable features of the philosophical ideas advocated in the Revolutionary era might have been, . . . a faith in all of the people was not one of them." Ibid., 267.
177. Locke, *Second Treatise*, sec. 54.
178. Garry Wills claims that Lincoln changed, in the Gettysburg Address, the meaning of the Declaration's conception of equality. According to Wills, Jefferson was simply arguing that the king had no right to govern America. He was not suggesting that equality should be a goal of American domestic policy. See Wills, *Lincoln at Gettysburg*. As in his specific work on the Declaration of Independence, Wills fails to account for Locke's influence on the Declaration. Wills's interpretation of Lincoln's role in the development of the American idea of equality is therefore provocative, but unconvincing. In addition, as I show in the text, Wills misinterprets Lincoln's conception of equality.
179. Abraham Lincoln, "Speech on the Dred Scott Decision at Springfield, Illinois," June 26, 1857, in *Abraham Lincoln: Speeches and Writings*, vol. 1, 398 (emphasis in original). See generally Diamond, "The Declaration and the Constitution," 48.
180. Abraham Lincoln, "Speech at Independence Hall, Philadelphia, Pennsylvania," February 22, 1861, in *Abraham Lincoln: Speeches and Writings*, vol. 2, 213.
181. Locke, *Second Treatise*, secs. 50, 34.
182. Ibid., sec. 42.
183. Ibid., secs. 7, 16, 134, 135, 149, 159, 171, 183 (emphasis supplied).
184. I explained above why "the pursuit of happiness" was substituted in the Declaration of Independence for "property" in its articulation of the Lockean trinity.
185. Ibid., secs. 6, 16.
186. Ibid.
187. Ibid., secs. 3, 6.
188. See generally Berlin, *Four Essays on Liberty*, 118–72.
189. Locke, *Second Treatise*, sec. 54.
190. Henry Steele Commager goes so far as to say that the eighteenth century was about the secular "religion of happiness." Commager, *Jefferson, Nationalism, and the Enlightenment*, 93.
191. In *The Works of John Adams*, vol. 4, 193.
192. See the 1780 Massachusetts Constitution written by Adams, in Poore, *Federal and State Constitutions*, vol. 1, 956–73.
193. "That all men . . . have certain inherent rights . . . [including] pursuing and obtaining happiness." In ibid., vol. 2, 1908.
194. In *The Writings of George Washington*, vol. 8, 440–41.

195. I therefore disagree with White's contention that replacing the word "ends" in Jefferson's rough draft with the word "rights" in the final version of the Declaration of Independence "might have altered the fundamental purpose of government as Jefferson conceived it." M. White, *The Philosophy of the American Revolution*, 250. According to White, Jefferson's rough draft supports my interpretation that an individual sometimes has legitimate claims on others, and on organized society and government, to strive to attain his happiness, but the final version does not (with the final version standing for no more than a commitment to making rights secure against invasion).

196. Commager's statement that the Founders sought "freedom from ... the superstition of the church" wrongly implies that they were antireligion. The Founders were not antireligion; they simply wished to leave religion to each individual's private conscience, free from state pressure. The classic statements of this position are by Thomas Jefferson, Virginia Bill for Establishing Religious Freedom, in *The Portable Thomas Jefferson*, 251–53, and by James Madison, *Memorial and Remonstrance against Religious Assessments*, in *The Writings of James Madison*, vol. 2, 183–91.

197. Commager, *Jefferson, Nationalism, and the Enlightenment*, 89.

198. Diamond, "The Declaration and the Constitution," 49 (emphasis supplied and omitted). Harry Jaffa is an example of those criticized by Diamond. See, for example, Jaffa, *How to Think about the American Revolution*, 75–140. As is evident from the Introduction, Edwin Meese, Robert Bork, Chief Justice William Rehnquist, and many other contemporary conservatives share Jaffa's emphasis on majority-rule democracy.

199. Diamond, "The Declaration and the Constitution," 50.

200. It is again important to keep in mind the distinction between a republican *form of government* and a republican *political philosophy*.

Notes to Chapter 2

1. Beard, *An Economic Interpretation of the Constitution*.
2. See, for example, Brown, *Charles Beard and the Constitution*; McDonald, *E Pluribus Unum*; McDonald, *We the People*.
3. There is still some sympathy for Beard's thesis. See, for example, Nedelsky, *Private Property and the Limits of American Constitutionalism*.
4. Morris, *The Forging of the Union*.
5. Greene, *Peripheries and Center*.
6. McDonald, *Novus Ordo Seclorum*.
7. Sunstein, "Beyond the Republican Revival." See also Ackerman, *We the People*; Michelman, "Law's Republic"; Sunstein, *The Partial Constitution*. For a critical assessment of the republic revival, see Gerber, "The Republican Revival in American Constitutional Theory."
8. Onuf, "Reflections on the Founding," 365. See also Lutz, *A Preface to*

American Political Theory, 42–43 (explaining that it is necessary to examine materials like those discussed in this chapter to understand the Constitution—an "incomplete text").

9. Here, my disagreement with the Straussians' approach to interpreting the
   texts of the American Founding is manifested. See generally Wood, *The
   Fundamentalists and the Constitution* (describing the Straussians' aver-
   sion to reading texts in historical context).

10. *Van Horne's Lessee v. Dorrance,* 2 U.S. (2 Dall.) 304, 308 (1795).

11. The Declaration of Independence, preamble.

12. The difference between means and ends in constitutional theory was well
    appreciated by Locke. "Politics contains two parts very different the one
    from the other," Locke writes, "the one containing the origin of societies
    and the rise and extent of political power, the other, the art of governing
    men in society"—with the *Second Treatise* being primarily concerned with
    the former. Locke, "Some Thoughts concerning Reading and Study for a
    Gentleman," in *The Educational Writings of John Locke,* 400. As has been
    shown in detail elsewhere, the Framers turned for assistance to Montes-
    quieu, Hume, and Blackstone, among others, rather than to Locke, when
    dealing with issues of institutional design. See, for example, Lutz, "The
    Relative Influence of European Writers on Late Eighteenth-Century Ameri-
    can Political Thought" (employing a citation count to identify the Framers'
    influences).

13. Historians have long disagreed about the relationship between the Declara-
    tion of Independence and the Constitution. For years, Merrill Jensen was
    the leading proponent of the view that there was a philosophical break
    between the revolutionary period and the constitutional period. See Jensen,
    The Articles of Confederation. Perhaps the most surprising statement op-
    posing a continuity thesis was made by Carl Becker in *The Declaration of
    Independence.* There, Becker, who made the definitive connection between
    the ideas of the Declaration and Locke's *Second Treatise* (see chapter 1),
    asserted that "in few if any of the constitutions now in force, do we find
    the natural rights doctrine of the eighteenth century reaffirmed—*not even,
    where we should perhaps most expect it, in the Constitution of the United
    States."* Becker, *The Declaration of Independence,* 234 (emphasis sup-
    plied). Becker, like Jensen, contended that the natural-rights principles of
    the Declaration of Independence are absent in the Constitution because
    the Framers wanted to avoid the radical implications of those principles.
    Those disagreeing with Jensen's and Becker's (and Beard's, among oth-
    ers) position included Edmund Morgan and Benjamin Wright. See E. S.
    Morgan, *The Birth of a Republic;* Wright, *Consensus and Continuity.*
    Gordon Wood is the leading contemporary proponent of the view that
    there was a break between the philosophical tenets of the revolutionary
    period and the constitutional period. See Wood, *The Creation of the Ameri-
    can Republic.* According to Wood, the revolutionary period was republican
    and the constitutional period was liberal. In response to Wood, much

contemporary historical debate centers on when and how the alleged classical republican principles of the American Revolution were supplanted by the liberal principles of modern America.

14. In chapter 1 I rejected the prevailing scholarly view that the American Revolution was inspired by classical republican concerns. As is the case with the scholarship on the American Revolution, some scholars are beginning to argue that the Constitution is best characterized as "liberal-republican." See, for example, Ackerman, *We the People;* Belz, Hoffman, and Albert, eds., *To Form a More Perfect Union;* Sinopoli, *The Foundations of American Citizenship;* Sunstein, *The Partial Constitution.* This chapter endeavors to show that with regard to the basic purpose of government, the Constitution is Lockean liberal.

15. Farrand, *The Framing of the Constitution of the United States,* 197.

16. Speech by James Wilson in the Pennsylvania Ratifying Convention, December 4, 1787, in Jensen, Kaminski, and Saladino, eds., *Documentary History of the Ratification of the Constitution,* vol. 2, 472–73.

17. U.S. Constitution, preamble. Hereafter, quotations from the Constitution's preamble will follow modern capitalization.

18. See *Jacobson v. Massachusetts,* 197 U.S. 11, 22 (1905); See generally Himmelfarb, "The Preamble in Constitutional Interpretation."

19. Adler, *We Hold These Truths,* 129–30.

20. Farrand, ed., *Records of the Federal Convention,* vol. 2, 137 (remarks of Edmund Randolph) (emphasis omitted).

21. In *The Papers of James Madison,* vol. 9, 354. See generally O'Brien, "The Framers' Muse on Republicanism, the Supreme Court, and Pragmatic Constitutional Interpretivism," 124–31 ("According to Madison, the denial of individual rights by legislative majorities was at the root of the crisis in republicanism in the 1780s").

22. See, for example, Brennan, "The Constitution of the United States."

23. D. F. Epstein, "The Political Theory of the Constitution," 82–83 (emphasis in original). See also Kramnick, *Republicanism and Bourgeois Radicalism,* 265 ("The commitment in the preamble to the Constitution to 'establish justice' meant for the framers that it would protect private rights").

24. Farrand, ed., *Records of the Federal Convention,* vol. 1, 134 (remarks of James Madison).

25. *The Federalist* no. 41, 257–58 (James Madison).

26. Ibid., no. 10, 78 (James Madison).

27. M. White, *Philosophy, The Federalist, and the Constitution,* 211 (emphasis in original).

28. Recall, for instance, Madison's remarks during the federal Convention: "the necessity of providing more effectually for the security of private rights, and the steady dispensation of Justice. Interferences with these were evils which had *more perhaps than any thing else* produced this convention." Farrand, ed., *Records of the Federal Convention,* vol. 1, 134 (emphasis supplied). The Framers were also concerned with, among other things,

conducting better foreign policy and more effectively administering an increasingly large territory. See Morris, *The Forging of the Union*; Greene, *Peripheries and Center*.

29. See M. White, *Philosophy, The Federalist, and the Constitution*, 211.

30. See Locke, *Second Treatise*, sec. 130. See also Locke, *Two Treatises of Government, First Treatise*, sec. 92:

> Government being for the Preservation of every Mans Right and Property, by preserving him from the Violence or Injury of others, is for the good of the Governed. For the Magistrates Sword being for a Terror to Evil Doers, and by that Terror to inforce Men to observe the positive Laws of the Society, made conformable to the Laws of Nature, for the *public good, i.e. the good of every particular Member of that Society*, as far as by common Rules, it can be provided for. (Emphasis supplied and omitted)

31. *The Federalist* no. 43, 279 (James Madison).

32. Jefferson thought it contrary to natural rights to make a "perpetual constitution." For Jefferson, the Constitution should be updated by each generation. See Letter from Thomas Jefferson to James Madison, September 6, 1789, in *The Portable Thomas Jefferson*, 449. See also Letter from Thomas Jefferson to Samuel Kercheval, July 12, 1816, in ibid., 558–61. Madison, among others, disagreed with Jefferson on this point. See Letter from James Madison to Thomas Jefferson, February 4, 1790, in *The Papers of Thomas Jefferson*, vol. 16, 147–50 (rejecting Jefferson's argument on Lockean tacit-consent grounds, as well as because frequent institutional change would render natural rights insecure).

33. See Hoffert, *A Politics of Tensions*, chap. 4; Jensen, *The Articles of Confederation*, xiii, xxiii, 245.

34. See Rakove, *The Beginnings of National Politics*, 183–91.

35. See Billias, "The Declaration of Independence," 47–48; Mahoney, "The Declaration of Independence as a Constitutional Document," 67–68.

36. Farrand, ed., *Records of the Federal Convention*, vol. 1, 425 (remarks of Elbridge Gerry).

37. Ibid., 48 (remarks of Elbridge Gerry).

38. Ibid., 49, vol. 2, 119 (remarks of George Mason).

39. Ibid., vol. 2, 124, vol. 1, 135 (remarks of James Madison).

40. Letter from James Madison to George Washington, April 16, 1787, in *The Papers of James Madison*, vol. 9, 384. Compare Locke, *Second Treatise*, sec. 87.

41. Farrand, ed., *Records of the Federal Convention*, vol. 1, 147 (remarks of Roger Sherman).

42. Ibid., vol. 2, 137 (remarks of Edmund Randolph) (emphasis omitted).

43. Ibid., 222 (remarks of Gouverneur Morris) (emphasis supplied). Of course, Morris lost this debate. The tension between the concept of equality embodied in the Declaration of Independence and the guarantees to slavery in the Constitution is addressed in chapter 5.

44. Ibid., vol. 1, 440 (remarks of Robert Yates). Other delegates who made express reference to natural-rights political philosophy during the Convention include Alexander Hamilton, Rufus King, and Luther Martin. See ibid., 324, 437, 477, 493.

45. The fact that the Constitution was submitted to the people for ratification displays the Framers' commitment to the Lockean liberal doctrine of consent. See Richards, *Foundations of American Constitutionalism*, 104.

46. [Mercy Otis Warren], *Observations on the New Constitution* (1788), in Ford, ed., *Pamphlets on the Constitution of the United States*, 13. Warren's pamphlet has been wrongly attributed to Elbridge Gerry. See Billias, *Elbridge Gerry*, 214–15, 394–95 (discussing the error in attribution).

47. Luther Martin, *Letter to the Citizens of Maryland*, March 21, 1788, in Ford, ed., *Essays on the Constitution of the United States*, 364–65.

48. George Mason, *Objections to the Proposed Federal Constitution*, in Ford, ed., *Pamphlets on the Constitution of the United States*, 329.

49. See, for example, Kaminski, "Restoring the Declaration of Independence," 145. See generally Storing, *What the Anti-Federalists Were For* (providing the classic analysis of the Antifederalists' often contradictory positions).

50. Letter from Thomas Jefferson to James Madison, December 20, 1787, in *The Portable Thomas Jefferson*, 430.

51. James Wilson, "Speech on the Federal Constitution, delivered in Philadelphia," October 4, 1787, in Ford, ed., *Pamphlets on the Constitution of the United States*, 156.

52. Farrand, ed., *Records of the Federal Convention*, vol. 3, 143 (remarks of James Wilson). In a powerful reply to Wilson's ratifying-convention speeches opposing a bill of rights, delegate John Smilie read the Declaration of Independence to the Pennsylvania convention and then demanded a bill of rights based on those natural-rights principles. See John Smilie, Speech in the Pennsylvania Ratifying Convention, November 28, 1787, in Kurland and Lerner, ed., *The Founders' Constitution*, vol. 1, 455–56.

53. James Madison, "Speech in the Virginia Convention," June 25, 1788, in *The Writings of James Madison*, vol. 5, 231.

54. *The Federalist* no. 84, 513 (Alexander Hamilton).

55. Ibid., 515 (emphasis in original).

56. An obvious problem with the Federalists' argument, which they were never able to overcome, was that the proposed Constitution already reserved several rights, most notably the writ of habeas corpus. As Jefferson succinctly remarked, the Federalists' argument was "a gratis dictum, opposed by strong inferences from the body of the instrument." Letter from Thomas Jefferson to James Madison, December 20, 1787, in *The Portable Thomas Jefferson*, 429.

57. In Meyers, ed., *The Mind of the Founder*, 175. For a less benevolent interpretation of Madison's motives for securing the Bill of Rights, see Levy, *Original Intent and the Framers' Constitution*, 164–75 (arguing that

Madison's chief objective was to thwart the Antifederalists' attempts to call a second constitutional convention).

58. Storing, "The Constitution and the Bill of Rights," 32.
59. Murphy, "The Art of Constitutional Interpretation," 140.
60. See U.S. Constitution, art. 6 (requiring state judges to enforce the federal Constitution). Although many, including some of those sympathetic to a substantive reading of the ninth amendment, argue that the ninth amendment, like amendments 1 through 8, was *not* originally intended to apply to the states, I disagree. I disagree because, as I explain below, the Framers believed there are certain rights—natural rights—beyond the power of any legitimate government, federal or state, to invade. The possibility of incorporating the ninth amendment to the states through the fourteenth amendment has mooted this question on the original reach of the ninth amendment for most scholars. Compare Patterson, *The Forgotten Ninth Amendment*, 36–43 (contending that the ninth amendment has always been applicable to the states), with Barnett, "James Madison's Ninth Amendment," 47–48 (maintaining that the ninth amendment did not originally apply to the states).
61. The ninth amendment was reawakened in the privacy case *Griswold v. Connecticut* (1965), particularly in Justice Arthur Goldberg's concurring opinion. Chapter 5 discusses the *Griswold* case in detail.
62. U.S. Constitution, amend. 9.
63. In Meyers, ed., *The Mind of the Founder*, 171. The argument to which Madison refers is that of James Wilson (discussed above). Initially opposed to a bill of rights to the Constitution, Madison was eventually persuaded by Jefferson of its importance. See, for example, Letter from Thomas Jefferson to James Madison, March 15, 1789, in *The Portable Thomas Jefferson*, 438–40.
64. Berger's and Bork's argument has been adopted by a host of commentators, most of whom, like Berger and Bork themselves, are politically conservative. See, for example, Cooper, "Limited Government and Individual Liberty"; McAffee, "The Original Meaning of the Ninth Amendment." I have more to say below about the connection between conservatism and opposition to a substantive reading of the ninth amendment. A few conservatives do look to the ninth amendment for a grant of unenumerated rights. See, for example, Macedo, *Liberal Virtues*, 57, 173, 187–88.
65. Berger, "The Ninth Amendment," 8; Bork, *The Tempting of America*, 185.
66. Barnett, "James Madison's Ninth Amendment," 12–13.
67. Letter from James Madison to Thomas Jefferson, October 17, 1788, in *The Writings of James Madison*, vol. 5, 271–72.
68. See, for example, Berger, "The Ninth Amendment," 3. Even scholars claiming that the ninth amendment has independent substantive content maintain that Madison's letter to Washington suggests otherwise. See, for example, Barnett, "James Madison's Ninth Amendment," 18–19.

69. Letter from James Madison to George Washington, December 5, 1789, in *The Writings of James Madison*, vol. 5, 431.
70. Ibid., 432.
71. U.S. Constitution, amend. 10 (emphasis supplied).
72. Morton, "John Locke, Robert Bork, Natural Rights, and the Interpretation of the Constitution," 751–55.
73. In an interesting twist on Berger's and Bork's argument, historian James Hutson declares that it is "ludicrous" to believe that the Bill of Rights, including the ninth amendment, protects natural rights, because the Constitution "was created not by individuals leaving a state of nature but by the people acting collectively through their state governments." According to Hutson, "individual natural rights were the concern of the states." Hutson, "The Bill of Rights and the American Revolutionary Experience," 89–95. Hutson's reading of the Bill of Rights has at least three problems. First, as the opening words of the preamble, "We the People," suggest, the Framers emphasized, in Lockean fashion, that the Constitution was created by the people, not by the states. Second, as is discussed throughout this chapter, the Framers were gravely concerned about the violations of natural rights occurring in the states and, therefore, did not want to leave rights solely to state protection. Third, as this chapter ultimately endeavors to show, the Framers remained committed during the constitutional period to the concept of government articulated in the Declaration of Independence: that all legitimate governments, including the federal government, exist chiefly to secure natural rights.
74. Grey, "Do We Have an Unwritten Constitution?" 715–16. See also Corwin, *The "Higher Law" Background of American Constitutional Law*, 5 (arguing that the ninth amendment illustrates the Framers' commitment to natural-rights doctrine "perfectly"); Kaminski, "Restoring the Declaration of Independence," 144 (maintaining that the ninth amendment was intended to secure "the self-evident truths of the Declaration of Independence"); Patterson, *The Forgotten Ninth Amendment*, 20 (same).
75. In Meyers, ed., *The Mind of the Founder*, 168.
76. The importance of natural rights in the Bill of Rights is also reflected in the only original draft of the Bill of Rights known to exist. The draft is written in Roger Sherman's hand. The second numbered paragraph reads as follows:

> 2. The people have certain natural rights which are retained by them when they enter into Society, Such are the rights of Conscience in matters of religion; of acquiring property and of pursuing happiness & Safety; of Speaking, writing and publishing their Sentiments with decency and freedom; of peaceably assembling to consult their common good, and of applying to Government by petition or remonstrance for redress of grievances. Of these rights therefore they Shall not be deprived by the Government of the united States. (Reprinted in Barnett, ed., *The Rights Retained by the People*, vol. 1, 351)

Sherman served with Madison on the committee assigned to draft the Bill of Rights. See generally Gerber, "Roger Sherman and the Bill of Rights."

77. For example, Berger writes that "Justice Goldberg would transform the ninth amendment into a bottomless well in which the judiciary can dip for the formation of undreamed of 'rights' in their limitless discretion, a possibility the Founders would have rejected out of hand." Berger, "The Ninth Amendment," 2.

78. Bickel, *The Least Dangerous Branch*, 18.

79. See generally Chemerinsky, "The Vanishing Constitution," 74–75; O'Brien, "The Framers' Muse on Republicanism, the Supreme Court, and Pragmatic Constitutional Interpretivism," 119–31.

80. See James Madison, *Vices of the Political System of the United States* (1787), in *The Papers of James Madison*, vol. 9, 345; *The Federalist* no. 10, 77–84 (James Madison); ibid., no. 51, 320–25 (James Madison).

81. Public-law scholars should, however, avoid relying *exclusively* on *The Federalist* for discerning the Framers' intent. See, for example, Ackerman, *We the People* (employing an originalist methodology, but relying exclusively on *The Federalist*). See generally Gerber, Review of *We the People*, by Bruce A. Ackerman (noting the methodological problems of relying exclusively on *The Federalist*).

82. See Wills, *Explaining America*.

83. See D. F. Epstein, *The Political Theory of the Federalist*.

84. See Diamond, "Democracy and *The Federalist*," in *As Far as Republican Principles Will Admit*, 27–30; Pangle, *The Spirit of Modern Republicanism*.

85. See M. White, *Philosophy, The Federalist, and the Constitution*, 227.

86. Letter from Thomas Jefferson to Thomas Mann Randolph, May 30, 1790, in *The Writings of Thomas Jefferson*, vol. 8, 31; Locke, "Some Thoughts concerning Reading and Study for a Gentleman," in *The Educational Writings of John Locke*, 400.

87. *The Federalist* no. 2, 37 (John Jay). Jay's contribution to *The Federalist* was limited by illness. Jay wrote five papers, Madison twenty-six, and Hamilton fifty-one. Three papers were a collaboration between Madison and Hamilton. Rossiter, Introduction to *The Federalist*, xi (citing the work of Douglass Adair).

88. *The Federalist* no. 40, 252–53 (James Madison) (emphasis omitted).

89. See M. White, *Philosophy, The Federalist, and the Constitution*, 261 n. 1; Sinopoli, *The Foundations of American Citizenship*, 89.

90. *The Federalist* no. 37, 227 (James Madison).

91. Madison advances a Lockean characterization of the state of nature and why men establish government in *The Federalist* no. 51. Echoing Jay's remarks in no. 2, Madison notes that in the state of nature even "the stronger individuals are prompted, by the uncertainty of their condition, to submit to a government which may protect the weak as well as themselves." Ibid., no. 51, 324–25. In essence, what Madison is doing in no. 51 is

developing an analogy so that he can persuade his audience—especially those comprising majority factions—that it is in their self-interest to adopt the Constitution's scheme of an extended federal republic. M. White, *Philosophy, The Federalist, and the Constitution*, 27–28. It should not go unnoticed that Madison chooses as the basis for his analogy the Lockean theory of government embodied in the Declaration of Independence.

92. *The Federalist* no. 10, 77–78 (James Madison) (emphasis supplied). *The Federalist* no. 10 is also illuminating because of the Lockean conception of property Madison adopts there (see chapters 1 and 5). Madison argues that an unequal distribution of property is natural because of the "different and unequal faculties of acquiring property" with which individuals are endowed. Ibid., 78.

93. Ibid., no. 14, 104–5 (James Madison).

94. Ibid., no. 45, 288–89 (James Madison). On a related note, *The Federalist* no. 39 finds Madison arguing in favor of the republican form of government proposed in the Constitution because "no other form would be reconcilable with the genius of the people of America; with the fundamental principles of the Revolution; or with that honorable determination which animates every votary of freedom to rest all our political experiments on the capacity of mankind for self-government." Ibid., no. 39, 240.

95. Ibid., no. 46, 298 (James Madison).

96. Ibid., no. 43, 279 (James Madison). No. 43 is also interesting because Madison adopts the Lockean characterization of government as a neutral "umpire" among competing interests, a role played by government that is essential to the protection of natural rights. Ibid., 279, 277.

97. Ibid., no. 31, 193 (Alexander Hamilton).

98. Ibid., no. 28, 180 (Alexander Hamilton).

99. Ibid., no. 26, 168 (Alexander Hamilton).

100. Ibid., no. 9, 72–73 (Alexander Hamilton).

101. Forrest McDonald rejects the nearly unanimous characterization of Madison as the "father" of the Constitution. McDonald emphasizes that Madison lost many votes during the Convention and that he wanted a purely national government. McDonald, *Novus Ordo Seclorum*, 205–9.

102. James Madison, *Preface to Debates in the Convention of 1787*, in Farrand, ed., *Records of the Federal Convention*, vol. 3, 551 (emphasis supplied). Further evidence of Madison's continued commitment late in life to the principles of the Declaration of Independence is found in a letter he wrote to Jefferson acknowledging that the Declaration is the first of the "best guides" to the "distinctive principles" of government. Letter from James Madison to Thomas Jefferson, February 8, 1825, in *The Writings of James Madison*, vol. 9, 221.

103. Letter from James Madison to Thomas Jefferson, October 24, 1787, in *The Papers of James Madison*, vol. 9, 212.

104. Letter from James Madison to George Washington, April 16, 1787, in

Letters and Other Writings of James Madison, vol. 1, 288 (emphasis in original).

105. See Letter from James Madison to Thomas Jefferson, September 6, 1787, in *The Papers of James Madison,* vol. 10, 163; Letter from James Madison to Thomas Jefferson, October 17, 1788, in ibid., vol. 11, 298.

106. In ibid., vol. 9, 355, 357. Madison was greatly influenced by David Hume's arguments in favor of an extended republic. See Adair, "'That Politics May Be Reduced to a Science.'"

107. James Madison, *Amendments to the Constitution,* June 8, 1789, in *The Papers of James Madison,* vol. 12, 200. Madison's initial proposal for a bill of rights differs somewhat from Jefferson's Declaration of Independence in that Madison, unlike Jefferson, mentions the right of "obtaining" happiness. Madison was undoubtedly influenced by George Mason's Virginia Declaration of Rights on this point. The implications of this distinction are discussed in chapters 1 and 5.

108. In *Letters and Other Writings of James Madison,* vol. 4, 478 (emphasis in original).

109. Ibid. (emphasis in original). In his classic 1785 essay on the natural right to religious freedom, *A Memorial and Remonstrance against Religious Assessments,* Madison echoes Locke's position—shared by Jefferson, most notably in Jefferson's Virginia Bill for Establishing Religious Freedom (which Madison helped pass)—on the relations between church and state. Madison argues that religious activities should be entirely exempt from state or societal interference, because of man's natural right to freedom of conscience. In *The Writings of James Madison,* vol. 2, 183–91. See generally Thomas Jefferson, Bill for Establishing Religious Freedom, in *The Portable Thomas Jefferson,* 251–53; Locke, *A Letter on Toleration,* 65. Madison also subscribed to Locke's controversial doctrine of tacit consent. See Letter from James Madison to Thomas Jefferson, February 4, 1790, in *The Papers of Thomas Jefferson,* vol. 16, 149. See generally Locke, *Second Treatise,* sec. 119.

110. Letter from James Madison to Joseph Cabell, September 7, 1829, *The Writings of James Madison,* vol. 9, 351. See also Letter from James Madison to Edward Everett, August 28, 1830, in ibid., 383 (recognizing the people's ultimate recourse "to original rights & the law of self-preservation").

111. James Wilson, *Lectures on Law* (1790–92), in Andrews, ed., *Works of James Wilson,* vol. 1, 60 ("The writings of Mr. Locke have facilitated the progress, and have given strength to the effects of scepticism"). On epistemology, Wilson was an adherent of the common-sense school of the Scottish Enlightenment.

112. James Wilson, Speech to the Pennsylvania Ratifying Convention, November 26, 1787, in McCloskey, ed., *The Works of James Wilson,* vol. 2, 769–70.

113. Speech by James Wilson in the Pennsylvania Ratifying Convention, De-

cember 4, 1787, in Jensen, Kaminski, and Saladino, eds., *Documentary History of the Ratification of the Constitution*, vol. 2, 472–73.

114. See, for example, Berns, "Judicial Review and the Rights and Laws of Nature," 49, 58–66; Storing, "The Constitution and the Bill of Rights," 44–48.

115. James Wilson, *Lectures on Law*, in Andrews, ed., *Works of James Wilson*, vol. 2, 303, 307. John Jay made the same point, albeit less eloquently, in *The Federalist* no. 2.

116. James Wilson, *Lectures on Law*, in Andrews, ed., *Works of James Wilson*, vol. 2, 335.

117. Wilson also emphasizes the related principle of popular sovereignty, a principle that he credits "the great and penetrating mind of Locke" with being the first to identify. Speech by James Wilson to the Pennsylvania Ratifying Convention, December 4, 1787, in Jensen, Kaminski, and Saladino, eds., *Documentary History of the Ratification of the Constitution*, vol. 2, 472. The Constitution of the United States was the first written national governing document based upon this principle of popular sovereignty.

118. Wright, *American Interpretations of Natural Law*, 89.

119. Kramnick, *Republicanism and Bourgeois Radicalism*, 261.

120. *The Federalist* no. 26, 168 (Alexander Hamilton).

121. Ibid., no. 84, 515 (Alexander Hamilton).

122. Farrand, ed., *Records of the Federal Convention*, vol. 1, 477 (remarks of Alexander Hamilton). George Washington makes a similar argument in his September 17, 1787, letter submitting the Convention's proposed Constitution to Congress. Just as individuals "entering into society must give up a share of liberty to protect the rest," Washington writes, so the states must give up a share of their sovereign powers to "promote the lasting welfare of the country so dear to us all, and secure her freedom and happiness." Ibid., vol. 2, 666–67.

123. In a provocative book on Jefferson's political philosophy, Garrett Ward Sheldon argues that Jefferson became more of a classical republican, and less of a Lockean liberal, in his postrevolutionary days. See Sheldon, *The Political Philosophy of Thomas Jefferson*. I read Jefferson differently, as this section shows.

124. Letter from James Madison to Thomas Jefferson, October 17, 1788, in *The Papers of James Madison*, vol. 11, 297.

125. Letter from Thomas Jefferson to James Madison, March 15, 1789, in *The Portable Thomas Jefferson*, 439.

126. Letter from Thomas Jefferson to Thomas Mann Randolph, May 30, 1790, in *The Writings of Thomas Jefferson*, vol. 8, 31.

127. In *The Portable Thomas Jefferson*, 210.

128. In ibid., 253. See also Thomas Jefferson, Address to the Danbury Baptist Association, January 1, 1804, in *The Writings of Thomas Jefferson*, vol. 16, 281.

129. Letter from Thomas Jefferson to F. W. Gilmer, 1816, in *Democracy by Thomas Jefferson*, 28. See also Letter from Thomas Jefferson to Dupont de Nemours, 1816, in ibid., 29 ("I believe ... that justice is the fundamental law of society; that the majority oppressing an individual, is guilty of a crime, abuses its strength, and by acting on the law of the strongest breaks up the foundations of society").

130. Letter from Thomas Jefferson to Colonel Smith, 1787, in ibid., 260. See also Letter from Thomas Jefferson to James Madison, January 30, 1787, in *The Portable Thomas Jefferson*, 417 ("A little rebellion, now and then, is a good thing, and as necessary in the political world as storms in the physical. ... It is a medicine necessary for the sound health of government").

131. Letter from Thomas Jefferson to Roger C. Weightman, June 24, 1826, in *The Portable Thomas Jefferson*, 585.

132. In *The Works of John Adams*, vol. 4, 271.

133. Madison called Adams's *Defence* "a powerful engine in forming the public opinion" both because of Adams's great stature in the United States and because "the book has merit." Letter from James Madison to Thomas Jefferson, June 6, 1787, in *The Papers of James Madison*, vol. 9, 29–30.

134. Parrington, *Main Currents in American Thought*, vol. 1, 319, 308.

135. In *The Works of John Adams*, vol. 4, 292.

136. Locke, *Second Treatise*, sec. 54.

137. Letter from John Adams to Thomas Brand-Hollis, June 11, 1790, in *The Works of John Adams*, vol. 9, 570.

138. Richards, *Foundations of American Constitutionalism*, 93.

139. In *The Works of John Adams*, vol. 5, 457–58.

140. See Webking, *The American Revolution and the Politics of Liberty*, 138–44.

141. In *The Works of John Adams*, vol. 6, 208. See also vol. 4, 554. See generally Sinopoli, *The Foundations of American Citizenship* (arguing that the Framers viewed virtue as a means to secure Lockean liberal ends).

142. In *The Works of John Adams*, vol. 6, 65.

143. Bryce, *The American Commonwealth*, vol. 1, 19. See also Lutz, *The Origins of American Constitutionalism*; Wright, *Consensus and Continuity*.

144. Nevins, *The American States during and after the Revolution*, 119.

145. The early state constitutions are collected in Poore, *Federal and State Constitutions*.

146. See, for example, Nevins, *The American States during and after the Revolution*, 147; Wright, *American Interpretations of Natural Law*, 115.

147. Howard, *Commentaries on the Constitution of Virginia*, vol. 2, 35 ("The rights claimed ... were ... natural rights, and the language of Locke informs the early sections of the Bill of Rights").

148. Poore, *Federal and State Constitutions*, vol. 2, 1908–9. As chapter 1 explained, the Declaration of Independence does not include the Virginia

Bill's right of "obtaining" happiness. The implications of this omission are discussed in chapter 5.

149. Poore, *Federal and State Constitutions*, vol. 1, 377–78.
150. Ibid., vol. 2, 1328, 1330–32.
151. See Howard, *Commentaries on the Constitution of Virginia*, vol. 1, 282.
152. Poore, *Federal and State Constitutions*, vol. 2, 1909.
153. Ibid., vol. 1, 956.
154. Quoted in Nevins, *The American States during and after the Revolution*, 171.
155. Interestingly, in only seven of the thirty-seven states admitted to the union since the nation's founding did Congress fail to reference the fundamental principles of the American Founding in enabling acts. The specific references were to one or more of the following: the Declaration of Independence, the Constitution of the United States, a republican form of government, and the Northwest Ordinance. I thank Mark Hall for this information.

Notes to Chapter 3

1. See Beard, *The Supreme Court and the Constitution*. Felix Frankfurter once wrote that Beard's study of the Founders' views on judicial review should put an end to the charge that the Supreme Court "usurped" that power in *Marbury v. Madison* (1803). Frankfurter, "A Note on Advisory Opinions," 1003 n. 4. As the plethora of books and articles on judicial review reveals, however, Beard's study merely exacerbated the usurpation charge.
2. The Supreme Court has not always done a good job in protecting rights (see chapter 5). In theory, however, the Court should be able to do so— as the present chapter attempts to show.
3. See Reid, *The Concept of Representation in the Age of the American Revolution*.
4. Blackstone, *Commentaries on the Laws of England*, vol. 1, 91.
5. 77 Eng. Rep. 646, 652 (1610).
6. See Sosin, *The Aristocracy of the Long Robe*, 56–58, 66–68.
7. There have been a few isolated occasions since the Glorious Revolution in which British judges appear to have exercised judicial review. One of the most well known is *The City of London v. Wood*, 88 Eng. Rep. 1592, 1602 (1702).
8. Nevins, *The American States during and after the Revolution*, 26.
9. Even in those states that formally separated powers in their constitutions, the legislature frequently trespassed on the judicial function. See Goebel, *Antecedents and Beginnings to 1801*, 98–99.
10. Chipman, Preface to Vermont Reports, bk. 2, 21, 22.

11. Rakove, "Parchment Barriers and the Politics of Rights," 120. The current practice of equating legislative supremacy with majoritarianism is, therefore, fundamentally flawed.

12. Thomas Jefferson, *Notes on the State of Virginia* (1782), in *The Portable Thomas Jefferson*, 164 (emphasis in original).

13. Seven states adopted bills of rights by 1784 and four others singled out specific rights for incorporation into the general provisions of their constitutions.

14. Farrand, ed., *Records of the Federal Convention*, vol. 1, 134 (remarks of James Madison).

15. Ibid., vol. 2, 288 (remarks of John Mercer). Many similar observations were offered. For example, Gouverneur Morris declared, "The public liberty is in greater danger from Legislative usurpations than from any other source," whereas James Wilson stated, "We have seen the Legislatures in our own country deprive the citizen of Life, of Liberty, & Property, we have seen Attainders, Banishments, & Confiscations." Ibid., 76 (remarks of Gouverneur Morris), vol. 1, 172 (remarks of James Wilson).

16. Even the delegates who opposed a strong national government understood the need to curb the abuses occurring in the state legislatures. As explained below, for many of those delegates more responsible state courts were the answer.

17. See, for example, James Madison, *Vices of the Political System of the United States* (1787), in *The Papers of James Madison*, vol. 9, 357; *The Federalist* no. 10, 83–84 (James Madison).

18. See *The Federalist* no. 10, 82–83 (James Madison).

19. The Senate, chosen under the Virginia plan not directly by the people nor by the state legislatures, but by the first branch of the national legislature, was also, as Edmund Randolph put it, to serve as a check on "the fury of democracy." Farrand, *Records of the Federal Convention*, vol. 1, 58.

20. See, for example, Letter from James Madison to George Washington, April 16, 1787, in *The Papers of James Madison*, vol. 9, 384.

21. Farrand, *Records of the Federal Convention*, vol. 2, 28 (remarks of James Madison).

22. Ibid., 76 (remarks of Luther Martin). Other delegates made similar observations. See, for example, ibid., vol. 1, 109 (remarks of Rufus King). Although several scholars of considerable renown—including Louis Boudin and William Crosskey—have argued that the Supreme Court was empowered to void only those acts of Congress that interfere with the prerogatives of the judiciary itself, the weight of the evidence is to the contrary. See Boudin, *Government by Judiciary*, vol. 1, 114; Crosskey, *Politics and the Constitution in the History of the United States*, vol. 2, 1007. For a convincing refutation of Boudin's and Crosskey's position, see Berger, *Congress v. The Supreme Court*, 154–64. I have more to say below about the scope of judicial review.

23. Madison's ability to win support for his notion of an extended federal

republic should not go unnoticed when considering how the Constitution secures rights. See, for example, Goldwin and Schambra, eds., *How Does the Constitution Secure Rights?*

24. U.S. Constitution, art. 6.

25. See Letter from James Madison to James Monroe, December 27, 1817, in *Letters and Other Writings of James Madison*, vol. 3, 56 (stating that if the Convention had accepted his proposal for a council of revision, this would have eliminated any need for judicial review of legislation for constitutional validity).

26. In *Congress v. The Supreme Court*, Raoul Berger makes a highly persuasive case that the Constitution *unequivocally* commissions the Supreme Court with broad power to review the acts of the co-equal branches of the national government, as well as the acts of the states. As Beard's study did years earlier, Berger has left many commentators unconvinced.

27. Elliot, ed., *Debates in the Several State Conventions*, vol. 2, 489 (remarks of James Wilson).

28. Ibid., vol. 3, 553 (remarks of John Marshall). Similar remarks were made in other state ratifying conventions. See, for example, ibid., vol. 2, 196 (remarks of Oliver Ellsworth in Connecticut).

29. *The Federalist* no. 78, 467 (Alexander Hamilton).

30. See Brutus, Essays 11–15 (1788), in Ketcham, ed., *The Anti-Federalist Papers and the Constitutional Convention Debates*, 293–309. J. M. Sosin argues that Brutus "sought to inflate judicial power to the dimensions of a bugbear, reading into the document what may not have existed." Sosin, *The Aristocracy of the Long Robe*, 264. According to Sosin, Brutus wanted to defeat the Constitution—and would go to any lengths, including grossly exaggerating the power of the Court, to do so—because he desired to maintain state power. Sosin's interpretation of Brutus's essays is interesting but unconvincing. There is no hint in any of Brutus's essays that he did not sincerely believe that the Constitution commissioned the Supreme Court with a broad power of judicial review.

31. A complete account of the role of natural-rights doctrine in judicial review must consider the arguments made by early American lawyers, as well as the decisions issued by judges. This is because, as Suzanna Sherry aptly observes, the lawyers' positions reflect "the types of arguments considered legitimate and within the bounds of the legal culture of the period." Sherry, "The Founders' Unwritten Constitution," 1136 n. 42. Moreover, innovations in judicial practice are often the product of persuasive lawyers' arguments.

32. Compare ibid. (arguing that the Founders envisioned natural-rights–based judicial review from the beginning), with Michael, "The Role of Natural Law in Early American Constitutionalism" (reviewing the same evidence and concluding that the Founders consistently rejected natural-rights–based judicial review).

33. See generally "Perspectives on Natural Law." Leading modern attempts to minimize the role of natural-law and rights doctrine in early judicial prac-

tice include Cover, *Justice Accused* (discussing slavery cases); Currie, *The Constitution in the Supreme Court*, 47–48, 130–32, 138, 152–53 (describing early Supreme Court practice); Wolfe, *The Rise of Modern Judicial Review*, 108–13 (same). See also McDowell, "Coke, Corwin, and the Constitution" (advancing a positivist critique of Corwin's famous article about natural law and the Constitution). Cover's, Currie's, McDowell's, and Wolfe's position represents current orthodoxy.

34. Consistent with his thesis that judicial review has no basis in history, Sosin makes much of the fact that Otis's argument, as well as most other precedents for judicial review, was not officially reported until years later. See Sosin, *The Aristocracy of the Long Robe*, 165–66. Sosin fails to appreciate, however, that news as significant as Otis's challenge to the writs of assistance circulated in myriad informal ways, such as through pamphlets, newspaper accounts, and correspondence. The Founders were well aware of the precedents for judicial review. See, for example, Farrand, ed., *Records of the Federal Convention*, vol. 1, 97 (remarks of Elbridge Gerry), vol. 2, 28 (remarks of James Madison); *The Federalist* no. 78, 470 (Alexander Hamilton); Elliot, ed., *Debates in the Several State Conventions*, vol. 3, 299 (remarks of Edmund Pendleton), 324–25 (remarks of Patrick Henry).

35. See James Otis, "Speech on the Writs of Assistance," February 24, 1761, in *The Works of John Adams*, vol. 2, 521–22.

36. See Flaherty, *Privacy in Colonial New England;* Lasson, *The History and Development of the Fourth Amendment to the United States Constitution.*

37. In *The Works of John Adams*, vol. 2, 522.

38. Letter from John Adams to William Tudor, March 29, 1817, in ibid., vol. 10, 248. Otis continued his attack on legislative acts that violate natural rights in two influential pamphlets published in 1762 and 1764. See chapter 1.

39. 1 Jeff. (Va.) 109, 114 (1772).

40. Colonel Bland, arguing the case for the defendants, emphasized legislative supremacy. Ibid., 118.

41. Ibid., 123.

42. See R. L. Clinton, *Marbury v. Madison and Judicial Review*, 48–55 (discussing the disagreement in the literature about the status of the early state cases as precedent for judicial review).

43. 4 Call (8 Va.) 5 (1782). Boudin and Crosskey accuse Daniel Call, the reporter of *Caton*, of fabricating the court's statements about judicial review. See Boudin, *Government by Judiciary*, vol. 1, 535; Crosskey, *Politics and the Constitution in the History of the United States*, vol. 2, 952, 960. In my judgment, Boudin and Crosskey do not adequately substantiate their charge. Because there is so much disagreement among scholars about the early state cases, as well as about the other historical materials on judicial review, I will not, as a rule, attempt to address the variety of interpretations advanced over the years. Instead, I will offer my own independent reading of the materials and will limit my comments on competing interpretations to those of particular significance.

44. There is some evidence that two years earlier, in *Holmes v. Walton* (N.J.,

1780), the New Jersey Supreme Court invalidated a state statute mandating the use of six jurors in certain cases instead of the traditional twelve. The evidence includes a series of petitions introduced in the New Jersey legislature denouncing the court's invalidation of the statute. However, because the court's opinion has never been found, I credit *Caton* with being the first recorded state case of judicial review. For more on *Holmes*, see Scott, "*Holmes v. Walton*." *Josiah Philips's Case* (Va., 1778) is also frequently mentioned as an early state precedent for judicial review. Like *Holmes v. Walton*, the opinion in *Josiah Philips's Case* has never been found, so I begin with *Commonwealth v. Caton*. For more on *Josiah Philips's Case*, see Trent, "The Case of Josiah Philips."

45. Chief Judge Edmund Pendleton's opinion is somewhat inconsistent in this regard. At one point, Pendleton stated that the propriety of judicial review need not be addressed by the court. See 4 Call (8 Va.), 18. Later, the chief judge engaged in judicial review. See ibid., 19–20 ("In passing [the law], the legislature have, in my opinion, pursued, and not violated, the constitution").

46. As Locke states, "politics contains two parts very different the one from the other, the one containing the origin of societies and the rise and extent of political power, the other, the art of governing men in society." Locke, "Some Thoughts concerning Reading and Study for a Gentleman," in *The Educational Writings of John Locke*, 400. See generally Sherry, "The Founders' Unwritten Constitution" (identifying the significance for judicial review of the difference between individual-rights cases and allocation-of-powers cases). I have more to say below about this distinction.

47. 4 Call (8 Va.), 8. Earlier in his opinion, Wythe favorably invoked the Cokean notion that it is the duty of a judge to "protect the rights of the subject." Ibid.

48. The case is reprinted in *The Law Practice of Alexander Hamilton*, vol. 1, 393–419.

49. Ibid., 373.

50. Ibid., 395, 400.

51. Ibid., 415.

52. 1 Kirby (Conn.) 444, 447 (1785).

53. See Varnum, *The Case, Trevett Against Weeden*. The contemporaneous accounting of the case by one of the principals makes *Trevett v. Weeden* more reliable than *Holmes v. Walton* and *Josiah Philips's Case*, two other alleged early state precedents for judicial review for which the courts' opinions have not been located.

54. Varnum, *The Case, Trevett Against Weeden*, 11. Varnum's other arguments were that the statute had expired and that the court lacked jurisdiction to hear the case. Ibid., 2–3.

55. Ibid., 25.

56. Ibid., 35.

57. Newspapers accounts indicate that in 1786 judges in New Hampshire voided a statute that deprived creditors of trial by jury in certain cases.

Those newspaper accounts intimate that the judges interpreted the New Hampshire constitution in light of natural-rights principles. Unfortunately, the opinions in the so-called *Ten Pound Act Cases* have not been located.

58. 1 N.C. (Martin) 5, 10 (1787).

59. A letter by Richard Dobbs Spaight to James Iredell, author of the letter "To the Public," reveals the influence Iredell's letter had on the court. I discuss Spaight's letter below.

60. James Iredell, "To the Public," August 17, 1786, in *Life and Correspondence of James Iredell*, vol. 2, 145.

61. Letter from Richard Dobbs Spaight to James Iredell, August 12, 1787, in ibid., 169–70.

62. Letter from James Iredell to Richard Dobbs Spaight, August 26, 1787, in ibid., 172 (emphasis omitted).

63. 3 U.S. (3 Dall.) 386, 399 (1798) (Iredell, J.). *Calder v. Bull* is discussed below.

64. See also Farrand, ed., *Records of the Federal Constitution*, vol. 1, 97 (remarks of Elbridge Gerry), vol. 2, 28 (remarks of James Madison).

65. *The Federalist* no. 78, 466 (Alexander Hamilton). See also 469–71. Morton White denies that *The Federalist* commissions the Court as an active guardian of the people's natural rights. White interprets Hamilton's argument in no. 78 in strictly negative terms, focusing as White does on phrases such as that which describes the Court as "the least dangerous branch" of the national government. According to White, "the main point of *Number* 78 about the judiciary is that it will be the least dangerous of the three branches of government to [natural] rights, not that it will exercise the most effective restraint upon the invasion of those rights." M. White, *Philosophy, The Federalist, and the Constitution*, 158. The problems with White's argument are that it fails to account for Hamilton's discussion, quoted in the text, of the Court's central role in protecting natural rights, and it leaves the Court with virtually no role to play in the American system of separation of powers and checks and balances. White also fails to recognize that much of Hamilton's deprecating characterization of the Court's power is a polemical device offered to rebut the influential charge of Brutus, discussed earlier, that the Court's power of judicial review and its independent status under the Constitution would make the Court despotic.

66. Elliot, ed., *Debates in the Several State Conventions*, vol. 2, 480–81 (remarks of James Wilson).

67. Ibid., vol. 3, 563, 567 (remarks of William Grayson).

68. Haines, *The Revival of Natural Law Concepts*, 85. See also Sherry, "Natural Law in the States," 173 ("The best evidence in support of a natural law heritage, then, is not what the founders [or the philosophers who influenced them] *said*, but what courts *did*" [emphasis in original]).

69. 1 Bay (S.C.) 93, 98 (1789).

70. 1 Wythe (Va.) 211, 213–15 (1793).
71. 4 Hen. & M. (14 Va.) 315, 341 (1809) (emphasis in original).
72. Ibid., 346–47 (Roane, J.) (emphasis in original). The act was upheld. Judge Roane concluded that applying the act retroactively was not unjust, whereas Judge William Fleming concurred on statutory construction grounds. Curiously, Judge Roane misstated Blackstone's position on judicial review. Blackstone's position was more rigid than Roane implies.
73. 2 Johns. Ch. 162, 166 (N.Y. 1816).
74. 1 N.H. 111, 114 (1817). The New Hampshire court's decision was reversed two years later by the U.S. Supreme Court. See *Trustees of Dartmouth College v. Woodward*, 17 U.S. (4 Wheat.) 518 (1819). That decision is discussed below. For more state precedents, see Haines, "Law of Nature in State and Federal Judicial Decisions"; Sherry, "Natural Law in the States." As Haines's and Sherry's articles make clear, the state cases I have discussed are representative of a larger pattern. The remainder of this section is devoted to examining early U. S. Supreme Court practice on the role of natural-rights doctrine in constitutional interpretation, a subject of perhaps more immediate interest to commentators on the Court than the state court decisions that served as precedent.
75. See Goebel, *Antecedents and Beginnings to 1801*, 143–250.
76. Currie, *The Constitution in the Supreme Court*, 3.
77. See, for example, Wolfe, *The Rise of Modern Judicial Review*, 108–13. See also Currie, *The Constitution in the Supreme Court*, 47–48, 130–32, 138, 152–53.
78. Currie, *The Constitution in the Supreme Court*, 4. These cases are further proof that Chief Justice Marshall was not saying anything new about the Court's authority to interpret the Constitution in *Marbury v. Madison*.
79. The three cases are *Chisholm v. Georgia*, 2 U.S. (2 Dall.) 419 (1793); *Hylton v. United States*, 3 U.S. (3 Dall.) 171 (1796); and *Calder v. Bull*, 3 U.S. (3 Dall.) 386 (1798). *Chisholm v. Georgia* and *Calder v. Bull* appealed to natural-rights principles. Neither Currie nor Wolfe mentions *Chisholm* as an example of natural-law and rights jurisprudence in their otherwise excellent histories of constitutional interpretation. They overlook later cases as well.
80. See *Van Horne's Lessee v. Dorrance*, 2 U.S. (2 Dall.) 304 (1795). Most of the cases decided by the Supreme Court during the formative years involved technical jurisdictional issues, a subject of obvious concern for any new court. For a discussion of those cases, see Currie, *The Constitution in the Supreme Court*, 6–30.
81. 2 U.S. (2 Dall.) 419 (1793).
82. See, for example, Warren, *The Supreme Court in United States History*, vol. 1, 93 n. 1 (describing the case as an action to recover on bonds given by debtors whose property the state had confiscated); Goebel, *Antecedents and Beginnings to 1801*, 726 (characterizing the case as an action for the price of goods furnished to the state).

83. The eleventh amendment reversed the Court's decision.
84. 2 U.S. (2 Dall.), 450–53 (Blair, J.).
85. Ibid., 469, 479 (Jay, C.J.).
86. Ibid., 466, 468 (Cushing, J.).
87. Ibid., 453–66 (Wilson, J.). Justice James Iredell dissented, arguing that a sovereign state could not be sued without its consent. He also warned that the Court's decision to the contrary would be viewed by the states as a dangerous assault upon their sovereignty. Ibid., 429–50 (Iredell, J., dissenting). The quick passage of the eleventh amendment indicates Justice Iredell correctly anticipated the states' reaction. See generally Graebe, "The Federalism of James Iredell in Historical Context." Justice Iredell had much to say about natural-rights–based judicial review in *Calder v. Bull*, discussed below.
88. 2 U.S. (2 Dall.) 304, 310 (1795) (Paterson, J.).
89. 3 U.S. (3 Dall.) 386 (1798).
90. Ibid., 400–401 (Cushing, J.).
91. Ibid., 395, 397 (Paterson, J.). Justice Paterson's opinion was mainly a technical exegesis on ex post facto laws.
92. Ibid., 386, 387–88 (Chase, J.).
93. See Letter from James Iredell to Richard Dobbs Spaight, August 26, 1787, in *Life and Correspondence of James Iredell*, vol. 2, 172.
94. 3 U.S. (3 Dall.), 397, 399 (Iredell, J.). Justice Iredell issued a virtually identical opinion on circuit the same year. See *Minge v. Gilmour*, 17 F. Cas. 440, 443–44 (C.C.D.N.C. 1798). Curiously, however, he engaged in an extended exegesis on natural-rights philosophy in a prize case only a few years earlier. See *Talbot v. Jansen*, 3 U.S. (3 Dall.) 133, 162–63 (1795).
95. See Bork, "The Struggle over the Role of the Court," 1138. See also Bork, "Natural Law and the Constitution."
96. *Hylton v. United States*, 3 U.S. (3 Dall.) 171 (1796), was the only full-scale constitutional law decision during the pre-Marshall era that did not invoke natural-rights principles. In *Hylton*, the Court held that a federal tax on carriages was not a "direct" tax required to be apportioned among the states. Importantly, in *Hylton*, federalism, not individual rights, was at issue. Appeal to natural-rights principles was therefore unnecessary.
97. 5 U.S. (1 Cr.) 137 (1803).
98. See Currie, *The Constitution in the Supreme Court*, 65–90.
99. Jurisdictional questions continued to be decided as well. See ibid., 91–126.
100. 10 U.S. (6 Cr.) 87 (1810).
101. Chief Justice Marshall put an end to the practice of each justice writing his own opinion. He also discouraged dissents.
102. Ibid., 133, 139.
103. Ibid (emphasis supplied). Currie, who tries to minimize the role of natural-law and rights doctrine in the early Court's constitutional jurisprudence, acknowledges that Marshall's opinion in *Fletcher v. Peck* "bristles" with such references. Currie, *The Constitution in the Supreme Court*, 130.

104. 10 U.S. (6 Cr.), 143–44 (Johnson, J., concurring).
105. The contract clause was used in more cases challenging state legislation during the Court's first one hundred years than any other constitutional provision. Wright, *The Contract Clause of the Constitution*, xiii.
106. 13 U.S. (9 Cr.) 43 (1815). *New Jersey v. Wilson*, 11 U.S. (7 Cr.) 164 (1812), is typically mentioned as one of the Marshall Court's major contract clause cases. See, for example, Currie, *The Constitution in the Supreme Court*, 136–37; Wright, *The Contract Clause of the Constitution*, 34–37. In that case the Court held that the state of New Jersey impaired a contract it made earlier with the Delaware Indians when the state sought to repeal a tax exemption granted to the Indians. As a sweeping statement of immunity from taxation, the case is significant. In terms of interpretive methodology, the Court did little more than cite *Fletcher v. Peck*.
107. 13 U.S. (9 Cr.), 52. Consistent with his more general attempt to minimize the role of natural-law and rights principles in the early Court's constitutional jurisprudence, Currie calls the quoted passage from Story's opinion "gratuitous." Currie, *The Constitution in the Supreme Court*, 138. Although Supreme Court opinions can certainly be read in a variety of ways, I find Currie's reading unconvincing for several reasons. First, a careful study of Story's opinion for the Court in *Terrett v. Taylor* reveals that he was using natural-law and rights doctrine as an exegetical tool. Second, as I have been endeavoring to show in this section, appeal to natural-law and rights doctrine in private rights cases was the rule, not the exception, for the early Court. Third, Story employed natural-law and rights jurisprudence on other occasions. For example, in *Wilkinson v. Leland*, 27 U.S. (2 Pet.) 627, 657 (1829), Story wrote, "The fundamental maxims of free government seem to require, that the rights of personal liberty and private property should be held sacred. At least no court of justice would be warranted in assuming that the power to violate and disregard them ... lurked under any general grant of legislative authority." Story also alluded to the importance of natural-law and rights doctrine in his acclaimed *Commentaries on the Constitution of the United States*.
108. 25 U.S. (12 Wheat.) 213 (1827). *Trustees of Dartmouth College v. Woodward*, 17 U.S. (4 Wheat.) 518 (1819), is often ranked second in importance to *Fletcher v. Peck* among the Marshall Court's contract clause decisions. See, for example, O'Brien, *Constitutional Law and Politics*, vol. 2, 192–93. The reason *Dartmouth College* is important is that the Court held that a corporate charter is a contract under the terms of the Constitution. The case said little about the methodology of constitutional interpretation, however.
109. The Court first applied the contract clause in the bankruptcy context in *Sturges v. Crowninshield*, 17 U.S. (4 Wheat.) 122 (1819).
110. Currie, *The Constitution in the Supreme Court*, 152–53.
111. 25 U.S. (12 Wheat.), 332, 346, 353–54 (Marshall, C. J., dissenting).
112. 17 U.S. (4 Wheat.) 316 (1819).

113. 22 U.S. (9 Wheat.) 1 (1824).
114. 32 U.S. (7 Pet.) 243 (1833).
115. See Haines, *The Revival of Natural Law Concepts*, 97; Wright, *American Interpretations of Natural Law*, 173–76.
116. 23 U.S. (10 Wheat.) 66 (1825).
117. In a trenchant analysis of the Marshall Court's racial minority cases, G. Edward White suggests that the Court's failure to afford Blacks and Indians natural-rights protection can be ascribed to the Court's unwilling-ness to consider Blacks and Indians fully human. See G. E. White, *The Marshall Court and Cultural Change*, chap. 9. White's interpretation is consistent with the way slavery was treated by many state judges at the time. As noted earlier, the pressure of disunion was also relevant.
118. Sherry, "The Founders' Unwritten Constitution," 1171. Natural-law and rights jurisprudence was not absent from the Court for long. Between 1889 and 1937 the Court appealed to natural-law and rights principles to protect private wealth. As I describe below, the modern Court fre-quently interprets the Constitution in light of natural-law–like concepts as well.
119. On a related note, Sotirios Barber suggests that the burden of proof should be on those who call for a minimal role for the Court in the American constitutional order. Barber astutely points out that critics of the Court as an institution simply assume or assert that their minimalist reading is correct. See Barber, *The Constitution of Judicial Power*, xi.
120. Even Roscoe Pound, who was critical of natural-law and rights jurispru-dence because it interfered with his vision of judges as social engineers, acknowledged that early American judges interpreted the law in light of those principles. See, for example, Pound, "Law in Books and Law in Action," 28.
121. Helen Michael maintains that Chief Judge Pendleton rejected natural-rights–based judicial review in an unpublished portion of his *Common-wealth v. Caton* (Va., 1782) opinion. Following Crosskey (and Boudin), Michael accuses Call of "doctoring" his report so as to provide a stronger precedent for judicial review. Michael, "The Role of Natural Law in Early American Constitutionalism," 453 n. 187. Even if this charge is true (and I do not believe it is), *two* rejections of natural-rights–based judicial review do not a jurisprudential pattern make. In fairness to Michael, there were probably instances that have not been uncovered in which judges other than Iredell rejected natural-rights–based judicial review. But, as this section advises, the weight of the evidence is to the contrary.
122. 4 Hen. & M. (14 Va.) 315, 341 (1809).
123. See, for example, *Cooper v. Aaron*, 358 U.S. 1 (1958); *Baker v. Carr*, 369 U.S. 186 (1962); *Powell v. McCormack*, 395 U.S. 486 (1969); *United States v. Nixon*, 418 U.S. 683 (1974). In all of these cases, the Court cited *Marbury v. Madison* for support. However, as has been discussed in detail by others, a close reading of *Marbury* indicates that Chief Justice

Marshall was *not* making the claim in that case that the Court is the supreme interpreter of the Constitution, but only that the Court is competent to—and has the authority to—address issues of constitutionality, as do the other branches of the government. See, for example, Engdahl, "John Marshall's 'Jeffersonian' Concept of Judicial Review." While *Marbury v. Madison* may not stand for the power of judicial finality the Court has been repeatedly asserting since *Cooper v. Aaron* in 1958, this section explains that the Court's role in the American constitutional order supports the Court's more recent claims to enjoy such power.

124. There are many scholars who argue for an egalitarian approach to constitutional interpretation. See, for example, Agresto, *The Supreme Court and Constitutional Democracy;* Bickel, *The Supreme Court and the Idea of Progress;* S. R. Burgess, *Contest for Constitutional Authority;* Burt, *The Constitution in Conflict;* Fisher, *Constitutional Dialogues.* The presidents who have expressly advanced an egalitarian approach to constitutional interpretation include Thomas Jefferson, Andrew Jackson, Abraham Lincoln, Franklin Roosevelt, Richard Nixon, and Ronald Reagan. See generally Gunther, *Individual Rights in Constitutional Law,* 22–25 (collecting the presidential statements); "Perspectives on the Authoritativeness of Supreme Court Decisions" (analyzing then attorney general Edwin Meese's controversial speech on behalf of the Reagan administration). There are differences among the egalitarian approaches (for example, Jefferson's position is less respectful of the Court's authority than Lincoln's is). What is important for purposes of this volume, however, is the rejection of judicial finality at the heart of all of them.

125. Jaffa's essays on the Declaration, originally published in the *University of Puget Sound Law Review,* are reprinted in Jaffa, *Original Intent and the Framers of the Constitution.*

126. Jaffa, "Judicial Conscience and Natural Rights," 242.

127. Although Jaffa agrees with the conservatives' position on the judicial function, he disagrees with their approach to the larger question of how the Constitution should be interpreted.

128. Corwin, *Court over Constitution,* 33. Berger argues to the contrary. See Berger, *Congress v. the Supreme Court,* 188–97. In my judgment, Berger's evidence is not nearly as convincing as he maintains.

129. *The Federalist* no. 81, 483 (Alexander Hamilton).

130. [Melancton Smith], "Letters of a Federal Farmer" (1787), in Ford, ed., *Pamphlets on the Constitution of the United States,* 306. For years, scholars thought the "Federal Farmer" was Richard Henry Lee. See, for example, Webking, "Melancton Smith and the Letters from the Federal Farmer."

131. Brutus, Essay 11 (1788), in Ketcham, ed., *The Anti-Federalist Papers and the Constitutional Convention Debates,* 295.

132. See, for example, Burt, *The Constitution in Conflict,* 56–76.

133. *The Federalist* no. 49, 314 (James Madison).

134. James Madison, Speech in the United States House of Representatives, in *Annals of Congress*, vol. 1, 520.
135. Letter from James Madison to Mr. ———, 1834, in *Letters and Other Writings of James Madison*, vol. 4, 350 (emphasis in original). See generally O'Brien, "The Framers' Muse on Republicanism, the Supreme Court, and Pragmatic Constitutional Interpretivism," 137–46.
136. The leading scholarly account of structural reasoning is C. L. Black, *Structure and Relationship in Constitutional Law*.
137. Articles 6 and 3 also strongly suggest that the Founders intended for the Supreme Court to have the final say in constitutional interpretation. Upon examining the relationship between the supremacy clause of Article 6 and the judicial provisions of Article 3, Justice Story was led to conclude that the Supreme Court is "the final judge or interpreter" of the Constitution. Story, *Commentaries on the Constitution of the United States*, 123–25.
138. *The Federalist* no. 48, 308 (James Madison).
139. Brennan, "The Constitution of the United States," 170.
140. In Meyers, ed., *The Mind of the Founder*, 171–72. Unenumerated rights are "expressly stipulated for" via the ninth amendment (see chapter 2), so Madison's use of that phrase should not be construed as a rejection of the view that unenumerated rights merit judicial protection. See Mitchell, "The Ninth Amendment and the 'Jurisprudence of Original Intention,'" 1740.
141. See, for example, the discussion of the jurisprudence of Meese, Bork, and Rehnquist in the Introduction, and of Jaffa at the beginning of this section, as well as Justice Antonin Scalia's opinion for the Court in *Employment Division, Department of Human Resources of Oregon v. Smith*, 110 S.Ct. 1595 (1990).
142. See also *The Federalist* no. 78, 467 (Alexander Hamilton) ("Without this [judicial review], all the reservations of particular rights or privileges would amount to nothing").
143. David Richards makes this point well:

    Judicial review is the natural culminating point of the architecture of America's experiment in Lockean constitutionalism because it is the most nearly adequate institutional embodiment of its supreme requirement: the impartial and independent judgment of the invoidable rights of the person that must be immune from political bargaining and compromise. (Richards, *Foundations of American Constitutionalism*, 166)

144. Bickel, *The Least Dangerous Branch*, 25–26. In his later works, Bickel backed away, though not completely, from his vision of the Court as "the institution best fitted to give us a rule of principle." Ibid., 261. Compare Bickel's view of the Court's role in *The Least Dangerous Branch* with that offered in his *The Supreme Court and the Idea of Progress*, 113, 177–78, and in his *The Morality of Consent*, 4.
145. Locke, *Essays on the Law of Nature*, 113–14. See also Locke, *Second Treatise*, sec. 124.

146. See *The Works of John Adams*, vol. 1, 195, vol. 3, 457, vol. 4, 259.
147. Letter from Thomas Jefferson to John Adams, 1813, in *Democracy by Thomas Jefferson*, 126–27.
148. Jefferson's distrust of Marshall is seen in an 1810 letter to Madison: "His [Marshall's] twistifications in the case of Marbury, in that of Burr, and the Yazoo case show how dexterously he can reconcile law to his personal biases." Letter from Thomas Jefferson to James Madison, 1810, in ibid., 275.
149. Letter from Thomas Jefferson to James Madison, March 15, 1789, in *The Portable Thomas Jefferson*, 438. See also Letter from Thomas Jefferson to A. H. Rowan, September 26, 1798, in *The Writings of Thomas Jefferson*, vol. 10, 61 ("The laws of the land, administered by upright judges, would protect you from any exercise of power unauthorized by the Constitution of the United States").
150. See, for example, *The Federalist* no. 10, 80–83 (James Madison); Elliot, ed., *Debates in the Several State Conventions*, vol. 3, 536–37 (remarks of James Madison).
151. Letter from James Madison to Mr. ———, 1834, in *Letters and Other Writings of James Madison*, vol. 4, 350. Madison's June 8, 1789, speech to the U.S. House of Representatives calling for the adoption of the Bill of Rights, quoted above, provides early signs of the leading role for the Court he was later to embrace, as well as evidence of the influence of Jefferson's 1789 letter, which made the same point, albeit more explicitly, about the advantages of institutional competence enjoyed by the Court. See also *The Federalist* no. 81, 483 (Alexander Hamilton).
152. Farrand, ed., *Records of the Federal Convention*, vol. 2, 429 (remarks of Charles C. Pinckney).
153. Although some, including Thomas Jefferson in the Kentucky Resolutions and John Calhoun during the nullification crisis, have claimed that the states may authoritatively declare the meaning of the Constitution within their borders, this claim has long been discredited. As James Madison aptly put it, the meaning of the Constitution "must be [left] to the authority of the whole, not to that of the parts separately and independently." Otherwise, the United States would be "a government in name only." James Madison, "On Nullification" (1835–36), reprinted in ibid., vol. 3, 537.
154. Levinson, "Could Meese Be Right This Time?" 1077.
155. President Andrew Jackson, Bank Veto Message (July 10, 1832), quoted in Gunther, *Individual Rights in Constitutional Law*, 22.
156. See Scigliano, *The Supreme Court and the Presidency*, 16.

Notes to Chapter 4

1. For a notable exception, see Agresto, *The Supreme Court and Constitutional Democracy*, chap. 5.

2. 14 U.S. (1 Wheat.) 304 (1816). Justice Story's position is somewhat ambiguous. The central portion of his opinion in *Martin v. Hunter's Lessee* asserted that Article 3 is "not mandatory, and that congress may constitutionally omit to vest the judicial power in courts of the United States," whereas several other paragraphs of the opinion argued that Article 3 jurisdiction is "mandatory upon the legislature."

3. See, for example, Eisenberg, "Congressional Authority to Restrict Lower Federal Court Jurisdiction" (arguing that the existence of the lower federal courts "in some form is [now] constitutionally required"); Sager, "Constitutional Limitations on Congress' Authority to Regulate the Jurisdiction of the Federal Courts" (contending that there must be *some* federal judicial forum for the enforcement of federal constitutional rights—*either* a lower federal court *or* the Supreme Court).

4. U.S. Constitution, art. 3, sec. 1 (emphasis supplied).

5. Ibid., sec. 2 (emphasis supplied).

6. See Merry, "Scope of the Supreme Court's Appellate Jurisdiction," 57. Merry makes the doubtful claim that Congress's power under the exceptions clause was intended to be limited to regulating the treatment of issues of fact. Not only is Merry's historical evidence unconvincing, but his interpretation is "contrary to the punctuation of the relevant phrase." (There are commas both before and after the phrase "both as to Law and Fact." The exceptions clause therefore modifies the words "appellate jurisdiction," rather than the word "Fact.") Gunther, "Congressional Power to Curtail Federal Court Jurisdiction," 901. See also Redish, "Congressional Power to Regulate Supreme Court Appellate Jurisdiction under the Exceptions Clause," 913–14.

7. All other occasions on which the Court has addressed the meaning of the exceptions clause have been dicta. See, for example, *The Francis Wright*, 105 U.S. 381, 386 (1881); *Daniels v. Railroad Company*, 70 U.S. (3 Wall.) 250, 254 (1865); *Barry v. Mercein*, 46 U.S. (5 How.) 103, 119 (1847); *Wiscart v. Dauchy*, 3 U.S. (3 Dall.) 321, 327 (1796). The dicta support a broad reading of Congress's power under the exceptions clause. In a more recent statement on the issue, Justice William Douglas asserted, "There is a serious question whether" the modern Court would approve a broad exercise of congressional power under the exceptions clause. *Glidden v. Zdanok*, 370 U.S. 530, 605 n. 11 (1961) (Douglas, J., dissenting).

8. 74 U.S. (7 Wall.) 506 (1868).

9. See, for example, Redish, "Congressional Power to Regulate Supreme Court Appellate Jurisdiction under the Exceptions Clause," 904.

10. 75 U.S. (8 Wall.) 85, 103 (1869) (stating that a complete denial of the Supreme Court's habeas corpus jurisdiction would "greatly weaken the efficacy of the writ ... and seriously hinder the establishment of ... uniformity in deciding upon questions of personal rights").

11. 80 U.S. (13 Wall.) 128 (1872).

12. See, for example, Rice, "Congress and the Supreme Court's Jurisdiction,"

972–73. The statute at issue in *United States v. Klein* directed that no pardon or amnesty be considered by the judiciary under the Abandoned and Captured Property Act, an important piece of Congress's post–Civil War Reconstruction policy.

13. See, for example, Gunther, "Congressional Power to Curtail Federal Court Jurisdiction," 898; Redish, "Congressional Power to Regulate Supreme Court Appellate Jurisdiction under the Exceptions Clause," 900.

14. Ratner, "Majoritarian Constraints on Judicial Review," 939.

15. Gunther, "Congressional Power to Curtail Federal Court Jurisdiction," 900.

16. Hart, "The Power of Congress to Limit the Jurisdiction of Federal Courts," 1365.

17. Ratner, "Majoritarian Constraints on Judicial Review," 934.

18. Ratner, "Congressional Power over the Appellate Jurisdiction of the Supreme Court."

19. Redish, "Congressional Power to Regulate Supreme Court Appellate Jurisdiction under the Exceptions Clause," 911.

20. Ratner, "Majoritarian Constraints on Judicial Review," 957.

21. Berger, *Congress v. the Supreme Court,* 268 (emphasis in original).

22. Scholars such as Gary McDowell and Martin Redish, who argue that the state courts would be available to protect individual and minority rights even if the Supreme Court's appellate jurisdiction were withdrawn and the lower federal courts were abolished, fail to appreciate that one of principal reasons for enacting the Constitution was to limit the infringements on individual and minority rights occurring in the states. See chapter 2. But see McDowell, *Curbing the Courts,* 129–30; Redish, "Constitutional Limitations on Congressional Power to Control Federal Jurisdiction," 166.

23. See *Bolling v. Sharpe,* 347 U.S. 497 (1954).

24. For example, Redish, "Congressional Power to Regulate Supreme Court Appellate Jurisdiction under the Exceptions Clause," 916.

25. Letter from Attorney General William French Smith to Senator Strom Thurmond, May 6, 1982, quoted in Gunther, *Individual Rights in Constitutional Law,* 44 n. 4.

26. Quoted in Baucus and Kay, "The Supreme Court Stripping Bills," 1017.

27. Orfield, *The Amending of the Federal Constitution,* 1.

28. Most of the scholarship on constitutional amendments focuses on the content of specific amendments, rather than on the amending process itself. There are a few notable exceptions. See, for example, Caplan, *Constitutional Brinkmanship;* Vile, *Rewriting the United States Constitution;* Weber and Perry, *Unfounded Fears.*

29. J. W. Burgess, *Political Science and Comparative Constitutional Law,* vol. 1, 137.

30. The Congress, whenever two thirds of both Houses shall deem it necessary, shall propose Amendments to this Constitution, or, on the Application of the Legislatures of two thirds of the several States, shall call a Convention for proposing Amend-

ments, which, in either Case, shall be valid to all Intents and Purposes, as Part of this Constitution, when ratified by the Legislatures of three fourths of the several States, or by Convention in three fourths thereof, as the one or the other Mode of Ratification may be proposed by the Congress; Provided that no Amendment which may be made prior to the Year One thousand eight hundred and eight shall in any Manner affect the first and fourth Clauses in the Ninth Section of the first Article; and that no State, without its Consent, shall be deprived of its equal Suffrage in the Senate. (U.S. Constitution, art. 5)

The provision that no state may be deprived of equal suffrage in the Senate without its consent was a concession to the small states. The provision protecting the institution of slavery until at least 1808 was a concession to the slaveholding states.

31. Farrand, ed., *Records of the Federal Convention*, vol. 1, 203 (remarks of George Mason).

32. See generally Jaffa, *Crisis of the House Divided*. But see Wills, *Lincoln at Gettysburg.*

33. Abraham Lincoln, "First Inaugural Address," March 4, 1861, in *Letters and Addresses of Abraham Lincoln*, 197 (emphasis supplied).

34. With his typical overstatement, Patrick Henry complained at the Virginia ratifying convention that "to suppose that so large a number as three fourths of the states will concur, is to suppose that they will possess genius, intelligence, and integrity, approaching to miraculous." Elliot, ed., *Debates in the Several State Conventions*, vol. 3, 49.

35. The constitutionality of the twenty-seventh amendment, which was ratified 203 years after it was proposed, is open to serious question because of the absence of "a contemporaneous consensus" for its ratification. See, for example, Van Alstyne, "What Do You Think about the Twenty-Seventh Amendment?" See generally *Dillon v. Gloss*, 256 U.S. 368, 374–76 (1921) (discussing the contemporaneous consensus requirement—and in the context of the original second [now the twenty-seventh] amendment). The twenty-seventh amendment requires a delay in congressional pay raise implementation until after an election.

36. *The Federalist* no. 49, 314 (James Madison).

37. Carter, "Constitutional Adjudication and the Indeterminate Text," 843.

38. 2 U.S. (2 Dall.) 419 (1793).

39. 60 U.S. (19 How.) 393 (1857).

40. 157 U.S. 429 (1895).

41. 400 U.S. 112 (1970).

42. Murphy, "Constitutional Interpretation," 1768–69.

43. Murphy, "An Ordering of Constitutional Values," 755–57.

44. *The Federalist* no. 78, 465 (Alexander Hamilton).

45. In *The Writings of George Washington*, vol. 12, 226.

46. *Annals of Congress*, vol. 1, 504 (remarks of Rep. Elbridge Gerry). See also *The Federalist* no. 78, 470 (Alexander Hamilton) (arguing that the Constitution is "binding"—"until the people have, by some *solemn and*

authoritative act, annulled or changed the established form" [emphasis supplied]).

47. See, for example, Abraham, *The Judicial Process,* 42–48. Two other lower federal court judges resigned before their impeachment processes were completed.

48. Letter from Thomas Jefferson to Judge Spencer Roane, September 6, 1819, in *The Writings of Thomas Jefferson,* vol. 15, 213; Letter from Thomas Jefferson to John Taylor, May 28, 1816, in ibid., 21; Letter from Thomas Jefferson to Edward Livingston, March 25, 1825, in ibid., vol. 16, 114. For a modern statement of this view, see McDowell, *Curbing the Courts,* 10.

49. Agresto, *The Supreme Court and Constitutional Democracy,* 120.

50. Rehnquist, "The Impeachment Clause," 903–4. The two occasions to which Rehnquist refers are the impeachment proceedings against Justice Samuel Chase and President Andrew Johnson. See generally Rehnquist, *Grand Inquests.*

51. Rehnquist, "The Impeachment Clause," 903–4.

52. For example, Berger, *Impeachment,* 3–4, 146–47.

53. U.S. Constitution, art. 1, sec. 3.

54. Ibid., art. 2, sec. 2.

55. The other questions include: Is impeachment the only constitutionally permissible means of removing federal judges? What procedures are appropriate for impeachment proceedings? Is it permissible to impeach a judge who has already resigned? Is judicial review of impeachment permissible? These questions have been exhaustively addressed in the literature on impeachment.

56. U.S. Constitution, art. 2, sec. 4.

57. See, for example, Farrand, ed., *Records of the Federal Convention,* vol. 2, 68–69 (remarks of Gouverneur Morris).

58. Ibid., 337, 550.

59. Ibid. (remarks of George Mason).

60. Ibid., 550 (remarks of Elbridge Gerry).

61. Ibid. (remarks of James Madison).

62. Ibid. (remarks of George Mason).

63. See, for example, Abraham, *The Judicial Process,* 42–43; Berger, *Impeachment,* 70–71; Bestor, Review of *Impeachment,* by Raoul Berger, 255; C. L. Black, *Impeachment,* 35; Feerick, "Impeaching Federal Judges," 1; Gerhardt, "The Constitutional Limits to Impeachment and Its Alternatives," 101.

64. See, for example, Brant, *Impeachment;* Burdick, *The Law of the American Constitution,* 87.

65. Congressional Record, 116th Cong., 2d sess., 1970, H3113–14 (daily ed. April 15) (remarks of Rep. Gerald R. Ford).

66. Berger, *Impeachment,* 53.

67. Charles Black makes an interesting argument against Ford's sweeping claim based on the constitutional prohibitions against bills of attainder and ex post facto laws:

When a congressman says, in effect, that Congress is entirely free to treat as impeachable any conduct it desires so to treat, he (or she) is giving a good textbook definition of a bill of attainder and an *ex post facto* law, rolled into one. Our Framers abhorred both of these things, and we have never wavered from that abhorrence. It cannot be right for Congress to act toward the president as though these prohibitions did not exist. There may be no way to keep Congress from violating their letter or spirit, but the conscientious congressman has to feel them, in spirit at least, as bounding and confining the operation of the vague words, "high Crimes and Misdemeanors." (C. L. Black, *Impeachment*, 32)

68. *The Federalist* no. 79, 474 (Alexander Hamilton).
69. For example, Berger, *Impeachment*; Rotunda, "An Essay on the Constitutional Parameters of Federal Impeachment," 723.
70. Bestor, Review of *Impeachment*, by Raoul Berger, 263–64.
71. Farrand, ed., *Records of the Federal Convention*, vol. 2, 550 (remarks of George Mason).
72. Ibid., 337, 550 (remarks of James Madison).
73. Gerhardt, "The Constitutional Limits to Impeachment and Its Alternatives," 85.
74. *The Federalist* no. 65, 396 (Alexander Hamilton).
75. Elliot, ed., *Debates in the Several State Conventions*, vol. 4, 113 (remarks of James Iredell).
76. Ibid., vol. 2, 169 (remarks of Samuel Stillman).
77. In McCloskey, ed., *The Works of James Wilson*, vol. 1, 426.
78. Letter from Thomas Jefferson to Joseph H. Nicholson, May 13, 1803, in *The Writings of Thomas Jefferson*, vol. 10, 390.
79. Chase's attacks were peppered with statements about natural-rights political philosophy. See, for example, *Annals of Congress*, vol. 14, 673–76 (a grand jury charge entered into the record in Chase's impeachment trial).
80. The English practice, from which the Founders drew heavily, included impeaching judges "for oppressive, unjust, or irregular practice contrary to the obvious rules of natural justice." Bacon's *Abridgment* (1768), 744, quoted in Berger, *Impeachment*, 66.
81. *Annals of Congress*, vol. 1, 504 (remarks of Rep. Elbridge Gerry).
82. Farrand, ed., *Records of the Federal Convention*, vol. 2, 550 (remarks of George Mason).
83. Letter from Thomas Jefferson to Judge Spencer Roane, September 6, 1819, in *The Writings of Thomas Jefferson*, vol. 15, 213.
84. President Jefferson may have underestimated the effectiveness of his attempted impeachment of the Federalist-dominated judiciary. Chief Justice Marshall, to name but the most significant example, curtailed his interference with presidential and congressional policy choices after Jefferson's attempts.
85. Unpublished Opinion of Justice Hugo Black (1966), in Schwartz, *The Unpublished Opinions of the Warren Court*, 274–75.
86. *The Federalist* no. 81, 485 (Alexander Hamilton). Hamilton was responding

to Robert Yates's charge that usurpations of power by the Supreme Court would go unchecked. See Brutus, Essay 15 (1788), in Ketcham, ed., *The Anti-Federalist Papers and the Constitutional Convention Debates*, 304–9.

87. See, for example, Agresto, *The Supreme Court and Constitutional Democracy*, 120; Rehnquist, "The Impeachment Clause," 903–4.

88. C. L. Black, *Impeachment*, 1.

89. See Maxman, "In Defense of the Constitution's Judicial Impeachment Standard," 423 ("The impeachment provisions were *designed* to be cumbersome, in order to protect judicial decisionmaking autonomy. To the Framers, mandating an intricate process for removal of federal judges seemed a small price to pay to ensure the American people an independent judiciary") [emphasis in original].

90. Quoted in Lash, *From the Diaries of Felix Frankfurter*, 113 n. 3.

91. *West Virginia Board of Education v. Barnette*, 319 U.S. 624, 647 (1943) (Frankfurter, J., dissenting) (emphasis supplied).

92. See Abraham, "Reflections on our Enduring and Evolving Constitution," 330.

93. Cardozo, *The Nature of the Judicial Process*, 168.

94. Quoted in Abraham, "Reflections on our Enduring and Evolving Constitution," 332.

95. Ibid., 333 (emphasis in original).

96. Over the years, the Court has itself developed "sixteen great maxims of judicial self-restraint." Abraham, *The Judicial Process*, 348. These maxims, or what Alexander Bickel termed the "passive virtues" (see Bickel, *The Least Dangerous Branch*, title of chapter 4), are well chronicled in Abraham, *The Judicial Process*, 347–73. They are: (1) a definite "case" or "controversy," (2) "standing," (3) no advisory opinions, (4) a live constitutional issue citing a specific provision of the Constitution, (5) a petitioner who has not sought the benefit of the action he is challenging, (6) exhaustion of lower court remedies, (7) a substantial, pivotal, and affirmative federal question, (8) a legal, as opposed to factual, basis for appeal, (9) adherence to precedent (though not absolute), (10) a question not "political" in nature, (11) a general presumption of the challenged statute's constitutionality (subject to the *Carolene Products* footnote 4 exception), (12) the avoidance, if possible, of deciding on the basis of federal constitutional law, (13) an unwillingness to impute illegal motives to the lawmakers, (14) limiting, as much as possible, any finding of unconstitutionality, (15) a general deference to legislative decisions, and (16) an unwillingness to serve as a check on an unwise or incompetent, yet constitutional, political judgment. These maxims have themselves been manipulated by the Court for result-oriented reasons. Gary McDowell calls for a more principled application of the maxims. See McDowell, *Curbing the Courts*.

97. For a thoughtful critique of a host of leading works on constitutional interpretation, see Barber, *The Constitution of Judicial Power*.

98. Thayer, "The Origin and Scope of the American Doctrine of Constitutional Review."

99. Quoted in Abraham, "The Judicial Function under the Constitution," 13.

100. See Gabin, *Judicial Review and the Reasonable Doubt Test.*

101. Thayer, "The Origin and Scope of the American Doctrine of Constitutional Review," 143–44.

102. One commentator goes so far as to say that "if conscientiously followed [Thayer's test] means the end of judicial review." Snowiss, *Judicial Review and the Law of the Constitution,* 191.

103. Ely, *Democracy and Distrust.*

104. Miller, *Toward Increased Judicial Activism,* 9.

105. See, for example, Bonner, *Battle for Justice;* Bork, *The Tempting of America,* 267–349; Phelps and Winternitz, *Capitol Games;* Simon, *Advice and Consent.* The Bork and Thomas confirmation battles also inspired countless articles. See, for example, "Confirmation Controversy"; "Gender, Race, and the Politics of Supreme Court Appointments."

106. Abraham, Preface, 2.

107. See generally Harris, *The Advice and Consent of the Senate,* 17–35.

108. For example, John Rutledge stated that he was not "disposed to grant so great a power to any single person. The people will think that we are leaning too much towards Monarchy." Farrand, ed., *Records of the Federal Convention,* vol. 1, 119.

109. James Wilson's remarks are representative. He "opposed the appointment of Judges by the national Legisl: Experience shewed the impropriety of such appointmts. by numerous bodies. Intrigue, partiality, and concealment were the necessary consequences. A principal reason for unity in the Executive was that officers might be appointed by a single, responsible person." Ibid.

110. See, for example, ibid., vol. 2, 41–43 (remarks of Nathaniel Gorham and James Madison). Hamilton was actually the first delegate to propose giving both the executive and the Senate roles in the appointment process, although the proposal received no consideration when he offered it. See ibid., vol. 1, 128.

111. See Friedlander, "Judicial Selection and the Constitution," 9.

112. *The Federalist* no. 76, 457 (Alexander Hamilton).

113. [Melancton Smith], "Letters of a Federal Farmer: III," October 10, 1787, in Ford, ed., *Pamphlets on the Constitution of the United States,* 298.

114. Elliot, ed., *Debates in the Several State Conventions,* vol. 4, 116 (remarks of Samuel Spencer).

115. Leahy, "Reflections on Federal Judicial Selection."

116. Hatch, "The Politics of Picking Judges."

117. C. L. Black, "A Note on Senatorial Consideration of Supreme Court Nominees," 661 (emphasis in original). The fact that the Convention seriously considered creating an advisory council to assist the president in making nominations provides additional support for Black's reading of the

Convention debates. See also Monaghan, "The Confirmation Process,"
1204:

> Nothing in the language of the appointments clause, in its origins, or in the actual
> history of the appointment process supports a constitutionally based presidential
> "right" to mold an independent branch of government for a period extending long
> beyond his electoral mandate. Rather (and to my surprise), all the relevant histori-
> cal and textual sources support the Senate's power when and if it sees fit to assert
> its vision of the public good against that of the President.

118. Here, practice conforms to theory. Henry Abraham captures the point:
"The Senate's role is second; but it is not secondary, as the record amply
demonstrates." Abraham, Preface, 1. The Senate has refused to consent
to 28 of the 148 presidential nominations to the Supreme Court (as of
July 1994).

119. Abraham, *Justices and Presidents*, 5. See also O'Brien, *Judicial Roulette*,
49 (referring to "political patronage, professional qualifications, and legal-
policy goals").

120. Abraham, *Justices and Presidents*, 39.

121. See O'Brien, *Judicial Roulette*, 95 ("It is the swing of electoral politics
that largely determines who makes it to the federal bench"). President
Franklin Roosevelt's ill-fated 1937 "court packing" plan is a notable example of the politics that have plagued the appointment process.

122. Letter from James Madison to Mr. ———, 1834, in *Letters and Other
Writings of James Madison*, vol. 4, 350.

123. Letter from Thomas Jefferson to James Madison, March 15, 1789, in *The
Portable Thomas Jefferson*, 438.

124. Abraham, *Justices and Presidents*, 25–26.

125. *The Federalist* no. 66, 405 (Alexander Hamilton). See also Monaghan, "The
Confirmation Process," 1205 (observing that the "goal of the [advice and
consent] provision was clearly to help secure meritorious appointees").

126. See, for example, O'Brien, *Judicial Roulette*, 98.

127. Abraham, Preface, 4–5. See also Goldman, "Judicial Selection and the
Qualities That Make a 'Good' Judge," 113–14.

128. Frankfurter, "The Supreme Court in the Mirror of Justices," 795.

129. Quoted in Abraham, *The Judicial Process*, 58–59.

130. For example, Tribe, *God Save This Honorable Court*, 92 ("The simple
truth [is] that the upper house of Congress has been scrutinizing Supreme
Court nominees and rejecting them on the basis of their political, judicial,
and economic philosophies ever since George Washington was President"). But see Danelski, "Ideology as a Ground for the Rejection of the
Bork Nomination" (questioning much of Tribe's evidence).

131. Fein, "A Circumscribed Senate Confirmation Role," 673. See also Carter,
"The Confirmation Mess," 1196–97:

> A reflective Senate would refuse to speculate about a potential nominee's likely
> votes, and would eschew any inquiry into judicial philosophy, not merely because

the body might be institutionally incapable of evaluating a nominee's philosophy, but also because the long-term interest of the American people requires what, at a deep level, most Americans probably want or believe that they have: an independent judiciary.

132. Bork, *The Tempting of America*, 347–48. Bork has apparently changed his mind (because a Democrat is in the White House?). See Bork, "The Senate's Power Grab."

133. Berger, "Academe vs. the Founding Fathers," 471.

134. C. L. Black, "A Note on Senatorial Consideration of Supreme Court Nominees," 663–64.

135. See Abraham, *Justices and Presidents*, 24–48.

136. O'Brien, *Judicial Roulette*, 50, 58–60.

137. David Strauss and Cass Sunstein argue that the White House and the Senate should discuss potential nominees *before* the president makes his choice. The authors claim that this prenomination consultation is required by the "advice" component of the Senate's "advice and consent" role. See D. A. Strauss and Sunstein, "The Senate, the Constitution, and the Confirmation Process."

138. Abraham, "The Judicial Function under the Constitution," 12 (emphasis in original).

139. See, for example, O'Brien, *Judicial Roulette*, 35–38.

140. See Abraham, *Justices and Presidents*, 5, 204–7.

Notes to Chapter 5

1. 3 U.S. (3 Dall.) 386, 399 (1798) (Iredell, J.).

2. Bork, "The Struggle over the Role of the Court," 1138. See also Bork, "Natural Law and the Constitution."

3. See, for example, Ely, *Democracy and Distrust*, 50 ("Natural law has been summoned in support of all manner of causes in this country—some worthy, others nefarious—and often on both sides of the same issue").

4. The Introduction described how the vast majority of conservative proponents of original intent maintain that the Founders' views on specific rights are *binding*, not merely suggestive. However, as I argued in the Introduction, originalism should not be so constrained. The Founders rejected the notion that future generations should adhere to their intentions on specific rights. See Levy, *Original Intent and the Framers' Constitution*, 1–29, 284–321; Powell, "The Original Understanding of Original Intent."

5. Locke, *Second Treatise*, sec. 54. See generally Diamond, "The American Idea of Equality," in *As Far as Republican Principles Will Admit*, 241–57. In a provocative book on equality and the Constitution, Judith Baer—who characterizes herself as a "bleeding-heart liberal"—argues that equality, under both the Declaration of Independence and the Constitution, is "*not*

a notion about capacities or abilities, but a notion of *entitlement.*" Baer, *Equality under the Constitution,* 10, 253 (emphasis supplied in part). As the discussions in this chapter and in part 1 suggest, I disagree strongly with Baer's egalitarian interpretation of the political philosophy of the American regime. Simply stated, the political philosophy of the American regime is Lockean liberalism, not Rawlsian or Dworkinian egalitarianism. I have more to say about the differences between Lockean liberalism and egalitarianism throughout this chapter.

6. Myrdal, *An American Dilemma.*
7. Locke also participated in the slave trade in various ways, a personal lapse that is inconsistent with the concept of equality embodied in his teachings. See Glausser, "Three Approaches to Locke and the Slave Trade."
8. Jefferson's original draft of the Declaration of Independence included the following grievance against the king:

> He has waged cruel war against human nature itself, violating its most sacred rights of life & liberty in the persons of a distant people who never offended him, captivating & carrying them into slavery in another hemisphere, or to incur miserable death in their transportation thither. ... Determined to keep open a market where MEN should be bought & sold, he has prostituted his negative for suppressing every legislative attempt to prohibit or to restrain this execrable commerce. (In *The Papers of Thomas Jefferson,* vol. 1, 426)

9. See Farrand, ed., *Records of the Federal Convention,* vol. 1, 135 (remarks of James Madison), 588 (remarks of Gouverneur Morris), vol. 2, 220 (remarks of Roger Sherman), 221 (remarks of Gouverneur Morris), 364 (remarks of Luther Martin), 370 (remarks of George Mason), 371 (remarks of Oliver Ellsworth), 372 (remarks of John Dickinson), 415 (remarks of James Madison and Hugh Williamson), 417 (remarks of James Madison).
10. "Neither slavery nor involuntary servitude, except as a punishment for crime whereof the party shall have been duly convicted, shall exist within the United States, or any place subject to their jurisdiction." U.S. Constitution, amend. 13, sec. 1. Slavery is recognized in three places in the original Constitution, though the words "slavery" and "slaves" are never used. For purposes of taxation and representation in the House of Representatives Article 1, section 2, counted "three fifths of all other [nonfree] Persons." Article 1, section 9, permitted the "Migration or Importation of such [nonfree] Persons" until at least 1808, and Article 4, section 2, required, on demand of the owner, the return of fugitive slaves.
11. Marshall, "Slavery, Civil Rights, and the Constitution," 304.
12. 60 U.S. (19 How.) 393 (1857).
13. Hughes, *The Supreme Court of the United States,* 50.
14. In *The Portable Thomas Jefferson,* 215.
15. 60 U.S. (19 How.), 410, 407–8.
16. The essential tenet of the Confederate States of America was that slavery was *not* contrary to natural law. Alexander Stephens, the vice president of

the Confederacy, acknowledged how different this belief was from the political philosophy of the American Founding, but he argued the Founders were mistaken. In Stephens's words:

> The prevailing ideas entertained by ... most of the leading statesmen at the time of the formation of the old Constitution, were that the enslavement of the African was in violation of the laws of nature; that it was wrong in principle, socially, morally, and politically. ... Those ideas were fundamentally wrong. They rested upon the assumption of the equality of the races. This was an error. (Alexander H. Stephens, The Cornerstone Speech, March 21, 1861, in Cleveland, *Alexander H. Stephens in Public and Private*, 721–23)

17. Abraham Lincoln, Speech on the Dred Scott Decision, June 26, 1857, in *Abraham Lincoln: Speeches and Writings*, vol. 1, 398 (emphasis supplied in bold face).
18. The classic account of this American system of apartheid is C. V. Woodward, *The Strange Career of Jim Crow*.
19. 163 U.S. 537 (1896).
20. 95 U.S. 485 (1878).
21. 109 U.S. 3 (1883).
22. *Strauder v. West Virginia*, 100 U.S. 303 (1880), was an exception to the Supreme Court's otherwise poor record in race cases. In *Strauder*, the Court struck down a state law that excluded Blacks from juries.
23. 163 U.S., 551, 544.
24. Ibid., 562, 559 (Harlan, J., dissenting).
25. 347 U.S. 483 (1954).
26. Here, it is necessary to reject Jefferson's claim that Blacks are mentally inferior to Whites. See Thomas Jefferson, *Notes on the State of Virginia* (1782), in *The Portable Thomas Jefferson*, 188. Again we see the shortcomings of "strict originalism," or binding modern Americans to the Founders' specific conclusion about an issue, as compared to "moderate originalism," or applying a principle—in this case, equality—to which they dedicated the nation.
27. Wasserstrom, "Racism, Sexism, and Preferential Treatment," 592.
28. The fourteenth amendment applies to the state governments, and the fifth amendment applies to the national government. The implicit equal protection guarantee in the due process clause of the fifth amendment was recognized in *Bolling v. Sharpe*, 347 U.S. 497 (1954).
29. See Berger, *Government by Judiciary*, 166–92.
30. See, for example, *In re Griffiths*, 413 U.S. 717, 729 (1973) (Rehnquist, J., dissenting).
31. See, for example, Baer, *Equality under the Constitution*; Graham, *Everyman's Constitution*; Kelly, "The Fourteenth Amendment Reconsidered"; ten Broek, *Equal under Law*. See also Richards, *Foundations of American Constitutionalism*, 255 ("Whereas the equal protection clause is a relatively late addition to our constitutional history, the underlying moral ideal

of the equality of persons is not. This is evident ... in the solemn aspirations of the Declaration of Independence"). See generally Richards, *Conscience and the Constitution.*

32. See Nelson, *The Fourteenth Amendment.*

33. Bickel, "The Original Understanding and the Segregation Decision," 61. See also Bickel, *The Least Dangerous Branch,* 98–110.

34. That the Founders, as well as the members of the Reconstruction Congress, *personally* thought little of women's abilities is beyond dispute. A letter written by John Adams contemporaneous to the drafting of the Declaration of Independence is illustrative. Adams wrote, "Nature has made [women] fittest for domestic cares" and unfitted them for "the great businesses of life, and the hardy enterprises of war, as well as the arduous cares of state." Letter from John Adams to James Sullivan, May 26, 1776, in *The Works of John Adams,* vol. 9, 376. As noted earlier, the purpose of this chapter is to apply, in a principled manner, the political philosophy of the Declaration of Independence to issues of constitutional-rights adjudication, not to parrot the Founders' views on the results to which that application leads.

35. Until recently, the Supreme Court's record on sex discrimination was terrible. While racial discrimination existed largely because Whites hated Blacks, sex discrimination resulted principally because men wanted to protect women. Justice David Brewer's opinion for the Court in a 1908 case upholding a state statute limiting female workers in certain industries to a ten-hour work day was typical. According to Justice Brewer:

> The two sexes differ in structure of body, in the functions to be performed by each, in the amount of physical strength, in the capacity for long-continued labor, particularly when done standing, ... the self-reliance which enables one to assert full rights, and in the capacity to maintain the struggle for subsistence. This difference justifies a difference in legislation and upholds that which is designed to compensate for some of the burdens which rest upon her. (*Muller v. Oregon,* 208 U.S. 412 [1908])

In the 1970s the Court began to view sex discrimination differently. See, for example, *Reed v. Reed,* 404 U.S. 71 (1971) (declaring unconstitutional a state statute that gave men preference over women in administering decedents' estates); *Frontiero v. Richardson,* 411 U.S. 677 (1973) (striking down a federal law under which male military officers automatically qualified for benefits for their wives, while female officers could obtain the same benefits only if they proved that their husbands were dependent upon them for support); *Craig v. Boren,* 429 U.S. 190 (1976) (invalidating a state law that prohibited the sale of 3.2 percent beer to males under the age of twenty-one, but to females only under eighteen). As cases like *Rostker v. Goldberg,* 453 U.S. 57 (1981) (a case in which the Court *upheld* the Military Selective Service Act's authorization for the president to require males, but not females, to register for potential military service), illustrate, however, the Court still has a long way to go to satisfy the Declaration of Independence's concept of equality.

36. See Thomas I. Emerson, Remarks to the Senate Judiciary Committee on the Equal Rights Amendment, October 9, 1970, quoted in Murray, "The Rights of Women," 542.

37. Section 1 of the proposed equal rights amendment provided that "Equality of rights under the law shall not be denied or abridged by the United States or by any State on account of sex." Quoted in O'Brien, *Constitutional Law and Politics*, vol. 2, 1423.

38. See Baer, *Equality under the Constitution*, 153.

39. 427 U.S. 307 (1976).

40. 440 U.S. 93 (1979).

41. 427 U.S., 313 (maintaining that the state police officers were not "subjected to unique disabilities on the basis of stereotyped characteristics not truly indicative of their abilities").

42. 387 U.S. 1, 17 (1967).

43. For an excellent discussion of the rights of children in Locke's theory, see Simmons, *The Lockean Theory of Rights*, 192–204.

44. Ibid., 202.

45. Locke, *Second Treatise*, sec. 63.

46. 406 U.S. 205 (1972).

47. Ibid., 241, 244–46 (Douglas, J., dissenting).

48. See, for example, *Regents of the University of California v. Bakke*, 438 U.S. 265 (1978).

49. *Wygant v. Jackson Board of Education*, 476 U.S. 267, 280 (1986).

50. See *De Funis v. Odegaard*, 507 P.2d 1169, 1189 (1973) (Hale, C.J., dissenting) (raising—and rejecting—this puzzling scenario). See generally Kull, *The Color-Blind Constitution* (demonstrating, as a matter of legal history, that the Constitution was intended to be color-blind).

51. See, for example, Bickel, *The Morality of Consent*, 132–33; Newton, "Reverse Discrimination as Unjustified"; Wortham, *The Other Side of Racism*.

52. Baer, *Equality under the Constitution*, 131–53. See also Dworkin, "Why Bakke Has No Case"; Wasserstrom, "Racism, Sexism, and Preferential Treatment," 586.

53. See, for example, Thomas, "The Higher Law Background of the Privileges or Immunities Clause of the Fourteenth Amendment"; Thomas, "Toward a 'Plain Reading' of the Constitution." See generally Gerber, "The Jurisprudence of Clarence Thomas."

54. Thomas, "Affirmative Action Goals and Timetables," 403 n. 3. See also Carter, *Reflections of an Affirmative Action Baby* (contending that class preferences are demeaning to Blacks, lower standards, and rob Blacks of the incentive to achieve excellence); Murray, "Affirmative Racism" (arguing that preferential treatment has created a "new racism").

55. For instance, the NAACP took the highly unusual step of opposing a Black nominee to the federal bench and opposed Justice Thomas's nomination to the Supreme Court because the group considered Thomas's record on civil rights to be "reactionary." Statement by Dr. William F. Gibson, Press Re-

lease no. 91–125, Chairman, The National Board of Directors of the NAACP on the Nomination of Judge Clarence Thomas to the U.S. Supreme Court (July 31, 1991). See also Higginbotham, "An Open Letter to Justice Clarence Thomas" (a letter from a respected, senior, Black federal judge criticizing Thomas's record on civil rights).

56. Thomas, "Civil Rights as a Principle versus Civil Rights as an Interest," 392 (emphasis in original). See also Thomas, "Affirmative Action Goals and Timetables," 403 n. 3 (arguing that class preferences "are an affront to the rights and dignity of individuals"). Although I agree with Justice Thomas's reading of the Declaration of Independence on preferential treatment, I disagree with his approach to many other important issues. See Gerber, "The Jurisprudence of Clarence Thomas," 109–29.

57. See Harrington, *The Other America.*

58. Johnson, "To Fulfill These Rights," 254.

59. Locke, *Second Treatise,* secs. 54, 42.

60. Ibid., secs. 7, 16, 134, 135, 149, 159, 171, 183.

61. Ibid., sec. 6.

62. The Founders did not consider the death penalty to be cruel and unusual punishment, as the prevalence of executions during the Founding plainly shows. As in the discussion of equality, however, I am concerned in this section with applying a principle to which the Founders dedicated our nation—here, life—not with how they personally felt about capital punishment.

63. "No person shall be . . . twice put in jeopardy of life or limb, . . . nor be deprived of life . . . without due process of law." U.S. Constitution, amend. 5. "No state shall . . . deprive any person of life . . . without due process of law." U.S. Constitution, amend. 14.

64. *Trop v. Dulles,* 356 U.S. 86, 101 (1958) (emphasis supplied).

65. Wolfe, *The Rise of Modern Judicial Review,* 376 n. 46.

66. 428 U.S. 153 (1976).

67. Ibid., 232 (Marshall, J., dissenting).

68. The Rehnquist Court has reaffirmed the constitutionality of the death penalty. See, for example, *Tison v. Arizona,* 481 U.S. 137 (1987).

69. Locke, *Second Treatise,* sec. 16.

70. Ibid., sec. 6.

71. See, for example, Brennan, "The Constitution of the United States," 173.

72. *Thompson v. Oklahoma,* 487 U.S. 815 (1988) (declaring as unconstitutional under the eighth amendment the imposition of the death penalty to one fifteen years old or younger at the time of his crime); *Stanford v. Kentucky* and *Wilkins v. Missouri,* 109 S.Ct. 2969 (1989) (holding that the death penalty may be imposed on those who are sixteen years or older).

73. In a dissenting opinion in *Thompson v. Oklahoma,* Justice Scalia criticized the Court for holding that a killer under sixteen can never be sentenced to death, no matter what his "individual . . . level of maturity and moral responsibility." 487 U.S., 859 (Scalia, J., dissenting). Later in his opinion,

Justice Scalia revealed that even he accepted the Court's argument that "at some age a line does exist ... below which a juvenile can *never* be considered fully responsible for murder." Ibid., 872 (emphasis in original).

74. See, for example, *Lockett v. Ohio*, 438 U.S. 586 (1978); *Bell v. Ohio*, 438 U.S. 637 (1978).

75. *Penry v. Lynaugh*, Ibid., 2934 (1989) (permitting the imposition of the death penalty on a mentally impaired convicted murderer, as long as an individualized determination of whether the death penalty is appropriate was conducted). In a separate opinion, Justice Brennan argued for a generalization that *all* mentally impaired persons lack sufficient blameworthiness to be put to death. Ibid., 2961 (Brennan, J., concurring in part and dissenting in part).

76. Locke, *Second Treatise*, sec. 6.

77. 110 S.Ct. 2841 (1990).

78. Ronald Dworkin provides a useful—and provocative—discussion of the traditional philosophical positions surrounding the right to die, including the Lockean liberal position (though, as I will show, by maintaining that Lockean liberalism opposes the right to die, Dworkin misreads that philosophy). See Dworkin, *Life's Dominion*, 179–217.

79. Locke, *Second Treatise*, sec. 6.

80. Scholars disagree on whether Locke sometimes permits suicide. Those arguing in the affirmative include Sibyl Schwarzenbach and George Windstrup. See Schwarzenbach, "Locke's Two Conceptions of Property," 144–45; Windstrup, "Locke on Suicide." Representative opposing views, emphasizing the theological basis of Locke's thought, are offered by John Dunn and Ronald Dworkin. See Dunn, *The Political Thought of John Locke*, 125; Dworkin, *Life's Dominion*, 195. Simmons's position is more difficult to discern. On the one hand, he states unequivocally that he "can find no textual warrant for claiming that [Locke] *does* allow [suicide]." Simmons, *The Lockean Theory of Rights*, 62 n. 120 (emphasis in original). On the other hand, he then proceeds to articulate both textual and philosophical reasons for concluding that Locke *should* allow for suicide. See ibid., 61–63.

81. Windstrup argues that Locke's statement seemingly forbidding suicide under all circumstances is simply a rhetorical device to justify his theory of revolution, the exposition of which is the chief purpose of the *Second Treatise*. Windstrup, "Locke on Suicide," 176. The rhetorical connection between a prohibition on suicide and the right of revolution is that people are entitled to resist arbitrary power because of the threat such power is to their lives.

82. Locke, *Second Treatise*, sec. 6.

83. Ibid., sec. 23.

84. Simmons, *The Lockean Theory of Rights*, 63.

85. 410 U.S. 113 (1973).

86. O'Brien, *Constitutional Law and Politics*, vol. 2, 1158.

87. Compare Justice Sandra Day O'Connor's dissenting opinion in *Akron v. Akron Center for Reproductive Health*, 462 U.S. 416, 458 (1983), in which she argued against the trimester approach because

> the Roe framework ... is clearly on a collision course with itself. As the medical risks of various abortion procedures decrease, the point at which the State may regulate for reasons of maternal health is moved forward to actual childbirth. As medical science becomes better able to provide for the separate existence of the fetus, the point of viability is moved further back toward conception.

88. See, for example, *Planned Parenthood v. Danforth*, 428 U.S. 552 (1976) (holding that government may not give a veto over a woman's abortion decision to the man who shares responsibility for the pregnancy or, in the case of a woman below the age of majority, to the young woman's parents); *Maher v. Doe*, 432 U.S. 464 (1977) (upholding a state statute that refused to reimburse Medicaid recipients for abortion expenses unless the attending physician certified that an abortion is medically necessary); *Harris v. McRae*, 448 U.S. 297 (1980) (upholding a federal statute that limited federal funding for nontherapeutic abortions); *Akron v. Akron Center for Reproductive Health*, 462 U.S. 416 (1983) (holding that statutes requiring parental consent must provide for alternative approval by a judge for a minor who is mature enough to make the abortion decision herself or who has a good reason for not seeking parental consent).

89. 109 S.Ct. 3040 (1989).

90. 112 S.Ct. 2791, 2804, 2820 (1992).

91. *Northern Securities Company v. United States*, 193 U.S. 197, 400 (1904) (Holmes, J., dissenting). Many scholars mistakenly attribute authorship of the phrase "hard case" to Ronald Dworkin. See, for example, Hirsch, *A Theory of Liberty*, 243 n. 10. Dworkin does use the phrase, but it did not originate with him. See, for example, Dworkin, *Taking Rights Seriously*, 81–130.

92. 410 U.S., 159.

93. Tribe, *Abortion*.

94. Locke, *Second Treatise*, sec. 16 (emphasis supplied).

95. Lehrman, "The Declaration of Independence and the Right to Life."

96. See, for example, Gerber, "The Jurisprudence of Clarence Thomas," 118–19.

97. Lehrman, "The Declaration of Independence and the Right to Life," 22–23.

98. Ibid., 22.

99. See, for example, Thomas Jefferson, Bill for Establishing Religious Freedom, in *The Portable Thomas Jefferson*, 251–53; James Madison, *Memorial and Remonstrance against Religious Assessments*, in *The Writings of James Madison*, vol. 2, 183–91; Locke, *A Letter on Toleration*, 65. See also *Webster v. Reproductive Health Services*, 109 S.Ct., 3070 (Stevens, J., dissenting) (arguing that a state abortion statute declaring that life begins at conception violates the establishment clause of the first amendment).

100. Compare Gardner, "Is an Embryo a Person?" 557 (arguing that an embryo is not a life) with John Willke, "Did You Know?" (arguing that an embryo is a life).
101. Dunn, "Justice and the Interpretation of Locke's Political Theory," 73, 81.
102. See Macpherson, *The Political Theory of Possessive Individualism*, 221, 225–66; L. Strauss, *Natural Right and History*, 243, 247–48. See also Pangle, *The Spirit of Modern Republicanism*, 143–44, 161, 306–7.
103. Locke, *Two Treatises of Government, First Treatise*, sec. 42 (emphasis in original).
104. Locke, *Second Treatise*, secs. 6, 70. See also secs. 5, 93.
105. John Locke, "Venditio" (1695), quoted in Dunn, "Justice and the Interpretation of Locke's Political Theory," 74. Locke's other works likewise recognize a right to and a duty of charity. See Simmons, *The Lockean Theory of Rights*, 328 (discussing, in addition to the works I have described, Locke's *Essays on the Law of Nature*, *Essay concerning Toleration*, and *Some Thoughts concerning Education*).
106. See, for example, Trattner, *From Poor Law to Welfare State*, 31–46.
107. 394 U.S. 618, 638, 627 (1969).
108. 397 U.S. 254 (1970).
109. 489 U.S. 189, 196 (1989). See also *Youngsberg v. Romeo*, 457 U.S. 307, 317 (1982) ("As a general matter, a State is under no constitutional duty to provide substantive services for those within its border"); *Harris v. McRae*, 448 U.S. 297, 317–18 (1980) ("Although the liberty protected by the Due Process Clause affords protection against unwarranted *government* interference . . ., it does not confer entitlement to such [governmental aid] as may be necessary to realize all the advantages of that freedom" [emphasis in original]); *Lindsey v. Norment*, 405 U.S. 56, 74 (1972) (holding that there is no government obligation to provide adequate housing).
110. See, for example, R. A. Epstein, *Takings*, 306–29 (maintaining that *all* public transfer and welfare programs are illegitimate, both as a matter of constitutional law and as a matter of political theory, including those for the poor and the needy); Thomas, "Civil Rights as a Principle versus Civil Rights as an Interest," 399 (arguing that if the Supreme Court determined there was a "right to welfare" in the ninth amendment, such a determination would be an illegitimate "discover[y]").
111. See, for example, Locke, *Two Treatises of Government, First Treatise*, sec. 42 (stating that an individual is entitled to relief only if he has "no means to subsist otherwise"). I noted earlier that it is not necessary to adhere to the Founders' conclusions about how a principle should be applied in a given situation. It is also not necessary to follow Locke's personal position on issues, including on charity. Locke's well-known proposal for the Board of Trade on the reform of the Poor Laws was excessively harsh. In his proposal Locke required, among other things, that children as young as three be separated from their mothers so the mothers could work.

112. 116 U.S. 616, 630 (1886).
113. Warren and Brandeis, "The Right of Privacy," 205.
114. See generally O'Brien, *Privacy, Law, and Public Policy*, 35–176 (discussing cases involving the first, fourth, and fifth amendments).
115. 381 U.S. 479 (1965).
116. Ibid., 484. Justice Douglas referenced the first, third, fourth, fifth, and ninth amendments.
117. Strong evidence exists that Justice Brennan devised the theory upon which Justice Douglas's opinion was based. See O'Brien, *Constitutional Law and Politics*, vol. 2, 307–8 (discussing an internal memorandum written by Justice Brennan to Justice Douglas).
118. See 381 U.S., 507–27 (Black, J., dissenting), 527–31 (Stewart, J., dissenting). Justice Black later expanded on his *Griswold* dissent, remarking that "even though I like my privacy as well as the next one, I am nevertheless compelled to admit that government has a right to invade it . . . [because I can] find in the Constitution no language which either specifically or impliedly grants to all individuals a constitutional right of privacy." H. L. Black, *A Constitutional Faith*, 9.
119. Bork, *The Tempting of America*, 99.
120. Justice Stewart was especially critical of Justice Goldberg's concurring opinion. According to Justice Stewart, Justice Goldberg's use of the ninth amendment "turns somersaults with history." 391 U.S., 529 (Stewart, J., dissenting).
121. Ibid., 488 (Goldberg, J., concurring) (citation omitted).
122. O'Brien, *Privacy, Law, and Public Policy*, 182–83.
123. Bork, "Neutral Principles and Some First Amendment Problems," 8.
124. Letter from John Locke to Denis Grenville, quoted in Simmons, *The Lockean Theory of Rights*, 53.
125. Conservatives like Bork are not the only modern commentators who reject the notion that there is a general right of privacy in the Constitution. Dworkin, one of the great liberal theorists of the second half of the twentieth century, argues that the general right possessed by all individuals is to equal concern and respect, from which particular rights, including privacy, may be inferred. See Dworkin, *Taking Rights Seriously*, chap. 12.
126. *Olmstead v. United States*, 277 U.S. 438, 478 (1928) (Brandeis, J., dissenting). Of course, the right to be let alone continues only so long as an individual is not violating the rights of others. See chapter 1. The evocative phrase the "right to be let alone" came from nineteenth-century torts commentator Judge Thomas Cooley. See Cooley, *Law of Torts*, 29. Cooley likely derived the phrase from the Anglo-American adage "a man's home is his castle."
127. 277 U.S., 478 (Brandeis, J., dissenting).
128. *Eisenstadt v. Baird*, 405 U.S. 438 (1972).
129. *Carey v. Population Services International*, 431 U.S. 678 (1977).
130. *Zablocki v. Redhail*, 434 U.S. 374 (1978).

131. *Moore v. City of East Cleveland*, 431 U.S. 494 (1977).
132. *Stanley v. Illinois*, 405 U.S. 645 (1972); *Wisconsin v. Yoder*, 406 U.S. 205 (1972).
133. *Roe v. Wade*, 410 U.S. 113 (1973).
134. The statute also made heterosexual sodomy illegal. The Court ignored that aspect of the statute.
135. 478 U.S. 186, 192–94 (1986) (citations omitted).
136. The penalty for a man was castration. The penalty for a woman was "cutting through the cartilage of her nose a hole of one half inch in diameter at the least." Thomas Jefferson, A Bill for Proportioning Crimes and Punishments in Cases Heretofore Capital, in *The Papers of Thomas Jefferson*, vol. 2, 497.
137. See, for example, Jaffa, "What Were the 'Original Intentions' of the Framers of the Constitution of the United States?"
138. Jaffa, "Judicial Conscience and Natural Rights," 252. Elsewhere, Jaffa remarks that there is no constitutional privacy right to engage in homosexual acts because such acts "treat men as if they were women." Jaffa, Review of *Gays/Justice*, by Richard D. Mohr, 314. See generally Jaffa, *Homosexuality and the Natural Law*.
139. Even under Jaffa's formalistic approach there would be a natural-liberty right to engage in what have long been called "deviant" heterosexual acts (provided they are done discreetly between consenting adults). Although Justice White carefully skirted the issue in *Bowers*, laws outlawing heterosexual sodomy are unconstitutional because, applying Jaffa's test, heterosexual sodomy does not run counter to regeneration. Indeed, by facilitating sexual arousal heterosexual sodomy may assist the regenerative process.
140. For the classic debate on the enforcement of morality in the context of homosexuality, see "The Hart-Devlin Debate," in Wasserstrom, ed., *Morality and the Law*, 24–54.
141. See *West Coast Hotel v. Parrish*, 300 U.S. 379 (1937) (upholding a state minimum wage law); *National Labor Relations Board v. Jones and Laughlin Steel Corporation*, 301 U.S. 1 (1937) (upholding the National Labor Relations Act).
142. See generally Abraham, *Freedom and the Court*, 11–37.
143. *Jones v. Opelika*, 316 U.S. 584, 608 (1942) (Stone, C. J., dissenting). "Preferred freedoms" is a concept originating with Justice Benjamin Cardozo's opinion in *Palko v. Connecticut*, 302 U.S. 325 (1937), and it was shortly thereafter incorporated into the famous "footnote four" of Justice (later Chief Justice) Harlan Stone's opinion for the Court in *United States v. Carolene Products Company*, 304 U.S. 144, 152 n. 4 (1938).
144. Hand, "Chief Justice Stone's Conception of the Judicial Function," 698.
145. *Morey v. Doud*, 354 U.S. 457 (1957) (striking down a state law exempting the American Express Company from licensing requirements for companies issuing money orders); *Allegheny Pittsburgh Coal Company v.*

County Commission, 488 U.S. 336 (1989) (invalidating a real estate tax law that assessed real estate in such a way that huge discrepancies in the taxable value of neighboring properties resulted).

146. R. A. Epstein, *Takings*; Levy, "Property as a Human Right"; Macedo, *The New Right v. the Constitution*; Posner, *The Economics of Justice*; Siegan, *Economic Liberties and the Constitution*.

147. Macedo, *The New Right v. the Constitution*, 47.

148. Siegan, *Economic Liberties and the Constitution*, 320. Not all of those who wish to abandon the double standard seek to protect individual economic liberty. Richard Funston believes that the double standard should be abolished in order to facilitate a more egalitarian distribution of wealth. See Funston, "The Double Standard of Constitutional Protection in the Era of the Welfare State."

149. 405 U.S. 538, 552 (1972).

150. See also Thomas, ABA Address, August 10, 1987, 9 ("What we need to emphasize is that the *entire* Constitution is a Bill of Rights; and economic rights are protected as much as any other rights" [emphasis in original]). Justice Thomas's writings and speeches attacking the double standard drew sharp criticism from several liberal members of the Senate Judiciary Committee during his confirmation hearing. See, for example, Senate Committee on the Judiciary, *Nomination of Clarence Thomas to Be Associate Justice of the Supreme Court of the United States*, 110–26 (remarks of Sen. Joseph R. Biden, Jr.).

151. *The Federalist* no. 10, 78 (James Madison).

152. In *The Works of John Adams*, vol. 6, 280. See also Farrand, ed., *Records of the Federal Convention*, vol. 1, 424 (remarks of Alexander Hamilton), 533 (remarks of Gouverneur Morris), 534 (remarks of John Rutledge), vol. 2, 123 (remarks of Elbridge Gerry); *Van Horne's Lessee v. Dorrance*, 2 U.S. (2 Dall.) 304, 310 (1795) (Paterson, J.).

153. See, for example, Macpherson, *The Political Theory of Possessive Individualism;* Tully, *A Discourse on Property*.

154. Locke, *Second Treatise*, sec. 42.

155. Schwartz, *The New Right and the Constitution*, 93. But see Wright, *American Interpretations of Natural Law*, 305 (writing in 1931, before the advent of the double standard, that "the justices of the Supreme Court and of the lower Federal and state courts who find in due process the means of giving protection to property rights may go to extremes in their interpretation of this principle of 'fundamental law.' There can be little doubt, however, but that they are holding steadfastly to the tradition of the founding fathers"). In his controversial book on the takings clause, Richard Epstein adopts a similarly simplistic view of economic liberty, generally, and of Locke, particularly. See R. A. Epstein, *Takings*.

156. Locke, "Some Considerations of the Consequences of the Lowering of Interest," in *The Works of John Locke*, vol. 5, 24–25.

157. Commager, *Jefferson, Nationalism, and the Enlightenment*, 93–121.

158. Letter from Thomas Jefferson to General Kosciusko, 1810, in *Democracy by Thomas Jefferson*, 239.
159. Adler and Gorman, *The American Testament*, 40.
160. See Reich, "The New Property." See also Reich, "Individual Rights and Social Welfare."
161. 397 U.S. 254, 264 (1970).
162. 489 U.S. 189 (1989).
163. 411 U.S. 1 (1973).

Notes to the Conclusion

1. Bickel, *The Least Dangerous Branch*, 18.
2. In his inaugural address, which identified "America's ideals" as "life, liberty, and the pursuit of happiness," President Bill Clinton reminded the American people that we are "an idea born in revolution." Reprinted in *Washington Post*, January 21, 1993, A26, cols. 1–2.
3. Letter from Thomas Jefferson to John Cartwright, June 5, 1824, in *The Portable Thomas Jefferson*, 580.
4. *The Federalist* no. 49, 314 (James Madison) (arguing that frequent constitutional change deprives the government of "that veneration" necessary to secure natural rights). Jefferson, more than any other Founder, valued occasional recourse to revolution to revitalize a regime. See, for example, Letter from Thomas Jefferson to James Madison, January 30, 1787, in *The Portable Thomas Jefferson*, 417 ("A little rebellion now and then is a good thing, and as necessary in the political world as storms in the physical. . . . It is a medicine for the sound health of government"); Letter from Thomas Jefferson to William Stephens Smith, November 13, 1787, in *Democracy by Thomas Jefferson*, 259 ("The tree of liberty must be refreshed from time to time with the blood of patriots and tyrants. It is its natural manure").
5. *The Federalist* no. 43, 279 (James Madison) (alluding to "the great principle of self-preservation; to the transcendent law of nature and of nature's God, which declares that the safety and happiness of society are the objects at which all political institutions aim and to which all such institutions must be sacrificed").
6. Ibid., no. 1, 33 (Alexander Hamilton).
7. The fact that some of the antimajoritarian features of the Founders' Constitution have been weakened (for example, direct election of the Senate) advises that those remaining—most notably, a strong and independent Court—must be vigorously embraced.

Works Cited

Government Documents

Annals of the Congress of the United States. Vol. 1 (1789–91), vol. 5 (1795–96), vol. 14 (1804–5). Edited by John Gales. Washington, D.C.: Gales and Seaton.

Congressional Record, 116th Cong., 2d sess., 1970. Congressional Record H3113–14 (daily ed. April 15).

Congressional Record, 133d Cong., 1st sess., 1987. S9188–89 (daily ed. July 1).

U.S. Senate Committee on the Judiciary. *Nomination of Clarence Thomas to Be Associate Justice of the Supreme Court of the United States,* 102d Cong., 1st sess., 1991.

———. *Nomination of Robert H. Bork to Be Associate Justice of the Supreme Court of the United States,* 100th Cong., 1st sess., 1987.

Books and Articles

Abraham, Henry J. *Freedom and the Court: Civil Rights and Liberties in the United States.* 5th ed. New York: Oxford University Press, 1988.

———. "The Judicial Function under the Constitution: Theory and Practice." Photocopy.

———. *The Judicial Process: An Introductory Analysis of the Courts of the United States, England, and France.* 6th ed. New York: Oxford University Press, 1993.

———. *Justices and Presidents: A Political History of Appointments to the Supreme Court.* 3d ed. New York: Oxford University Press, 1992.

———. Preface to *Journal of Law and Politics* 6 (Fall 1989): 1–5.

———. "Reflections on Our Enduring and Evolving Constitution." Photocopy.

Ackerman, Bruce A. *We the People 1: Foundations.* Cambridge, Mass.: Belknap Press, 1991.

Adair, Douglass. "'That Politics May Be Reduced to a Science': David Hume, James Madison, and the Tenth *Federalist.*" *Huntington Library Quarterly,* no. 4 (1957): 343–60.

Adams, John. *The Works of John Adams.* Edited by Charles F. Adams. 10 vols. Boston: Little, Brown, 1850–59.

Adams, Samuel. *The Writings of Samuel Adams.* Edited by Harry A. Cushing. 4 vols. New York: Putnam's Sons, 1904–8.

Adler, Mortimer J. *We Hold These Truths.* New York: Macmillan, 1987.

Adler, Mortimer J., and William Gorman. *The American Testament.* New York: Praeger, 1975.

Agresto, John. *The Supreme Court and Constitutional Democracy.* Ithaca: Cornell University Press, 1984.

Appleby, Joyce. *Liberalism and Republicanism in the Historical Imagination.* Cambridge: Harvard University Press, 1992.

Arkes, Hadley. *Beyond the Constitution.* Princeton: Princeton University Press, 1990.

Ashcraft, Richard. *Locke's Two Treatises of Government.* London: Unwin Hyman, 1987.

———. *Revolutionary Politics and Locke's Two Treatises of Government.* Princeton: Princeton University Press, 1986.

Baer, Judith A. *Equality under the Constitution: Reclaiming the Fourteenth Amendment.* Ithaca: Cornell University Press, 1983.

Bailyn, Bernard. *The Ideological Origins of the American Revolution.* Cambridge: Harvard University Press, 1967.

———. *The Origins of American Politics.* New York: Alfred A. Knopf, 1968.

———, ed. *Pamphlets of the American Revolution, 1750–1776.* Cambridge: Harvard University Press, 1965.

Baker, John S., Jr. "The Establishment Clause as Intended: No Preference among Sects and Pluralism in a Large Commercial Republic." In *The Bill of*

Rights: Original Meaning and Current Understanding, edited by Eugene W. Hickok, Jr., 42–53. Charlottesville: University Press of Virginia, 1991.

Ball, Terrence, and J. G. A. Pocock. Introduction to *Conceptual Change and the Constitution*, edited by Terrence Ball and J. G. A. Pocock, 1–12. Lawrence: University Press of Kansas, 1988.

Bancroft, George. *History of the United States*. 10 vols. Boston: Little, Brown, 1834–75.

Banning, Lance. "The Republican Interpretation: Retrospect and Prospect." In *The Republican Synthesis Revisited: Essays in Honor of George Athan Billias*, edited by Milton H. Klein, Richard D. Brown, and John B. Hench, 91–117. Worcester, Mass.: American Antiquarian Society, 1992.

Barber, Sotirios A. *The Constitution of Judicial Power*. Baltimore: Johns Hopkins University Press, 1993.

Barnett, Randy E. "James Madison's Ninth Amendment." In *The Rights Retained by the People*, edited by Randy E. Barnett. Vol. 1, 1–49. Fairfax, Va.: George Mason University Press, 1989.

———, ed. *The Rights Retained by the People*. Vol. 1. Fairfax, Va.: George Mason University Press, 1989.

Bassham, Gregory. *Original Intent and the Constitution: A Philosophical Study*. Lanham, Md.: Rowman and Littlefield, 1992.

Baucus, Max, and Kenneth R. Kay. "The Supreme Court Stripping Bills: Their Impact on the Constitution, the Courts, and Congress." *Villanova Law Review* 27 (May 1982): 988–1018.

Beard, Charles A. *An Economic Interpretation of the Constitution of the United States*. New York: Macmillan, 1913.

———. *The Supreme Court and the Constitution*. New York: Macmillan, 1912.

Becker, Carl L. *The Declaration of Independence: A Study in the History of Political Ideas*. Rev. ed. New York: Vintage Books, 1958.

———. *History of Political Parties in the Province of New York, 1760–1776*. 1909; reprint, Madison: University of Wisconsin Press, 1960.

Belz, Herman, Ronald Hoffman, and Peter J. Albert, eds. *To Form a More Perfect Union: The Critical Ideas of the Constitution*. Charlottesville: University Press of Virginia, 1992.

Berger, Raoul. "Academe vs. the Founding Fathers." *National Review*, April 14, 1978, 468–71.

———. *Congress v. the Supreme Court*. Cambridge: Harvard University Press, 1969.

———. *Government by Judiciary: The Transformation of the Fourteenth Amendment*. Cambridge: Harvard University Press, 1977.

———. *Impeachment: The Constitutional Problems*. Cambridge: Harvard University Press, 1973.

———. "The Ninth Amendment." *Cornell Law Review* 66 (November 1980): 1–26.

———. "'Original Intent' in Historical Perspective." *George Washington University Law Review* 54 (January–March 1986): 296–337.

Berlin, Isaiah. *Four Essays on Liberty.* New York: Oxford University Press, 1970.

Berns, Walter. "The Constitution as a Bill of Rights." In *How Does the Constitution Secure Rights?* edited by Robert A. Goldwin and William A. Schambra, 50–73. Washington, D.C.: AEI Press, 1985.

———. "Judicial Review and the Rights and Laws of Nature." In *1982 Supreme Court Review,* edited by Philip B. Kurland, Gerhard Casper, and Dennis J. Hutchinson, 49–83. Chicago: University of Chicago Press, 1983.

———. *Taking the Constitution Seriously.* New York: Simon and Schuster, 1987.

Bestor, Arthur. Review of *Impeachment: The Constitutional Problems,* by Raoul Berger. *Washington Law Review* 49 (November 1973): 255–85.

Bickel, Alexander M. *The Least Dangerous Branch: The Supreme Court at the Bar of Politics.* Indianapolis: Bobbs-Merrill, 1962.

———. *The Morality of Consent.* New Haven: Yale University Press, 1975.

———. "The Original Understanding and the Segregation Decision." *Harvard Law Review* 69 (1955): 1–65.

———. *The Supreme Court and the Idea of Progress.* New York: Harper and Row, 1970.

Billias, George Athan. "The Declaration of Independence: A Constitutional Document." *This Constitution: A Bicentennial Chronicle* (Spring 1985): 47–48.

———. *Elbridge Gerry: Founding Father and Republican Statesman.* New York: MacGraw Hill, 1976.

Black, Charles L., Jr. *Impeachment: A Handbook.* New Haven: Yale University Press, 1974.

———. "A Note on Senatorial Consideration of Supreme Court Nominees." *Yale Law Journal* 79 (March 1970): 657–64.

———. *Structure and Relationship in Constitutional Law.* Baton Rouge: Louisiana State University Press, 1969.

Black, Hugo L. *A Constitutional Faith.* New York: Alfred A. Knopf, 1968.

Blackstone, William. *Commentaries on the Laws of England.* Edited by Stanley Nader Katz. 4 vols., 1765–69; facsimile, Chicago: University of Chicago Press, 1979.

Bonner, Ethan. *Battle for Justice: How the Bork Nomination Shook America.* New York: W. W. Norton, 1989.

Boorstin, Daniel. *The Lost World of Thomas Jefferson.* New York: Henry Holt, 1948.

Bork, Robert H. "Natural Law and the Constitution." *First Things* 21 (March 1992): 16–20.

———. "Natural Law and the Law: An Exchange." *First Things* 23 (May 1992): 45.

———. "Neutral Principles and Some First Amendment Problems." *Indiana Law Journal* 47 (Fall 1971): 1–35.

————. "Original Intent and the Constitution." *Humanities* 7 (February 1986): 22–26.

————. "The Senate's Power Grab." *New York Times*, June 23, 1993, A23, cols. 2–5.

————. "The Struggle over the Role of the Court." *National Review*, September 17, 1982, 1137–39.

————. *The Tempting of America: The Political Seduction of the Law.* New York: Free Press, 1990.

————. "Tradition and Morality in Constitutional Law." In *Views from the Bench: The Judiciary and Constitutional Politics,* edited by Mark W. Cannon and David M. O'Brien, 166–72. Chatham, N.J.: Chatham House, 1985.

Boudin, Louis B. *Government by Judiciary.* 2 vols. New York: Godwin, 1932.

Boyd, Julian P. *The Declaration of Independence: The Evolution of the Text.* Princeton: Princeton University Press, 1945.

Brant, Irving. *Impeachment: Trials and Errors.* New York: Alfred A. Knopf, 1972.

Brennan, William J., Jr. "The Constitution of the United States: Contemporary Ratification." In *The U.S. Constitution and the Supreme Court,* edited by Steven Anzovin and Janet Podell, 166–79. New York: H. W. Wilson, 1988.

Brest, Paul. "The Misconceived Quest for the Original Understanding." In *Interpreting the Constitution: The Debate over Original Intent,* edited by Jack N. Rakove, 227–62. Boston: Northeastern University Press, 1990.

Brown, Robert E. *Charles Beard and the Constitution: A Critical Analysis of An Economic Interpretation of the Constitution.* Chicago: University of Chicago Press, 1956.

Bryce, James. *The American Commonwealth.* 2 vols. New York: Macmillan, 1888.

Burdick, Charles K. *The Law of the American Constitution.* New York: G. P. Putnam & Sons, 1922.

Burgess, John W. *Political Science and Comparative Constitutional Law.* 2 vols. Boston: Ginn, 1890.

Burgess, Susan R. *Contest for Constitutional Authority: The Abortion and War Powers Debates.* Lawrence: University Press of Kansas, 1992.

Burt, Robert A. *The Constitution in Conflict.* Cambridge, Mass.: Belknap Press, 1992.

Caplan, Russell L. *Constitutional Brinkmanship: Amending the Constitution by National Convention.* New York: Oxford University Press, 1988.

Cardozo, Benjamin N. *The Nature of the Judicial Process.* New Haven: Yale University Press, 1921.

Carter, Stephen L. "The Confirmation Mess." *Harvard Law Review* 101 (April 1988): 1185–1201.

————. "Constitutional Adjudication and the Indeterminate Text: A Preliminary Defense of an Imperfect Muddle." *Yale Law Journal* 94 (March 1985): 821–72.

————. *Reflections of an Affirmative Action Baby.* New York: Basic Books, 1991.

Chemerinsky, Erwin. *Interpreting the Constitution.* New York: Praeger, 1987.

————. "The Vanishing Constitution." *Harvard Law Review* 103 (November 1989): 43–104.

Chesterton, G. K. *What I Saw in America.* New York: Dodd, Mead, 1922.

Chinard, Gilbert. *Thomas Jefferson: The Apostle of Americanism.* Boston: Little, Brown, 1929.

Chipman, Daniel. Preface to Vermont Reports. Book 2, 9–36. Middlebury: D. Chipman & Son, 1824.

Choper, Jesse H. *Judicial Review and the National Political Process: A Functional Reconsideration of the Role of the Supreme Court.* Chicago: University of Chicago Press, 1980.

Cleveland, Henry. *Alexander H. Stephens in Public and Private: With Letters and Speeches, before, during, and since the War.* Philadelphia: National Publishing, 1866.

Clinton, Bill. "Inaugural Address." *Washington Post,* January 21, 1993, A26, cols. 1–2.

Clinton, Robert Lowry. *Marbury v. Madison and Judicial Review.* Lawrence: University Press of Kansas, 1989.

Clinton, Robert N. "Original Understanding, Legal Realism, and the Interpretation of 'This Constitution.'" *Iowa Law Review* 72 (July 1987): 1177–1279.

Commager, Henry Steele, ed. *Documents of American History.* 9th ed. New York: Appleton-Century-Crofts, 1973.

————. *Jefferson, Nationalism, and the Enlightenment.* New York: George Braziller, 1975.

"Confirmation Controversy: Selection of a Supreme Court Justice." Symposium. *Northwestern University Law Review* 84 (Spring/Summer 1990): 832–1046.

Cooley, Thomas M. *Law of Torts.* 2d ed. Chicago: Callaghan, 1888.

Cooper, Charles J. "Limited Government and Individual Liberty: The Ninth Amendment's Forgotten Lessons." *Journal of Law and Politics* 4 (Summer 1987): 63–80.

Cord, Robert L. *Separation of Church and State: Historical Fact and Current Fiction.* New York: Lambeth Press, 1982.

Corwin, Edward S. *Court over Constitution: A Study of Judicial Review as an Instrument of Popular Government.* Princeton: Princeton University Press, 1938.

————. *The "Higher Law" Background of American Constitutional Law.* Ithaca: Cornell University Press, 1929.

Cover, Robert M. *Justice Accused: Antislavery in the Judicial Process.* New Haven: Yale University Press, 1975.

Cox, Richard. *Locke on War and Peace.* Washington, D.C.: University Press of America, 1982.

Crosskey, William W. *Politics and the Constitution in the History of the United States.* 2 vols. Chicago: University of Chicago Press, 1953.

Currie, David P. *The Constitution in the Supreme Court: The First Hundred Years, 1789–1888.* Chicago: University of Chicago Press, 1985.

Curti, Merle. *Probing Our Past.* Gloucester, Mass.: Peter Smith, 1962.

Danelski, Daniel J. "Ideology as a Ground for the Rejection of the Bork Nomination." *Northwestern University Law Review* 84 (Spring/Summer 1990): 900–920.

Davis, Derek. *Original Intent: Chief Justice Rehnquist and the Course of American Church-State Relations.* New York: Prometheus, 1991.

Diamond, Martin. *As Far as Republican Principles Will Admit: Essays by Martin Diamond.* Edited by William A. Schambra. Washington, D.C.: AEI Press, 1992.

———. "The Declaration and the Constitution: Liberty, Democracy, and the Founders." *Public Interest* 41 (Fall 1975): 39–55.

Dickinson, John. *The Political Writings of John Dickinson.* 2 vols. Wilmington, Del.: Bonsal and Niles, 1801.

Diggins, John Patrick. *The Lost Soul of American Politics: Virtue, Self-Interest and the Foundations of Liberalism.* New York: Basic Books, 1984.

Dumbauld, Edward. *The Declaration of Independence: And What It Means Today.* Norman: University of Oklahoma Press, 1950.

Dunn, John. "Justice and the Interpretation of Locke's Political Theory." *Political Studies* 16 (February 1968): 68–87.

———. *The Political Thought of John Locke: An Historical Account of the Argument of the Two Treatises of Government.* Cambridge: Cambridge University Press, 1969.

———. "The Politics of Locke in England and America in the Eighteenth Century." In *John Locke: Problems and Perspectives,* edited by John W. Yolton, 45–80. Cambridge: Cambridge University Press, 1969.

Dworetz, Steven M. *The Unvarnished Doctrine: Locke, Liberalism, and the American Revolution.* Durham, N.C.: Duke University Press, 1990.

Dworkin, Ronald. "The Jurisprudence of Richard Nixon." *New York Review of Books,* May 4, 1972, 27–35.

———. *Law's Empire.* Cambridge: Harvard University Press, 1986.

———. *Life's Dominion: An Argument about Abortion, Euthanasia, and Individual Freedom.* New York: Alfred A. Knopf, 1993.

———. *Taking Rights Seriously.* Cambridge: Harvard University Press, 1978.

———. "Why Bakke Has No Case." *New York Review of Books,* November 10, 1977, 11–15.

Eisenberg, Theodore. "Congressional Authority to Restrict Lower Federal Court Jurisdiction." *Yale Law Journal* 83 (January 1974): 498–533.

Elliot, Jonathan, ed. *The Debates in the several State Conventions on the adoption of the Federal Constitution, as recommended by the General Convention at Philadelphia.* 2d ed. 5 vols. 1836; reprint, Philadelphia: J. B. Lippincott, 1901.

Ely, John Hart. *Democracy and Distrust: A Theory of Judicial Review.* Cambridge: Harvard University Press, 1980.

Engdahl, David E. "John Marshall's 'Jeffersonian' Concept of Judicial Review." *Duke Law Journal* 42 (November 1992): 279–339.

Epstein, David F. "The Political Theory of the Constitution." In *Confronting the Constitution*, edited by Allan Bloom, 77–141. Washington, D.C.: AEI Press, 1990.

———. *The Political Theory of the Federalist.* Chicago: University of Chicago Press, 1984.

Epstein, Richard A. *Takings: Private Property and the Power of Eminent Domain.* Cambridge: Harvard University Press, 1985.

Farber, Daniel A., and John E. Muench. "The Ideological Origins of the Fourteenth Amendment." *Constitutional Commentary* 1 (Summer 1984): 235–79.

Farrand, Max. *The Framing of the Constitution of the United States.* New Haven: Yale University Press, 1913.

———, ed. *The Records of the Federal Convention of 1787.* 3 vols. New Haven: Yale University Press, 1911.

The Federalist. Edited by Clinton Rossiter. New York: New American Library, 1961.

Feerick, John. "Impeaching Federal Judges: A Study of the Constitutional Provisions." *Fordham Law Review* 39 (October 1970): 1–58.

Fein, Bruce. "A Circumscribed Senate Confirmation Role." *Harvard Law Review* 102 (January 1989): 672–87.

Fisher, Louis. *Constitutional Dialogues: Interpretation as a Political Process.* Princeton: Princeton University Press, 1988.

Flaherty, David H. *Privacy in Colonial New England.* Charlottesville: University Press of Virginia, 1972.

Ford, Paul L., ed. *Essays on the Constitution of the United States.* New York: Burt Franklin, 1892; reprint, 1970.

———, ed. *Pamphlets on the Constitution of the United States.* Brooklyn: 1888; reprint, New York: De Capo Press, 1968.

Frankfurter, Felix. "A Note on Advisory Opinions." *Harvard Law Review* 36 (June 1924): 1002–9.

———. "The Supreme Court in the Mirror of Justices." *University of Pennsylvania Law Review* 105 (April 1957): 781–96.

———. "The Zeitgeist and the Judiciary." In *Law and Politics: Occasional Papers of Felix Frankfurter, 1913–1938*, edited by Archibald Macleish and E. F. Prichard, Jr., 3–9. New York: Harcourt, Brace, 1939.

Franklin, Benjamin. *The Life and Writings of Benjamin Franklin.* Edited by Albert Henry Smyth. 10 vols. New York: Macmillan, 1906.

Friedlander, Robert A. "Judicial Selection and the Constitution: What Did the Framers Originally Intend?" *Saint Louis University Public Law Review* 8 (1989): 1–11.

Funston, Richard. "The Double Standard of Constitutional Protection in the Era of the Welfare State." *Political Science Quarterly* 90 (Summer 1975): 261–87.

Gabin, Sanford B. *Judicial Review and the Reasonable Doubt Test*. Port Washington, N.Y.: Kennikat Press, 1981.

Gardner, Charles A. "Is an Embryo a Person?" *Nation*, November 13, 1989, 557.

"Gender, Race, and the Politics of Supreme Court Appointments: The Impact of the Anita Hill/Clarence Thomas Hearings." Symposium. *Southern California Law Review* 65 (March 1992): 1278–1582.

Gerber, Scott D. "The Jurisprudence of Clarence Thomas." *Journal of Law and Politics* 8 (Fall 1991): 107–41.

———. "Justice Clarence Thomas: First Term, First Impressions." *Howard Law Journal* 35 (Winter 1992): 115–53.

———. "Original Intent and Its Obligations: Rediscovering the Principles of the American Founding." *Hamline Journal of Public Law and Policy* 11 (Spring 1990): 1–18.

———. "The Republican Revival in American Constitutional Theory." *Political Research Quarterly* 47 (December 1994): 985–95.

———. "Roger Sherman and the Bill of Rights." College of William and Mary. Typescript. 1994.

———. Review of *We the People 1: Foundations*, by Bruce A. Ackerman, and *Rights Talk: The Impoverishment of Political Discourse*," by Mary Ann Glendon. *Journal of Law and Politics* 9 (Fall 1992): 232–38.

———. "Whatever Happened to the Declaration of Independence? A Commentary on the Republican Revisionism in the Political Thought of the American Revolution." *Polity* 26 (Winter 1993): 207–31.

Gerhardt, Michael J. "The Constitutional Limits to Impeachment and Its Alternatives." *Texas Law Review* 68 (November 1989): 1–104.

Gerhardt, Michael J., and Thomas D. Rowe, Jr. *Constitutional Theory: Arguments and Perspectives*. Charlottesville, Va.: Michie, 1993.

Germino, Dante. *Machiavelli to Marx: Modern Western Political Thought*. Chicago: University of Chicago Press, 1972.

Gibson, William F. Press Release No. 91–125, Chairman, The National Board of Directors of the NAACP on the Nomination of Judge Clarence Thomas to the U.S. Supreme Court (July 31, 1991).

Glausser, Wayne. "Three Approaches to Locke and the Slave Trade." *Journal of the History of Ideas* 51 (April–June 1990): 199–216.

Goebel, Julius, Jr. *Antecedents and Beginnings to 1801*. New York: Macmillan, 1971.

Goldman, Sheldon. "Judicial Selection and the Qualities That Make a 'Good' Judge." *Annals of the American Academy of Social and Political Science* 62 (July 1982): 112–24.

Goldwin, Robert A., and William A. Schambra, eds. *How Does the Constitution Secure Rights?* Washington, D.C.: AEI Press, 1985.

Graber, Mark A. "Asking Better Questions: The Problems of Constitutional Theory." *PS: Political Science and Politics* 26 (June 1993): 216–22.

Graebe, Christopher T. "The Federalism of James Iredell in Historical Context." *North Carolina Law Review* 69 (November 1990): 251–72.

Graham, Howard Jay. *Everyman's Constitution.* Madison: State Historical Society of Wisconsin, 1968.

Greene, Jack P. *Peripheries and Center: Constitutional Development in the Extended Polities of the British Empire and the United States, 1607–1788.* Athens: University of Georgia Press, 1986.

Grey, Thomas C. "Do We Have an Unwritten Constitution?" *Stanford Law Review* 27 (February 1975): 703–18.

Guest, Stephen. *Ronald Dworkin.* Edinburgh: University Press, 1992.

Gunther, Gerald. *Cases and Materials on Constitutional Law.* 10th ed. Mineola, N.Y.: Foundation Press, 1980.

———. "Congressional Power to Curtail Federal Court Jurisdiction: An Opinionated Guide to the Ongoing Debate." *Stanford Law Review* 36 (July 1984): 895–922.

———. *Individual Rights in Constitutional Law.* 4th ed. Mineola, N.Y.: Foundation Press, 1986.

Haines, Charles Grove. "The Law of Nature in State and Federal Judicial Decisions." *Yale Law Journal* 25 (June 1916): 617–57.

———. *The Revival of Natural Law Concepts.* 1930; reprint, New York: Russell and Russell, 1965.

Hall, Roland, and Roger Woolhouse. *80 Years of Locke Scholarship.* Edinburgh: University Press, 1983.

Hamilton, Alexander. *The Law Practice of Alexander Hamilton: Documents and Commentary.* Edited by Julius Goebel, Jr. 4 vols. New York: Columbia University Press, 1964.

———. *The Papers of Alexander Hamilton.* Edited by Harold C. Syrett and Jacob E. Cooke. 27 vols. New York: Columbia University Press, 1962.

Hamoway, Ronald. "*Cato's Letters,* John Locke, and the Republican Paradigm." In *John Locke's Two Treatises of Government: New Interpretations,* edited by Edward J. Harpham, 148–72. Lawrence: University Press of Kansas, 1992.

———. "Jefferson and the Scottish Enlightenment: A Critique of Garry Wills' *Inventing America: Jefferson's Declaration of Independence.*" *William and Mary Quarterly* 36 (October 1979): 504–23.

Hand, Learned. "Chief Justice Stone's Conception of the Judicial Function." *Columbia Law Review* 46 (September 1946): 696–99.

Harpham, Edward J., ed. *John Locke's Two Treatises of Government: New Interpretations.* Lawrence: University Press of Kansas, 1992.

Harrington, Michael. *The Other America.* Baltimore: Penguin Books, 1963.

Harris, Joseph B. *The Advice and Consent of the Senate.* Berkeley: University of California Press, 1953.

Hart, Henry M., Jr. "The Power of Congress to Limit the Jurisdiction of Federal Courts: An Exercise in Dialectic." *Harvard Law Review* 66 (June 1953): 1362–402.

Hartz, Louis. *The Liberal Tradition in America: An Interpretation of American Political Thought since the American Revolution.* New York: Harcourt Brace Jovanovich, 1955.

Hatch, Orrin G. "The Politics of Picking Judges." *Journal of Law and Politics* 6 (Fall 1989): 35–53.

Hazelton, John H. *The Declaration of Independence: Its History.* New York: Dodd, Mead, 1905.

Hellenbrand, Harold. *The Unfinished Revolution: Education and Politics in the Thought of Thomas Jefferson.* Newark: University of Delaware Press, 1990.

Higginbotham, A. Leon. "An Open Letter to Justice Clarence Thomas from a Federal Judicial Colleague." *University of Pennsylvania Law Review* 140 (January 1992): 1005–28.

Himmelfarb, Dan. "The Preamble in Constitutional Interpretation." *Seton Hall Constitutional Law Journal* 2 (Fall 1991): 127–209.

Hirsch, H. N. *A Theory of Liberty: The Constitution and Minorities.* New York: Routledge, 1992.

Hittinger, Russell. "Natural Law in Positive Laws: A Legislative or Adjudicative Issue?" *Review of Politics* 55 (Winter 1993): 5–34.

Hoffert, Robert W. *A Politics of Tensions: The Articles of Confederation and American Political Ideas.* Niwot: University Press of Colorado, 1992.

Horwitz, Morton J. "Republicanism and Liberalism in American Constitutional Thought." *William and Mary Law Review* 29 (Fall 1987): 57–74.

Howard, A. E. Dick. *Commentaries on the Constitution of Virginia.* 2 vols. Charlottesville: University Press of Virginia, 1974.

Hughes, Charles Evans. *Addresses and Papers of Charles Evans Hughes.* New York: Putnam's Sons, 1908.

———. *The Supreme Court of the United States.* New York: Columbia University Press, 1926.

Hume, David. *Moral and Political Philosophy.* Edited by Henry D. Aiken. New York: Hafner, 1948.

Hutson, James H. "The Bill of Rights and the American Revolutionary Experience." In *A Culture of Rights: The Bill of Rights in Philosophy, Politics, and Law—1791 and 1991*, edited by Michael J. Lacey and Knud Haakonssen, 62–97. New York: Cambridge University Press, 1991.

———. "The Creation of the Constitution: The Integrity of the Documentary Record." In *Interpreting the Constitution: The Debate over Original Intent*, edited by Jack N. Rakove, 151–78. Boston: Northeastern University Press, 1990.

Iredell, James. *Life and Correspondence of James Iredell.* Edited by Griffith J. McRee. 2 vols. New York: Appleton, 1857–58.

Isaacs, Nathan. "John Marshall on Contracts: A Study in Early American Juristic Theory." *Virginia Law Review* 7 (March 1921): 413–28.

Jaffa, Harry V. *American Conservatism and the American Founding.* Durham, N.C.: Carolina Academic Press, 1984.

———. *Crisis of the House Divided: An Interpretation of the Issues in the Lincoln-Douglas Debates.* Garden City, N.Y.: Doubleday, 1959.

———. *Homosexuality and the Natural Law.* Montclair, Calif.: Center for the Study of the Natural Law, Claremont Institute, 1990.

———. *How to Think about the American Revolution: A Bicentennial Cerebration.* Durham, N.C.: Carolina Academic Press, 1978.

———. "Judicial Conscience and Natural Rights: A Reply to Professor Ledewitz." *University of Puget Sound Law Review* 11 (Winter 1988): 219–53.

———. *Original Intent and the Framers of the Constitution: A Disputed Question.* Washington, D.C.: Regnery Gateway, 1994.

———. Review of *Gays/Justice: A Study of Ethics, Society, and Law,* by Richard D. Mohr. *Constitutional Commentary* 8 (Winter 1991): 313–17.

———. "What Were the 'Original Intentions' of the Framers of the Constitution of the United States?" *University of Puget Sound Law Review* 10 (Spring 1987): 351–448.

Jefferson, Thomas. *Democracy by Thomas Jefferson.* Edited by Saul K. Padover. New York: D. Appleton-Century, 1939.

———. *The Papers of Thomas Jefferson.* Edited by Julian Boyd. 28 vols. Princeton: Princeton University Press, 1950–94.

———. *The Portable Thomas Jefferson.* Edited by Merrill D. Peterson. New York: Penguin Books, 1975.

———. *The Works of Thomas Jefferson.* Edited by Paul L. Ford. 12 vols. New York: Putnam's Sons, 1904–5.

———. *The Writings of Thomas Jefferson.* Edited by Andrew A. Lipscomb and Albert E. Bergh. 20 vols. Washington, D.C.: Thomas Jefferson Memorial Association, 1904–5.

Jensen, Merrill. *The Articles of Confederation: An Interpretation of the Social-Constitutional History of the American Revolution, 1774–1781.* 3d printing. Madison: University of Wisconsin Press, 1959.

Jensen, Merrill, John P. Kaminski, and Gasper J. Saladino, eds. *Documentary History of the Ratification of the Constitution.* 2 vols. Madison: State Historical Society of Wisconsin, 1976.

Johnson, Lyndon B. "To Fulfill These Rights." In *The Great Society Reader: The Failure of American Liberalism,* edited by Marvin E. Gettleman and David Mermelstein. New York: Random House, 1967.

Kaminski, John P. "Restoring the Declaration of Independence: Natural Rights and the Ninth Amendment." In *The Bill of Rights,* edited by Jon Kukla, 141–50. Richmond: Virginia State Library and Archives, 1987.

Kay, Richard S. "Adherence to the Original Intentions in Constitutional Adjudication: Three Objections and Responses." *Northwestern University Law Review* 82 (Winter 1988): 226–92.

Kelly, Alfred H. "The Fourteenth Amendment Reconsidered: The Segregation Question." *Michigan Law Review* 54 (June 1956): 1049–86.

Kendall, Willmore. *John Locke and the Doctrine of Majority-Rule.* Urbana: University of Illinois Press, 1959.

Ketcham, Ralph, ed. *The Anti-Federalist Papers and the Constitutional Convention Debates.* New York: New American Library, 1986.

————. *Framed for Posterity: The Enduring Philosophy of the Constitution*. Lawrence: University Press of Kansas, 1993.

Klein, Milton H., Richard D. Brown, and John B. Hench, eds. *The Republican Synthesis Revisited: Essays in Honor of George Athan Billias*. Worcester, Mass.: American Antiquarian Society, 1992.

Koch, Adrienne. *The Philosophy of Thomas Jefferson*. New York: Columbia University Press, 1943.

Kramnick, Isaac. *Republicanism and Bourgeois Radicalism: Political Ideology in Late Eighteenth-Century England and America*. Ithaca: Cornell University Press, 1990.

Kull, Andrew. *The Color-Blind Constitution*. Cambridge: Harvard University Press, 1992.

Kurland, Philip B., and Ralph Lerner, eds. *The Founders' Constitution*. 5 vols. Chicago: University of Chicago Press, 1987.

Lash, Joseph P. *From the Diaries of Felix Frankfurter*. New York: W. W. Norton, 1975.

Lasson, Nelson B. *The History and Development of the Fourth Amendment to the United States Constitution*. Baltimore: Johns Hopkins University Press, 1937.

Leahy, Patrick. "Reflections on Federal Judicial Selection." *Journal of Law and Politics* 6 (Fall 1989): 25–30.

Lehrman, Lewis. "The Declaration of Independence and the Right to Life: One Leads Unmistakably from the Other." *The American Spectator*, April 1987, 21–23.

Levinson, Sanford. "Could Meese Be Right This Time?" *Tulane Law Review* 61 (April 1987): 1071–78.

Levinson, Sanford, and Steven Mailloux. Preface to *Interpreting Law and Literature: A Hermeneutic Reader*, edited by Sanford Levinson and Steven Mailloux, xi. Evanston, Ill.: Northwestern University Press, 1988.

————, eds. *Interpreting Law and Literature: A Hermeneutic Reader*. Evanston, Ill.: Northwestern University Press, 1988.

Levy, Leonard W. *The Establishment Clause: Religion and the First Amendment*. New York: Macmillan, 1986.

————. *The Law of the Commonwealth and Chief Justice Shaw*. Cambridge: Harvard University Press, 1957.

————. *Original Intent and the Framers' Constitution*. New York: Macmillan, 1988.

————. "Property as a Human Right." *Constitutional Commentary* 5 (Winter 1988): 169–84.

Lewis, Paul. *The Grand Incendiary: A Biography of Samuel Adams*. New York: Dial Press, 1973.

Lincoln, Abraham. *Abraham Lincoln: Speeches and Writings*. Edited by Don E. Fehrenbacher. 2 vols. New York: New American Library, 1989.

————. *Abraham Lincoln's Speeches*. Edited by L. L. Chittenden. New York: Dodd, Mead, 1896.

——. *The Collected Works of Abraham Lincoln.* Edited by Roy P. Basler. 9 vols. New Brunswick, N.J.: Rutgers University Press, 1953.

——. *Complete Works of Abraham Lincoln.* Edited by John G. Nicolay and John Hay. 12 vols. New York: Lamb Publishing, 1905.

——. *Letters and Addresses of Abraham Lincoln.* Edited by Howard Wilford Bell. New York: Trow Press, 1903.

Locke, John. *The Educational Writings of John Locke.* Edited by James L. Axtell. Cambridge: Cambridge University Press, 1968.

——. *An Essay concerning Human Understanding.* Edited by Alexander C. Fraser. 2 vols. Oxford: Clarendon Press, 1894.

——. *Essays on the Law of Nature.* Edited by Wolfgang von Leyden. Oxford: Clarendon Press, 1954.

——. *A Letter on Toleration.* Edited by J. W. Gough. Oxford: Clarendon Press, 1968.

——. *The Second Treatise of Government.* Edited by Thomas Peardon. New York: Macmillan, 1952.

——. *Two Treatises of Government.* Edited by Peter Laslett. 2d ed. Cambridge: Cambridge University Press, 1967.

——. *The Works of John Locke.* 11th ed. 20 vols. London: W. Otrige, 1824.

Lofgren, Charles A. "The Original Understanding of Original Intent?" In *Interpreting the Constitution: The Debate over Original Intent,* edited by Jack N. Rakove, 117–50. Boston: Northeastern University Press, 1990.

Lutz, Donald S. *The Origins of American Constitutionalism.* Baton Rouge: Louisiana State University Press, 1988.

——. *A Preface to American Political Theory.* Lawrence: University Press of Kansas, 1992.

——. "The Relative Influence of European Writers on Late Eighteenth-Century American Political Thought." *American Political Science Review* 78 (March 1984): 189–97.

Macedo, Stephen. *Liberal Virtues: Citizenship, Virtue, and Community in Liberal Constitutionalism.* Oxford: Clarendon Press, 1990.

——. *The New Right v. the Constitution.* Washington, D.C.: Cato Institute, 1986.

Macpherson, C. B. *The Political Theory of Possessive Individualism: Hobbes to Locke.* Oxford: Oxford University Press, 1962.

Madison, James. *Letters and Other Writings of James Madison.* 4 vols. Philadelphia: J. B. Lippincott, 1865.

——. *The Papers of James Madison.* Edited by W. T. Hutchinson and William M. E. Rachal. 13 vols. Chicago: University of Chicago Press, 1962–77.

——. *The Writings of James Madison.* Edited by Gaillard Hunt. 9 vols. New York: G. P. Putnam's Sons, 1900–1910.

Mahoney, Dennis J. "The Declaration of Independence as a Constitutional Document." In *The Framing and Ratification of the Constitution,* edited by Leonard W. Levy and Dennis J. Mahoney, 54–68. New York: Macmillan, 1987.

Marcus, Maeva, ed. *The Documentary History of the Supreme Court of the*

United States, 1789–1800. 4 vols. New York: Columbia University Press, 1988.

Marshall, Thurgood. "Slavery, Civil Rights, and the Constitution." In *The New Federalist Papers*, edited by J. Jackson Barlow, Dennis J. Mahoney, and John G. West, Jr., 303–5. New York: University Press of America, 1988.

Maxman, Melissa H. "In Defense of the Constitution's Judicial Impeachment Standard." *Michigan Law Review* 86 (November 1987): 420–63.

Mayer, David N. "The Natural Rights Basis of the Ninth Amendment: A Reply to Professor McAffee." *Southern Illinois University Law Journal* 16 (Winter 1992): 313–26.

McAffee, Thomas B. "The Original Meaning of the Ninth Amendment." *Columbia Law Review* 90 (June 1990): 1215–320.

McCants, David A. *Patrick Henry, The Orator.* New York: Greenwood, 1990.

McDonald, Forrest. *E Pluribus Unum: The Formation of the American Republic, 1776–1790.* Boston: Houghton Mifflin, 1965.

———. *Novus Ordo Seclorum: The Intellectual Origins of the Constitution.* Lawrence: University Press of Kansas, 1985.

———. *We the People: The Economic Origins of the Constitution.* Princeton: Princeton University Press, 1958.

McDowell, Gary L. "Coke, Corwin, and the Constitution: The 'Higher Law Background' Reconsidered." *Review of Politics* 55 (Summer 1993): 393–420.

———. *Curbing the Courts: The Constitution and the Limits of Judicial Power.* Baton Rouge: Louisiana State University Press, 1988.

———. "Postscript: A Debate on Judicial Activism." In Stephen Macedo, *The New Right v. the Constitution.* Washington, D.C.: Cato Institute, 1986.

Meese, Edwin III. "Address before the American Bar Association." In *The Great Debate: Interpreting Our Written Constitution*, 1–10. Washington, D.C.: Federalist Society, 1986.

———. "The Law of the Constitution." *Tulane Law Review* 61 (April 1987): 979–90.

———. "Toward a Jurisprudence of Original Intention." In *American Court Systems*, edited by Sheldon Goldman and Austin Sarat, 584–87. 2d ed. New York: Longman, 1989.

Merry, Henry J. "Scope of the Supreme Court's Appellate Jurisdiction: Historical Basis." *Minnesota Law Review* 47 (November 1963): 53–69.

Meyers, Marvin, ed. *The Mind of the Founder: Sources of the Political Thought of James Madison.* Rev. ed. Hanover, N.H.: University Press of New England, 1983.

Michael, Helen K. "The Role of Natural Law in Early American Constitutionalism: Did the Founders Contemplate Judicial Enforcement of 'Unwritten' Individual Rights?" *North Carolina Law Review* 69 (January 1991): 421–90.

Michelman, Frank I. "Law's Republic." *Yale Law Journal* 97 (July 1988): 1493–537.

Miller, Arthur S. *Toward Increased Judicial Activism: The Political Role of the Supreme Court.* Westport, Conn.: Greenwood, 1982.

Mitchell, Lawrence E. "The Ninth Amendment and the 'Jurisprudence of Original Intention.'" *Georgetown Law Journal* 74 (August 1986): 1719–42.

Monaghan, Henry P. "The Confirmation Process: Law or Politics?" *Harvard Law Review* 101 (April 1988): 1202–12.

Morgan, Edmund S. *The Birth of a Republic, 1763–89.* Chicago: University of Chicago Press, 1956.

Morgan, Edmund S., and Helen M. Morgan. *The Stamp Act Crisis: Prologue to Revolution.* Chapel Hill: University of North Carolina Press, 1953.

Morris, Richard B. *The Forging of the Union, 1781–1789.* New York: Harper and Row, 1987.

Morton, Bruce N. "John Locke, Robert Bork, Natural Rights, and the Interpretation of the Constitution." *Seton Hall Law Review* 22 (1992): 709–88.

Murphy, Walter F. "The Art of Constitutional Interpretation: A Preliminary Showing." In *Essays on the Constitution of the United States,* edited by M. Judd Harmon, 130–59. Port Washington, N.Y.: Kennikat Press, 1978.

———. "Constitutional Interpretation: The Art of the Historian, Magician, or Statesmen?" Review of *Government by Judiciary,*" by Raoul Berger. *Yale Law Journal* 87 (1978): 1752–71.

———. "An Ordering of Constitutional Values." *Southern California Law Review* 53 (January 1980): 703–60.

Murphy, Walter F., James E. Fleming, and William Harris II. *American Constitutional Interpretation.* Mineola, N.Y.: Foundation Press, 1986.

Murray, Charles. "Affirmative Racism." Reprinted in *Philosophical Problems in the Law,* edited by David M. Adams, 357–64. Belmont, Calif.: Wadsworth, 1992.

Murray, Pauli. "The Rights of Women." In *The Rights of Americans,* edited by Norman Dorsen, 521–45. New York: Pantheon Books, 1971.

Myrdal, Gunnar. *An American Dilemma: The Negro Problem and Modern Democracy.* New York: Harper and Row, 1944.

Namier, Lewis B. *England in the Age of the American Revolution.* London: Macmillan, 1930.

Nedelsky, Jennifer. *Private Property and the Limits of American Constitutionalism: The Madisonian Framework and Its Legacy.* Chicago: University of Chicago Press, 1990.

Nelson, William E. *The Fourteenth Amendment: From Political Principle to Judicial Doctrine.* Cambridge: Harvard University Press, 1988.

Nevins, Allan. *The American States during and after the Revolution, 1775–1789.* New York: Macmillan, 1924; reprint, n.p.: Augustus M. Kelley, 1969.

Newton, Lisa. "Reverse Discrimination as Unjustified." Reprinted in *Philosophical Problems in the Law,* edited by David M. Adams, 354–57. Belmont, Calif.: Wadsworth, 1992.

O'Brien, David M. *Constitutional Law and Politics.* 2 vols. New York: W. W. Norton, 1991.

———. "The Framers' Muse on Republicanism, the Supreme Court, and Pragmatic Constitutional Interpretivism." *Constitutional Commentary* 8 (Winter 1991): 119–48.

———. *Judicial Roulette*. New York: Priority Press, 1988.

———. *Privacy, Law, and Public Policy*. New York: Praeger, 1979.

Onuf, Peter S. "Reflections on the Founding: Constitutional Historiography in Bicentennial Perspective." *William and Mary Quarterly* 46 (April 1989): 341–75.

Orfield, Lester Bernhardt. *The Amending of the Federal Constitution*. Chicago: Callaghan, 1942.

Ortiz, Daniel R. "The Price of Metaphysics: Deadlock in Constitutional Theory." In *Pragmatism in Law and Society*, edited by Michael E. Brint and William G. Weaver, 311–22. Boulder, Colo. Westview, 1991.

Pangle, Thomas L. *The Spirit of Modern Republicanism: The Moral Vision of the American Founders and the Philosophy of Locke*. Chicago: University of Chicago Press, 1988.

Parrington, Vernon L. *Main Currents in American Thought*. 2 vols. New York: Harcourt, Brace, 1927.

Patterson, Bennett B. *The Forgotten Ninth Amendment*. Indianapolis: Bobbs-Merrill, 1955.

Perry, Michael J. *The Constitution in the Courts: Law or Politics?* New York: Oxford University Press, 1994.

"Perspectives on the Authoritativeness of Supreme Court Decisions." Symposium. *Tulane Law Review* 61 (April 1987): 977–1095.

"Perspectives on Natural Law." Symposium. *University of Cincinnati Law Review* 61 (1992): 1–222.

Phelps, Timothy M., and Helen Winternitz. *Capitol Games: Clarence Thomas, Anita Hill, and the Behind-the-Scenes Story of a Supreme Court Nomination*. New York: Hyperion, 1992.

Pocock, J. G. A. *The Machiavellian Moment: Florentine Political Thought and the Atlantic Republican Tradition*. Cambridge: Harvard University Press, 1975.

———. "*The Machiavellian Moment* Revisited: A Study in History and Ideology." *Journal of Modern History* 53 (March 1981): 49–72.

———. *Politics, Language, and Time: Essays on Political Thought and History*. New York: Atheneum, 1971.

———. "Virtue and Commerce in the Eighteenth Century." *Journal of Interdisciplinary History* 3 (Summer 1972): 120–34.

———. *Virtue, Commerce, and History: Essays on Political Thought and History, Chiefly in the Eighteenth Century*. Cambridge: Cambridge University Press, 1985.

Poore, Benjamin P. *Federal and State Constitutions*. 2d ed. 2 vols. Washington, D.C.: Government Printing Office, 1878.

Posner, Richard A. *The Economics of Justice*. Cambridge: Harvard University Press, 1981.

———. *Law and Literature: A Misunderstood Relation.* Cambridge: Harvard University Press, 1988.

Pound, Roscoe. "Law in Books and Law in Action: Historical Causes of Divergence between the Nominal and Actual Law." *American Law Review* 44 (1910): 12–28.

Powell, H. Jefferson. "The Original Understanding of Original Intent." *Harvard Law Review* 98 (March 1985): 885–948.

Rahe, Paul A. *Republics Ancient and Modern: Classical Republicanism and the American Revolution.* Chapel Hill: University of North Carolina Press, 1992.

Rakove, Jack N. *The Beginnings of National Politics: An Interpretive History of the Continental Congress.* New York: Alfred A. Knopf, 1979.

———. "Parchment Barriers and the Politics of Rights." In *A Culture of Rights: The Bill of Rights in Philosophy, Politics, and Law—1791 and 1991,* edited by Michael J. Lacey and Knud Haakonssen, 98–143. New York: Cambridge University Press, 1991.

———. Review of *Taking the Constitution Seriously,* by Walter Berns. *ABA Journal,* September 1, 1987, 120.

———, ed. *Interpreting the Constitution: The Debate over Original Intent.* Boston: Northeastern University Press, 1990.

Ramsey, David. *History of the American Revolution.* 2 vols. Philadelphia: R. Aitken & Son, 1789.

Ratner, Leonard G. "Congressional Power over the Appellate Jurisdiction of the Supreme Court." *University of Pennsylvania Law Review* 109 (December 1960): 157–202.

———. "Majoritarian Constraints on Judicial Review: Congressional Control of Supreme Court Jurisdiction." *Villanova Law Review* 27 (May 1982): 929–58.

Redish, Martin H. "Congressional Power to Regulate Supreme Court Appellate Jurisdiction under the Exceptions Clause: An Internal and External Examination." *Villanova Law Review* 27 (May 1982): 900–928.

———. "Constitutional Limitations on Congressional Power to Control Federal Jurisdiction: A Reaction to Professor Sager." *Northwestern University Law Review* 77 (April 1983): 143–67.

Rehnquist, William H. *Grand Inquests: The Historic Impeachments of Justice Samuel Chase and President Andrew Johnson.* New York: William Morrow, 1992.

———. "The Impeachment Clause: A Wild Card in the Constitution." *Northwestern University Law Review* 85 (Summer 1991): 903–18.

———. "The Notion of a Living Constitution." In *Views from the Bench: The Judiciary and Constitutional Politics,* edited by Mark W. Cannon and David M. O'Brien, 127–36. Chatham, N.J.: Chatham House, 1985.

———. *The Supreme Court: How It Was, How It Is.* New York: William Morrow, 1987.

Reich, Charles. "Individual Rights and Social Welfare: The Emerging Legal Issues." *Yale Law Journal* 74 (June 1969): 1245–57.

———. "The New Property." *Yale Law Journal* 73 (April 1964): 733–87.

Reid, John Phillip. *The Concept of Representation in the Age of the American Revolution.* Chicago: University of Chicago Press, 1989.

———. *Constitutional History of the American Revolution: The Authority of Rights.* Madison: University of Wisconsin Press, 1987.

Rice, Charles E. "Congress and the Supreme Court's Jurisdiction." *Villanova Law Review* 27 (May 1982): 959–87.

Richards, David A. J. *Conscience and the Constitution: History, Theory, and Law of the Reconstruction Amendments.* Princeton: Princeton University Press, 1993.

———. *Foundations of American Constitutionalism.* New York: Oxford University Press, 1989.

Rossiter, Clinton. Introduction to *The Federalist.* New York: New American Library, 1961.

———. *Seedtime of the Republic: The Origin of the American Tradition of Political Liberty.* New York: Harcourt Brace Jovanovich, 1953.

Rotunda, Ronald D. "An Essay on the Constitutional Parameters of Federal Impeachment." *Kentucky Law Journal* 76 (1987–88): 707–61.

Rousseau, Jean-Jacques. *The Social Contract and Discourses.* Edited by G. H. D. Cole. London: Dent, 1973.

Sager, Lawrence. "Constitutional Limitations on Congress' Authority to Regulate the Jurisdiction of the Federal Courts." *Harvard Law Review* 95 (November 1981): 17–89.

Schlesinger, Arthur M., Sr. *The Colonial Merchants and the American Revolution.* New York: Columbia University Press, 1918.

Schwartz, Bernard. *The New Right and the Constitution: Turning Back the Legal Clock.* Boston: Northeastern University Press, 1990.

———. *The Unpublished Opinions of the Warren Court.* New York: Oxford University Press, 1985.

Schwarzenbach, Sibyl. "Locke's Two Conceptions of Property." *Social Theory and Practice* 14 (Summer 1988): 141–72.

Scigliano, Robert. *The Supreme Court and the Presidency.* New York: Free Press, 1971.

Scott, Austin. "*Holmes v. Walton:* The New Jersey Precedent." *American Historical Review* 4 (April 1899): 456–69

Shalhope, Robert E. "Toward a Republican Synthesis: The Emergence of an Understanding of Republicanism in American Historiography." *William and Mary Quarterly* 29 (January 1972): 49–80.

Sheldon, Garrett Ward. *The Political Philosophy of Thomas Jefferson.* Baltimore: Johns Hopkins University Press, 1991.

Sherry, Suzanna. "The Founders' Unwritten Constitution." *University of Chicago Law Review* 54 (Fall 1987): 1127–77.

———. "Natural Law in the States." *University of Cincinnati Law Review* 61 (1992): 171–222.

Sidney, Algernon. *Discourses concerning Government.* 1698; reprint, New York: Arno Press, 1979.

Siegan, Bernard H. *Economic Liberties and the Constitution.* Chicago: University of Chicago Press, 1980.

Simmons, A. John. *The Lockean Theory of Rights.* Princeton: Princeton University Press, 1992.

———. *Moral Principles and Political Obligations.* Princeton: Princeton University Press, 1979.

Simon, Paul. *Advice and Consent: Clarence Thomas, Robert Bork, and the Intriguing History of the Supreme Court's Nomination Battles.* Bethesda, Md.: National Press Books, 1992.

Sinopoli, Richard C. *The Foundations of American Citizenship: Liberalism, the Constitution, and Civic Virtue.* New York: Oxford University Press, 1992.

Smith, Page. "David Ramsey and the Causes of the American Revolution." *William and Mary Quarterly* 17 (January 1960): 51–77.

Smith, Rogers M. *Liberalism and American Constitutional Law.* Rev. ed. Cambridge: Harvard University Press, 1990.

Snowiss, Sylvia. *Judicial Review and the Law of the Constitution.* New Haven: Yale University Press, 1990.

Sosin, J. M. *The Aristocracy of the Long Robe: The Origins of Judicial Review in America.* Westport, Conn.: Greenwood, 1989.

Stimson, Shannon. *The American Revolution in Law: Anglo-American Jurisprudence before John Marshall.* Princeton: Princeton University Press, 1990.

Storing, Herbert. "The Constitution and the Bill of Rights." In *Essays on the Constitution of the United States,* edited by M. Judd Harmon, 32–48. Port Washington, N.Y.: Kennikat Press, 1978.

———. *What the Anti-Federalists Were For.* Chicago: University of Chicago Press, 1981.

Story, Joseph. *Commentaries on the Constitution of the United States.* Boston: Hilliard, Gray, 1833.

Strauss, David A., and Cass R. Sunstein. "The Senate, the Constitution, and the Confirmation Process." *Yale Law Journal* 101 (May 1992): 1491–524.

Strauss, Leo. *Natural Right and History.* Chicago: University of Chicago Press, 1953.

———. "On Natural Law." In *Studies in Political Philosophy,* edited by Thomas L. Pangle, 137–46. Chicago: University of Chicago Press, 1983.

Sunstein, Cass R. "Beyond the Republican Revival." *Yale Law Journal* 97 (July 1988): 1539–90.

———. *The Partial Constitution.* Cambridge: Harvard University Press, 1993.

Tarcov, Nathan, and Thomas L. Pangle. "Epilogue: Leo Strauss and the History of Political Philosophy." In *History of Political Philosophy,* edited by Leo

Strauss and Joseph Cropsey, 907–35. 3d ed. Chicago: University of Chicago Press, 1987.

ten Broek, Jacobus. *Equal under Law*. New York: Collier, 1965.

Thayer, James Bradley. "The Origin and Scope of the American Doctrine of Constitutional Review." *Harvard Law Review* 7 (October 1893): 129–56.

Thomas, Clarence. "ABA Address, Luncheon Meeting of the Business Law Section." August 10, 1987. Photocopy.

———. "Affirmative Action Goals and Timetables: Too Tough? Not Tough Enough!" *Yale Law and Policy Review* 5 (Spring/Summer 1987): 402–11.

———. "Civil Rights as a Principle versus Civil Rights as an Interest." In *Assessing the Reagan Years*, edited by David Boaz, 391–402. Washington, D.C.: Cato Institute, 1988.

———. "The Higher Law Background of the Privileges or Immunities Clause of the Fourteenth Amendment." *Harvard Journal of Law and Public Policy* 12 (Winter 1989): 63–68.

———. "Toward a 'Plain Reading' of the Constitution—The Declaration of Independence in Constitutional Interpretation." *Howard Law Journal* 30 (1987): 983–95.

Trattner, Walter I. *From Poor Law to Welfare State: A History of Social Welfare in America*. 3d ed. New York: Free Press, 1984.

Trent, William P. "The Case of Josiah Philips." *American Historical Review* 1 (April 1896): 444–54.

Trevelyan, George Otto. *The American Revolution*. 4 vols. New York: Longmans, Green, 1898–1907.

Tribe, Laurence H. *Abortion: The Clash of Absolutes*. New York: W.W. Norton, 1990.

———. *God Save This Honorable Court*. New York: Random House, 1985.

Tully, James. *A Discourse on Property: John Locke and His Adversaries*. Cambridge: Cambridge University Press, 1980.

Tushnet, Mark. *Red, White, and Blue: A Critical Analysis of Constitutional Law*. Cambridge: Harvard University Press, 1988.

Van Alstyne, William. "What Do You Think about the Twenty-Seventh Amendment?" *Constitutional Commentary* 10 (Winter 1993): 9–18.

Varnum, James Mitchell. *The Case, Trevett Against Weeden: On Information and Complaint, for refusing Paper Bills in Payment for Butcher's Meat, in Market, at Par with Specie* (1787). University of Virginia.

Vile, John R. *Rewriting the United States Constitution: An Examination of Proposals from Reconstruction to the Present*. New York: Praeger, 1991.

Walker, Thomas G., and Lee Epstein. *The Supreme Court of the United States: An Introduction*. New York: St. Martin's Press, 1993.

Warren, Charles. *The Supreme Court in United States History*. Rev. ed. 2 vols. Boston: Little, Brown, 1926.

Warren, Samuel D., and Louis D. Brandeis. "The Right of Privacy." *Harvard Law Review* 4 (December 1890): 193–220.

Washington, George. *The Writings of George Washington.* Edited by Jared Sparks. 12 vols. Boston: Little, Brown, 1858.

Wasserstrom, Richard A., ed. *Morality and the Law.* Belmont, Calif.: Wadsworth, 1971.

———. "Racism, Sexism, and Preferential Treatment: An Approach to the Topics." *UCLA Law Review* 24 (February 1977): 581–622.

Weber, Paul J., and Barbara A. Perry. *Unfounded Fears: Myths and Realities of a Constitutional Convention.* New York: Greenwood, 1989.

Webking, Robert H. *The American Revolution and the Politics of Liberty.* Baton Rouge: Louisiana State University Press, 1988.

———. "Melancton Smith and the Letters from the Federal Farmer." *William and Mary Quarterly* 44 (July 1987): 510–28.

White, G. Edward. *The Marshall Court and Cultural Change, 1815–35.* New York: Macmillan, 1988.

White, Morton. *The Philosophy of the American Revolution.* New York: Oxford University Press, 1978.

———. *Philosophy, The Federalist, and the Constitution.* New York: Oxford University Press, 1987.

———. *Social Thought in America: The Revolt against Formalism.* Boston: Beacon Press, 1957.

Will, George F. "Person of the Millennium." *Washington Post,* December 16, 1990, K7.

Willke, John. "Did You Know?" Pamphlet.

Wills, Garry. *Explaining America: The Federalist.* New York: Doubleday, 1981.

———. *Inventing America: Jefferson's Declaration of Independence.* Garden City, N.Y.: Doubleday, 1978.

———. *Lincoln at Gettysburg: The Words That Remade America.* New York: Simon and Schuster, 1992.

Wilson, James. *Works of James Wilson.* Edited by James D. Andrews. 2 vols. Chicago: Callaghan, 1896.

———. *The Works of James Wilson.* Edited by Robert G. McCloskey. 2 vols. Cambridge, Mass.: Belknap Press, 1967.

Wilson, James Q. *American Government.* 4th ed. Lexington, Mass.: D. C. Heath, 1989.

Windstrup, George. "Locke on Suicide." *Political Theory* 8 (May 1980): 169–82.

Wolfe, Christopher. *Judicial Activism: Bulwark of Freedom or Precarious Security?* Pacific Grove, Calif.: Brooks/Cole, 1991.

———. *The Rise of Modern Judicial Review: From Constitutional Interpretation to Judge-Made Law.* New York: Basic Books, 1986.

Wood, Gordon S. Afterword to *The Republican Synthesis Revisited: Essays in Honor of George Athan Billias,* edited by Milton H. Klein, Richard D. Brown, and John B. Hench, 143–51. Worcester, Mass.: American Antiquarian Society, 1992.

———. *The Creation of the American Republic, 1776–1787.* Chapel Hill: University of North Carolina Press, 1969.

――――. *The Fundamentalists and the Constitution.* Charlottesville: Virginia Commission on the Bicentennial of the United States Constitution, 1989.

――――. *The Radicalism of the American Revolution.* New York: Alfred A. Knopf, 1992.

Woodward, Bob, and Scott Armstrong. *The Brethren: Inside the Supreme Court.* New York: Simon and Schuster, 1979.

Woodward, C. Vann. *The Strange Career of Jim Crow.* 3d ed. New York: Oxford University Press, 1974.

Wortham, Anne. *The Other Side of Racism.* Columbus: Ohio State University Press, 1981.

Wright, Benjamin F., Jr. *American Interpretations of Natural Law.* Cambridge: Harvard University Press, 1931.

――――. *Consensus and Continuity, 1776–1787.* Boston: Boston University Press, 1958.

――――. *The Contract Clause of the Constitution.* Cambridge: Harvard University Press, 1938.

Cases

Akron v. Akron Center for Reproductive Health, 462 U.S. 416 (1983).

Allegheny Pittsburgh Coal Company v. County Commission, 488 U.S. 336 (1989).

The Antelope Case, 23 U.S. (10 Wheat.) 66 (1825).

Baker v. Carr, 369 U.S. 186 (1962).

Barron v. Baltimore, 32 U.S. (7 Pet.) 243 (1833).

Barry v. Mercein, 46 U.S. (5 How.) 103 (1847).

Bayard v. Singleton, 1 N.C. (Martin) 5 (1787).

Bell v. Ohio, 438 U.S. 637 (1978).

Bolling v. Sharpe, 347 U.S. 497 (1954).

Bowers v. Hardwick, 478 U.S. 186 (1986).

Boyd v. United States, 116 U.S. 616 (1886).

Brown v. Board of Education, 347 U.S. 483 (1954).

Calder v. Bull, 3 U.S. (3 Dall.) 386 (1798).

Carey v. Population Services International, 431 U.S. 678 (1977).

Chisholm v. Georgia, 2 U.S. (2 Dall.) 419 (1793).

The City of London v. Wood, 88 Eng. Rep. 1592 (1702).

Civil Rights Cases, 109 U.S. 3 (1883).

Commonwealth v. Caton, 4 Call (8 Va.) 5 (1782).

Cooper v. Aaron, 358 U.S. 1 (1958).

Craig v. Boren, 429 U.S. 190 (1976).

Cruzan v. Director of the Missouri Department of Health, 110 S.Ct. 2841 (1990).

Currie's Administrator v. Mutual Assurance Society, 4 Hen. & M. (14 Va.) 315 (1809).

Daniels v. Railroad Company, 70 U.S. (3 Wall.) 250 (1865).
De Funis v. Odegaard, 507 P.2d 1169 (1973).
DeShaney v. Winnebago County Department of Social Services, 489 U.S. 189 (1989).
Dillon v. Gloss, 256 U.S. 368 (1921).
Dr. Bonham's Case, 77 Eng. Rep. 646 (1610).
Dred Scott v. Sandford, 60 U.S. (19 How.) 393 (1857).
Eisenstadt v. Baird, 405 U.S. 438 (1972).
Employment Division, Department of Human Resources of Oregon v. Smith, 110 S.Ct. 1595 (1990).
Fletcher v. Peck, 10 U.S. (6 Cr.) 87 (1810).
The Francis Wright, 105 U.S. 381 (1881).
Frontiero v. Richardson, 411 U.S. 677 (1973).
Fullilove v. Klutznick, 448 U.S. 448 (1980).
Furman v. Georgia, 408 U.S. 238 (1972).
Gardner v. Newburgh, 2 Johns. Ch. 162 (N.Y. 1816).
Re Gault, 387 U.S. 1 (1967).
Gibbons v. Ogden, 22 U.S. (9 Wheat.) 1 (1824).
Glidden v. Zdanock, 370 U.S. 530 (1961).
Goldberg v. Kelly, 397 U.S. 254 (1970).
Gregg v. Georgia, 428 U.S. 153 (1976).
In re Griffiths, 413 U.S. 717 (1973).
Griswold v. Connecticut, 381 U.S. 479 (1965).
Hall v. DeCuir, 95 U.S. 485 (1878).
Ham v. M'Claws, 1 Bay (S.C.) 93 (1789).
Harris v. McRae, 448 U.S. 297 (1980).
Hylton v. United States, 3 U.S. (3 Dall.) 171 (1796).
Jacobson v. Massachusetts, 197 U.S. 11 (1905).
Jones v. Opelika, 316 U.S. 584 (1942).
Kamper v. Hawkins, 1 Va. Cas. 20 (1793).
Lindsey v. Norment, 405 U.S. 56 (1972).
Lockett v. Ohio, 438 U.S. 586 (1978).
Lynch v. Household Finance Corporation, 405 U.S. 538 (1972).
Maher v. Doe, 432 U.S. 464 (1977).
Marbury v. Madison, 5 U.S. (1 Cr.) 137 (1803).
Martin v. Hunter's Lessee, 14 U.S. (1 Wheat.) 304 (1816).
Massachusetts Board of Retirement v. Murgia, 427 U.S. 307 (1976).
Ex Parte McCardle, 74 U.S. (7 Wall.) 506 (1868).
McCulloch v. Maryland, 17 U.S. (4 Wheat.) 316 (1819).
Minge v. Gilmour, 17 F. Cas. 440 (C.C.D.N.C. 1798).
Moore v. City of East Cleveland, 431 U.S. 494 (1977).
Morey v. Doud, 354 U.S. 457 (1957).
Muller v. Oregon, 208 U.S. 412 (1908).
National Labor Relations Board v. Jones and Laughlin Steel Corporation, 301 U.S. 1 (1937).

New Jersey v. Wilson, 11 U.S. (7 Cr.) 164 (1812).
Northern Securities Company v. United States, 193 U.S. 197 (1904).
Ogden v. Saunders, 25 U.S. (12 Wheat.) 213 (1827).
Olmstead v. United States, 277 U.S. 438 (1928).
Oregon v. Mitchell, 400 U.S. 112 (1970).
Osborn v. United States Bank, 22 U.S. (9 Wheat.) 739 (1830).
Page v. Pendleton, 1 Wythe (Va.) 211 (1793).
Palko v. Connecticut, 302 U.S. 325 (1937).
Penry v. Lynaugh, 109 S.Ct. 2934 (1989).
Planned Parenthood v. Danforth, 428 U.S. 552 (1976).
Planned Parenthood of Southeastern Pennsylvania v. Casey, 112. S.Ct. 2791
    (1992).
Plessy v. Ferguson, 163 U.S. 537 (1896).
Plyler v. Doe, 457 U.S. 202 (1982).
Pollack v. Farmers' Loan and Trust Company, 157 U.S. 429 (1895).
Powell v. McCormack, 395 U.S. 486 (1969).
Reed v. Reed, 404 U.S. 71 (1971).
Regents of the University of California v. Bakke, 438 U.S. 265 (1978).
Robin v. Hardaway, 1 Jeff. (Va.) 109 (1772).
Roe v. Wade, 410 U.S. 113 (1973).
Rostker v. Goldberg, 453 U.S. 57 (1981).
San Antonio v. Rodriguez, 411 U.S. 1 (1973).
Shanks v. Dupont, 28 U.S. (3 Pet.) 239 (1830).
Shapiro v. Thompson, 394 U.S. 618 (1969).
Southern Pacific Company v. Jensen, 245 U.S. 202 (1917).
Stanford v. Kentucky and *Wilkins v. Missouri*, 109 S.Ct. 2969 (1989).
Stanley v. Illinois, 405 U.S. 645 (1972).
Strauder v. West Virginia, 100 U.S. 303 (1880).
Sturges v. Crowninshield, 17 (4 Wheat.) 122 (1819).
Symsbury Case, 1 Kirby (Conn.) 444 (1785).
Talbot v. Jansen, 3 U.S. (3 Dall.) 133 (1795).
Terrett v. Taylor, 13 U.S. (9 Cr.) 43 (1815).
Thompson v. Oklahoma, 487 U.S. 815 (1988).
Tison v. Arizona, 481 U.S. 137 (1987).
Trop v. Dulles, 356 U.S. 86 (1958).
Trustees of Dartmouth College v. Woodward, 1 N.H. 111 (1817).
Trustees of Dartmouth College v. Woodward, 17 U.S. (4 Wheat.) 518 (1819).
United States v. Carolene Products Company, 304 U.S. 144 (1938).
United States v. Klein, 80 U.S. (13 Wall.) 128 (1872).
United States v. Nixon, 418 U.S. 683 (1974).
Vance v. Bradley, 440 U.S. 93 (1979).
Van Horne's Lessee v. Dorrance, 2 U.S. (2 Dall.) 304 (1795).
Wallace v. Jaffree, 472 U.S. 38 (1985).
Ware v. Hylton, 3 U.S. (3 Dall.) 199 (1796).
Webster v. Reproductive Health Services, 109 S.Ct. 3040 (1989).

West Coast Hotel v. Parrish, 300 U.S. 379 (1937).
West Virginia Board of Education v. Barnette, 319 U.S. 624 (1943).
Wilkinson v. Leland, 27 U.S. (2 Pet.) 627 (1829).
Wiscart v. Dauchy, 3 U.S. (3 Dall.) 321 (1796).
Wisconsin v. Yoder, 405 U.S. 205 (1972).
Wygant v. Jackson Board of Education, 476 U.S. 267 (1986).
Ex Parte Yerger, 75 U.S. (8 Wall.) 85 (1869).
Youngsberg v. Romeo, 457 U.S. 307 (1982).
Zablocki v. Rehail, 434 U.S. 374 (1978).

Index